The International Organization for Migration in North Africa

This book examines the International Organization for Migration's (IOM) practices of international migration management and studies current transformations of migration governance and the role of international organizations outside Europe.

While so-called migration crises in North Africa in 2005 and 2011 made the instability of the increasingly militarized border regime visible, they also created space for new actors and instruments to emerge under the label of international migration management, promising softer forms to control migration outside Europe. Who are these actors, and how do they think and practice migration control without the use of physical force and obvious repression? This book develops an innovative theoretical framework that mobilizes Bourdieu's Theory of Practice to critically investigate the work of the IOM in Morocco and Tunisia between 2005 and 2015. Analyzing its information campaigns, voluntary return programs, and anti-trafficking politics, the book shows how this organization teaches (potential) migrants and North African actors to understand migration as their own problem and its management as their own responsibility.

This book advances our understanding of the complex and ambivalent practices of controlling migration through information, protection and repatriation, and the implications of ubiquitous but underresearched institutions, such as the IOM, in this contested field. It will appeal to postgraduates, researchers, and academics in International Relations Theory, Border and Migration Studies, International Political Sociology, international organizations, and contemporary politics in North Africa.

Inken Bartels is a postdoctoral researcher at the Institute for Migration Research and Intercultural Studies at the University of Osnabrück. She is a member of the research group "The Production of Knowledge on Migration," specializing in statistical knowledge production on migration in West Africa. She holds a PhD from the Humboldt University in Berlin. Her research focuses on international actors and their governing practices within migration and border regimes in Africa, and is situated in the disciplines of (International) Political Sociology, International Relations, and (Critical) Migration and Border Studies.

Interventions

The series provides a forum for innovative and interdisciplinary work that engages with alternative critical, post-structural, feminist, postcolonial, psychoanalytic and cultural approaches to international relations and global politics. In our first 5 years, we have published 60 volumes.

We aim to advance understanding of the key areas in which scholars working within broad critical post-structural traditions have chosen to make their interventions, and to present innovative analyses of important topics. Titles in the series engage with critical thinkers in philosophy, sociology, politics and other disciplines and provide situated historical, empirical and textual studies in international politics.

We are very happy to discuss your ideas at any stage of the project: just contact us for advice or proposal guidelines. Proposals should be submitted directly to the series editors:

- Jenny Edkins (jennyedkins@hotmail.com) and
- Nick Vaughan-Williams (N.Vaughan-Williams@Warwick.ac.uk).

> As Michel Foucault has famously stated, "knowledge is not made for understanding; it is made for cutting." In this spirit, The Edkins–Vaughan-Williams Interventions series solicits cutting-edge, critical works that challenge mainstream understandings in International Relations (IR). It is the best place to contribute post-disciplinary works that think rather than merely recognize and affirm the world recycled in IR's traditional geopolitical imaginary.
> Michael J. Shapiro, University of Hawai'i at Manoa, USA

Disappearances and Police Killings in Contemporary Brazil
The Politics of Life and Death
Sabrina Villenave

For more information about this series, please visit: https://www.routledge.com/series/INT

The International Organization for Migration in North Africa

Making International Migration Management

Inken Bartels

LONDON AND NEW YORK

Doctoral thesis written at Humboldt-Universität, Faculty of Humanities and Social Sciences.

First published 2022
by Routledge
2 Park Square, Milton Park, Abingdon, Oxon OX14 4RN

and by Routledge
605 Third Avenue, New York, NY 10158

Routledge is an imprint of the Taylor & Francis Group, an informa business

© 2022 Inken Bartels

The right of Inken Bartels to be identified as author of this work has been asserted in accordance with sections 77 and 78 of the Copyright, Designs and Patents Act 1988.

All rights reserved. No part of this book may be reprinted or reproduced or utilised in any form or by any electronic, mechanical, or other means, now known or hereafter invented, including photocopying and recording, or in any information storage or retrieval system, without permission in writing from the publishers.

Trademark notice: Product or corporate names may be trademarks or registered trademarks, and are used only for identification and explanation without intent to infringe.

British Library Cataloguing-in-Publication Data
A catalogue record for this book is available from the British Library

Library of Congress Cataloging-in-Publication Data
Names: Bartels, Inken, 1984- author.
Title: The International Organization for Migration in North Africa : making international migration management / Inken Bartels.
Description: Abingdon, Oxon ; New York, NY : Routledge, 2022. | Series: Interventions | Includes bibliographical references and index.
Identifiers: LCCN 2021037535 (print) | LCCN 2021037536 (ebook) | ISBN 9781032068541 (hardback) | ISBN 9781032068572 (paperback) | ISBN 9781003204169 (ebook)
Subjects: LCSH: International Organization for Migration. | Africa, North—Emigration and immigration—Government policy.
Classification: LCC JV8977 .B37 2022 (print) | LCC JV8977 (ebook) | DDC 304.8/6—dc23/eng/20211026
LC record available at https://lccn.loc.gov/2021037535
LC ebook record available at https://lccn.loc.gov/2021037536

ISBN: 9781032068541 (hbk)
ISBN: 9781032068572 (pbk)
ISBN: 9781003204169 (ebk)

DOI: 10.4324/9781003204169

Typeset in Times New Roman
by codeMantra

Contents

Acknowledgments ix
List of abbreviations xi

Introduction 1
Crises and conflicts of the expanding border regime in Morocco and Tunisia 3
IOs and the politics of migration management in North Africa 6
A praxeological perspective to migration control in the Mediterranean 9
Outline of the book 13

1 **A praxeological approach to the politics of international migration management** 24
   1.1 The framework of a border regime and the Autonomy of Migration thesis 25
   1.2 Practice-theoretical approaches to international politics 30
   1.3 A Bourdieusian perspective on the politics of international migration management 34
      1.3.1 Field 36
      1.3.2 Habitus 39
      1.3.3 Symbolic capital, power, and violence 41
      1.3.4 Struggles as the engine of stability and change 45
   1.4 Outline of a praxeological research perspective on the politics of international migration management 47

2 **The IOM in the trans-Mediterranean field of migration management** 59
   2.1 The emergence of the IOM in international migration politics 60
   2.2 From securitization to international migration management in North Africa 63

vi Contents

    2.2.1 Migration in and from North Africa 64
    2.2.2 The securitization and externalization of migration control 65
    2.2.3 Contested positions and relations in trans-Mediterranean migration politics 68
  2.3 *Shifting discourses, practices, and actors in trans-Mediterranean migration management 71*

3 Information campaigns: migration management as a global duty for education   87
  3.1 *Preventing populations at risk of migration in Morocco 90*
    3.1.1 Practices and meanings of prevention: The SALEM project in Morocco 91
    3.1.2 The symbolic violence of constructing and infantilizing risk groups 93
    3.1.3 The symbolic power of informing and forming responsible individuals 94
    3.1.4 "But they know it is dangerous"—contradictions and contestations in the field 98
  3.2 *Participatory migration management in Tunisia 102*
    3.2.1 Communicating opportunities to the benefit of all? The START project 103
    3.2.2 The symbolic power of the IOM's cinematography: The SALEMM project 106
    3.2.3 "If the people were really convinced, they would not have left"—the doubtful impact of virtual migration management 113
  3.3 *The symbolic power of neoliberal risk management: why potential migrants would (not) participate in their own management 115*

4 Voluntary return programs: migration management as a moral responsibility to protect   123
  4.1 *The IOM's promise of a cost-effective and humane alternative to deportation 125*
    4.1.1 Competition in the voluntary return business 128
    4.1.2 Migrants' encounters with an international bureaucracy 129
    4.1.3 Donor influence and the international play of funding (ir)rationalities 133
    4.1.4 Rising demand in the context of repressive state politics 138
    4.1.5 The IOM as a travel agency: practices of appropriation and repair 145
  4.2 *Voluntary return as humanitarian crisis management in Tunisia 148*
    4.2.1 The symbolic production of a humanitarian crisis at the Tunisian-Libyan border 149

- 4.2.2 Practices of divide, rule, and return in the North African borderlands 152
- 4.2.3 In the camp: postcolonial relations and patriarchal logic 154
- 4.2.4 In the office: The illusio of humanitarian migration management 156
- 4.2.5 Making invisible: Tunisia's Local Integration Program and IOs' retreat from the field 158
- 4.2.6 "At least Choucha is free": a space of rumors and hope 163
- 4.2.7 Voluntary return within cycles of criminalization and illegalization 165
- 4.2.8 Struggles for durable solutions: beyond charity and "associative things" 167

4.3 *The humanitarian politics of return: revisiting strategies, struggles, and stakes in the field of international migration management* 171

5 Anti-trafficking politics: migration management as a struggle for hard facts and soft influence 185

5.1 *Mainstreaming migration politics in times of transition* 188
- 5.1.1 Producing knowledge on human trafficking 190
- 5.1.2 The play of international conferences 195

5.2 *Victims of trafficking as a new target group of migration management* 202
- 5.2.1 Forced, sold, prostituted—defining VoTs through female suffering 203
- 5.2.2 Protecting vulnerable migrants 205
- 5.2.3 The prevention of risk groups 207

5.3 *Building capacities and negotiating laws* 209
- 5.3.1 The symbolic power of law- and policy-making in Tunisia 209
- 5.3.2 Repressive migration control in the name of anti-trafficking in Morocco 214
- 5.3.3 "They take everything!"—perceptions of the IOM's position and influence 218

5.4 *Compassion and repression in mainstreaming anti-trafficking politics* 220

Conclusion 229

Change and stability in the trans-Mediterranean field of migration management 230
The IOM as a global expert for (not only) migration 236
The praxeological approach reconsidered 239

Index 243

Acknowledgments

Writing this book would not have been possible without the advice, inspiration, and support of many people, whom I want to thank here.

First, I thank Gökçe Yurdakul, Steffen Mau, and Naika Foroutan, who supervised the dissertation at the Humboldt Universität on which this book is based. I am thankful for their advice, confidence, and patience in my work. In particular, I want to thank my first supervisor, Gökçe Yurdakul, for her continuous encouragement and enthusiasm for my research and her detailed and valuable feedback during the research process from the very first to the final drafts. I am grateful for the institutional, administrative, and financial support of the Berlin Graduate School of Social Sciences at the Humboldt University in Berlin. The scholarship I received from the European Doctoral Program made this research project, in its multi-sitedness and extensive mobility, possible.

Moreover, I thank my interview partners and their institutions for having shared their stories and knowledge with me. In Rabat, my special thanks go to Abdelkrim Belguendouz, Amat Hafssa, Bachir Hamdouch, and Fatima El Majd. In Tunis, Anais Elbassil and Walid Fellah were particularly helpful during my fieldwork. In Florence, I want to thank Jean-Pierre Cassarino and Jonathan Zaragoza Cristiani for sharing their valuable insights and contacts in the field (and Laia, Mira, and Nuria for the great time at the EUI). I also want to express my thanks and admiration to all those migrants and activists, who I met during my journeys for this work, struggling for the freedom of movement on both shores of the Mediterranean.

This research project would not have been possible without the support of many colleagues and friends. Among them, special thanks go to Giulia Borri and Samia Dinkelaker for going through many struggles of (researching) migration together. I am also thankful to Jana Hönke for introducing me to the world of practices, and to Martin Geiger for supporting my interest in researching international organizations and migration management. I thank Katrin Becker, Thomas Böwing, Katherine Braun, Lisa Carstensen, Silvia Griepentrog, Lee Hielscher, Katja Imberi, Anna Köster-Eiserfunke, Laura-Solmaz Litschel, Clemens Reichhold, Helge Schwiertz, Simon Sperling, Olaf Tietje, and Ronja Wagner, as well as members of the PhD colloquium under the supervision of Gökçe Yurdakul, the kritnet group in Hamburg, and the Bürokollektiv Wandalenweg for commenting on, correcting, and discussing earlier versions and important parts of the manuscript.

For their valuable advice and encouragement to turn this manuscript into a book, I want to thank my colleagues at the Institute for Migration Research and Intercultural Studies at the Osnabrück University, in particular Isabella Löhr, Andreas Pott, Christiane Reinecke, Philipp Schäfer, Laura Stielike, Helen Schwenken, and the members of the Forschungswerkstatt of the Department of Migration and Society. A special thanks also goes to Stephan Scheel for introducing me to the rules and practices of the field of international publishing. For the attentive supervision of the publication, I would like to thank the editors of the Interventions Series, Jenny Edkins and Nick Vaughan-Williams, the Routledge editorial team, as well as the two anonymous reviewers for their critical evaluation and constructive comments on the manuscript.

Finally, I am very thankful to my family, who made it possible for me to take up the challenge of doing this research and supported me throughout these years, to Joscha Metzger for his challenging questions and his borderless support from the first steps to the final moments of this work, and to Aaron for being there.

Hamburg, May 2021 Inken Bartels

Abbreviations

AECID	Agencia Española de Cooperación Internacional para el Desarrollo, Spanish Agency for International Development Cooperation
AVR	Assisted Voluntary Return
AVRR	Assisted Voluntary Return and Reintegration
BE	Belgian Embassy
CNDH	Conseil National des Droits de l'Homme, National Human Rights Council
EMP	Euro-Mediterranean Partnership
ENP	European Neighbourhood Policy
EU	European Union
GAM	Global Approach to Migration
ICMPD	International Centre for Migration Policy Development
IDC	Italian Development Cooperation
ILO	International Labor Organization
IO	International Organization
IOM	International Organization for Migration
IR	International Relations
MDIC	Ministry of Development and International Cooperation
MRE	Marocains Résidants à l'Étranger, Moroccans Living Abroad
MSA	Ministry of Social Affairs
MSF	Médecins Sans Frontières, Doctors Without Borders
NGO	Non-Governmental Organization
OAU	Organization for Africa Unity
OTE	Office des Tunisiens à l'Étranger, Office for Tunisians Living Abroad
PRIRAC	Promoting the Return and Reintegration of Rejected Asylum Seekers
SALEM	Solidarity with the Children in Morocco
SALEMM	Solidarity with the Children of the Maghreb and the Mashriq
SDC	Swiss Development Cooperation

SHARE	Support and Hand-over of Assistance and Referral Mechanism as well as Exchange of Practices in Anti-Trafficking
START	Stabilizing At-Risk Communities and Reinforcing Migration Management to Enable Smooth Transitions in Egypt, Tunisia, and Libya
TRE	Tunisiens Résidants à l'Étranger, Tunisians Living Abroad
UN	United Nations
UNHCR	United Nations High Commissioner for Refugees
US	United States
VoT	Victim of Trafficking
WSF	World Social Forum

Introduction

When the International Organization for Migration (IOM) intervenes in a country, its presence "often starts as a one-man or two-man show," one staff member explained during an interview in Morocco in 2014 (interview with IOM staff member, Morocco 2014).

> Or you have situations [...] where it is immediately linked to a concrete crisis. And there, we don't start with two people, we start with 50 people. And so, it is very demand-driven. But the demand is not always by the government. It might very well be that there is a crisis situation, and that is where the demand is created.
>
> (Ibid.)

In contrast to the routinized, labor-intensive procedure of establishing its business at a new site, my interview partner directed my attention to exceptional situations in which the IOM's involvement is required—not by the governments of its (financially strong) member states—but by a "concrete crisis." Unlike other international bureaucracies, the IOM's work is "very demand-driven," which assigns the organization a specific role in international migration politics. While governments of European and North American states usually commission and fund IOM's activities based on economic, political, or moral justifications, "crisis situations" form a seemingly self-explanatory need for its projects, especially if they are to be implemented in the Global South. Consequently, such moments of rupture and change in dominant ideas, everyday routines, and unquestioned morals of international migration politics provide an opportunity for the IOM to enter a country, not just as a "one-man or two-man-show," but to mobilize massive (wo)man-power with the IOM's readiness and flexibility to offer its services when international assistance seems to be most urgently needed.

The IOM is an international organization (IO) with a remarkable history of global expansion and growing influence in international migration politics over the last few decades.[1] In North Africa, its presence changed from a "one-man show" to a well-recognized spectacle, in what the IOM staff called "a crisis situation." While the organization wanted to cooperate with

DOI: 10.4324/9781003204169-1

North African states since the 1990s, it only convinced the Moroccan and Tunisian governments, as well as European donors, of its services in the aftermath of collective border crossings, challenging the militarized border regime in Morocco in 2005 and in Tunisia in 2011. Well before what became known in public and political discourses as Europe's 'refugee crisis' in 2015, these deadly incidents were referred to as 'migration crises'[2] in North Africa and beyond. Both moments of unexpected, extensive border crossings manifested the conflicts of an expanding *European border regime*[3] (Tsianos and Karakayalı 2010; Hess 2012) for increased securitization of its external borders as well as for cooperation with repressive governments on the Southern side of the Mediterranean. Confronted with practical failure, fading legitimacy, and public criticism of existing border and migration control instruments, European actors searched for new ways of governing migration in transit countries. As moments of rupture in existing control logic and governing techniques, the 'migration crises' in Morocco and Tunisia allowed new actors to emerge in the name of migration management, promising softer forms to control migration outside of Europe.

It is one of these actors, its practices, and logic that is at the center of this book which seeks to reveal how control of human mobility outside Europe was changed during a crucial period, in which the militarized border regime of the Mediterranean was challenged by several 'migration crises.' It critically investigates the emergence of the IOM in North Africa and reconstructs its migration control measures that work through incentives and education, rather than force and repression. Analyzing the IOM's information campaigns, voluntary return programs, and anti-trafficking politics, the book demonstrates how the organization teaches (potential) migrants and North African actors to understand migration as their own problem and its management as their own responsibility. It argues that the IOM's influence is based on subtle forms of *symbolic power* (Bourdieu and Wacquant 1992), mobilizing those who are governed to become (more) involved in their own management. The book traces how the IOM established itself as a recognized expert on these issues, and expanded its influence to national and transnational policy-making processes through North Africa. It concludes that the IOM's emergence is based on the organization's ability to interact with different actors and combine security with neoliberal and humanitarian logic at the expense of a rights-based approach, contributing to shifts in international migration governance between 2005 and 2015.

With the help of Pierre Bourdieu's *Theory of Practice* (Bourdieu 1977, 1990), I examine governance shifts as the result of struggles among and within diverse social actors in the *trans-Mediterranean field of migration management*. This praxeological perspective offers a relational approach for the actors and their histories, including their strategies and struggles in making and negotiating migration management in social situations (Adler and Pouliot 2011; Bueger and Gadinger 2014). Investigating the micropolitics of international migration in Morocco and Tunisia, I question the

IOM's interventions to be smooth top-down processes of European externalization. Instead, I aim to show what is *at stake* (and for whom) when migration is managed in transit countries outside of Europe. In this way, this book contributes to a better understanding of the externalization of European migration control and the role of IOs from the perspective of the North African borderlands in which migration management projects are implemented and/or contested. In addition, it promotes theoretical debates that critically appraise recent transformations of the globalized politics of migration control.

Crises and conflicts of the expanding border regime in Morocco and Tunisia

Located on the main migration routes from Africa to Europe, Morocco and Tunisia have been the preferred target countries for European efforts to outsource migration control policies for over two decades (Bartels 2015; Infantino 2016). Despite long-standing attempts by European states to externalize migration policies to North Africa, authorities resisted, or did not implement the policies of the cooperation agreements, political initiatives, and declared partnerships concluded throughout the 1990s (Fargues 2006; Cassarino 2010). At that time, IOs working in the field only played a minor role in these countries. Their work was tolerated, though it was focused on small-scale projects, mainly offering direct assistance to migrants in need or information campaigns to prevent potential migrants from emigrating (Valluy 2007; Caillault 2012; Tazzioli 2014). In 2003 and 2004, King Mohammed VI of Morocco and Tunisian President Zine El Abidine Ben Ali introduced a securitized logic of border control through laws that criminalized unauthorized emigration and enhanced control of their external sea borders (Belguendouz 2005; Di Bartolomeo, Fakhoury, and Perrin 2010). In Morocco, fences around two Spanish enclaves of the African territory, Ceuta and Melilla, were built with Spanish support (Migreurop 2006). These policies assisted the Moroccan and Tunisian governments in meeting European expectations to cooperate in irregularized migration and enhanced their legitimacy in international relations (Natter 2015). They sought to satisfy the demands of the European Union (EU) and its member states and thus gain financial support from Europe in fields of international cooperation, e.g., development and economic integration (El Qadim 2010).

However, both countries share a long tradition of emigration to Europe and profit from remittances sent from their citizens residing abroad, so they were reluctant to implement further restrictive measures to the declared 'fight against irregular migration.' Instead, they demanded an extension of legal ways for emigration to Europe. Questions of immigration and asylum, in turn, ranked low in government priorities, not understanding themselves to be countries of transit or immigration at the time (cf. Di Bartolomeo, Fakhoury, and Perrin 2010; De Haas 2014). When collective struggles of migration in Morocco in 2005 and in Tunisia in 2011 made the apparent failure and fatal consequences of the existing border regime becoming visible, these countries became laboratories for seemingly global, comprehensive, and mutually beneficial forms of migration control—beyond the restrictive doctrines of fortifying borders and conditioning international cooperation (Wunderlich 2010; Gaibazzi, Bellagamba, and Dünnwald 2017).

"Do you know what happened in Spain in 2005 when they fired on the immigrants?" a migrant from West Africa asked me during an interview in Rabat in 2014 (interview with migrant, Mor. 2014). "When they climbed the fences?" I responded. He completed my question after a meaningful pause: "With barbed wire, yes" (ibid.). He then continued his story about the deadly border struggles in the western Mediterranean. "So, in this moment, we arrived at the Canary Islands. When they killed the people there [at the fences of Ceuta and Melilla], we were pushed back, which is how we arrived in Morocco" (ibid.). This passage from an interview with someone who arrived in Morocco through a Spanish push-back in 2005 illustrates how the deadly incidents of Ceuta and Melilla have become a hallmark in international migration politics, and a crucial reference in the collective memory of Sub-Saharan migrants in North Africa. Moreover, this story conveys how border struggles were not singular incidents—as indicated in official statements and references—but happened in a context of increasingly violent repression and raids against Sub-Saharan migrants on both sides of the EU's external borders.

In Morocco, Sub-Saharan migrants had taken refuge in the mountain forests near the Spanish enclaves, waiting for months or years in precarious conditions for when to climb the 6-meter-high fences, armed with barbed wire that separate Moroccan territory from the Schengen Area. In camps on the mountain Gourougourou near Melilla and in the forest Bel Younech near Ceuta, they faced constant repression and arrests by the Moroccan police trying to evict self-organized spaces. Once after they tried to cross the highly militarized border with self-made wooden ladders, they were hunted down and pushed back with rubber bullets and batons by the Spanish National Guards.

In late September 2005, more than 500 migrants collectively stormed the fortifications around Ceuta. Five migrants died and many more were injured by gunshot wounds, unclear if of Moroccan or Spanish origin. Six migrants also died in a similar event climbing the fences around Melilla, the second Spanish enclave on Moroccan territory (GADEM 2007). At least 20 people were killed by Moroccan police forces in the autumn of 2005. The number of migrants deported to the desert of the Moroccan-Algerian border was much higher, but remains unclear (cf. Migreurop 2006). The border struggles were thus part of an increasingly hostile and repressive atmosphere with growing violence against Sub-Saharan migrants in Morocco. This led to public criticism and protest among local and transnational civil society networks against the militarized 'Fortress Europe.' European media also reported on the "Murderous crisis of Ceuta and Melilla" and the desperate and dangerous situation of migrants at the external borders of the EU (ibid.). The widely publicized pictures of death and violence lessened the existing repressive practices of border control in their unquestioned legitimacy. When obvious violence had to contain the collective struggles of migration in the North African borderlands, the EU and its member states searched for new measures to prevent unauthorized crossings from turning deadly and spectacular. They rethought their deterrence strategy, realizing that migration movements toward Europe could not be stopped by building fences and enhanced security measures along territorial borders. While repressive means were strengthened in the aftermath of this Moroccan 'migration crisis,' the search for practical alternatives gained relevance in political and academic debates.

In this context, IOs became important partners for the EU and its member states to implement projects dealing with what was perceived as the 'problem of irregular migration' in North Africa and channeling it into manageable and productive ways. IOs were expected to take care of migrants blocked at the EU's external borders more diplomatically, efficiently, and sustainably than North African state actors had done. As a consequence, Morocco became a testing ground for new transnational practices to control migration outside European territory without the use of obvious force and repression. The IOM took this historical opportunity to offer its services of international migration management to Moroccan authorities and European member states to deal with Sub-Saharan migrants and potential Moroccan emigrants in 2005.

In Tunisia, it was the proclamation of a 'migration crisis' in the context of the Arab Spring that provided the basis of the work by the IOM to gain visibility and recognition six years later. It started as part of a joint international operation called humanitarian crisis management in 2011. When the Arab Spring looked at Tunisia as the focus of international attention, European states redirected and increased their funding for different aid programs (Tazzioli 2015). In addition to financial support for the country's democratic transition, funding to improve border control and to introduce instruments of migration management were ranked high among the priorities of European states. In this way, they sought to stop the 'flood' of migrants coming from the southern shores of the Mediterranean, as predicted by European media and politicians (see De Haas and Sigona 2012). European states were anxious about the threat of an 'exodus' or 'invasion' (cf. Ben Achour and Ben Jemia 2011; Bartels 2015) when political instability and growing repression against Sub-Saharan migrant workers in Libya led to unauthorized crossings to the northern shores of the Mediterranean after former dictator Gadhafi was ousted from the country under international fire. The removal of two long-standing dictators created political destabilization of the North African borderlands, and the EU lost its preferred partners for migration control.

As a result, many people indeed used this opportunity to cross the Mediterranean Sea. With the outbreak of war in Libya in February 2011, more than 350,000 people, Libyans and third-country nationals, also crossed the land border into Tunisia. While approximately 97,000 of those crossing were returning Tunisian nationals, tens of thousands third-country nationals entered the country in political transition—almost 200,000 people according to the IOM statistics (IOM 2011). Many had lived and worked in Libya, but fled from economic instability and racist repression against migrant workers, motivated by revenge at potential mercenaries of the Gadhafi regime.

Migrants fleeing or returning from Libya were initially helped by the Tunisian army; non-governmental organizations (NGOs) and the local population provided them with basic needs (Boubakri and Potot 2011). Proud of Tunisian hospitality in difficult times of the country's own transition, Tunisian politicians whom I interviewed during my fieldwork in 2015 pointed to extraordinary solidarity and generosity (interview with a representative of the Ministry of Development and International Cooperation (MDIC), Tunisia 2015). At the same time, they emphasized that Tunisia was a "small country which would not be able to absorb all the influx" (ibid.). They seemed aware that European states wanted to solve the 'problem of irregular migration' on the southern side of the Mediterranean. In contrast to the repressive reactions of the Moroccan state in 2005, Tunisian politicians—in their official rhetoric—reiterated their commitment to develop migration policies and institutions for the unprecedented influx of immigrants in 2011 (see Crépeau 2012). Practically, however, these measures were not among the top priorities for interim governments after the revolution (cf. Schäfer 2011). With growing democratic accountability in Tunisian policy-making, the newly appointed authorities had to legitimize their decisions in front of an increasingly active civil society and electorate, rather than bow to international demands (Natter 2015). Consequently, they initially refused European pressure to reinstate violent methods of border control employed to stop irregularized emigration under Ben Ali (cf. Boubakri 2013).

Realizing that migration control by former European gatekeepers, Ben Ali and Gadhafi, could neither be easily reinstalled with new bilateral agreements, nor with enhanced funds or stronger conditionality, European states opted for new solutions to repair the unstable border regime in the central Mediterranean. IOs took over management of international migration in the North African model country, Tunisia. They were primarily financed by European states that feared this Tunisian 'migration crisis' would spread North and therefore aimed to send humanitarian and operational support to the border with Libya. After years of a marginal existence, the IOM became part of a humanitarian intervention in 2011.

IOs and the politics of migration management in North Africa

In reaction to these crises and conflicts of the European border regime, Morocco and Tunisia became laboratories for new actors, their means and methods of migration control. Today, they are the most integrated North African countries in the expanding trans-Mediterranean border regime. While many migrants have searched for new routes and redirected their old ones toward Libya, Morocco and Tunisia have become comparatively stable and reliable partners for cooperation in international migration politics. This situation makes them perfect sites to investigate the emerging politics of international migration management. Proactively promoted by IOs, this new global policy discourse emerged in the early 2000s. It promised a global and proactive approach that could turn migration into a 'triple win' process for the benefit of all parties: receiving and sending states, as well as migrants themselves (see Kalm 2012). This "new twist" in international migration politics was a split from the negative view that migration must be prevented and borders closed (ibid., 50). Instead, it promotes an optimistic perspective that seeks to transfer migration into an orderly, predictable, and manageable process, and to maximize its impact for all stakeholders (ibid. 2010). It rests on the belief that migration movements can be effectively state-controlled if management is improved (Oelgemüller 2017).

This optimistic, technocratic view of migration had a profound influence on the design of the EU's first Global Approach to Migration (GAM) (European Council 2006). Signed by the EU and its member states in 2005, it extended existing security-oriented policies, in which the primary aim was to 'fight the threat of irregular migration' since the 1990s (Walters 2010). Based on a new understanding of migration as a normal and potentially positive phenomenon, migration policies should productively anticipate, control, and channel migration movements before reaching external borders of the Schengen Area (Geiger and Pécoud 2010). For practical expanding control measures beyond its external borders, the EU strengthened cooperation with multiple state and non-state actors, who would govern migration within third-countries (Gammeltoft-Hansen and Nyberg-Sørensen 2013). As a result, Morocco and Tunisia became part of a transnational field, in which multiple actors, practices, and discourses engage in making and challenging international migration management (Casas-Cortes, Cobarrubias, and Pickles 2013; Gaibazzi, Bellagamba, and Dünnwald 2017).

Under the GAM framework, IOs intensified their participation and gained influence in the EU's external migration governance. From the EU perspective, IOs' involvement in migration management within third-countries was regarded as "very helpful," since "such organizations could confirm that measures do comply fully with justified needs for protection" (European Commission 2001, 9). Moreover, the EU considered it more efficient to use existing international infrastructures than to create new ones (ibid.). Finally, European actors expected IOs to create formats of dialogue that would ensure cooperation between different actors (ibid.). Migration scholars, therefore, argue that IOs are "useful vehicles for transporting European concerns and policy solutions via multilateral frameworks to sending and transit countries" (Lavenex 2007, 259). According to Martin Geiger (2014, 225),

> EU institutions in their approach to exterritorialize, or territorially "shift out," prevention strategies are highly dependent on specialized

intermediary actors, most notable intergovernmental organizations. [...] On the basis of their expert knowledge and their wide portfolio of operational opportunities they provide states [...] exceptional opportunities to find practical solutions and outsource their mobility-related measures.

Implementing migration control measures within sending and transit countries, IOs take an important role in European migration governance on the African continent. Due to their perception of being neutral and objective international experts, IOs are expected to be able to influence diverse actors. As trusted intermediaries, IOs were engaged by European states to establish frameworks, practical knowledge, and the skills to encourage the governments of sending and transit countries to participate in new forms of migration control. In this respect, they were expected to help Morocco and Tunisia understand irregularized migration as their own problem and to establish a relation to make international cooperation on migration issues acceptable for them.

Martin Geiger and Antoine Pécoud (2014, 874) characterize the relationship between IOs and third-countries as a matter of self-discipline and socialization:

> Even without exercising direct coercive power, they would determine the "right" policies to be implemented by governments and develop the instruments through which to assess their compliance with these principles. Governments would not perceive the norms of IOs as imposed on them from more powerful external actors; on the contrary, they would "self-discipline" themselves, "socialize" with and adhere to these norms, understood as unquestionable universal values.

Following similar arguments, many migration scholars interpret the power of IOs as a form of "global governmentality" (Hess 2014, 258) or the "international conduct of conduct of countries" (Andrijasevic and Walters 2010, 989). Drawing on Foucault's work on discourse, discipline, and governmentality, they highlight how the power of a subtle "art of governing" migration (Karakayalı and Tsianos 2007, 7, translation IB) influences how migration is perceived, interpreted, and dealt with in specific contexts. They direct attention to activating modes that make state and non-state actors, as well as migrants, participate in the governance of migration (Geiger and Pécoud 2013).

At the same time, some IOs have developed a vision of how to govern migration and play a significant role in the construction of the 'reality of migration' by identifying and framing 'problems of migration' (Geiger and Pécoud 2014). Advancing specific issues, IOs take a proactive part in the struggles over the direction of international migration policymaking (Georgi 2010, 48). As scholars of international relations point out, IOs have their "own ideas and pursue their own agendas" (Barnett and Finnemore

2004, 2). Despite their service orientation and dependence on external funding, they do not simply do "what states want," but as bureaucracies, they can also "change the world around them" (ibid., 2f.). The negotiations between IOs and their member states, however, have received little attention in border and migration studies. This holds especially true for their relations with state and non-state actors in countries of the Global South where they implement most programs. The internal dynamics of IOs and the implications on their performance are also rarely considered by existing studies. The ways in which emerging politics of migration management are shaped by implementing actors, as well as by the contexts to which they were applied, have thus seldom been subject to independent scrutiny.

To compensate for this neglect, this book turns to the IOM's *practices* in Morocco and Tunisia. The IOM is a particularly interesting case to study recent dynamics of the expanding and changing border regime, since it is formally both, a major implementation partner for migration-related projects financed by the EU and European states beyond their territories, and actively promoting a global vision of 'managing migration to the benefit of all' (Geiger and Pécoud 2010; Georgi 2010; Ashutosh and Mountz 2011). With this promise, the IOM became known as a cost-effective, human rights-respecting service provider in the expanding global market of migration management, in which diverse state and non-state actors compete for the most convincing offer in the decisive moment of reorientation of European migration politics with the GAM (Gammeltoft-Hansen and Nyberg-Sørensen 2013; Andersson 2014). While the organization was present in Morocco and Tunisia previously, it successfully offered services to North African governments and European member states in moments of crisis, and became one of the key intermediary actors within European attempts to stabilize the North African borderlands in the early 2000s (see Bartels 2017, 2018). Analyzing its practices of social work and education, humanitarian aid and assistance, as well as knowledge production and dissemination, this book promotes critical knowledge about the ubiquitous but underresearched role of the IOM in North Africa. Studying the IOM's practices becomes even more urgent, as they are increasingly circulating to control and constrain migration on the African continent (see Frowd 2018). In this way, this book aims to contribute to a better understanding of how human mobility is governed outside of Europe.

A praxeological perspective to migration control in the Mediterranean

In order to study the contested *making* of international migration management in Morocco and Tunisia, this book advances a praxeological perspective that combines the framework of a border regime and the *Autonomy of Migration* thesis with practical-theoretical approaches in International Relations (IR) (see Chapter 1). The border regime framework, that this book draws on, was developed by antiracist activists and critical border and migration scholars in order to conceptualize the dynamics between migration movements and the political and administrative attempts to govern them (see Transit Migration Forschungsgruppe 2007; Hess and Kasparek 2010; Hess, Kasparek, and Schwertl 2018). This particular notion of a regime is defined as a more or less ordered ensemble of social practices, actors, and discourses, whose composition is not pregiven or centrally regulated, but provides answers to questions and problems raised by these interactions (Karakayalı and Tsianos 2007). Emphasizing the use of technologies and knowledge in making and negotiating migration management, this regime perspective notably reveals economic and biopolitical arts of governing (Tsianos and Karakayalı 2010; Hess 2012). As such, it indicates how power is not only exercised through coercion and repression but also through more informal and subtle forms of mobilizing and guiding subjects, that influence how they think, act, and perceive (Walters 2006).

This border regime literature refers to the theory of the Autonomy of Migration to understand the struggles of migration as a force of transformation (Moulier Boutang 2002; Bojadzijev and Karakayalı 2007; Mezzadra 2007; Scheel 2019). It highlights the dynamic and conflictual relation between people on the move and the politics of their restriction and regulation. As a "heuristic model" (Moulier Boutang 2007), it makes the practices of migrants the starting point to investigate and theorize changes in border and migration regimes. Accordingly, I do not understand migration movements merely as objects of governance or management, but as a constituent force in international migration politics, driving and structuring its transformations. Challenging control measures, they require policies and governing techniques to adjust, transform, and develop (Papadopoulos, Stephenson, and Tsianos 2008). In this sense, I regard crises and struggles of migration as integral parts of the expanding border regime in the Mediterranean. Consequently, I analyze shifts of control practices and regulatory logic as contingent and contested results of asymmetrical interactions between migration movements and governing techniques.

Within this relational framework, the book mobilizes practice-theoretical approaches in IR (see Bueger and Gadinger 2014) to zoom into the micropolitics of international migration management. Using concepts that were developed by Pierre Bourdieu as part of his Theory of Practice (Bourdieu 1977, 1990, 1998), I direct attention to the struggles among social actors who engage in the making of migration management, according to specific histories, strategies, and stakes. This praxeological perspective makes it possible to analyze changing techniques, rationalities, and power relations of migration control as a result of conflictive material and symbolic interaction among and within collective actors (Bueger and Gadinger 2008; Scheel et al. 2016). This approach thus moves social actors into the center of analysis and reveals their relations and negotiations about what is at stake in the *transnational field of migration management*. According to Pierre Bourdieu and Loïc Wacquant (1992, 94ff), a field refers to a social space defined by the (power) relations between (asymmetric) positions and stakes, about which actors compete. These stakes go beyond purely economic interests, including strategies to maximize different kinds of individual and institutional resources, relations, and recognition that are recognized as relevant (*forms of capital*), and to improve actors' positions in the field (Bourdieu 1986). As a field of struggles, this is an inherently *contested* space defined by the central *logic* in which the actors believe, rather than by national boundaries.

The notion of a transnational field of migration management allows me to grasp the implementation, appropriation, and rejection of international migration management as a negotiation process between different positions in an asymmetrically structured transnational and transcontinental space. This field is not predefined, but exists in practice, as actors participate in it because they believe in its logic, rules, and gains. In the transnational field of migration management, the EU and European states design and finance programs that are realized by the IOM in North Africa. In contrast to much of the literature on the externalization of European migration policies, I view neither North African actors nor migrants as "passive spectators in the background," but examine how diverse actors actively shape developments in this field (Gaibazzi, Bellagamba, and Dünnwald 2017, 11). While this book focuses on one transnationally operating actor, the IOM, it does not regard the implementation of migration management "in a vacuum but in specific historical, sociopolitical, economic, and cultural realities" that influence practices in certain contexts (ibid., 12). This way, the book advances a *relational* approach that focuses on the interaction of both those who implement transnational programs of migration control and those who accept, appropriate, or reject them. Asking what is at stake, according to which logic for the different actors involved in this struggle field, I aim to show why Moroccan and Tunisian actors or migrants become engaged in the making of international migration management. I argue that Bourdieu's concepts of symbolic power and symbolic violence are key to understanding the IOM's influence in externalizing control to sending and transit countries.

Moreover, Bourdieu's concept of *habitus* allows me to open the box of collective actors (such as states or IOs) that are regarded as monolithic in much of the literature. It makes it possible to consider how internal dynamics, unquestioned assumptions, and embodied routines inform how they make, challenge, and appropriate migration control in concrete situations (Jackson 2008). It further directs attention to the taken-for-granted knowledge that makes their action possible. Taking the meanings, values, and morals into account that guide the practice of migration management, this book is not only interested in new *modes* of governing migration but also in its *content* (see Bigo 2002; Fassin 2009). To include the inarticulate assumptions, working routines, and habitus of those who work for the organization into the analysis, I investigate the IOM as a social field of its own.

12 *Introduction*

In sum, analyzing the IOM's practices in the trans-Mediterranean field of migration management makes it possible to link struggles over material resources with symbolic struggles among different actors at different levels. The advantage of this approach is that it directs attention to the relational and conflictive character of the externalization of European migration control, its historical embeddedness, and concrete sites of negotiation, contestation, and appropriation.

This book is based on qualitative data that I generated through participant observation, semi-structured interviews, and document analysis during fieldwork in Morocco and Tunisia, between 2013 and 2015. The fieldwork was conducted in Morocco in September and October 2013, and in May to August of 2014, as well as in Tunisia in March 2013 and January to April 2015. During these visits, my aim was to grasp the everyday practices and their contextually specific meanings of migration management. The analytical focus on practices in international politics and organizations made participant observation the preferred research method (Ybema et al. 2009; Pouliot 2013). This was carried out at political, social, and cultural events, including conferences and workshops organized by IOs themselves. Taking part in these epistemic places allowed me to study actors "in their own settings, in the midst of doing whatever it is that they do every day, with whatever is required to do it" (Miettinen, Samra-Fredericks, and Yanow 2009, 1315). Based on firsthand monitoring of practices and negotiations from a knowledgeable but distanced perspective, it was possible to observe the dynamics, particularities, and complexities which otherwise seem too ordinary to enter into conversations and written documents (Pritzlaff 2006; Ybema and Kamsteeg 2009). This situated analysis allowed me to gain empirical insights into the interaction of different actors, their self-evident, embodied practices, and everyday discourses that coproduce international migration management at specific sites.

Since access to the everyday work of the IOM and other relevant actors in the field is very limited to outsiders, I complemented my observations with approximately 30 semi-structured interviews and many more informal conversations with representatives of various actors, including IOs, state institutions, embassies of donor countries, and NGOs, as well as with researchers, activists, and migrants.[4] Through these interviews and conversations,[5] I gained access to the meanings that actors assign to the IOM's migration management and to the strategies that these actors proceed to implementation, cooperation, or contestation (Pouliot 2013, 49). In addition, I analyzed textual and visual material collected during fieldwork.[6] In a field in which the production of so-called expert literature is a common and central practice, this material offers important insights into official narratives and (self-)representations, their continuities and ruptures, as well as background information on the positions and relations in the field (Yanow 2009; Hess 2012; Schwertl 2013). Through the combination of these research methods and materials, this book offers profound empirical insights into practices and negotiations of migration control in North Africa, highlighting the tensions and discrepancies between different writings, sayings, and doings.

Operating across countries, scales, and sites, the IOM's work in North Africa allowed me to follow migration management practices to different "sites of struggle" (Garelli and Tazzioli 2013, 246), or as Ruben Andersson (2014, 285) puts it, to the "interfaces where the border machinery rubs against specific places, people, and structures." The multi-sited research on which this book is based offers a transnational perspective that investigates the making of international migration management in "singular but connected sites" (Burawoy 2000, 5; see also Marcus 1995). An understanding of these sites are *sites of struggles* highlights how this research is itself intertwined with the contested making of international migration management that is embedded in the politics of production of (scientific) knowledge about migration and its possibilities of control (Mato 2000; De Genova 2013). Conducted in a field in which knowledge production and dissemination belong to the core practices under study, with boundaries between science and politics often blurred, it is "inevitably caught up in the system that it sets out to analyse" (Andersson 2014, 15). In contrast to the multiple policy reports commissioned or published by IOs and thinks tanks in this field, however, the aim of this book is not to improve the problem-solving capacity of migration management by indicating how practices could more efficiently contribute to serve proclaimed project objectives, but to question the dominant framings, taken-for-granted assumptions, and routinized practices, rendering migration management as a widely unquestioned reality that expands to ever new fields of implementation today.

Outline of the book

The chapter following the Introduction outlines the theoretical framework of this study. It explains how the book combines the concept of border regime and the Autonomy of Migration thesis with a practice-theoretical lens inspired by Bourdieu's Theory of Practice. As detailed above, these approaches enable conceptualization of the practices of international migration management as inherently relational, contested, and made by social actors involved in the trans-Mediterranean field of migration management. Given this conceptual framework, transformations in means and methods of migration control are shaped by social actors—including migration movements—acting within specific historical conditions and relations. 'Migration crises' are regarded as moments of rupture and change in dominant ideas, routines, and morals of governing migration that make it possible for new actors, practices, and logic to emerge and gain influence in a certain field of struggles.

Chapter 2 demonstrates how the IOM emerged in North Africa with fading stability and legitimacy in the expanding European border regime, promoting its services to govern migration in more efficient, sustainable, and dignified ways than security-oriented forms of migration control. The chapter proceeds in three steps: the first part introduces the IOM with its historical dynamics, internal structures, and relations in the trans-Mediterranean field of migration politics. The second part recalls the historical developments in European and North African migration politics since the 1990s to reconstruct the emergence and shifts in logic of today's trans-Mediterranean field of migration management. It introduces relevant actors and their stakes, and carves out the logic and *doxic beliefs* that structure the field. The last part reviews academic literature about the politics of international migration management, examining this new paradigm in terms of changing discourses, practices, and institutional reconfigurations. The chapter concludes that the IOM presents a paradigmatic case to study the practices of international migration management in North Africa.

The following three chapters analyze in detail different transnational projects that were implemented by the IOM in Morocco and Tunisia and negotiated with regard to different actors in the field. The chapters roughly follow a chronological order of events that reveal critical situations, constitutive conflicts, and main issues negotiated. They provide a transnational perspective, tracing practices and negotiations from one setting to the next, indicating how they inform and resonate with each other. Each chapter brings a different practice of migration management to the spotlight and looks at how different logics mobilize action in the field. They draw on different concepts of Bourdieu's Theory of Practice to examine diverse relations, practices, and logic, and to intervene in key debates about neoliberal, humanitarian, and securitized migration governance.

Chapter 3 focuses on proactive practices of migration management in a context that was widely perceived as being shaped by traditions and dynamics of emigration. It analyzes the IOM's information campaigns to convince young Moroccans and Tunisians to voluntarily stay and to engage in the development of their countries of origin. Based on an analysis of the IOM's textual and visual documents, as well as interviews in both countries, I demonstrate how the organization uses individual incentives and (self-)discipline to educate marginalized youth in North Africa about their place in an asymmetrically structured field of international mobility rights and to change their behavior. While existing literature describes such techniques as modes of neoliberal governing at a distance (Rose and Miller 2010), through freedom (Ong 2007), and responsibilization (Ferguson and Gupta 2002), I focus on the relations between the IOM and potential North African emigrants to consider why those who are supposed to be managed would (not) participate in programs of neoliberal governance. I argue that it is the symbolic power of the IOM's education and social work practices that address morals, emotions, and beliefs to make entrepreneurial subjects participate in their own management. I conclude that these practices of individualized risk management are based on an unquestioned understanding of IOM's work as that of *global duty for education* that contributes to spread neoliberal logic and values to North African politics and societies.

Chapter 4 examines the IOM's practices of voluntary return, introduced when transit migration became a visible phenomenon in the two North African 'migration crises' outlined above. When the limits of a repressive border regime became obvious, the IOM offered migrants, blocked at the external borders of the EU, its assistance to return 'in dignity' to their countries of origin. Based on voluntary offers and incentives rather than physical force and state repression, migrants were mobilized to engage in their own return. Contrary to its promotion in public and political discourses, this chapter shows how voluntary return was conditioned by constant threat and "deportability" (De Genova 2002). It contributes to the growing field of return studies (see Coutin 2015) by demonstrating the inherent interactions and mutual conditions of modes of repatriation. Secondly, the chapter also analyzes how voluntary return became an instrument of mass migration management in the context of a 'humanitarian crisis' at the Tunisian-Libyan border in 2011. As such, the IOM's practices acquired a new meaning and practical logic of aid and assistance that informed a change in seeing its work as humanitarian. I argue that from the perspective of the IOM, migration management became an unquestioned *moral responsibility to protect* certain groups of migrants from the dangers of moving to Europe. Based on this understanding, the organization sorted and reoriented migration trajectories during transit. With assistance to Sub-Saharan migrants who were regarded as passive recipients of the aid, versus individuals with rights to asylum (or the potential to empower), the chapter concludes that the IOM contributed to shifting logic from a rights-based approach to one of humanitarian aid, rearranging strategies, struggles, and stakes of other actors including migrants.

Chapter 5 turns to the IOM's politics of anti-trafficking. An analysis of knowledge production, dissemination, capacity building, law and policy making shows how the IOM institutionalized the 'fight against human trafficking' into newly designed migration policies in Morocco and Tunisia. Focusing on the organization's long-term, strategic engagement, and relation to state actors in both countries, I discuss the IOM's *symbolic capital* as an international expert, its *collective habitus*, and the *asymmetrical relations* (re)produced between international experts and North African actors. Based on participant observation at different conferences and workshops, I show how the IOM incites state actors to introduce new categories of protection for Victims of Trafficking (VoT) and criminal persecution for smuggling and trafficking. This way, the IOM mainstreams its own vision of migration management for these countries' policies and holds authorities accountable to manage migration with international standards. Mobilizing the concepts of symbolic capital, symbolic power, and symbolic violence, I conclude that the IOM emerged in a position of a recognized expert that is able to influence doxic beliefs and enlarge boundaries for new issues, measures, and actors. Against this background, I propose an understanding of international migration management as a *struggle for hard facts and soft influence*.

The Conclusion summarizes empirical findings and reflects on the theoretical framework advanced in this book. I argue that migration management means to teach (potential) migrants, as well as Moroccan and Tunisian actors, to understand the control of migration as their own problem and to take appropriate action with the dominant logics in the field: neoliberalism, humanitarianism, and security. The IOM supports this process through social work and education, aid and assistance, and the production and dissemination of knowledge and capacity building. Through these practices, the IOM exercises a symbolic power about how migration is framed as problematic and determines what would legitimize its management. Based on a constant will to improve and reinvent its services and to productively deal with external protest, the organization expands to new spheres of action, funding, and influence—despite the questionable impact of many projects. While the IOM distinguishes its work from repressive state politics, this book shows how different logics, which reinforce but sometimes contradict each other, contribute to stabilize the border regime in the Mediterranean. It concludes that the IOM is neither a sheer instrument of states nor is it independent of them. The organization rather interferes in the complex relations in the trans-Mediterranean field of migration management, in which it can shape dominant logic and doxic beliefs and stretch boundaries to include new modes and content. In this way, the book is not only about new forms of governing migration in transit but also about new contents of control, such as gendered and racialized hierarchies for international mobility and protection. In light of the *symbolic violence* that obliterates the actual consequences of these practices, the IOM's migration management is widely accepted as legitimate and thus remains misrecognized as being imposed from a specific position in the field. While advancing our understanding of current transformations in how human mobility is controlled outside of Europe, this book directs particular attention to ubiquitous but underresearched institutions (such as the IOM) in this contested field.

Notes

1 The organization was founded in 1951 by Western European states to help them with the logistics of relocating displaced people after the Second World War. Until the end of the 20th century, the organization, whose main office is based in Geneva, expanded its activities thematically and its membership globally. The projects, that the IOM implements world-wide today, are largely financed by its European and North American member states. After decades of deliberately chosen independence, the IOM became a related agency under the framework of the United Nations (UN). For more details, see Georgi (2019); Geiger and Pécoud (2020).
2 Single inverted commas are used for quotes within quotes as well as for distancing in the text, e.g. to indicate policy relevant terms and labels which are typically used in the field, even when they are not directly quoted from a specific reference.

3 I use *italics* to highlight the conceptual terms that derive their specific meaning from the theoretical framework of this study the first time they appear in a chapter, without explaining or referencing them each time of their appearance. They are explained in the theoretical chapter in more detail. I also use *italics* to express emphasis on specific terms in the text as well as in interview citations.
4 All names and places are anonymized in this book. However, I include references to professions if they provide important contextual information, indicating position and relations in the field (see Kruse 2014, 358). Since anonymization (especially in smaller organizations) can be difficult, positions in the organization are kept vague. The book is not interested in the individual person interviewed or in abstract discourse formations, but seeks to grasp the social position in the field and the habitus of the collective actor represented. Consequently, the text does not refer to any characteristics that make informants and interview partners recognizable. Yet, categories such as nationality, gender, age, education are indicated if relevant; this would be to analyze the collective habitus of actors and power relations in the field.
5 Most interviews were conducted in French, a few in English and German. Most interview partners agreed to record our conversations, so that they can be turned into written transcripts for qualitative analysis. While analyzing the transcribed texts in their original language, I translated the quotes into English for selected presentation in the book to make the text more coherent. While translation into another language must be seen as a potential source of modifying the meaning, it also helps to know that transcriptions and translations are always interpretations based on selective reconstructions by the researcher (see Kowal and O'Connell 2009, 440).
6 These include political and scientific formats, notably manuals, reports, websites, videos, press releases, newspaper articles, magazines, and other printed, online and journalistic coverage.

Literature cited

Adler, Emanuel, and Vincent Pouliot. 2011. *International Practices*. Cambridge: Cambridge University Press. doi:10.1017/CBO9780511862373.

Andersson, Ruben. 2014. *Illegality, Inc. Clandestine Migration and the Business of Bordering Europe*. Oakland: University of California Press. doi:10.1525/9780520958289.

Andrijasevic, Rutvica, and William Walters. 2010. "The International Organization for Migration and the International Government of Borders." *Environment and Planning D: Society and Space* 28 (6): 977–999. doi:10.1068/d1509.

Ashutosh, Ishan, and Alison Mountz. 2011. "Migration Management for the Benefit of Whom? Interrogating the Work of the International Organization for Migration." *Citizenship Studies* 15 (1): 21–38. doi:10.1080/13621025.2011.534914.

Barnett, Michael, and Martha Finnemore. 2004. *Rules for the World: International Organizations in Global Politics*. Ithaka, NY: Cornell University Press. doi:10.7591/9780801465161.

Bartels, Inken. 2015. "Reconfigurations of Tunisian Migration Politics after the 'Arab Spring' – The Role of Young Civil Society Movements." In *Youth, Revolt, Recognition – The Young Generation during and after the "Arab Spring"*, edited by Isabel Schäfer, 62–79. Berlin: Humboldt Universität zu Berlin.

Bartels, Inken. 2017. "'We Must Do It Gently.' The Contested Implementation of the IOM's Migration Management in Morocco." *Migration Studies* 5 (3): 315–336. doi:10.1093/migration/mnx054.

18 Introduction

Bartels, Inken. 2018. "Practices and Power of Knowledge Dissemination." *Movements. Journal for Critical Migration and Border Regime Studies* 4 (1): 47–66. https://movements-journal.org/issues/06.wissen/03.bartels--practices-and-power-of-knowledge-dissemination-international-organizations-in-the-externalization-of-migration-management-in-morocco-and-tunisia.html [16.04.2021].

Belguendouz, Abdelkrim. 2005. "Expansion et Sous-Traitance des Logiques d'Enfermement de l'Union Européenne: L'Exemple du Maroc." *Cultures & Conflits* 57: 155–219. doi:10.4000/conflits.1754.

Ben Achour, Souhayma, and Monia Ben Jemia. 2011. *Révolution Tunisienne et Migration Clandestine vers Europe: Réactions Européennes et Tunisiennes*. 2011/65. CARIM Notes d'Analyse et de Synthèse. Florence: EUI.

Bigo, Didier. 2002. "Security and Immigration: Toward a Critique of the Governmentality of Unease." *Alternatives* 27 (Special Issue): 63–92. doi:10.1177/03043754020270S105.

Bojadzijev, Manuela, and Serhat Karakayalı. 2007. "Autonomie der Migration. 10 Thesen zu einer Methode." In *Turbulente Ränder. Neue Perspektiven auf Migration an den Rändern Europas*, edited by Transit Migration Forschungsgruppe, 203–210. Bielefeld: transcript. doi:10.14361/9783839407813-011.

Boubakri, Hassan. 2013. *Revolution and International Migration in Tunisia*. 2013/04. MPC Research Report. Florence: EUI.

Boubakri, Hassan, and Swante Potot. 2011. "Migrations tunisiennes: quand les Visas se tarissent, la Mer prend le Relais," March 11th, 2011. http://blogs.mediapart.fr/blog/swpotot/100311/exode-et-migrations-en-tunisie-quand-la-societe-civile-se-reveille [01.09.2020].

Bourdieu, Pierre. 1977. *Outline of a Theory of Practice*. Cambridge: Cambridge University Press. doi:10.1017/CBO9780511812507.

Bourdieu, Pierre. 1986. "The Forms of Capital." In *Handbook of Theory and Research for the Sociology of Education*, edited by John G. Richardson, 241–258. Westport, CT: Greenwood Press.

Bourdieu, Pierre. 1990. *The Logic of Practice*. Stanford, CA: Stanford University Press.

Bourdieu, Pierre. 1998. *Practical Reason. On the Theory of Action*. Stanford, CA: Stanford University Press.

Bourdieu, Pierre, and Loïc Wacquant. 1992. *An Invitation to Reflexive Sociology*. Chicago, IL: University of Chicago Press.

Bueger, Christian, and Frank Gadinger. 2008. "Praktisch Gedacht! Praxistheoretischer Konstruktivismus in den Internationalen Beziehungen." *Zeitschrift Für Internationale Beziehungen* 15 (2): 273–302. doi:10.5771/0946-7165-2008-2-273.

Bueger, Christian, and Frank Gadinger. 2014. *International Practice Theory – New Perspectives*. Basingstoke: Palgrave Macmillan. doi:10.1057/9781137395535.

Burawoy, Michael. 2000. "Introduction: Reaching for the Global." In *Global Ethnography. Forces, Connections, and Imaginations in a Postmodern World*, edited by Michael Burawoy, Joseph Blum, Sheba George, Zsuzsa Gille, Teresa Gowan, Lynne Haney, Maren Klawiter, Steven H. Lopez, Seán Ó Rian, and Millie Thayer, 1–40. Berkley and Los Angeles: The Regents of the University of California.

Caillault, Clotilde. 2012. "The Implementation of Coherent Migration Management through IOM Programs in Morocco." *IMIS-Beiträge* 40: 133–156.

Casas-Cortes, Maribel, Sebastian Cobarrubias, and John Pickles. 2013. "Re-Bordering the Neighbourhood: Europe's Emerging Geographies of Non-Accession

Integration." *European Urban and Regional Studies* 20 (1): 37–58. doi:10.1177/ 0969776411434848.
Cassarino, Jean-Pierre. 2010. "Dealing with Unbalanced Reciprocities: Cooperation on Readmission and Implications." In *Unbalanced Reciprocities: Cooperation on Readmission in the Euro-Mediterranean Area*, edited by Jean-Pierre Cassarino, 1–29. Washington, DC: Middle East Institute. doi:10.2139/ssrn.1730633.
Coutin, Susan Bibler. 2015. "Deportation Studies: Origins, Themes and Directions." *Journal of Ethnic and Migration Studies* 41 (4): 671–681. doi:10.1080/ 1369183X.2014.957175.
Crépeau, François. 2012. *Le Rapporteur Spécial des Nations Unies pour les Droits de l'Homme des Migrants conclut sa première Visite de Pays dans son Étude régionale des Droits de l'Homme des Migrants aux Frontières de l'Union Européenne: Visite en Tunisie*. Geneva: Office of the High Commissioner for Human Rights.
De Genova, Nicholas. 2002. "Migrant 'Illegality' and Deportability in Every-Day Life." *Annual Review of Anthropology* 31 (1): 419–447. doi:10.1146/annurev. anthro.31.040402.085432.
De Genova, Nicholas. 2013. "'We Are of the Connections': Migration, Methodological Nationalism, and 'Militant Research.'" *Postcolonial Studies* 16 (3): 250–258. doi:10.1080/13688790.2013.850043.
de Haas, Hein. 2014. "Morocco: Setting the Stage for Becoming a Migration Transition Country?" *Migrationpolicy.org*. https://www.migrationpolicy.org/article/morocco-setting-stage-becoming-migration-transition-country [01.09.2020].
de Haas, Hein, and Nando Sigona. 2012. "Migration and Revolution." *Forced Migration Review Online* 39: 4–5.
Di Bartolomeo, Anna, Tamirace Fakhoury, and Delphine Perrin. 2010. *CARIM – Migration Profile Tunisia*. CARIM Migration Profiles. Florence: EUI.
El Qadim, Nora. 2010. "La politique migratoire européenne vue du Maroc: contraintes et opportunités." *Politique européenne* 31 (2): 91–118. doi:10.3917/ poeu.031.0091.
European Commission. 2001. *Communication from the Commission to the Council and the European Parliament. On a Common Policy on Illegal Immigration*. COM (2001) 627 final. Brussels: European Commission.
European Council. 2006. *Presidency Conclusions of the Brussels European Council of 15 and 16 December*. SN 15914/01/05. Brussels: European Council.
Fargues, Philippe. 2006. "Arab Migration to Europe: Trends and Policies." *International Migration Review* 38 (4): 1348–1371. doi:10.1111/j.1747-7379.2004.tb00240.x.
Fassin, Didier. 2009. "Another Politics of Life Is Possible." *Theory, Culture and Society* 26 (5): 44–60. doi:10.1177/0263276409106349.
Ferguson, James, and Akhil Gupta. 2002. "Spatializing States: Toward an Ethnography of Neoliberal Governmentality." *American Ethnologist* 29 (4): 981–1002. doi:10. 1525/ae.2002.29.4.981.
Frowd, Philippe M. 2018. *Security at the Borders. Transnational Practices and Technologies in West Africa*. Cambridge: Cambridge University Press. doi:10. 1017/9781108556095.
GADEM (Groupe Antiraciste de Défense et d'Accompagnement des Étrangers et Migrants). 2007. *La Chasse aux Migrants aux Frontières Sud de l'Europe – Conséquences des Politiques Migratoires Européennes. Les Refoulements de Décembre 2006 au Maroc*. Rabat: GADEM.

Gaibazzi, Paolo, Alice Bellagamba, and Stephan Dünnwald. 2017. "Introduction: An Afro-Europeanist Perspective on EurAfrican Borders." In *EurAfrican Borders and Migration Management. Political Cultures, Contested Spaces, and Ordinary Lives*, edited by Paolo Gaibazzi, Alice Bellagamba, and Stephan Dünnwald, 3–28. Basingstoke: Palgrave Macmillan. doi:10.1057/978-1-349-94972-4_1.

Gammeltoft-Hansen, Thomas, and Ninna Nyberg-Sørensen. 2013. *The Migration Industry and the Commercialization of International Migration*. New York: Routledge. doi:10.4324/9780203082737.

Garelli, Glenda, and Martina Tazzioli. 2013. "Challenging the Discipline of Migration: Militant Research in Migration Studies, an Introduction." *Postcolonial Studies* 16 (3): 245–249. doi:10.1080/13688790.2013.850041.

Geiger, Martin. 2014. "The Production of a Safe Neighborhood and the Disciplining of International Mobility." In *Territoriality and Migration in the E.U. Neighbourhood: Spilling over the Wall*, edited by Margaret Walton-Roberts and Jenna Hennebry, 225–243. Dordrecht: Springer. doi:10.1007/978-94-007-6745-4_14.

Geiger, Martin, and Antoine Pécoud. 2010. "The Politics of International Migration Management." In *The Politics of International Migration Management*, edited by Martin Geiger and Antoine Pécoud, 1–20. Basingstoke: Palgrave Macmillan. doi:10.1057/9780230294882_1.

Geiger, Martin, and Antoine Pécoud. 2013. *Disciplining the Transnational Mobility of People*. Basingstoke: Palgrave Macmillan. doi:10.1057/9781137263070.

Geiger, Martin, and Antoine Pécoud. 2014. "International Organisations and the Politics of Migration." *Journal of Ethnic and Migration Studies* 40 (6): 865–887. doi:10.1080/1369183x.2013.855071.

Geiger, Martin, and Antoine Pécoud. 2020. *The International Organization for Migration: The New 'UN Migration Agency' in Critical Perspective*. Basingstoke: Palgrave Macmillan. doi:10.1007/978-3-030-32976-1.

Georgi, Fabian. 2010. "International Organization for Migration (IOM). Eine kritische Analyse." In *Grenzregime. Diskurse, Praktiken, Institutionen in Europa*, edited by Sabine Hess and Bernd Kasparek, 145–160. Berlin and Hamburg: Assoziation A.

Georgi, Fabian. 2019. *Managing Migration? Eine kritische Geschichte der Internationalen Organisation für Migration (IOM)*. Berlin: Bertz + Fischer.

Hess, Sabine. 2012. "De-Naturalising Transit Migration. Theory and Methods of an Ethnographic Regime Analysis." *Population Space Place* 18 (4): 428–440. doi:10.1002/psp.632.

Hess, Sabine. 2014. "Das Regieren der Migration als wissensbasierte Netzwerkpolitik. Eine ethnografische Policy-Analyse des International Centre for Migration Policy Development." In *Formationen des Politischen. Anthropologie politischer Felder*, edited by Asta Vonderau and Jens Adam, 241–273. Bielefeld: transcript. doi:10.14361/transcript.9783839422632.241.

Hess, Sabine, and Bernd Kasparek. 2010. *Grenzregime. Diskurse, Praktiken, Institutionen in Europa*. Berlin and Hamburg: Verlag Assoziation A.

Hess, Sabine, Bernd Kasparek, and Maria Schwertl. 2018. "Regime ist nicht Regime ist nicht Regime. Zum theoriepolitischen Einsatz der ethnografischen (Grenz-)Regimeanalyse." In *Was ist ein Migrationsregime? What Is a Migration Regime?* edited by Andreas Pott, Christoph Rass, and Frank Wolff, 257–283. Wiesbaden: Springer. doi:10.1007/978-3-658-20532-4_12.

Infantino, Federica. 2016. *Outsourcing Border Control. Politics and Practice of Contracted Visa Policy in Morocco*. Basingstoke: Palgrave Macmillan. doi:10.1057/ 978-1-137-46984-7.
IOM. 2011. *Humanitarian Evacuation on the Libyan Border. Three Monthly Report on IOM's Response*. March 2011. Geneva: IOM.
Jackson, Peter. 2008. "Pierre Bourdieu, the 'Cultural Turn' and the Practice of International History." *Review of International Studies* 34 (2): 155–181. doi:10.1017/ S0260210508008073.
Kalm, Sara. 2010. "Liberalizing Movement? The Political Rationality of Global Migration Management." In *The Politics of International Migration Management*, edited by Martin Geiger and Antoine Pécoud, 21–44. Basingstoke: Palgrave Macmillan. doi:10.1057/9780230294882_2.
Kalm, Sara. 2012. "Global Migration Management, Order and Access to Mobility." *IMIS-Beiträge* 40: 49–74.
Karakayalı, Serhat, and Vassilis Tsianos. 2007. "Movements that Matter. Eine Einleitung." In *Turbulente Ränder. Neue Perspektiven auf Migration an den Grenzen Europas*, edited by Transit Migration Forschungsgruppe, 7–22. Bielefeld: transcript. doi:10.14361/9783839407813-intro.
Kowal, Sabine, and Daniel C. O'Connell. 2009. "Zur Transkription von Gesprächen." In *Qualitative Forschung: Ein Handbuch*, edited by Uwe Flick, Ernst von Kardoff, and Ines Steinke, 437–447. Reinbek: Rowohlt.
Kruse, Jan 2014. *Qualitative Interviewforschung. Ein integrativer Ansatz*. Weinheim: Beltz Juventa.
Lavenex, Sandra. 2007. "The External Face of Europeanization: Third Countries and International Organizations." In *The Europeanization of National Policies and Politics of Immigration: Between Autonomy and the European Union*, edited by Thomas Faist and Andreas Ette, 246–264. Basingstoke: Palgrave Macmillan. doi:10.1057/9780230800717_12.
Marcus, George E. 1995. "Ethnography in/of the World System: The Emergence of Multi-Sited Ethnography." *Annual Review of Anthropology* 24 (1): 95–117. doi:10.1146/annurev.an.24.100195.000523.
Mato, Daniel. 2000. "Not 'Studying the Subaltern', but Studying with 'Subaltern' Social Groups, or, at Least, Studying the Hegemonic Articulations of Power." *Nepantla: Views from South* 1 (3): 479–502.
Mezzadra, Sandro. 2007. "Kapitalismus, Migrationen, Soziale Kämpfe. Vorbemerkungen zu einer Theorie der Autonomie der Migration." In *Empire und die biopolitische Wende. Die internationale Diskussion im Anschluss an Hardt und Negri*, edited by Marianne Pieper, Thomas Atzert, Serhat Karakayalı, and Vassilis Tsianos, 179–191. Frankfurt aM: Campus.
Miettinen, Reijo, Dalvir Samra-Fredericks, and Dvora Yanow. 2009. "Re-Turn to Practice: An Introductory Essay." *Organization Studies* 30 (12): 1309–1327. doi:10.1177/0170840609349860.
Migreurop. 2006. *Guerre aux Migrants: Le Livre Noir de Ceuta et Melilla*. http:// www.migreurop.org/IMG/pdf/livrenoir-ceuta.pdf [01.09.2020].
Moulier Boutang, Yann. 2002. "Thesen zur Autonomie der Migration und zum notwendigen Ende des Regimes der Arbeitsmigration." *Jungle World* 15 (April 3rd, 2002).
Moulier Boutang, Yann. 2007. "Europa, Autonomie der Migration, Biopolitik." In *Empire und die biopolitische Wende. Die internationale Diskussion im Anschluss an*

Negri und Hardt, edited by Marianne Pieper, Thomas Atzert, Serhat Karakayalı, and Vasilis Tsianos, 69–178. Frankfurt aM: Campus.

Natter, Katharina. 2015. "Revolution and Political Transition in Tunisia: A Migration Game Changer?" *Migrationpolicy.org.* https://www.migrationpolicy.org/article/revolution-and-political-transition-tunisia-migration-game-changer [01.09.2020].

Oelgemüller, Christina. 2017. *The Evolution of Migration Management in the Global North.* London and New York: Routledge. doi:10.4324/9781315644547.

Ong, Aihwa. 2007. "Neoliberalism as a Mobile Technology." *Transactions of the Institute of British Geographers* 32 (1): 3–8. doi:10.1111/j.1475-5661.2007.00234.x.

Papadopoulos, Dimitris, Niamh Stephenson, and Vassilis Tsianos. 2008. *Escape Routes. Control and Subversion in the 21st Century.* London: Pluto. doi:10.2307/j.ctt183q4b2.

Pouliot, Vincent. 2013. "Methodology. Putting Practice Theory into Practice." In *Bourdieu in International Relations: Rethinking Key Concepts in IR*, edited by Rebecca Adler-Nissen, 45–58. New York: Routledge.

Pritzlaff, Tanja. 2006. "Ethnographische Politikforschung." In *Methoden der Politikwissenschaft. Neuere Qualitative und Quantitative Analyseverfahren*, edited by Kai-Uwe Schnapp, Delia Schindler, Thomas Gschwend, and Joachim Behnke, 125–132. Baden-Baden: Nomos.

Rose, Nicholas, and Peter Miller. 2010. "Political Power beyond the State: Problematics of Government." *The British Journal of Sociology* 61 (1): 271–303. doi:10.1111/j.1468-4446.2009.01247.x.

Schäfer, Isabel. 2011. "Von der Revolution ins Reformlabor. Wer gestaltet den Übergang in Tunesien?" *Internationale Politik* 2 (März/April): 20–25.

Scheel, Stephan. 2019. *Autonomy of Migration? Appropriating Mobility within Biometric Border Regimes.* London and New York: Routledge. doi:10.4324/9781315269030.

Scheel, Stephan, Baki Cakici, Francisca Grommé, Evelyn Ruppert, Ville Takala, and Funda Ustek-Spilda. 2016. *Transcending Methodological Nationalism through a Transversal Method? On the Stakes and Challenges of Collaboration.* 1. ARITHMUS Working Paper Series. London: Goldsmiths, University of London.

Schwertl, Maria. 2013. "Vom Netzwerk zum Text: Die Situation als Zugang zu globalen Regimen." In *Europäisch-Ethnologisches Forschen. Neue Methoden und Konzepte*, edited by Sabine Hess, Johannes Moser, and Maria Schwertl, 106–126. Berlin: Dietrich Reimer Verlag.

Tazzioli, Martina. 2014. "'People Not of Our Concern'. Rejected Refugees in Tunisia." *Radical Philosophy* 184. https://www.radicalphilosophy.com/commentary/people-not-of-our-concern [01.09.2020].

Tazzioli, Martina. 2015. *Spaces of Governmentality. Autonomous Migration and the Arab Uprisings.* London: Rowman&Littlefield.

Transit Migration Forschungsgruppe. 2007. *Turbulente Ränder. Neue Perspektiven auf Migration an den Grenzen Europas.* Bielefeld: transcript. doi:10.14361/9783839407813.

Tsianos, Vassilis, and Serhat Karakayalı. 2010. "Transnational Migration and the Emergence of the European Border Regime: An Ethnographic Analysis." *European Journal of Social Theory* 13 (3): 373–387. doi:10.1177/1368431010371761.

Valluy, Jerome. 2007. *Contribution à une Sociologie Politique du HCR: Le Cas des Politiques Européennes et du HCR au Maroc.* Collection 'Etudes.' Recueil Alexandries. http://www.reseau-terra.eu/article571.html [01.09.2020].

Walters, William. 2006. "Border/Control." *European Journal of Social Theory* 9 (2): 187–203. doi:10.1177/1368431006063332.
Walters, William. 2010. "Imagined Migration Worlds: The European Union's Anti-Illegal Immigration Discourse." In *The Politics of International Migration Management*, edited by Martin Geiger and Antoine Pécoud, 73–95. Basingstoke: Palgrave Macmillan. doi:10.1057/9780230294882_4.
Wunderlich, Daniel. 2010. "Differentiation and Policy Convergence against Long Odds: Lessons from Implementing EU Migration Policy in Morocco." *Mediterranean Politics* 15 (2): 249–272. doi:10.1080/13629395.2010.485052.
Yanow, Dvora. 2009. "Organizational Ethnography and Methodological Angst: Myths and Challenges in the Field." *Qualitative Research in Organizations and Management: An International Journal* 4(2): 186–199. doi:10.1108/17465640910978427.
Ybema, Sierk, and Frans H. Kamsteeg. 2009. "Making the Familiar Strange: A Case for Disengaged Organizational Ethnography." In *Organizational Ethnography. Studying the Complexities of Everyday Life*, edited by Sierk Ybema, Dvora Yanow, Harry Wels, and Frans H. Kamsteeg, 101–119. London: Sage Publications. doi:10.4135/9781446278925.n6.
Ybema, Sierk, Dvora Yanow, Harry Wels, and Frans H. Kamsteeg. 2009. *Organizational Ethnography. Studying the Complexities of Everyday Life*. London: Sage Publications. doi:10.4135/9781446278925.

1 A praxeological approach to the politics of international migration management

The theoretical framework developed in this chapter combines different strands of literature that concern the everyday practices of international politics as the outcome of situated struggles within social structures. Drawing on recent debates in the fields of both International Political Sociology and Critical Border and Migration Studies, this chapter offers an interpretive perspective for studying the constructed and performative character of social phenomena that is taken for granted by many classical approaches in International Relations (IR) and Migration Studies.

Border and migration scholars have suggested a wide range of terms to indicate the shift in focus from borders 'as lines on a map' to the omnipresent processes and practices of bordering that develop within (in this case, European and African) territories (Parker and Vaughan-Williams 2009; Johnson et al. 2011). Analyzing these practices and processes, these scholars speak about "borderzones" (Christiansen, Petito, and Tonra 2000), "borderscapes" (Parker and Vaughan-Williams 2009), "border space" (Raeymaekers 2014), "border spectacle" (De Genova 2002), or "borderwork" (Rumford 2006) that takes place before, within, and/or beyond the border lines. Notably, social anthropologists have conceptualized the increasingly complex formations of borders and migration control as a "border regime" (Transit Migration Forschungsgruppe 2007), a "migration apparatus" (Feldman 2011), a "migration assemblage" (Schwertl 2015), a "migration industry" (Andersson 2014), or a "migration infrastructure" (Biao and Lindquist 2014). These terms seek to incorporate the dynamic and constructed nature of emerging constellations of actors, discourses, practices, knowledge, and technologies engaged in the making and challenging of migration control within, at, and around the edges of Europe.

As I will demonstrate in this chapter, of these terms, the concept of the *border regime* highlights the contested character of these dynamics. By introducing the agency of migrants into the complex picture of mobility and its control, this concept provides a heuristic perspective that recognizes migration as a constituent force in the production of international migration management. Approaching current transformations in governing practices and logic from a perspective of mobility, this perspective seeks to overcome rationalist, functionalist, and economist approaches of Migration Studies.

DOI: 10.4324/9781003204169-2

In the first part of this chapter, I argue that the border regime concept is useful for capturing the complexity of international migration governance beyond the state, as it directs attention to the role of non-state actors, soft forms of governing, and their embeddedness in political and economic structures. Moreover, the specific notion of a border regime, as it has been developed by critical border and migration scholars, opens up a relational and praxeographic perspective that understands migration practices and border struggles as the driving and structuring forces of the contingent developments in international migration politics. Drawing on the *Autonomy of Migration* thesis, this perspective allows for consideration of the *practices* and *struggles of migration* as integral components of the analysis of the reconfigurations of actors, logic, and practices of migration control in the North African borderlands.

Although this research perspective indicates the importance of struggles and practices as constitutive elements in the production of international migration governance, it provides little guidance on how to conceptualize and operationalize them as accounting for the transformations and stabilizations of a border regime that is under study. Therefore, in the second part of this chapter, I supplement the regime framework with a practice-theoretical perspective that proposes analyzing international politics as the result of an interplay of symbolic and material structures, along with diverse state and non-state actors, with their historical trajectories, internal dynamics, implicit knowledge, and embodied routines. Drawing on a praxeological approach in IR that is informed by Bourdieu's *Theory of Practice* allows for *symbolic and material struggles* at different levels of the *trans-Mediterranean field of migration management* to be placed at the center of my analysis. At the same time, this approach enables me to introduce the structuring agency and practical knowledge of a collective actor (the International Organization for Migration, IOM) into the analysis of current developments in international migration governance, without limiting its role to an instrument in the hands of rational acting states or to an autonomous international bureaucracy, in the sense of IR constructivism.

In the following two sections, I present the main theoretical concepts and arguments of these two strands of literature. In the final part, I argue that their combination provides rich ground for analyzing the IOM's practices as constitutive elements of the recent transformations of the expanding European border regime in North Africa.

1.1 The framework of a border regime and the Autonomy of Migration thesis

The regime concept is widely used among different social science disciplines and has recently drawn much attention in Border and Migration Studies (Horvath, Amelina, and Peters 2017; Pott, Rass, and Wolff 2018). Its main strength lies in its ability to account for the complexity and contestations of changing actor constellations and multilevel dynamics in international migration politics (Horvath, Amelina, and Peters 2017, 302). While emphasizing the role of norms and discourses, most migration regime approaches seek to study these political processes as contingent outcomes of practices (Pott, Rass, and Wolff 2018, 6). Beyond these common features, however, analyzing migration or border regimes[1] implies a variety of thematic perspectives, conceptual references, and methodological approaches (cf. Rass and Wolff 2018).

In order to clarify the specific theoretical, epistemological, and methodological underpinnings of the regime concept mobilized in this study, I refer to a particular research perspective that has been developed since the early 2000s in political and scientific discussions initiated by critical border and migration scholars (Transit Migration Forschungsgruppe 2007; Hess and Kasparek 2010; Heimeshoff et al. 2014; Hess, Kasparek, and Schwertl 2018). According to these scholars, the concept of the border regime aims to capture the dynamic, often conflicting, but mutually constitutive interactions between migration movements and the various attempts to control them. These scholars commonly draw on a definition by Giuseppe Sciortino (2004, 32), who argues that a border or migration regime is

> usually not the outcome of consistent planning. It is rather a mix of implicit conceptual frames, generations of turf wars among bureaucracies and waves after waves of "quick fix" to emergencies, triggered by changing political constellations of actors.

In a similar sense, Nicholas De Genova (2017, 5) calls states' diverse efforts at border control "reaction formations": they are "responses to a prior fact— the mass mobility of human beings on the move." According to the thesis of an Autonomy of Migration, the struggles and practices of migration are constitutive of the border regime—epistemologically speaking, they are the driving and structuring forces of its reconfigurations, interacting with and challenging existing modes of regulation (Moulier Boutang 2002; Bojadzijev and Karakayalı 2007; Mezzadra 2007). As a "heuristic model" (Moulier Boutang 2007, 169), the Autonomy of Migration thesis advances an understanding of migration as a "constituent creative force" that necessitates the reorganization of control (Papadopoulos, Stephenson, and Tsianos 2008, xviii).

Struggles of migration—as well as "migrant struggles" (Casas-Cortes et al. 2014) or "border struggles" (Mezzadra and Neilson 2013), as some authors phrase it—include two different phenomena. First, they refer to organized struggles in which migrants explicitly challenge the dominant politics of their management and control. Second, they also indicate the everyday struggles in which migrants "enact their (contested) presence" and resist their regulation (Casas-Cortes et al. 2014, 80). These are not explicitly framed as political battles or demands, but rather "imperceptible moments of social life" that fall outside of existing forms of control (Papadopoulos, Stephenson, and Tsianos

2008, xiii). Struggles of migration include a variety of visible and invisible practices of migrants at, inside, and (far) beyond the border. Importantly, these practices are not understood as individual acts but are conceptualized as part of a collective social and political movement (Karakayalı 2008; Hess, Kasparek, and Schwertl 2018) that, with reference to Asef Bayat (2010), can be called a "nonmovement." While they are neither formally organized nor share an overarching ideology or political project, nonmovements are collective struggles that mainly consist of ordinary people's strategies of resistance and refusal in everyday life (ibid.). However, these nonmovements are able to challenge existing regimes and prompt transformation—as Bayat demonstrates with regard to the Arab revolutions in 2011.

Furthermore, Vasilis Tsianos and Sabine Hess (2010, 244) highlight that practices of migration not only include the empirical practices of migrants but also the discourses, power relations, and wide range of political actions that condition these practices. According to Dimitris Papadopoulos, Niahm Stephenson, and Vasilis Tsianos (2008, 202), to take the perspective of the Autonomy of Migration thesis does not mean to "consider migration in isolation from social, cultural and economic structures. The opposite is true: migration is understood as a creative force within these structures." Thus, a border regime analysis that recognizes the constituent force of migration distances itself not only from the perception of migrants as victims or passive objects of management but also from the heroic figure of an entrepreneur or agent of development, which is pervasive in discourses of migration and development and in other attempts to romanticize the practices of migrants (cf. Karakayalı and Tsianos 2007, 15). In a relational perspective, social actors—whether migration movements or administrative institutions—make migration and borders, but they do so within the structural conditions that they (re)produce. Consequently, changes in control practices and shifts in regulatory logic are understood as the contingent and contested result(s) of asymmetrical interactions among the numerous political, technical, and administrative attempts of various actors to govern the "mobility of the migrants who seek to pass through, around, over, or under them" (Casas-Cortes et al. 2014, 57). Accordingly, I do not regard migration as a mere object of governance or management but as a social relation, the agency of which must be included in an analysis of the IOM's practices of migration management.

Based on this relational perspective, the Transit Migration Research Group (2007) developed a specific understanding of a regime as a more or less ordered ensemble of social practices and structures whose composition is not pregiven or centrally regulated but does provide an answer to questions and problems raised by these interactions. As a space of "negotiating practices" (Tsianos, Karakayalı, and Hess 2009, 2), this understanding refers to a complex set of norms, discourses, actors, and practices, and it emphasizes the use of technologies and knowledge that produce borders and migration in Europe and beyond (Karakayalı and Tsianos 2007, 14).

This constructivist perspective seeks to "denaturalize" the border (Walters 2002); to "decentralize" the migrant and the state in Border and Migration Studies; and to overcome merely structuralist, functionalist, and rationalist approaches in these disciplines (Kasparek and Hess 2010, 17).

This particular "praxeographic border regime analysis" (Tsianos and Hess 2010, 260, translation IB) is informed by references to different schools and traditions.[2] Most obviously, it shares significant similarities with the use of the regime concept in IR to theorize the entwinement of multiple actors—such as the supranational entity of the European Union (EU), international organizations (IOs), non-governmental organizations (NGOs), and private companies—as well as the rules, norms, and procedures that regulate international politics beyond the state (Keohane and Nye 1972; Krasner 1983). The regime concept, as it has been developed in IR since the 1970s, helps to avoid methodological nationalism without denying the key role that states play in global migration governance (Cvajner, Echeverría, and Sciortino 2018, 68). Against this background, the discussion of a European border regime comprises the heterogeneous

> complex and contradictory formations of diverse European authorities and jurisdictions – notably including not only the supranational state formation of the EU and the various nation-states involved, whether EU members or not (across and beyond "Europe"), as well as an array of nonstate actors, from private capitalist enterprises to "smuggling" networks to humanitarian agencies.
>
> (De Genova 2017, 5)

With references to the French regulation school and Poulantzas's materialist theory of the state, the border regime approach goes beyond a unified conception of a monolithic state and a linear understanding of politics as a centrally regulated, smooth, top-down process (Karakayalı 2008, 37; Hess 2012, 430). Instead, political regulations and instruments are regarded as the contingent outcomes of ongoing struggles in the global capitalist order, with the conflictive negotiations between diverse, asymmetrical positions (Poulantzas 1978) and their different forms of stabilization over time (Lipietz 1985) taken into account. This emphasis on the political economy of migration control allows an analysis of the reconfigurations of the border regime not only as a state-owned process of enhancing restrictive control and exclusion but also as a matter of materialist struggles in the global capitalist order that builds on the productivity of spatial and temporal regulation of labor and on new forms of inclusion and hierarchization of people on the move (Mezzadra 2007; Mezzadra and Neilson 2013).

Finally, referring to Foucault's studies of genealogy, governmentality, and discourse theory, the border regime concept is sensitive to the productivity of different forms of power, notably through knowledge production, technologies of subjectification, and (self-)disciplining. This "art of governing"

(Karakayalı and Tsianos 2007, 7, translation IB) helps delineate how power is not only exercised through coercion and repression but also through more informal and subtle methods of guiding and mobilizing subjects that influence the way they think, act, and perceive (Walters 2002, 2006). These soft modes of governing allow and secure the circulation of movement and the mobilization of a wider range of actors for their regulation and control (Hess and Karakayalı 2007, 53). In sum, by combining these different theoretical references, the border regime framework offers an innovative heuristic framework for studying the productivity of migration management within the global capitalist order, changing discursive rationalities, and complex institutional arrangements without reproducing the myth of the controllability of migration (Tsianos and Karakayalı 2010).

In the tradition of Social Anthropology and Ethnography, empirically the border regime approach has mostly been used to focus on the negotiation processes of international migration politics in micro-level situations. In line with newer approaches to an Anthropology of the State (e.g., Sharma and Gupta 2006, 165ff), it assumes that local policies, norms, and laws do not result from smooth, top-down implementation processes of transnational policy programs; rather, it focuses on the practical work of bureaucracies and the conflicts among and within governing or implementing institutions. However, the border regime perspective extends this focus by taking into account how the struggles and practices of migration prompt the (re)construction, transformation, and expansion of regulatory dynamics. By using this research perspective to study the politics of migration management in North Africa, I can integrate changing actor constellations beyond the state, various forms of governing, and shifting discursive, political, and economic structures all into one conceptual framework, as well as to relate them to the turbulences of migration that make these reconfigurations necessary. Accordingly, I do not position the practices of migration management in Morocco and Tunisia as a question of good or bad implementation of global discourses or of transnational governance programs, but as the contingent and contested outcomes of "continuous repair work" (Sciortino 2004, 33) in which IOs play a decisive but underresearched role. Investigating the projects of the IOM, I seek to direct analytical attention to the social actors who make migration management materialize in a certain context.

The question of how this *making* can be theoretically understood remains insufficiently answered in the border regime literature. While this literature offers a fruitful transnational, relational, and praxeographic perspective that highlights the contested character of international migration politics, it provides little guidance on how to conceptualize and operationalize its key elements for empirical research. First, I see the need to further conceptualize the *practices* and *struggles* that are essential to this approach, and to elaborate how they account for stability and change in a certain regime. Second, since potentially almost everything can be regarded as being part of a regime (cf. Pott, Rass, and Wolff 2018; Rass and Wolff 2018), it seems necessary to clarify who belongs to a formation under study, and why. In other words, we need criteria to delineate the *boundaries* of a border regime, which do not necessarily coincide with the borders of a state or continent. Finally, if I am to take the *social actors* making migration management as the analytical starting point for this study, I need to develop a theoretical approach that goes beyond the monolithic understanding of collective entities and that unpacks the particular experiences, strategies, and resources that account for their actions. In the following sections, I explain how I seek to fill these gaps by supplementing the border regime framework with practice-theoretical approaches in IR (1.2) and with selected concepts from Bourdieu's Theory of Practice (1.3).

1.2 Practice-theoretical approaches to international politics

Practice-theoretical approaches share the assumption that practices are crucial to the construction of social reality and thus also to the way international politics are made (Reckwitz 2002; Bueger and Gadinger 2008, 2015; Adler and Pouliot 2011a). These approaches are based on epistemological, ontological, and methodological perspectives promoted through the "practice turn" in social sciences (Schatzki, Knorr Cetina, and von Savigny 2000), which has recently become influential in the study of international politics (see Adler and Pouliot 2011a; Bueger and Gadinger 2014). Generally speaking, these perspectives aim to bring attention to "what actors do and say, and how these activities are embedded in larger arrangements" (Bueger and Gadinger 2014, 3). Moreover, they seek to reveal the practical or background knowledge shared by actors in a certain field, as well as the things and technologies these actors use in order to *do* international politics (ibid.). Practice-theoretical perspectives permit conceptualization of the social practices and the taken-for-granted knowledge of institutions that govern migration (such as the IOM) as constitutive elements in the struggles over migration and its control. Accordingly, the *making* of migration management results neither from rational interests nor from institutional change or discursive shifts alone, but from historically formed and embodied, partly implicit knowledge and routinized action of collective actors within a transnational field of material and symbolic struggles. In this way, practice-theoretical approaches offer new avenues for examining changes in governing techniques as well as the (re)production of a social and political order (such as the European border regime).

However, practice-theoretical approaches do not present a coherent, systematic "theory of practice," but rather "quite a heterogeneous set of ideas and concepts" (Bueger and Gadinger 2014, 8) that shares a common perspective on social action that differs epistemologically and ontologically from other social theories (Reckwitz 2002). Reaching beyond traditional dichotomies in levels and units of analysis, practice-theoretical perspectives commonly regard the interplay of agency and structures as constitutive of social action and of the making of the social world. In this respect, they make up a specific form of cultural-theoretical perspectives within social science theories in general (ibid.) and within constructivist approaches in IR in particular (Pouliot 2010, 14ff).

In contrast to structuralist, individualist, and normative theories, culturalist and constructivist theories include a level of symbolic, meaningful structures (usually called *culture*[3]) in their understanding of the social. However, while culturalist and constructivist theories share the interpretive, cultural, and linguistic turns in the social sciences, they differ in their location of the shared systems of meanings: in *mental orders* (such as internal cognitive schemata), *textual orders* (such as external discourses),[4] or *practical orders* (such as practical knowledge, know-how, everyday techniques, shared routines, and incorporated knowledge) (Reckwitz 2002, 246f.). According to Theodore Schatzki (1996, 89), such practical orders are a "temporally unfolding and spatially dispersed nexus of doings and sayings": in other words, they are a set of linguistic and non-linguistic actions that have some stability over time and space. Schatzki (ibid.) defines practice as a "routinized way in which bodies are moved, objects are handled, subjects are treated, things are described and the world is understood"; therefore, practices are inherently *social* practices. "A practice is social, as it is a 'type' of behaving and understanding that appears at different locals and at different points of time and is carried out by different body/minds" (ibid.). Social practices are different from mere action: collective, patterned, and embedded in a particular organized context, they always entail a collective component (Shove, Pantzar, and Watson 2012, 6). From a practice-theoretical perspective, politics of international migration management consist of distinct but intertwined concrete practices that are embedded in shared social knowledge, bodies, material artifacts, and routinized, collective action. Similar to discourse theoretical approaches, this perspective follows the linguistic turn but differs in its emphasis on the structuring agency of actors and the ontological status of practices (cf. Bueger and Gadinger 2008).

According to Andreas Reckwitz (2003), practice-theoretical approaches essentially share three core characteristics. First, using practices (and not discourses or norms) as the smallest unit of analysis assigns them a certain *materiality*. Practices are incorporated in human bodies and are materialized in artifacts, such as the use of technologies, the media, or means of transport; therefore, they are inherently material as well as ideal (ibid., 290). Linking individual actions and material objects in order to signify bodily, routinized practices rejects the materiality-versus-ideas duality (Bueger and Gadinger 2008; Shove, Pantzar, and Watson 2012).

The second core characteristic refers to the *implicit or informal logic of practices* (Reckwitz 2003, 291). Even though practice-theoretical approaches include elements of intentionality, normativity, and symbolism along with the explicit, relevant rules of action in a certain field (a *knowing that*), these elements are based on an implicit *practical sense* that is enclosed in practice.

Vincent Pouliot (2010, 38) argues that "which logic of reflexive action is to apply typically depends on an unreflexive practical mastery of the world." This *knowing how* as interpretive, methodical, and emotional knowledge is not universal but is rather historically specific, and contingent—so-called local knowledge. It consists of tacit, inarticulate background knowledge and is therefore not necessarily evident and/or transparent to the actors involved in a certain field (Duvall and Chowdhury 2011)—on the contrary: this knowledge, and the way it structures a certain social phenomenon, only becomes visible in practice.

Finally, the *routinized and unpredictable* character of social practices that accounts for continuity and change builds a common theme (Reckwitz 2003, 294). Within practice-theoretical literature, a tension is observed between two extremes. On the one hand, routinized practices that are based on implicit practical knowledge are expected to provide orderliness and *stability*, as they are responsible for repetitive administrative processes. On the other hand, the improvisational, innovative, or conflictual interpretation of practices also permits *change* in moments when the actors' routinized action does not fit a situation. Such a situation is often perceived as a crisis. A useful way to resolve this tension is to understand stability and change as two sides of the social world; accordingly, practices share different characteristics and depend on context, time, the way they interlock with larger complexes (such as social fields), and the subjects who sustain them. Regardless of which side is emphasized, practice-theoretical approaches foster a context-sensitive and process-oriented way of thinking. Social change and political transformations can be conceptualized as the interplay of routine and crises via an understanding of the relationship between agency and structure (Bueger and Gadinger 2008; Shove, Pantzar, and Watson 2012).

These three characteristics are also central to the study of *international practices*. According to the pioneering work on the subject by Emanuel Adler and Vincent Pouliot (2011b), international practices are "socially organized activities that pertain to world politics" (ibid., 7); they form the "ontological core concept that amalgamates the constitutive parts of social international life" (ibid., 10). Pouliot (2010, 12) emphasizes that

> in everything that people do, in world politics as in any other social field, there is always a practical substrate that does not derive from conscious deliberation or thoughtful reflection—instrumental, rule-based, communicative or otherwise. An essential dimension of practice is the result of inarticulate, practical knowledge that makes what is to be done appear self-evident or commonsensical.

In this respect, scholars of international politics trace how their objects of study are constructed through a rage of routinized practices that are based on a tacitly shared understanding of legitimate, appropriate action and are negotiated in a particular social context. This approach is not to be confused with policy-relevant implementation studies, which distinguish the negotiation process of *policy making* from its apparently apolitical, administrative *policy implementation*—which is represented as a neutral, rational, hierarchical, top-down process and reduces local implementers to mere decision-takers (cf. Stepputat and Larsen 2015, 15). Instead, these scholars advocate a performative understanding of international politics as the contingent, provisional, and unstable results of social practices and working routines; these politics do not occur in a vacuum, but are shaped by individual and collective agency as well as by the historical conditions and power relations in their respective fields of implementation (e.g., Nicolini 2009; Johnson et al. 2011).

Studying international politics from a practice-theoretical point of view reveals how the "world is constantly being produced in practice" (Bueger and Gadinger 2014, 19). This perspective directs attention to the situated and contextualized ways in which various state and non-state actors[5] interact (Sending and Neumann 2011). Importantly, within these interactions, IOs are understood neither as "passive servants" (Barnett and Finnemore 2004, 12) in the hands of powerful states nor as autonomous institutions that are able to shape and transform state interests. Thus, practice-theoretical perspectives share the constructivist view that moves the "interactive relationship between states and IOs at the center of analysis rather than presuming that the relationship is a one-way street in which states simply dictate to IOs" (ibid.). However, practice-theoretical perspectives go beyond a focus on the internal dynamics of IOs as bureaucracies that develop their own ideas and agendas (ibid., 3), seeking to design a consequently relational view on their role in international politics. In this respect, Ole Jacob Sending and Iver Neumann (2011, 234) argue that

> just as state understandings of the world and their attendant governing practices are shaped by IOs, so IOs are shaped by their environment and notably by the sovereign states that are their constitutive members.

In consequence, a practice-theoretical approach to the politics of international migration management invites us to open the black box of implementation actors (such as the IOM), but does not consider their behavior in isolation from other actors in the field. Instead, it suggests a relational and situated perspective that examines how their practices are structured by both their internal dynamics and implicit know-how as well as by their relations within larger social formations. Drawing attention to this mutually constitutive interplay of structuring agency and social structures, a practice-theoretical approach enables us to explain how larger formations (such as the border regime) are constantly (re)produced, negotiated, and transformed in practice. Accordingly, migration management becomes *real* through the way in which social actors (such as the IOM) interpret and do it. However, their interpretation and implementation are conditioned by institutional and professional understandings, strategies, and ambitions—the *collective habitus* or *practical sense*, to draw from Bourdieu—as well as the historically and geographically situated, cultural, and sociopolitical context of implementation, what I will call the trans-Mediterranean field of migration management. Mobilizing selected concepts of Bourdieu's Theory of Practice, in the next section I explain how the situated practices, meanings, and logic of migration control, along with their maintenance and change in North Africa, can be conceptualized as the contested outcome of the material and symbolic struggles among and within actors involved in a transnational field.

However, before introducing the Bourdieusian concepts, I wish to highlight the epistemological and methodological consequences of such a practice-theoretical perspective. Built on social-constructivist assumptions, practice theories question not only the distinction between knowledge and reality, but also the distinction between theory and practice in the social sciences (Pouliot 2007, 363). Accordingly, the research I draw on is not regarded as a "disinterested practice of objective knowledge production," but as a social practice itself (Berling 2013, 71). This book shares the assumption that science cannot be conducted from a detached, objective viewpoint; it is situated within the power relations of the field under study. This leads to the importance of reflexivity for both epistemological and methodological questions—concerning (among others) the relation between the researcher and the researched—as being themselves situated in a field of practice (Bueger and Gadinger 2008). This *social epistemology* calls for a responsibility in the power of definition and a sensibility of the contingency of interpretation from a particular perspective and position within the field (ibid.). In this respect, this book does not aim to produce 'neutral' or 'objective' knowledge about the IOM's migration management, instead offering a critical, situated perspective that intervenes in the symbolic struggles around the needs and possibilities of migration control in North Africa. It advances a critical and constructivist perspective that views international migration management as the result of shared practices and continued struggles in which the production of (scientific) knowledge plays an integral and powerful role.

1.3 A Bourdieusian perspective on the politics of international migration management

As outlined above, practice-theoretical approaches do not offer a universal theory of everything social; rather, they help spell out and question different aspects that are taken for granted by other social theories (Adler and Pouliot 2011b, 3). In this regard, one of the most prominent approaches was developed by Pierre Bourdieu in his empirically grounded research on the perpetuation of social inequalities (Bourdieu 1977, 1990a, 1992a). He did not develop one consistent theory of practice, although practices are at the center of his praxeological approach. With this approach, Bourdieu and his colleagues[6] sought to rethink the relation between structure and agency as an unnecessary but predominant dichotomy in the social sciences. "Of all the oppositions that artificially divide social science the most fundamental, and the most ruinous is the one that is set up between *subjectivism and objectivism*" (ibid. 1990b, 135, emphasis in original). According to Bourdieu (ibid.), this fundamental division underpins the existence of other dichotomies, including the "material and symbolic dimensions in social life," "interpretation and explanation," and theoretical and empirical research. To overcome these divisions, Bourdieu (ibid., 147) proposed a *constructivist structuralism* or *structuralist constructivism:*

> By structuralism, or structuralist, I mean that there exists in the social world, and not only in symbolic systems (language, myths etc.), objective structures, independent of the consciousness or the will of agents, which are capable of orienting or constraining practices and representations. By constructivism, I mean that there is a social genesis to both schemes of perception, thought and action on the one hand, and social structures on the other.

In short, "what people do or say is neither just a reflection of what is going on in their heads nor a production of social and material structures," but a result of practices (Jackson 2008, 164), of the actualization of past experiences and internalized knowledge in a certain situation. It is the "habitus, history turned into nature" that remains unrecognized but accounts for the practical reproduction of structures (Bourdieu 1977, 78). Accordingly, practices emerge from the interplay between the subjective perspectives and predispositions of social actors (the habitus) on the one hand, and the structural conditions of the particular social context in which they are acting (the field) on the other.

Bourdieu's Theory of Practice offers a number of useful concepts for empirical IR studies (Hopf 2002; Guilhot 2005; Williams 2007; Leander 2010; Pouliot 2010). Despite their differences, these studies commonly turn to the "micro-sociological practices" of international politics (Adler-Nissen 2013, 5). They ask how inarticulate, taken-for-granted knowledge and habitual, embodied, and unreflective behavior enter into and influence world politics, and they analyze the shared logic, symbolic power, and modes of domination in their specific fields of interest (Pouliot 2008, 269). In this respect, many scholars use Bourdieu's concepts as thinking tools, further developing and adjusting them to the needs of their respective research context.

However, Bourdieu's concepts are all connected and develop their analytical power only in relation to each other. In the following sections, I introduce the concepts relevant to this study, directing particular attention to the concepts of field and habitus. I argue that the field concept is particularly useful, as it bridges traditional levels of analysis and it allows us to delineate a transnational social formation that positions the state in relative terms

36 *A praxeological approach*

vis-à-vis other actors. The concept of habitus helps unpack the internal dynamics, embodied routines, and diverse resources that drive the practices of social actors in a given field. Together, they enable conceptualization of the reconfigurations in what I call the trans-Mediterranean field of migration management as the result of material and symbolic struggles at different levels among and within the various actors involved.

1.3.1 Field

According to Pierre Bourdieu and Loïc Wacquant's description (1992, 97), a field is a

> network, or a configuration of objective relations between positions. These positions are objectively defined, in their existence and in the determinations they impose upon their occupants, agents or institutions, by their present and potential situations *(situs)* in the structure of the distribution of species of power (or capital) whose possession commands access to the specific profits that are at stake in the field, as well as by their objective relations to other positions (domination, subordination, homology etc.).

In short, the notion of field refers to a particular social space defined by the (power) relations between actors' *positions* and the *stakes* (or objects of struggle) for which the actors compete (ibid., 98ff). Bourdieu often used the metaphor of a *game* to describe a field: actors are taken in by the game and pursue its stakes based on their emotional or corporal investments. Bourdieu and Wacquant (ibid., 117) called these unquestionable beliefs in the value, benefits, and rules of the game *illusio*. Participation in a game or field means a tacit acknowledgment of its informal and unspoken rules and structures, which constitute an effective constraint on action even as they operate at the semi- or unconscious level. In their entirety, these rules and structures constitute what Bourdieu defined as *doxa:* they comprise "all that is accepted as obvious, in particular the classifying schemes which determine what deserves attention and what does not" (quoted in Pouliot 2010, 34); or, in other words, the "silent experience of the world," that which "goes without saying" (Jackson 2008, 167; see also Bourdieu 1977, 167f.). These learned, fundamental, and mostly self-evident beliefs and values include unquestioned hierarchies and forms of domination. Functioning as tacitly acknowledged rules of the game, they do not dictate but rather inform participants' actions and behavior in the field (Bourdieu 1990a, 80ff). In this respect, they establish a *common sense* among diverse actors of what is at stake (here, regarding migration control in North Africa), but no *consensus* (on how this control should be exercised). Importantly, today's doxic beliefs result from previous struggles between those who govern and those who are governed (ibid. 2017, 308). Being constantly actualized in routinized action, these beliefs contribute to the stabilization of hierarchies and the reproduction of social orders, making them appear natural and legitimate; however, they can also be questioned and renegotiated, especially in situations of crisis.

Studies of international politics employ the concept of the field to analyze international and transnational spaces, notably of security experts (Bigo 2002a; Bigo et al. 2007; Abrahamsen and Williams 2011; Adler-Nissen 2014), of private military organizations (Williams 2007; Leander 2010), and of democracy promotion (Guilhot 2005). A crucial advantage of the field concept is that it helps to understand transnational social spaces while overcoming the "level of analysis problem" (Pouliot and Mérand 2013, 36). Whether a field is local, national, international, or functional is contingent on the nature of the struggle and is not defined a priori by the analysis (ibid., 32ff). Notably, the concept permits transcendence of nationally bounded case studies (Scheel et al. 2016), since the boundaries of a field, and the definition of who populates it, are the product of historical and constant struggles—a by-product of attempts to establish legitimate domination within the field. According to Bourdieu and Wacquant (1992, 100), the "limits of the field are situated at the point where the effects of a field cease." Transnational fields can thus be conceptualized as social spaces in which multiple state and non-state actors interact according to more and less explicit rules and various forms of power on different levels. On the one hand, this means that states constitute a key point of reference in a given field; on the other hand, states are not the only—and perhaps not the main—actors involved in its constitutive struggles. Bourdieu's field concept allows us to analyze social actors within their scope of action and their hierarchical relations to each other without determining a priori which actors are relevant and on which level or scale they interact.

Directing attention to the positions, relations, and struggles of the different actors involved in what can be called the *game of international migration management*, I use the field concept to reveal what is at stake in the making and challenging of migration control in North Africa. While I generally use the term *field of migration politics*, I speak of a particular *field of migration management* to indicate its centering around the particular logic, rules, and stakes that have evolved in international migration politics since the early 2000s (see Chapter 2). I call this field *trans-Mediterranean* to delineate the social space of migration control around the edges of the EU or, more accurately, around the "Schengenland" (Walters 2002). In academic literature, a wide range of geographical terms are employed to label this space: Euro-African (Andersson 2014), EurAfrican (Gaibazzi, Bellagamba, and Dünnwald 2017a), Euro- or Southern Mediterranean (Raeymaekers 2014), and the European neighborhood (Casas-Cortes, Cobarrubias, and Pickles 2013) are the most prominent. These labels refer, with different emphases and perspectives, to a relational space emerging between the two continents that is subject to the dynamics and problematizations of migration movements and border controls.

38 A praxeological approach

In this study, I use the term *Mediterranean field* in order to question the idea of two necessarily separated continents as distinct geographical, demographic, cultural, and moral units (Mudimbe 1988). In the Bourdieusian sense, this Mediterranean field is not defined by its geographical territory or cultural essence, but by the "dynamic, transformative and heterogenous figurations" that constitute this negotiation space, reinventing its histories, legacies, and affiliations (Pugliese 2010, 10). This way, it transports the asymmetric relationships and (imperial) imaginations reflected in current migration management interventions. Fernand Braudel (quoted in Raeymaekers 2014, 168, emphasis in original) noted that a "Mediterranean Frontier simultaneously focuses attention on the *conjuncture* of historical experiences, while taking seriously the *structure* (or the geopolitics) of Europe's expanding border enforcement." According to Timothy Raeymaekers (2014, 168), the notion of the Mediterranean refers to a "fluid landscape built on overlapping, and often contradictory, histories of mobility and exchange." In a similar sense, Paolo Gaibazzi, Alice Bellagamba, and Stephan Dünnwald (2017b, 11) argue that

> Europe's externalization of border and migration management towards Africa writes a new chapter in a long history of intertwined and concomitantly unequal trajectories between the two continents, once marked by exchanges and mutual appropriation and fascination, as well as by stark power inequalities, colonial domination, exploitation and racial discrimination.

I add the prefix *trans* in order to highlight the "transversal movement that cuts across authorized borders, moving not vertically or horizontally but diagonally across space" (Pugliese 2010, 11). In this way, I aim to emphasize the dynamics of this space which is crossed, contested, and managed both by the movements of migration as well as by the political and administrative policies, practices, and people that try to control them. Speaking of a *trans-Mediterranean field*, I seek to extend Bourdieu's field concept to include perspectives on the colonial histories and the postcolonial hierarchical relations that constitute this social space.

By referring to a *trans-Mediterranean* instead of a *European* field, I explicitly include North African state and non-state actors in my analysis as active participants who shape the developments in this field. This perspective highlights how transnational interventions (such as IOM projects in North Africa) do not take place in a vacuum but rather in specific contexts that influence their implementation (Gaibazzi, Bellagamba, and Dünnwald 2017b, 12). In other words, I expect that the contexts of implementation matter to the practical outcome and to the concrete meaning of migration management beyond the EU's territory. As I will show in the following chapters, the IOM introduces new elements in these contexts, but it also builds its work on the assumptions, modes, and strategies of migration control already existing in Morocco and Tunisia. Using the concept of the trans-Mediterranean field of migration management, I aim to delineate the relational character of the politics of international migration management; its historical embeddedness; and the specific sites of negotiation, contestation, and appropriation that challenge, transform, and stabilize the expanding European border regime in North Africa.[7]

1.3.2 Habitus

Bourdieu's concept of habitus directs attention to the cultural sources and subjectivity of the social actors involved in a field. Bourdieu (2000, 261 quoted in Pouliot 2010, 31) defined habitus as

> a system of durable, transposable dispositions, which integrates past experiences and functions at every moment as a matrix of perception, appreciation, and action, making possible the accomplishment of infinitely differentiated tasks.

The habitus gives analytical access to the semiconscious orientations and the engines of social actors. It is generated by the sum of external structures that have been internalized by actors in order to enable them to function effectively in a wide range of different situations. While the habitus does not automatically determine specific practices, it leads actors to engage in certain behaviors; it is generative rather than iterative. It accounts for practices "not by the process of a mechanical determinism," but by orienting, limiting, and conditioning their invention as a "system of generative schemes" (Bourdieu 1977, 95). In this respect, the habitus is an art of inventing that introduces contingency into social action, as the same disposition can potentially lead to different practices, depending on the social context. At the same time, however, the habitus also negates complete free will or creativity: social actors improvise within the bounds of historically constituted practical knowledge and bodily dispositions. As it is historical and dispositional, the habitus provides actors with "an endless capacity to engender products—thoughts, perceptions, expressions, actions—whose limits are set by the historically and socially situated conditions of its production" (ibid., 85).

For Bourdieu and Wacquant (1992, 107), these actors were not individuals or subjects, but *agents* who are "socially constituted as active and acting in the field under consideration by the fact that they possess the necessary properties to be effective, to produce effects, in this field." Therefore, it is the

> knowledge of the field itself in which they evolve that allows us best to grasp the roots of their singularity, their point of view or position (in the field) from which their particular vision of the world (and of the field itself) is constructed.

40 A praxeological approach

The habitus can be described as a generative grammar providing a basis for the production of practices; however, it does so only in relation to a social configuration—the field. It is relational in the sense that agents are the product of social relations. Even though the habitus is located at the subjective level, it constitutes the intersection of structure and agency (Bourdieu 1977, 72).

For scholars of international politics, the concept of habitus is mostly employed to place those responsible for formulating and implementing politics at the center of analysis (see Schlichte 1998; Hopf 2002; Pouliot 2008). According to Peter Jackson (2008, 156), the concept helps demonstrate the cultural roots of policymaking and provides a "framework for analyzing the dynamic relationship between the cultural predispositions of policymakers and the external structures that limit their policy choices." While the habitus is theorized to animate practices of both collective and individual actors, studies of international politics mostly focus on the individual level.

Scholars studying the sociology of organizations propose a twofold relational perspective to analyze the interdependence of structural developments in a field and the corresponding positions, strategies, and resources of organizations (e.g., Dederichs and Florian 2002; Janning 2002). This interplay can result in positional changes in the field, in its differentiation, in new stakes, and in changes within organizations, which are often not passively endured but proactively driven forward. In this perspective, organizations are analyzed as organized, cooperate actors with a proper individual character—both within a specific constellation of actors as well as regarding the internal processes and dynamics in producing its actorness and agency. This perspective aims to conceptualize an organization itself as a social field resulting from internal relations of power and capital distribution (Dederichs and Florian 2002, 91). Thus, the notion of the field is applied at different levels; strategies, positions, and capital distribution are not only analyzed among collective actors but also equally among the individual actors within them (ibid., 86). This relational approach provides a useful way to conceptualize IOs simultaneously as both *collective actors*—in the sense of "international bureaucracies" (Barnett and Finnemore 2004)—within a transnational field, and as *bureaucratic fields* assembling individual actors. When individual actors compete for positions within organizations, they "are likely to develop similar dispositions and thus similar practices," which crystalize a collective habitus (Jackson 2009, 107). The collective habitus, in turn, informs the outward performance and agency of the organization within the transnational field.

This twofold relational perspective on collective actors in international politics avoids examining (new) actors in isolation but instead asks how their internal dynamics lead them to adapt to, transform, or undermine a field under study. Applying this perspective to the emergence and the growing importance of the IOM within the field of migration politics directs attention to the organization's accumulation and transformation of different sorts of *capital* that fit recent reconfigurations of rules and logic in the field. As I will reconstruct in more detail in the following chapter, migration control has increasingly become a matter of technical, knowledge-based management rather than of militarized border control (Chapter 2). This development has enhanced the possibilities and increased the capacities of IOs to claim expertise in this field. Empowered by neoliberal logic and by expanding markets for migration management services, IOs have become "well-resourced corporate structures possessing the material, organizational and ideational capacities to operate on increasingly global scales" (Abrahamsen and Williams 2011, 315). Taking on the role of competent and competitive service providers, they can act as rational, reasonable, and reliable partners for states that seek to cost-effectively outsource the implementation of international migration governance (Gammeltoft-Hansen and Nyberg-Sørensen 2013; Andersson 2014). Mobilizing the concept of habitus permits an examination of how the internal structures and dynamics of the IOM make the organization particularly well equipped to fit recent developments in the field of migration management and to occupy an increasingly influential position.

1.3.3 Symbolic capital, power, and violence

Both individual and collective actors develop (often-unconscious) strategies to improve and maintain their positions in a field. These positions are determined by the distribution of different forms of capital. Bourdieu and Wacquant (1992, 119) mainly distinguished among *economic*, *social*, and *cultural capital*, each of which can be converted from one into the other through the actor's effort. Economic capital refers to material resources; social capital stems from the possibility of actors to mobilize "a durable network of more or less institutionalized relationships of mutual acquaintance and recognition" (Bourdieu 1986, 21); and cultural capital consists of competencies, skills, qualifications, etc. that can be mobilized by the actor as sources of cultural authority. Bourdieu (1998, 47) also introduced the notion of *symbolic capital* as a particular form of capital that the other three types take when they are recognized and valued as legitimate by other actors in the field. The possession and use of symbolic capital most obviously manifests in rituals of recognition and the accumulation of prestige, which secure and maintain distinction and dominance (Jackson 2009, 110).

Symbolic capital provides a crucial source of power, since it makes it possible to define what counts as common sense in a certain field (Nicolini 2012, 59). According to Bourdieu (1992a, 153, translation IB), it is "the power to make things with words." This "power to constitute the given by stating it, to act upon the world by acting upon the representation of the world," Bourdieu and Wacquant argued (1992, 148),

> does not reside in "symbolic systems" in the form of an "illocutionary force." It is defined in and by a definite relation that creates belief in the

legitimacy of the words and of the person who utters them, and operates only inasmuch as those who undergo it recognizes those who wield it.

As a consequence, "if you want to change the world, you have to change the way, how the world is 'made'" (Bourdieu 1992a, 151, translation IB). Bourdieu (ibid., 147f.) emphasized the importance of symbolic struggles over the imposition of a universal vision and division of the world and its legitimate social order for the opportunity to reproduce unquestioned, seemingly natural forms of hierarchies and domination. Language plays a crucial role in this regard: it is not a mere mode of communication, but in fact provides a medium of power relations. Bourdieu and Wacquant (1992, 142, emphasis in original) argued that "*linguistic relations are always relations of symbolic power* through which relations of force between the speakers and their respective groups are actualized in a transfigured form." The difference between Bourdieu's work and poststructuralist approaches, therefore, is "not the emphasis on discourse, but rather how to study it" (Adler-Nissen 2013, 6). While the latter treat discourses "as practices that systematically form the objects of which they speak" (Foucault 1972, 29), Bourdieu proposed a sociological approach to discourses, in which they are produced from specific positions within an asymmetrically structured social space and an existing web of meanings and categorizations. He argued that

> language is embedded in social hierarchies and in bodies. Particular agents, utterances and words may signal a person's social position. Language is part of distinction and classification games.
> (quoted in Adler-Nissen 2013, 6)

Thus, the power of language stems from the authority that comes from the position of the speaker and their relations within the material and symbolic struggles in a certain field (Wacquant 2017, 23). As Bourdieu (2004, 115) wrote: "the truth of the social world is the object of struggles in the social world and in the sociological world which is committed to producing the truth of the social world." This means that "the truth" about migration and its control emerges from the struggles among social actors in the trans-Mediterranean field of migration management—not only struggles over material gains but also struggles over the *symbolic power* to define the reality of migration and its possibilities of control within transit countries.

Bourdieu's understanding of power and violence is based on the idea that it must be recognized and acknowledged by those who are dominated (ibid. 2017, 291). Those actors addressed by IOM projects (be it North African politicians or (potential) migrants) are constitutive of the struggles in the trans-Mediterranean field of migration management. Therefore, the relations between those who manage and those who are managed will be systematically considered in this study. In the symbolic struggles over the imposition of meanings and the representations of social reality, the use of *symbolic violence* provides the key to understanding

> why people comply with hierarchy even though this might be against their interest, and why they do not dissent even though their objective situation of subordination and exploitation would seem to spur them to do so.
> (Christoforou and Lainé 2014, 8)

Symbolic violence works through schemes of classification and evaluation, categories of perception, and a dominant use of language that becomes "internalized by other actors as both natural and legitimate" (Jackson 2009, 111). According to Bourdieu (2005, 82), symbolic violence is more powerful than physical violence, since it is embedded and embodied in actors' modes of action, cognition, and beliefs, therefore often remaining *misrecognized* as a form of violence. Relying on the cooperation of Moroccan and Tunisian politicians and administrations as well as on the participation of (potential) migrants, the IOM is able to exercise a tacit but effective form of *"violence which is exercised upon a social agent with his or her complicity"* (Bourdieu and Wacquant 1992, 167, emphasis in original; see also Bourdieu 2017, 290).

While the symbolic form of power and violence is often characterized as *soft*, it is "not soft at all because it constitutes, in the same manner as material power, a potential instrument of domination" (Pouliot and Mérand 2013, 40). For Bourdieu and Wacquant (1992, 171), *symbolic domination* is particularly powerful, since it is "so deeply grounded as to need no justification: it imposes itself as self-evident, universal." This means that actors in the field take the system of domination for granted, because of "the quasi-perfect and immediate agreement" that has been reached between their schemes of perception and the seemingly objective structures in the field (ibid.). While presenting itself as universal and neutral, the discourse of international migration management nonetheless creates a symbolic order that legitimates the symbolic power of and produces the symbolic violence exercised by the IOM. Working with the tacit complicity of Moroccan and Tunisian actors, the IOM relies on this soft form of power to introduce concepts, categories, and 'best practices' into emerging North African migration politics. For the European donors of these projects, it provides a welcome alternative to the physical fortification of the external borders of the EU.

Bourdieu's conceptions of power and domination underline the importance of the production of expert knowledge and the entwinement of science and international politics. While traditional approaches in IR view knowledge as objective and independent from actors and structures (cf. Laffey and Weldes 1997), Bourdieu advocated reflecting on the position of individual or institutionalized research within a field of study. In this respect,

> the impossibility of a "view from nowhere" can be replaced by a "view from somewhere" in which researchers come into focus not just as

"factors" (or discourses) but also as "actors" in the co-constitution of social reality.

(Berling 2013, 64)

This implies a need to broaden the study of the science–policy nexus to a more general scope that includes the struggles for power in the political field in which science takes an influential position (ibid., 65). Knowledge should not only be analyzed within the scientific field, as science and other forms of expertise exercise a symbolic power in other fields, including international migration politics. In terms of empirical analysis, this approach enables analysis of the practically generated knowledge of IOs as stakes within transnational fields of struggles "for the power to impose universalist claims" as "the legitimate vision of the social world" (Bourdieu 2003, 181). In this context, the notion of *misrecognition* allows us to explore the "disguised practices of power that operate through the imposition of categories of meaning that are aimed at reproducing social relationships of domination" (Jackson 2009, 113). Giving discourses, categories, and definitions a "doxic aura of legitimacy, universality and naturalness" (Pouliot 2004, 13), the symbolic power of expert knowledge produced and distributed by IOs can both bring about and hinder change in international politics.

Paraphrasing Max Weber, Bourdieu (1992a, 149f.; 2017, 226) argued that the state typically holds the monopoly over the legitimate use of symbolic violence[8]; however, this is not an absolute monopoly, since different (symbolic) powers are in permanent conflict over the legitimate view of the world in what Bourdieu called the *field of power*. In this *meta-field*, the state acts as "central bank for symbolic credit" (ibid. 2017, 222), disposing of "the state capital granting power over the different species of capital and over their reproduction" (ibid. 1998, 42). Through this "*objectified symbolic capital* codified, delegated and guaranteed by the state, in a word *bureaucratized*" (ibid., 50f., emphasis in original), the state wields "a genuinely *creative*, quasi-divine power" (ibid., 52, emphasis in original) to name things, to make them official, and to manufacture what seems normal and legitimate in the eyes of its citizens (ibid. 2017, 128). Based on this *meta-capital*, the state is able to maintain its social and political orders without constantly applying repressive means (ibid., 295). At the same time, Bourdieu viewed the state not as a unified actor acting without contradiction, but itself as a place, object, and resource of material and symbol struggles.[9]

Within and beyond the state, "transnational guilds of professionals" (Bigo 2011, 247) today increasingly accumulate *transnational symbolic capital* to attribute power over concepts, classifications, and information. In this way, they question the state as the legitimate holder of meta-capital as well as its monopolistic position on symbolic power (Adler-Nissen 2014, 659). Acting as a "global elite," these professionals claim a dominant position in the "global field of power" (Bourdieu 1996) that affects their reputation in the national bureaucratic fields of different countries (Pouliot and Mérand 2013, 37).[10]

A praxeological approach 45

This relational perspective paves the way for new actors to emerge in international politics. Instead of an isolated view, this perspective invites us to consider how these professionals gain authority relative to the state. In this way, the rise of IOs in the global governance of migration does not automatically signal a decrease in the power of the state; rather, different actors are seen as interacting, conditioning, and distinguishing each other's positions in dynamic tension within a transnational social space (Abrahamsen and Williams 2011, 313).

If international migration politics is regarded as a conflictive production field of fundamental ideas, "the truth" about migration and its control results from the struggles between various state and non-state actors with different stocks of capital. One's power to impose a certain view depends on their authority and recognition (symbolic capital) gained in previous struggles. Accordingly, the position of international experts in the trans-Mediterranean field of migration management builds on prior accumulation of symbolic capital. When actors are recognized as experts, their visions of the social world no longer need to be imposed on other actors in the field: the visions appear as self-evident and therefore legitimate to the other actors. In this respect, not only states but also a number of bureaucratic institutions (such as IOs) are able to play a crucial role in producing and disseminating meanings and representations, as they continuously accumulate capital to routinely (re)invest in the struggles over the legitimate views of and means for migration control. In this book, I show how the IOM gained recognition as an international expert through continuous proactive engagement in the symbolic struggles over different kinds of migratory issues, and how this symbolic capital was successfully reinvested in struggles over power and positions in different contexts and levels of the trans-Mediterranean field of migration management.

1.3.4 Struggles as the engine of stability and change

Besides the emphasis on the symbolic dimension, Bourdieu often highlighted the conflictive character of social processes. He regarded social fields as *fields of struggles* in

> which agents confront each other, with differentiated means and ends according to their position in the structure of the field of forces, thus contributing to conserving or transforming its structure.
> (Bourdieu 1998, 32)

They do so according to "the regularities and the rules constitutive of this space of play," which designate a specific place to each actor that informs their room for maneuver (Bourdieu and Wacquant 1992, 102). The *sense of one's place* makes the actor's and others' positions in the field appear self-evident (Bourdieu 1992b, 141ff). This sense of one's and others' place is an important element of the notion of *practical sense*, or the actor's "socially constituted 'sense of the game,'" which results from the interplay between habitus and field as the intersection of embodied dispositions and structured positions (Bourdieu and Wacquant 1992, 120f.). This implicit practical logic functions without conscious reflection or reference to explicit knowledge; rather, it is through an unreflexive actualization in the present of past experiences that actors know what is to be done in the future—not in a strictly iterative sense, but in partly improvisatory fashion. Therefore, it is due to practical sense—to the compliance with explicit rules and norms, rational interests and calculations, and/or the best argument—that actors do what they can, instead of what they should (Pouliot and Mérand 2013, 30ff). Accordingly, a social practice is "the done thing, because one cannot do otherwise" from the perspective of a certain position in the field (Bourdieu 1990a, 69).

In terms of the struggles in the trans-Mediterranean field of migration management, it follows that actors in more powerful positions are able "to make it function to their advantage" (Bourdieu and Wacquant 1992, 102). For example, those actors who are recognized as international experts (such as the IOM) are able to define 'migration crises' or the 'dangers of human trafficking' as phenomena that can be solved through their proper management services. However, even the most powerful actors in a field must "contend with the resistance, the claims, the contention, 'political' or otherwise, of the dominated" (ibid.). Other actors continually question dominant concepts and categorizations and propose different understandings and modes of actions regarding the continuous struggles of migration in the Mediterranean. In resonance with the Autonomy of Migration thesis, Bourdieu and Wacquant (ibid.) concluded that "[t]here is history only as long as people revolt, resist, act." In this sense, they understood change and renewal as neither the result of rational action nor of structural determination, but as effected by actors and their strategies in the field. These are not conscious intentions or explicit plans of individuals, but practices that emerge from the fit of their habitus with a certain constellation of the field—in other words, the space of opportunities for a certain actor. Similarly, the reproduction of social order and hierarchies does not result from "the direct and simple action exercised by a set of agents" but is rather "the indirect effect of a complex set of actions engendered within the network of intersecting constraints" (Bourdieu 1998, 34).

Importantly, these constraints contain not only repressive means but also symbolic, seemingly non-violent structures and mechanisms of domination, which provide for the acceptance of the dominant conditions and the complicity of those who are dominated. For example, migrants from Sub-Saharan Africa are not only pushed back from the external borders of the EU by police forces, their mobility is also restricted by the IOM's suggestion to 'voluntarily' return to their countries of origin (see Chapter 4). Thus, a Bourdieu-inspired approach to questions of stability and change in the global political and social order directs particular attention to the "ways that existing social hierarchies and power relations are legitimated and reproduced by cultural representations and by practices" (Jackson 2009, 102). In this sense, Bourdieu is often (mis)taken as a theorist of reproduction rather than of transformation; however, as this book will demonstrate, his work alludes to both. It helps reveal how changing practices of migration control account for the reproduction of social and political orders, such as the European border regime (Gorski 2012, 11f.).

1.4 Outline of a praxeological research perspective on the politics of international migration management

Bourdieu's concepts direct attention to widely unnoticed and undertheorized aspects of international politics, such as social practices and embodied routines; the unconscious, unquestioned assumptions that shape actors' thoughts and action; and the symbolic resources employed in political struggles. As Rebecca Adler-Nissen (2013, 1) summarizes, using Bourdieu's approach in IR enables one to

> rediscover the everyday practices, symbolic structures and arenas of conflict that bring many other actors into perspective, rather than just focusing on nation states that produce (what we call) international politics. [...] Bourdieu allows us to explore how people create international relations in their daily activities. In short, Bourdieu helps us to take the discursive, visual and embodied practices in international politics more seriously.

In terms of the politics of international migration management, Bourdieu's thinking tools invite us to look beyond the official discourses and organizational charts of the implementing actors and to question the common beliefs, routinized practices, and seemingly self-evident meanings of migration control. Examining the bureaucratic struggles and power relations among and within collective actors, these thinking tools help explore what is at stake and for whom in increasingly transnational fields of migration governance. As a result, using Bourdieu's concepts permits us to rethink international migration politics beyond (but still relative to) the state and to analyze transformations in the practices and logic of migration control as the contingent and contested outcomes of situated struggles within larger social formations.

Placing the constitutive role of social practices at the center of analysis, Bourdieu's concepts enrich the relational and praxeographic perspectives proposed in the border regime literature. They allow us to clarify how new practices and logic of migration control emerge out of the dynamic relationship between historically formed dispositions—the collective habitus—of transnationally operating bureaucratic institutions (such as IOs), and the wider structural social space constituted by general rules and various forms of power that are at stake both domestically and internationally—the trans-Mediterranean field of migration politics. A Bourdieusian approach highlights the ongoing material and symbolic struggles about positions, resources, legitimacy, meanings, and values among different actors at different levels within this field. Such an approach conceptualizes the practices, meanings, and materializations of migration management as neither exclusively constituted through discourses nor made by individual assignments of meaning, but as a collective and contested process of negotiations conditioned by power structures and the experiences, knowledge, and strategies of actors in the field.

Turning to Bourdieu's Theory of Practice therefore extends border regime approaches that draw mostly on Foucauldian analytics of power, discourse, and governmentality in order to analyze new rationalities of migration control and emerging governing techniques. While both types of perspective highlight the importance of practices, they differ in the way they explain their emergence and change. Authors mobilizing a Foucauldian thinking conceptualize practices of migration management primarily as technologies or arts of governing that result from dominant rationalities and hegemonic discourses. These practices are primarily understood as the effects of powerful—and above all, neoliberal—discourses that trickle down to and materialize in different contexts of implementation (Kalm 2010, 2012). In this respect, economic rationalities and biopolitical governing technologies in particular, along with their complex effects on the way migration is problematized and regulated in certain situations, become visible and analyzable (Walters 2010). Sharing an understanding with the Bourdieusian perspective of power as productive and soft, studies inspired by Foucault's work highlight the subtle and discursive forms of migration governance that structure how migrants are thought about and dealt with in specific contexts, as well as how they are activated to participate in their own management (Geiger and Pécoud 2013). These studies offer useful perspectives on the discourses and governance programs of migration management, their emergence, their contradictions, and their depoliticizing effects. In this way, they provide important insights into the programmatic reconfigurations of international migration politics.

The praxeological perspective informed by Bourdieu's Theory of Practice that is proposed in this book, in turn, moves the conflictive negotiations among and within the social actors to the center of the analysis. According to Didier Bigo (2002b, 73f.), one of the few authors who employ Bourdieu's concepts to analyze international migration politics, new practices in the field do not only result from "everyday technologies" and "effects of power" but also emerge out of "political struggles, and especially through institutional competition," that take place "inside institutions and between institutions for what is to count as the legitimate truth." In this perspective, practices of migration management do not stem from discourses or governance programs but from the interplay of actors acting within structures. The situated manifestations of migration management are unstable and incomplete, not only because they face external resistance and appropriations in specific contexts but also because they are made by actors within a field of asymmetrical power relations and positions that structure their action. Consequently, "truth" in the field of migration management does not result from a dominant discourse or rationality, but from the symbolic struggles among and within the involved actors over the imposition of legitimate means of migration control.

Assuming that actors' practices depend on the understanding of the problem with which they are dealing, this praxeological approach opens the black box of the actors involved in these struggles. It seeks to reveal the unquestioned and often embodied knowledge that makes their action possible and to unpack the sense they make of the issues at stake. A practice-theoretical approach that mobilizes Bourdieusian thinking is not only interested in the *explicit discursive knowledge* and *subjectivations* that define, classify, and produce subjects of governance; it complements Foucauldian studies with a focus on how the *implicit knowledge*, incorporated *know-how*, and *routines* that are practically mastered by actors within a certain field are decisive in producing a social phenomenon (Reckwitz 2011, 49). This line of thinking brings the social actors—along with their experiences, strategies, unquestioned assumptions, and embodied routines—into the regime framework and locates them within a field of material and symbolic struggles, power relations, and asymmetric positions.

The integration of such a praxeological perspective into the border regime framework emphasizes the importance of struggles but shifts the focus away from their *modes* and *effects* to their *content* (Bigo 2002b; Fassin 2009). By asking what is at stake for different actors involved in a certain field, it sheds light on the values, morals, and convictions that motivate different actors to actually get engaged in the field. Importantly, these stakes are conceived as more than purely economic interests and utilitarian dynamics: they include strategies to maximize different kinds of individual and institutional resources and to expand actors' recognition in other fields. A praxeological perspective not only reveals the disconnections between the promises of migration management discourses and their moderate impact on the control and constraint of (potential) migrants; it also highlights the gains these practices provide to the IOM in order to distinguish and expand its activities in the trans-Mediterranean field of migration management.

Practices of migration management are not only interesting for the modes and procedures of governing that they express but also for their contents, directions, meanings, and values. Didier Fassin (2009, 48) argues that

> politics is not just a "game of arts of governing" but is about "the issues at stake in the practices of government" [...]: in other words, the matter of governing matters for governmentality.

50 *A praxeological approach*

In this sense, this book is interested not only in understanding *how* irregularized migration to Europe is prevented within countries of transit but also in clarifying *who* is supposed to stay (compared to others who are free to travel and work on a global scale) according to the dominant criteria, moral assumptions, and unquestioned rules in the field. Consequently, this book offers new perspectives on the reproduction of postcolonial relations and global social inequalities in international migration politics. To this end, the analysis of the practices and meanings of migration management in Morocco and Tunisia becomes a "question of the concrete way in which individuals and groups are treated, under which principles and in the name of which morals, implying which inequalities and misrecognitions" (ibid., 55). Moreover, these inequalities and misrecognitions hint at how and why those who are supposed to be managed accept and even participate in their own governing, which appears as natural and common sense to them. For these reasons, Fassin (ibid., 52) suggests moving "from the 'rules of the game' to its stakes." However, he also highlights that these "perspectives are not contradictory, but complementary: by analyzing the new forms of the art of governing one may apprehend what its political content is" (ibid.).

In sum, by applying this praxeological perspective to a study of the IOM's practices of migration management in North Africa, I emphasize the practical and inarticulate nature of international migration politics, and I focus on the structuring agency of one transnationally operating bureaucratic institution that is recognized as a relevant actor in the expanding European border regime. I treat the IOM as both a collective actor implementing the politics of international migration management outside Europe and as a transnational bureaucratic field with its own internal rules, stakes, and struggles over positions among departments, offices, staff members, etc. With this perspective, I open the black box of IOs and take into account the role of transnational policymaking elites who have a practical sense or feel for the game—who practically know not only what is possible and impossible but also how the written and unwritten rules of the game of international migration management can be changed. In this regard, the empirical chapters will demonstrate how the IOM succeeds in establishing a common sense among the involved actors that makes migration management a self-evident way of governing migration in the trans-Mediterranean field of migration politics.

A Bourdieu-inspired take on the politics of international migration management moves the struggles, negotiations, and experiences of actors to the foreground of border regime analysis. While I primarily use this perspective to investigate the institutional machinery that puts the politics of international migration management into practice, I also examine it in relation to the struggles of migration and the recurring crises and instabilities of their control as driving forces of the contingent developments in and of the European border regime. Integrating a praxeological perspective into the border regime framework allows me to empirically investigate the micropolitics of migration management in Tunisia and Morocco as a contingent and contested process marked by global dynamics, historical and geographical contexts, and the practical sense and tacit knowledge of the actors involved. This combination allows me to comprehend the reconfigurations in migration control as a matter of social practices and the taken-for-granted knowledge of governing institutions within the context of material and symbolic power relations, in which migration movements play an integral part.

Throughout the following chapters, I reconstruct how changing practices, meanings, and logic of migration control account for the reconfiguration and the expansion of the border regime in North Africa. In each empirical chapter, I elaborate on a different practice and corresponding logic of the regime, using the concepts mentioned above with varying degrees of emphasis.

Notes

1 Both the terms *border regime* and *migration regime* are used within these discussions, depending on the focus of analysis. I use the term border regime to indicate a distinctive approach to analyzing the 'problem of migration' through the prism of the border (Mezzadra and Neilson 2013).
2 For discussions of the theoretical background, see also Karakayalı (2008); Tsianos and Hess (2010); Hess and Karakayalı (2017).
3 Referring to Clifford Geertz's definition of culture as "webs of significance" (1973, 5); see also Jackson (2008).
4 However, Christian Bueger and Frank Gadinger (2014, 10) highlight that these perspectives are themselves pluralist and share many concerns with practice-theories.
5 Some authors would add "material artefacts"; for further discussion, see Bueger and Gadinger (2014, 19).
6 His praxeological approach has been further elaborated by his colleagues Abdelmalek Sayad and Loïc Wacquant, whose works also provide important references for this study.
7 I refer to a *European* border regime instead of a *trans-Mediterranean* border regime in order to capture the larger structure and trajectory of migration control that originates in Europe. While it is not regulated or controlled by a single actor or a central logic, this expansive transnational project has nevertheless largely been initiated, funded, and driven forward by the EU and its member states (see Chapter 2).
8 Bourdieu (1998, 41) saw the state not only as the holder of physical force of coercion but, more importantly, as the holder of "a sort of meta-capital granting power over other species of capital." This concentration of capital leads to the "emergence of a specific, properly state capital which enables the state to exercise power over the different fields and over the different particular species of capital, and especially over the rates of conversion between them" (ibid.).
9 While Bourdieu referred to the state "as a key point of reference" in many fields, he also argued that "the state cannot be considered as only an actor; it is first and foremost a space of positions" (Pouliot and Mérand 2013, 37) or a "specific field populated by bureaucracies, professionals of politics and private agents" (Bigo 2011, 248). Consequently, it is the "game's main stake more than it is an institution" (Pouliot and Mérand 2013, 36).

10 Bourdieu (1998) mostly equated the "field of power" with the state. However, other authors contend that a relational perspective on the field of power needs to "encompass the entirety of the power relations of the agents involved, including those of the dominated classes"; therefore, they conceptualize the field of power as a "meta-field" that is not only comprised of the elites but is also defined by the power relations of specific fields (Schmitz, Witte, and Gengnagel 2017, 63).

Literature cited

Abrahamsen, Rita, and Michael C. Williams. 2011. "Privatization in Practice: Power and Capital in the Field of Global Security." In *International Practices*, edited by Emanuel Adler and Vincent Pouliot, 310–332. Cambridge: Cambridge University Press. doi:10.1017/cbo9780511862373.017.

Adler, Emanuel, and Vincent Pouliot. 2011a. *International Practices*. Cambridge: Cambridge University Press. doi:10.1017/CBO9780511862373.

Adler, Emanuel, and Vincent Pouliot. 2011b. "International Practices: Introduction and Framework." In *International Practices*, edited by Emanuel Adler and Vincent Pouliot, 3–35. Cambridge: Cambridge University Press. doi:10.1017/cbo9780511862373.003.

Adler-Nissen, Rebecca. 2013. "Introduction. Bourdieu and International Relations Theory." In *Bourdieu in International Relations: Rethinking Key Concepts in IR*, edited by Rebecca Adler-Nissen, 1–23. New York: Routledge.

Adler-Nissen, Rebecca. 2014. "Symbolic Power in European Diplomacy: The Struggle between National Foreign Services and the EU's External Action Service." *Review of International Studies* 40 (4): 657–681. doi:10.1017/S0260210513000326.

Andersson, Ruben. 2014. *Illegality, Inc. Clandestine Migration and the Business of Bordering Europe*. Oakland: University of California Press. doi:10.1525/9780520958289.

Barnett, Michael, and Martha Finnemore. 2004. *Rules for the World: International Organizations in Global Politics*. Ithaka, NY: Cornell University Press. doi:10.7591/9780801465161.

Bayat, Asef. 2010. *Life as Politics. How Ordinary People Change the Middle East*. Amsterdam: Amsterdam University Press. doi:10.5117/9789053569115.

Berling, Trine Villumsen. 2013. "Knowledges." In *Bourdieu in International Relations: Rethinking Key Concepts in IR*, edited by Rebecca Adler-Nissen, 59–79. New York: Routledge.

Bigo, Didier. 2002a. "Border Regimes, Police Cooperation and Security in an Enlarged European Union." In *Europe Unbound. Enlarging and Reshaping the Boundaries of the European Union*, edited by Jan Zielonka, 213–239. New York: Routledge.

Bigo, Didier. 2002b. "Security and Immigration: Toward a Critique of the Governmentality of Unease." *Alternatives* 27 (Special Issue): 63–92. doi:10.1177/03043754020270s105.

Bigo, Didier. 2011. "Pierre Bourdieu and International Relations: Power of Practices, Practices of Power." *International Political Sociology* 5 (3): 225–258. doi:10.1111/j.1749–5687.2011.00132.x.

Bigo, Didier, Laurent Bonelli, Dario Chi, and Christian Olsson. 2007. *Mapping the Field of the EU Internal Security Agencies*. Centre d'Études sur les Conflits. Harmattan. http://www.open.ac.uk/researchprojects/iccm/files/iccm/Bigo_Bonelli_Chi_Olsson.pdf [01.09.2020].

Bojadzijev, Manuela, and Serhat Karakayalı. 2007. "Autonomie der Migration. 10 Thesen zu einer Methode." In *Turbulente Ränder. Neue Perspektiven auf Migration an den Rändern Europas*, edited by Transit Migration Forschungsgruppe, 203–210. Bielefeld: transcript. doi:10.14361/9783839407813-011.
Bourdieu, Pierre. 1977. *Outline of a Theory of Practice*. Cambridge: Cambridge University Press. doi:10.1017/CBO9780511812507.
Bourdieu, Pierre. 1986. "The Forms of Capital." In *Handbook of Theory and Research for the Sociology of Education*, edited by John G. Richardson, 241–258. New York: Greenwood Press.
Bourdieu, Pierre. 1990a. *The Logic of Practice*. Stanford, CA: Stanford University Press.
Bourdieu, Pierre. 1990b. *In Other Words: Essays toward a Reflexive Sociology*. Stanford, CA: Stanford University Press.
Bourdieu, Pierre. 1992a. *Language and Symbolic Power*. Cambridge: Polity Press.
Bourdieu, Pierre. 1992b. *Rede und Antwort*. Frankfurt aM: Suhrkamp.
Bourdieu, Pierre. 1996. *State Nobility: Elite Schools in the Field of Power*. Cambridge: Polity Press.
Bourdieu, Pierre. 1998. *Practical Reason. On the Theory of Action*. Stanford, CA: Stanford University Press.
Bourdieu, Pierre. 2003. *Méditations Pascaliennes*. Paris: Seuil.
Bourdieu, Pierre. 2004. *Science of Science and Reflexivity*. Chicago, IL: Polity Press.
Bourdieu, Pierre. 2005. *Die verborgenen Mechanismen der Macht. Schriften zu Politik & Kultur 1*, edited by Margareta Steinrücke, translated by Jürgen Bolder. Hamburg: VSA Verlag.
Bourdieu, Pierre. 2017. *Über den Staat: Vorlesungen am Collège de France 1989–1992*, translated by Horst Brühmann and Petra Willim. Berlin: Suhrkamp Verlag.
Bourdieu, Pierre, and Loïc Wacquant. 1992. *An Invitation to Reflexive Sociology*. Chicago, IL: The University of Chicago Press.
Bueger, Christian, and Frank Gadinger. 2008. "Praktisch Gedacht! Praxistheoretischer Konstruktivismus in den Internationalen Beziehungen." *Zeitschrift Für Internationale Beziehungen* 15 (2): 273–302. doi:10.5771/0946–7165-2008-2–273.
Bueger, Christian, and Frank Gadinger. 2014. *International Practice Theory – New Perspectives*. Basingstoke: Palgrave Macmillan. doi:10.1057/9781137395535.
Bueger, Christian, and Frank Gadinger. 2015. "The Play of International Practice." *International Studies Quarterly* 59 (3): 449–460. doi:10.1111/isqu.12202.
Casas-Cortes, Maribel, Sebastian Cobarrubias, Nicholas De Genova, Glenda Garelli, Giorgio Grappi, Charles Heller, Sabine Hess, Bernd Kasparek, Sandro Mezzadra, Brett Neilson, Irene Peano, Lorenzo Pezzani, John Pickles, Federico Rahola, Lisa Riedner, Stephan Scheel, and Martina Tazzioli. 2014. "New Keywords: Migration and Borders." *Cultural Studies* 29 (1): 55–87. doi:10.1080/09502386.2014.891630.
Casas-Cortes, Maribel, Sebastian Cobarrubias, and John Pickles. 2013. "Re-Bordering the Neighbourhood: Europe's Emerging Geographies of Non-Accession Integration." *European Urban and Regional Studies* 20 (1), 37–58. doi:10.1177/0969776411434848.
Christiansen, Thomas, Fabio Petito, and Ben Tonra. 2000. "Fuzzy Politics around Fuzzy Borders: The European Union's 'Near Abroad.'" *Cooperation and Conflict* 35 (4): 389–415. doi:10.1177/00108360021962183.
Christoforou, Asimina, and Michaël Lainé. 2014. *Re-Thinking Economics: Exploring the Work of Pierre Bourdieu*. New York: Routledge. doi:10.4324/9780203797136.

54 *A praxeological approach*

Cvajner, Martina, Gabriel Echeverría, and Giuseppe Sciortino. 2018. "What Do We Talk When We Talk about Migration Regimes? The Diverse Theoretical Roots of an Increasingly Popular Concept." In *Was ist ein Migrationsregime? What Is a Migration Regime?* edited by Andreas Pott, Christoph Rass, and Frank Wolff, 65–80. Wiesbaden: Springer. doi:10.1007/978-3-658-20532-4_3.

Dederichs, Andrea Maria, and Michael Florian. 2002. "Felder, Organisationen und Akteure – eine organisationssoziologische Skizze." In *Bourdieus Theorie der Praxis: Erklärungskraft – Anwendung – Perspektiven*, edited by Jörg Ebrecht and Frank Hillebrandt, 69–96. Wiesbaden: Westdeutscher Verlag. doi:10.1007/978-3-322-99803-3_4.

De Genova, Nicholas. 2002. "Migrant 'Illegality' and Deportability in Every-Day Life." *Annual Review of Anthropology* 31 (1): 419–447. doi:10.1146/annurev.anthro.31.040402.085432.

De Genova, Nicholas. 2017. "Introduction. The Borders of 'Europe' and the European Question." In *The Borders of "Europe". Autonomy of Migration, Tactics of Bordering*, edited by Nicholas De Genova, 1–36. Durham, NC and London: Duke University Press. doi:10.2307/j.ctv11smr05.4.

Duvall, Raymond D., and Arjun Chowdhury. 2011. "Practices of Theory." In *International Practices*, edited by Emanuel Adler and Vincent Pouliot, 335–354. Cambridge: Cambridge University Press. doi:10.1017/cbo9780511862373.019.

Fassin, Didier. 2009. "Another Politics of Life Is Possible." *Theory, Culture and Society* 26 (5): 44–60. doi:10.1177/0263276409106349.

Feldman, Gregory. 2011. *The Migration Apparatus: Security, Labor, and Policymaking in the European Union*. Stanford, CA: Stanford University Press. doi:10.1515/9780804779128.

Foucault, Michel. 1972. *The Archaeology of Knowledge*. New York: Pantheon Books.

Gaibazzi, Paolo, Alice Bellagamba, and Stephan Dünnwald. 2017a. *EurAfrican Borders and Migration Management. Political Cultures, Contested Spaces, and Ordinary Lives*. Basingstoke: Palgrave Macmillan. doi:10.1057/978-1-349-94972-4.

Gaibazzi, Paolo, Alice Bellagamba, and Stephan Dünnwald. 2017b. "Introduction: An Afro-Europeanist Perspective on EurAfrican Borders." In *EurAfrican Borders and Migration Management. Political Cultures, Contested Spaces, and Ordinary Lives*, edited by Paolo Gaibazzi, Alice Bellagamba, and Stephan Dünnwald, 3–28. Basigstoke: Palgrave Macmillan. doi:10.1057/978-1-349-94972-4_1.

Gammeltoft-Hansen, Thomas, and Ninna Nyberg-Sørensen. 2013. *The Migration Industry and the Commercialization of International Migration*. New York: Routledge. doi:10.4324/9780203082737.

Geertz, Clifford. 1973. "Thick Description: Toward an Interpretive Theory of Culture." In *The Interpretation of Cultures: Selected Essays*, edited by Clifford Geertz, 3–30. New York: Basic Books.

Geiger, Martin. and Antoine Pécoud. 2013. *Disciplining the Transnational Mobility of People*. Basingstoke: Palgrave Macmillan. doi:10.1057/9781137263070.

Gorski, Philip S. 2012. "Introduction: Bourdieu as a Theorist of Change." In *Bourdieu and Historical Analysis*, edited by Philip S. Gorski, 1–15. Durham, NC: Duke University Press. doi:10.1215/9780822395430-001.

Guilhot, Nicolas. 2005. *The Democracy Makers. Human Rights, and the Politics of Global Order*. New York: Columbia University Press. doi:10.7312/guil13124.

Heimeshoff, Lisa-Marie, Sabine Hess, Stefanie Kron, Helen Schwenken, and Miriam Trzeciak. 2014. *Grenzregime II. Migration, Kontrolle, Wissen, Transnationale Perspektiven*. Berlin and Hamburg: Assoziation A.

Hess, Sabine. 2012. "De-Naturalising Transit Migration. Theory and Methods of an Ethnographic Regime Analysis." *Population Space Place* 18 (4): 428–440. doi:10.1002/psp.632.
Hess, Sabine, and Serhat Karakayalı. 2007. "New Governance oder die imperiale Kunst des Regierens. Asyldiskurs und Menschenrechtsdispositiv im neuen EU-Migrationsmanagement." In *Turbulente Ränder. Neue Perspektiven auf Migration an den Grenzen Europas*, edited by Transit Migration Forschungsgruppe, 39–56. Bielefeld: transcript. doi:10.14361/9783839407813-002.
Hess, Sabine, and Serhat Karakayalı. 2017. "Fluchtlinien der Migration. Grenzen als soziale Verhältnisse." In *Der lange Sommer der Migration. Grenzregime III*, edited by Sabine Hess, Bernd Kasparek, Stefanie Kron, Mathias Rodatz, Maria Schwertl, and Simon Sontowski, 25–37. Berlin and Hamburg: Assoziation A.
Hess, Sabine, and Bernd Kasparek. 2010. *Grenzregime. Diskurse, Praktiken, Institutionen in Europa*. Berlin and Hamburg: Verlag Assoziation A.
Hess, Sabine, Bernd Kasparek, and Maria Schwertl. 2018. "Regime ist nicht Regime ist nicht Regime. Zum theoriepolitischen Einsatz der ethnografischen (Grenz-) Regimeanalyse." In *Was ist ein Migrationsregime? What Is a Migration Regime?* edited by Andreas Pott, Christoph Rass, and Frank Wolff, 257–283. Wiesbaden: Springer. doi:10.1007/978-3-658-20532-4_12.
Hopf, Ted. 2002. *Social Construction of International Politics: Identities and Foreign Policies, Moscow, 1955–1999*. Ithaca, NY: Cornell University Press.
Horvath, Kenneth, Anna Amelina, and Karin Peters. 2017. "Re-Thinking the Politics of Migration. On the Uses and Challenges of Regime Perspectives for Migration Research." *Migration Studies* 5 (3): 301–314. doi:10.1093/migration/mnx055.
Jackson, Peter. 2008. "Pierre Bourdieu, the 'Cultural Turn' and the Practice of International History." *Review of International Studies* 34 (1): 155–181. doi:10.1017/S0260210508008073.
Jackson, Peter. 2009. "Pierre Bourdieu." In *Critical Theorists and International Relations*, edited by Jenny Edkins and Nick Vaughan-Williams, 102–113. London and New York: Routledge.
Janning, Frank. 2002. "Habitus und Organisation. Ertrag der Bourdieuschen Problemformulierungen und alternativer Konzeptualisierungsvorschläge." In *Bourdieus Theorie der Praxis: Erklärungskraft – Anwendung – Perspektiven*, edited by Jörg Ebrecht and Frank Hillebrandt, 97–123. Wiesbaden: Westdeutscher Verlag. doi:10.1007/978-3-322-99803-3_5.
Johnson, Corey, Reece Jones, Anssi Paasi, Louise Amoore, Alison Mountz, Mark Salter, and Chris Rumford. 2011. "Interventions on Rethinking 'the Border' in Border Studies." *Political Geography* 30 (2): 61–69. doi:10.1016/j.polgeo.2011.01.002.
Kalm, Sara. 2010. "Liberalizing Movement? The Political Rationality of Global Migration Management." In *The Politics of International Migration Management*, edited by Martin Geiger and Antoine Pécoud, 21–44. Basingstoke: Palgrave Macmillan. doi:10.1057/9780230294882_2.
Kalm, Sara. 2012. "Global Migration Management, Order and Access to Mobility." *IMIS-Beiträge* 40: 49–74.
Karakayalı, Serhat. 2008. *Gespenster der Migration. Zur Genealogie illegaler Einwanderung in der Bundesrepublik Deutschland*. Bielefeld: transcript. doi:10.14361/9783839408957.
Karakayalı, Serhat, and Vassilis Tsianos. 2007. "Movements That Matter. Eine Einleitung." In *Turbulente Ränder. Neue Perspektiven auf Migration an den*

56 A praxeological approach

Grenzen Europas, edited by Transit Migration Forschungsgruppe, 7–22. Bielefeld: transcript. doi:10.14361/9783839407813-intro.

Kasparek, Bernd, and Sabine Hess. 2010. "Einleitung. Perspektiven einer kritischen Migrations- und Grenzregimeforschung." In *Grenzregime. Diskurse, Praktiken, Institutionen in Europa*, edited by Sabine Hess and Bernd Kasparek, 7–22. Berlin and Hamburg: Assoziation A.

Keohane, Robert Owen, and Joseph S. Nye. 1972. *Transnational Relations and World Politics*. Cambridge, MA: Harvard University Press. doi:10.4159/harvard.9780674593152.

Krasner, Stephen D. 1983. *International Regimes*. Ithaca, NY: Cornell University Press.

Laffey, Mark, and Jutta Weldes. 1997. "Beyond Belief: Ideas and Symbolic Technologies in the Study of International Relations." *European Journal of International Relations* 3 (2): 193–237. doi:10.1177/1354066197003002003.

Leander, Anna. 2010. "Practices Providing Order: The Private Military/Security Business and Global (in)Security Governance." In *Business and Global Governance – Business in Global Governance*, edited by Morten Ougaard and Anna Leander, 57–77. London: Routledge.

Lipietz, Alain. 1985. "Akkumulation, Krisen und Auswege aus der Krise: Einige methodische Überlegungen zum Begriff Regulation." *Prokla* 15 (58): 109–138. doi:10.32387/prokla.v15i58.1158.

Mezzadra, Sandro. 2007. "Kapitalismus, Migrationen, soziale Kämpfe. Vorbemerkungen zu einer Theorie der Autonomie der Migration." In *Empire und die biopolitische Wende. Die internationale Diskussion im Anschluss an Hardt und Negri*, edited by Marianne Pieper, Thomas Atzert, Serhat Karakayalı, and Vassilis Tsianos, 179–191. Frankfurt aM: Campus.

Mezzadra, Sandro, and Brett Neilson. 2013. *Border as Method, or, the Multiplication of Labor*. Durham, NC and London: Duke University Press. doi:10.1215/9780822377542.

Moulier Boutang, Yann. 2002. "Thesen zur Autonomie der Migration und zum notwendigen Ende des Regimes der Arbeitsmigration." *Jungle World* 15 (April 3rd, 2002).

Moulier Boutang, Yann. 2007. "Europa, Autonomie der Migration, Biopolitik." In *Empire und die Biopolitische Wende. Die internationale Diskussion im Anschluss an Negri und Hardt*, edited by Marianne Pieper, Thomas Atzert, Serhat Karakayalı, and Vasilis Tsianos, 69–178. Frankfurt aM: Campus.

Mudimbe, Valentin-Yves. 1988. *Invention of Africa: Gnosis, Philosophy and the Order of Knowledge*. Bloomington: Indiana University Press.

Nicolini, Davide. 2009. "Zooming in and Zooming Out: A Package of Method and Theory to Study Work Practices." In *Organizational Ethnography. Studying the Complexities of Everyday Life*, edited by Sierk Ybema, Dvora Yanow, Harry Wels, and Frans Kamsteeg, 120–138. London: Sage Publications. doi:10.4135/9781446278925.n7.

Nicolini, Davide. 2012. *Practice Theory, Work, and Organization: An Introduction*. Oxford: Oxford University Press.

Papadopoulos, Dimitris, Niamh Stephenson, and Vassilis Tsianos. 2008. *Escape Routes. Control and Subversion in the 21st Century*. London: Pluto. doi:10.2307/j.ctt183q4b2.

Parker, Noel, and Nick Vaughan-Williams. 2009. "Lines in the Sand? Towards an Agenda for Critical Border Studies." *Geopolitics* 14 (3): 582–587. doi:10.1080/14650040903081297.

Pott, Andreas, Christoph Rass, and Frank Wolff. 2018. *Was ist ein Migrationsregime? What Is a Migration Regime?* Wiesbaden: Springer. doi:10.1007/978-3-658-20532-4.

Poulantzas, Nicos. 1978. *Staatstheorie. Politischer Überbau, Ideologie, Sozialistische Demokratie.* Hamburg: VSA Verlag.

Pouliot, Vincent. 2004. "Toward a Bourdieusian Constructivism in IR: Outline of a Theory of Practice of Security Communities." Presented at the Fifth pan-European Conference, Standing Group on International Relations, The Hague.

Pouliot, Vincent. 2008. "The Logic of Practicality: A Theory of Practice of Security Communities." *International Organization* 62 (2): 257–288. doi:10.1017/s0020818308080090.

Pouliot, Vincent. 2010. *International Security in Practice. The Politics of NATO-Russian Diplomacy.* New York: Cambridge University Press. doi:10.1017/cbo9780511676185.

Pouliot, Vincent, and Frédéric Mérand. 2013. "Bourdieu's Concepts. Political Sociology in International Relations." In *Bourdieu in International Relations: Rethinking Key Concepts in IR*, edited by Rebecca Adler-Nissen, 24–44. New York: Routledge.

Pugliese, Joseph. 2010. "Introduction. Transmediterranean Cultures in Transnational Contexts." In *Trans-Mediterranean. Diasporas, Histories, Geopolitical Spaces*, edited by Joseph Pugliese, 11–20. Brussels: Peter Lang Verlag.

Raeymaekers, Timothy. 2014. "Introduction: Europe's Bleeding Border and the Mediterranean as a Relational Space." *ACME: An International E-Journal for Critical Geographies* 13 (2): 163–172.

Rass, Christoph, and Frank Wolff. 2018. "What Is in a Migration Regime? Genealogical Approach and Methodological Proposal." In *Was ist ein Migrationsregime? What Is a Migration Regime?* edited by Andreas Pott, Christoph Rass, and Frank Wolff, 19–64. Wiesbaden: Springer. doi:10.1007/978-3-658-20532-4_2.

Reckwitz, Andreas. 2002. "Toward a Theory of Social Practices: A Development in Culturalist Theorizing." *European Journal of Social Theory* 5 (2): 243–263. doi:10.1177/13684310222225432.

Reckwitz, Andreas. 2003. "Grundelemente einer Theorie sozialer Praktiken. Eine sozialtheoretische Perspektive." *Zeitschrift Für Soziologie* 32 (4): 282–301. doi:10.1515/zfsoz-2003-0401.

Reckwitz, Andreas. 2011. "Habitus oder Subjektivierung? Subjektanalyse nach Bourdieu und Foucault." In *Pierre Bourdieu und die Kulturwissenschaften: Zur Aktualität eines undisziplinierten Denkens*, edited by Daniel Šuber, Hilmar Schäfer, and Sophia Prinz, 41–61. Konstanz: UVK Verlag.

Rumford, Chris. 2006. "Rethinking European Spaces: Territory, Borders, Governance." *Comparative European Politics* 4 (2–3): 127–140. doi:10.1057/palgrave.cep.6110089.

Schatzki, Theodore R. 1996. *Social Practices. A Post-Wittgensteinian Approach to Human Activity and the Social.* Cambridge: Cambridge University Press.

Schatzki, Theodore R., Karin Knorr Cetina, and Eike von Savigny. 2000. *The Practice Turn in Contemporary Theory.* London: Routledge. doi:10.4324/9780203977453.

Scheel, Stephan, Baki Cakici, Francisca Grommé, Evelyn Ruppert, Ville Takala, and Funda Ustek-Spilda. 2016. *Transcending Methodological Nationalism through a Transversal Method? On the Stakes and Challenges of Collaboration.* 1. ARITHMUS Working Paper Series. London: Goldsmiths, University of London.

Schlichte, Klaus. 1998. "La Françafrique – Postkolonialer Habitus und Klientelismus in der französischen Afrikapolitik." *Zeitschrift für Internationale Beziehungen* 5 (2): 309–344.

Schmitz, Andreas, Daniel Witte, and Vincent Gengnagel. 2017. "Pluralizing Field Analysis: Toward a Relational Understanding of the Field of Power." *Social Science Information* 56 (1): 49–73. doi:10.1177/0539018416675071.

Schwertl, Maria. 2015. *Faktor Migration: Projekte, Diskurse und Subjektivierungen des Hypes um Migration&Entwicklung*. Münster: Waxmann Verlag GmbH.

Sciortino, Giuseppe. 2004. "Between Phantoms and Necessary Evils. Some Critical Points in the Study of Irregular Migrations to Western Europe." *IMIS-Beiträge* 24: 17–43.

Sending, Ole Jacob, and Iver B. Neumann. 2011. "Banking on Power: How Some Practices in an International Organization Anchor Others." In *International Practices*, edited by Emanuel Adler and Vincent Pouliot, 231–254. Cambridge: Cambridge University Press. doi:10.1017/cbo9780511862373.014.

Sharma, Aradhana, and Akhil Gupta, 2006. *The Anthropology of the State: A Reader*. Malden, MA and Oxford: Blackwell Publishing.

Shove, Elizabeth, Mika Pantzar, and Matt Watson. 2012. *The Dynamics of Social Practice. Everyday Life and How It Changes*. New Delhi: Sage Publications. doi:10.4135/9781446250655.

Stepputat, Finn, and Jessica Larsen. 2015. *Global Political Ethnography: A Methodological Approach to Studying Global Policy Regimes*. 1. DIIS Working Paper. Copenhagen: Danish Institute for International Studies (DIIS).

Transit Migration Forschungsgruppe. 2007. *Turbulente Ränder. Neue Perspektiven auf Migration an den Grenzen Europas*. Bielefeld: transcript. doi:10.14361/9783839407813.

Tsianos, Vassilis, and Sabine Hess. 2010. "Ethnographische Grenzregimeanalyse." In *Grenzregime. Diskurse, Praktiken, Institutionen in Europa*, edited by Sabine Hess and Bernd Kasparek, 243–264. Berlin and Hamburg: Assoziation A.

Tsianos, Vassilis, and Serhat Karakayalı. 2010. "Transnational Migration and the Emergence of the European Border Regime: An Ethnographic Analysis." *European Journal of Social Theory* 13 (3): 373–387. doi:10.1177/1368431010371761.

Tsianos, Vassilis, Serhat Karakayalı, and Sabine Hess. 2009. *Transnational Migration: Theory and Method of an Ethnographic Analysis of Border Regimes*. Working Paper 55. Sussex: Sussex Centre for Migration Research, University of Sussex.

Wacquant, Loïc. 2017. "Pierre Bourdieu und die demokratische Politik. Einige Anmerkungen." In *Symbolische Gewalt: Politik, Macht und Staat bei Pierre Bourdieu*, edited by Michael Hirsch and Rüdiger Voigt, 17–34. Baden-Baden: Nomos. doi:10.5771/9783845276441-17.

Walters, William. 2002. "Mapping Schengenland: Denaturalizing the Border." *Environment and Planning D: Society and Space* 20 (5): 561–580. doi:10.1068/d274t.

Walters, William. 2006. "Border/Control." *European Journal of Social Theory* 9 (2): 187–203. doi:10.1177/1368431006063332.

Walters, William. 2010. "Foucault and Frontiers: Notes on the Birth of the Humanitarian Border." In *Governmentality: Current Issues and Future Challenges*, edited by Ulrich Bröckling, Susanne Krasmann, and Thomas Lemke, 138–164. London: Routledge.

Williams, Michael C. 2007. *Culture and Security. Symbolic Power and the Politics of International Security*. London and New York: Routledge.

Xiang, Biao, and Johan Lindquist. 2014. "Migration Infrastructure." *International Migration Review* 48 (1): 122–148. doi:10.1111/imre.12141.

2 The IOM in the trans-Mediterranean field of migration management

> If properly managed, migration can be beneficial for all states and societies. If left unmanaged, it can lead to the exploitation of individual migrants, particularly through human trafficking and migrant smuggling and be a source of social tension, insecurity and bad relations between nations. Effective management is required to maximize the positive effects of migration and minimize potentially negative consequences.
>
> (McKinley 2004, 3)

In 2004, Brunson McKinley, former director general of the International Organization for Migration (IOM), summarized the organization's global mission to "properly" and "effectively" manage human mobility in order to become "beneficial for all states and societies." In that light, the IOM has been regarded as a "laboratory" for the globally expanding politics of migration management (Ashutosh and Mountz 2011, 23). The key agency in defining and globally promoting the concept of international migration management also acts as a formal implementing partner of European policies within sending and transit countries (Georgi 2010; Geiger 2012). Combining coercion and care while eschewing democratic control, the IOM thus contributes to the broader trend in international politics toward transnationalized forms of neoliberal governance (Brachet 2016, 274). As such, the organization "finds itself at the heart of power struggles that structure contemporary international [migration] politics" (Maâ 2020, 3).

This chapter introduces the IOM in terms of its historical dynamics, internal structures, and relations in the *trans-Mediterranean field of migration politics*. I argue that focusing on the IOM helps us to understand the reconfigurations of migration control in the Mediterranean under the paradigm of migration management. In support, the second part of the chapter recalls developments in European and North African migration politics since the 1990s and reconstructs the shifting control logics in the trans-Mediterranean field. After that, the third part turns to the recent politics of international migration management and outlines prominent changes in discourses, practices, and actors therein. Altogether, the chapter provides

DOI: 10.4324/9781003204169-3

60 *IOM in the field of migration management*

a historical background for the IOM's *making* of migration management in North Africa, as examined in the chapters that follow.

2.1 The emergence of the IOM in international migration politics

Founded in 1951 as the Provisional Committee for the Movement of Migrants from Europe by the United States (US) and its Western allies, the IOM was meant to temporally serve the economic and security interests of those states in opposition to the putatively neutral, humanitarian United Nations High Commissioner for Refugees (UNHCR) and Eastern European states during the Cold War. Its initial task was to offer its member states logistics and transportation services to facilitate migration to and from their territories (Perruchoud 1989). As the organization continued to expand its activities thematically and geographically, it renamed itself four times until reaching its current designation, the International Organization for Migration.[1] After the end of the Cold War, the IOM was transformed into a permanent international organization (IO) with global reach, albeit initially remaining outside the framework of the United Nations (UN) and accountable only to its 173 member states.[2] Although the IOM joined the UN as a related organization in 2016, its work has not been guided by an international legal or normative framework—for instance, the Geneva Convention for the UNHCR—and therefore not been bound to the standards of international law (Pécoud 2018, 1627). Not only does the IOM lack a formal protection mandate, but its constitution does not refer to the fundamental rights of migrants, either (ibid. 2020, 12f.). Nevertheless, the "non-normative organization" has been assigned the lead in developing the human rights-driven project known as the Global Compact on Safe, Orderly and Regular Migration (Guild, Grant, and Groenendijk 2017, 4).

Characterized by high decentralization, the IOM is oriented toward entrepreneurial service provision, or "projectization," meaning that its funding is almost exclusively acquired for specific projects (Geiger and Pécoud 2014, 872). While the IOM's headquarters in Geneva is responsible for major decision- and policymaking, national offices around the world are tasked with not only implementing national projects and coordinating with national and local authorities but also attracting financial support. Therefore, the offices continuously seek to expand their services. Projects are largely funded by the US and member states of the European Union (EU) and increasingly directly supported by EU funding programs. The IOM's director generals are also appointed by the US.

Since neoliberal policies and economic restructuring emerged in the 1990s, the IOM has rapidly grown from "a small members' organization for migrant receiving states" to the "most prominent international organization working on international migration" in the world (Betts 2008, 9; cf. Georgi 2019). Steeply rising numbers in member states, field offices, projects, and staff, not to mention an ever-increasing budget, reflect the organization's growing importance in recent decades (Lavenex 2007, 256). Presenting itself as "the migration agency," the IOM today operates as a major source of intelligence, assessment, consultation, and technical assistance for the full spectrum of people on the move (IOM 2011, 101). Claiming to work to ensure 'the orderly and humane management of migration' on a worldwide basis, the organization has also played a key role in defining and elaborating the concept of migration management, as well as in promoting and practically implementing it, since the 1990s (Georgi 2010; Geiger 2012). Thus operating at the intersection of politics and science, the IOM acts not only as a think tank for migration-related issues but also as a global service agency offering states the proper tools for managing migration (Speer 2014). Presenting itself as a (cost-)effective, professional, flexible service provider for states, the organization represents a prototype of neoliberal politics of migration management, all following the credo that well-regulated migration can ensure everyone's well-being.

In the 2000s, when the IOM established itself as a key actor in international migration politics (Geiger 2012), it began cooperating and competing with other IOs, notably the UNHCR which is devoted to refugees and asylum seekers; the International Labor Organization (ILO) which addresses labor migration issues; and the International Centre for Migration Policy Development (ICMPD), which operates merely in Europe (Lavenex 2007; Koch 2014; Korneev 2014). At the time, the IOM also became a major partner in implementing transnational projects in Africa, Asia, and Eastern Europe, especially in the context of humanitarian interventions addressing disaster-induced displacement (Bradley 2017). In that role, the organization (re)distributes international funding among smaller organizations, notably non-governmental organizations (NGOs) (Geiger 2014, 239). In many countries in the Global South, the IOM additionally coordinates the migration-related activities of state and non-state actors as well as trains their staff. As such, the organization can "'export' both concerns and practical 'solutions' from one part of the world to another" (Geiger and Pécoud 2014, 875). According to Martin Geiger and Antoine Pécoud (ibid.), the "capacity to guide the behavior of weak states through persuasion, in a manner that formally respects their sovereignty," is "the IOM's added value" that distinguishes the organization in the competitive field of international migration politics. Thus, considering the general history of its emergence in the field, many scholars have characterized the IOM as "a 'neoliberal organization' whose raison d'être is to govern human mobility in the interest of the capitalist ruling class" (Pécoud 2020, 5).

Although scholars of migration routinely use the IOM's material as data and often participate in its research and policy programs (Andrijasevic and Walters 2010, 982), the IOM has rarely been the object of academic research and instead remained an "omnipresent but unknown institution" in the literature (Pécoud 2012, 76, translation IB). Likewise, only recently did scholars begin to systematically investigate the organization's role in the international politics of migration management (Andrijasevic and Walters 2010; Ashutosh and Mountz 2011; Georgi 2019; Bradley 2020; Geiger and Pécoud 2020) and pay attention to its tasks and practices in the expanding European border regime (Pécoud 2010; Brachet 2016; Bartels 2017, 2018; Fine 2017; Maâ 2020). The literature thus reveals IOM's long history of cooperation with the EU and its member states as well as its implications in implementing migration management beyond Europe's borders.

From an EU perspective, the IOM figures as a "trustworthy service provider," one that "strictly follows the lines defined in the projects" and is

> always ready to adapt to the changing needs of the EU and manage to establish stable relationships with governmental structures in the countries that fall under the scope of its action.
>
> (quoted in Korneev 2014, 894)

According to Geiger (2014), funding the IOM to implement projects is particularly attractive to the EU because the organization can act as a seemingly "independent" third party that mediates European cooperation with sending and transit countries. In turn, from the perspective of those countries, the IOM appears to be a "partner" or "consultant" that assists states aiming to get "their own borders in order" (Andrijasevic and Walters 2010, 987). Cooperating with the IOM provides an opportunity for those states to adopt international standards without entering asymmetrical negotiations with the EU (Pécoud 2018). However, it would be misleading to reduce the IOM to a mere forum or instrument of states. On the contrary, the IOM proactively participates in expanding migration control beyond Europe and in elaborating and implementing new regional migration schemes. In that way, the organization constantly creates new demand for its services in order to consolidate its role (Geiger 2014, 238).

The IOM occupies an increasingly important position in the externalization of migration control. Although not directly involved in fortifying the EU's external borders, the organization does serve as an outpost for European border and migration control in new territories. Rutvica Andrijasevic and William Walters (2010, 985) have thus argued that the IOM

> plays a constructive and constitutive role, making important interventions which actually shape and define the way in which states, through their national experts, policy makers, border guards, etc. understand the "problem" of borders.

For Eastern Europe, Geiger (2010) has shown, for example, how the IOM has introduced new countries to the political strategies and interests of the EU. Claire Potaux (2011) has characterized the IOM's role in developing and implementing Mobility Partnerships in Eastern Europe and West Africa, while Susanne Schatral (2011) has explored its anti-trafficking practices in Russia.[3] Such case studies have revealed that the IOM does not "simply function like a missionary, preaching the gospel of good migration management to a series of reluctant and recalcitrant governments situated at the modern-day *limes* of the EU," but encourages sending and transit states outside the EU to "learn" its global mission of "managing migration to the benefit of all" (Andrijasevic and Walters 2010, 992).

Due to its geographical location and mounting political transitions, North Africa offered the IOM an "entrepreneurial field" or "testing ground" to expand its management practices in the early 2000s (Geiger 2013, 15). Since then, persistent uncertainty and arbitrariness have reinforced the IOM's position in the North African borderlands (Brachet 2016, 284). However, despite its continued expansion and growing influence in the region, the IOM's practices in North Africa have not been systematically scrutinized by external observers.

2.2 From securitization to international migration management in North Africa

The IOM's migration management emerged in a dynamic context shaped not only by complex political and socioeconomic developments within the North Africa countries but also by their relations with the EU and its member states. European attempts to externalize border and migration control in North Africa are nothing new but have been active since the early 1990s. In 2003, those efforts were intensified by the European Neighbourhood Policy (ENP) and the EU's shift in focus from Eastern Europe to North Africa. Briefly put, the attempts aimed to establish a so-called safe neighborhood without having to accommodate integration into the EU. Soon after, under the Global Approach to Migration (GAM) in 2005, European migration politics revamped their overly restrictive, security-oriented framing of border control into a comprehensive approach toward international migration management. In parallel, an array of actors—newly established EU agencies, private institutions, NGOs, and IOs, among others—were included in the transnational governance of borderlands beyond the Schengen space. As a result, North African borderlands have become contested fields in which multiple actors, practices, and discourses have engaged in implementing and negotiating the politics of international migration management.

This section provides a historical background for the study of the IOM's interventions in North Africa. It outlines how European migration politics grew out of the institutionalization of the Schengen space in the mid-1990s into a global approach toward international migration management under the GAM in 2005. In the process, I examine how those developments have affected, and been affected by, Morocco and Tunisia as two principal target countries of implementation.

2.2.1 Migration in and from North Africa

Large-scale emigration from Tunisia and Morocco, as from most North African countries, began half a century ago.[4] However, the most intense emigration directed toward Europe has been observed since the beginning of the 21st century (Di Bartolomeo, Fakhoury, and Perrin 2010; Khachani 2011).[5] Apart from the general political situation in North African states, increased pressure from young people on domestic labor markets has contributed to such high levels of emigration (Fargues 2006, 1351). Labor markets unable to offer education-appropriate employment opportunities have frustrated a growing, well-educated, urban youth population with un- and underemployment (Lahlou 2006, 113). Beyond that, as past constraints imposed by family have been lifted and personal freedom of movement has expanded, young women have increasingly entered the labor market to compete for the few jobs available (Fargues 2012). Local economic and political discontent have only intensified in juxtaposition with higher living standards in Europe, not least due to the availability of new information technology. For many youths in Tunisia and Morocco, Europe has represented "the best you can get in terms of living conditions, freedom, guarantees of one's rights, leisure activities, etc." (Lahlou 2006, 110). For that reason, more than 75% of youth living in Tunisia in 2005 considered emigration (Fargues 2011), and, in 2007, approximately 20% of Morocco's employed population reported wanting to emigrate (Sadiqi 2007, 1).

Despite Southern Europe's financial and economic crisis, the region's export-oriented agriculture, construction, and tourism sectors have shown continuously high demand for seasonal, flexible, and low-skilled workers in recent decades (Fargues 2013, 12). Those sectors have been willing to employ irregularized migrants. On top of that, the demographics of an aging population across Europe have prompted states to seek out young, well-educated workers not only in Europe but increasingly in North Africa as well. Against that trend, the implementation of a visa system and introduction of restrictive border controls have rendered emigration to Europe an increasingly difficult, dangerous task. Restrictive migration policies were first enacted by (north-western) European states following the economic crisis in the early 1970s. Until then, people in Tunisia and Morocco, similar to most migrant workers from North Africa, could travel to Europe legally. Due to increased restrictions, however, the limited mobility of migrant workers induced the permanent settlement of migrant families, for family reunification remained one of the few accepted reasons for legal entry into Europe. Otherwise, migrants have sought alternative routes and forms of travel to Europe, including clandestine entries, overstays following legal stays, and applications for asylum (Elmadmad 2007).

Since the end of the 1980s, trans-Mediterranean migration has changed significantly. Aside from economic, social, and political factors in North African countries, changes in European migration politics, including the implementation of the Schengen Agreement, the visa system, readmission agreements, the concept of safe third countries, prescreening practices, and carrier sanctions, have altered the quantity and quality of trans-Mediterranean migration (Lahlou 2006, 109). Those measures have also detained migrants from more distant African and Asian countries during their attempts to enter Europe via the Mediterranean. In fact, many migrants who initially considered Morocco and Tunisia as countries of transit ultimately settled in the North African borderlands after finding no way to enter Europe and refusing to return to their countries of origin. As a consequence, North Africa, already a region marked by emigration, has become one of transit and destination as well. Although North African states were once open to Sub-Saharan migrants, their reception has changed under increasing pressure from Europe since the 1990s (Fargues 2013, 29).

2.2.2 The securitization and externalization of migration control

As early as the 1980s, European states, notably Italy and France, approached North African states with the goal of enhancing cooperation in controlling international migration. Although such cooperation was initially based on bilateral agreements, the European coordination of such efforts commenced in the mid-1990s, when European states harmonized their visa procedures and began jointly governing their external borders as their internal borders opened within the Schengen area.[6] In turn, the Europeanization of migration politics served to institutionalize cooperation between European states and their functional organizations.[7] Thus, whereas joint European migration policies had initially emerged from (informal) intergovernmental forums outside the EU, they soon became incorporated into its constitutional structure.[8] As a result, the EU became a central actor in and arena for decision- and policymaking on migration-related issues.

In terms of content, the EU and its member states "embarked on a course of transforming immigration from a political question to a technical one, by presenting it as a matter of security" (Bigo 1998, 151). Within that framework, they developed predominantly restrictive, security-oriented migration policies throughout the 1990s, in a trend later reinforced by the events of September 11, 2001. At that point, major political documents determining the process of European integration and its relationship with neighboring regions began to understand immigration as a threat to internal security and called for more restrictive control.[9] The Conclusions of the European Council of Laeken (European Council 2001), for example, stated that the "better management of the Union's external border controls will help in the fight against terrorism, illegal immigration networks, and the traffic in human beings." Animated by those new security concerns at the turn of the 21st century, the EU fortified its external borders, experimented with new surveillance technologies, and initiated new forms and forums of security cooperation to stop uncontrolled migration (Bigo 1998, 2002; Huysmans 2000).

In the late 1990s, the EU sought to extend its security-oriented migration policies beyond its formal territory. Although European states had attempted to integrate sending and transit countries into migration control since the late 1970s, an explicit external dimension was added to EU migration policies with the Tampere Program in 1999, one that focused on cooperation with neighboring countries but not on integration (see Casas-Cortes, Cobarrubias, and Pickles 2013). As a consequence, though framed by notions of partnership, shared responsibility, and common challenges, subsequent joint Mediterranean initiatives designed by the EU and its member states largely prioritized European interests (Tocci and Cassarino 2011). Regarding the movement of people in particular, they adopted a focus on reducing irregularized migration. In that respect, the Euro-Mediterranean Partnership (EMP) enhanced the circulation of goods and services but restricted the circulation of people (Joffé 2008). Thus, the EMP tasked North African countries with controlling their external borders as Europe's "policemen" (Bilgin and Bilgiç 2011, 1).

The combined securitization and externalization of European migration policies[10] was further elaborated in the post-9/11 context with the European Security Strategy which introduced new measures aimed at creating a "safe neighborhood" in North Africa (Jeandesboz 2007, 400). The European Security Strategy (European Council 2003, 8) literally stated that

> it is in the European interest that countries on our borders are well governed. Neighbors who are engaged in violent conflicts, weak states where organized crime flourishes, dysfunctional societies or exploding population growth all pose problems for Europe.

Whereas the promotion of shared values—democracy, human rights, and market liberalization—remained mere rhetoric, the practical incentives were conditioned on cooperation in restrictive migration control. At Seville, the European Council (2002, 11) even concluded the following:

> Any further cooperation, association or equivalent agreement which the European Union or the European Community concludes with any country should include a clause on joint management of migration flows and on the compulsory readmission in the event of illegal immigration.

Migration and its control also became core topics in the ENP, the 2004 revision of the EMP. Designed to "prevent the emergence of new dividing lines between the enlarged EU and its neighbors," the ENP offered the latter "a chance to participate in various EU activities through greater political, security, economic, and cultural cooperation" (European Commission 2004, 3).

In that context, the EU Commission's president, Romano Prodi (2003, 5), proposed that North African states should share "everything with the Union but the institutions." However, "everything" did not include their citizens' freedom of movement.

In sum, the externalization of European migration policies decoupled control from the territorial borders of European states (Rumford 2006; Vaughan-Williams 2009). Control measures were exported to where the migrant is in order to surveil, intercept, deter, and prevent migratory movements before leading to the EU's external borders (Casas-Cortes, Cobarrubias, and Pickles 2013). In terms of content, the external dimension of European migration policies sought to combine short-term security-oriented measures to strengthen border controls and stop irregularized migration, smuggling, and trafficking, with long-term development strategies to prevent migration by addressing its 'root causes.' Extending the rhetoric of securitization, these strategies were based on a discourse envisioning development via cooperation and partnership with sending and transit countries. Such policies exceeded the scope of restrictive border controls by accommodating longer-sighted policies to keep potential migrants away from Europe. While the EU regarded the two approaches as complementary, critics observed a striking imbalance in their implementation (Boswell 2003; Turner, Rincon, and Nyberg-Sørensen 2006). Indeed, the EU had elaborated its policies and initiatives with measures to address what it called the root causes of migration. The Declaration of the Summit of Seville (European Council 2002), for example, concluded that closer economic cooperation, trade expansion, development assistance, and conflict prevention should promote economic development in the countries of origin and reduce the underlying causes of migration into Europe. In its practical recommendations, however, the Declaration merely sought to promote cooperation to combat irregularized migration, improve border controls, and facilitate readmission (cf. Lavenex and Kunz 2008, 445).

The EU's external migration governance (Lavenex 2004) thus resulted in practical initiatives addressing security risks outside the EU by extending regulations beyond its territory. Although with varying rhetoric and instruments, European policies to externalize migration control in the early 2000s all pursued the exclusion of migrants from the EU. According to Martin Lemberg-Pedersen (2013, 37), however, that externalization should not be misinterpreted as powerful EU states conditioning "less powerful states to boost and expand their border control, with pervasive effects for the plight of migrants as well as the countries instrumentalized as 'buffer zones' in this manner." The multiple means of such conditioning, region-specific power constellations, different national responses to European pressure, and the diverse strategies of actors in those states have nevertheless remained largely underexplored in literature on the externalization of European migration control, which instead remains concerned with European institutions and their decision- and policymaking. The next section therefore turns to the transnational negotiation of those policies and initiatives from the perspectives of Morocco and Tunisia. I examine how those states have negotiated, appropriated, and contested European initiatives and, as a result, actively shaped the outcomes of trans-Mediterranean migration politics.

2.2.3 Contested positions and relations in trans-Mediterranean migration politics

Focusing on bilateral instead of multilateral cooperation, the ENP assigned North African states a more active position in addressing their priorities, including co-development, enhanced mobility, and labor migration (Aubarell and Aragall 2005, 11). The ENP also provided a framework for more informal, non-standard agreements preferred by many states for their flexibility and operability (Cassarino 2010). In turn, those agreements enabled the EU to selectively cooperate with a broader range of actors and introduce a new form of "positive conditionality" into the relations with North African countries (Del Sarto and Schumacher 2005, 22). In the metaphor of carrots and sticks, the carrot of accession, though succeeding with Eastern European countries, was not applicable in North Africa, and the EU feared instability in this region if sanctions were used as sticks. Therefore, it offered new carrots in the form of trade agreements, visa facilitation, investments, and development aid to North African states in exchange for cooperation on migration control. Although the ENP remained programmatically committed to an overall security-oriented approach, the practical outcome depended on the elaboration and implementation of bilateral national action plans, with Morocco and Tunisia as the principal target countries.

In the implementation of European migration initiatives, Tunisia had long played the role of "passive witness" (Fargues 2006, 1358ff). It had signed numerous conventions with other North African states since the 1960s and entered into a bilateral agreement with Italy in 1998 intended to facilitate the readmission of irregularized Tunisian migrants and third-country nationals transiting through Tunisia (Adepoju, van Noorloos, and Zoomers 2010). When direct cooperation with the EU commenced in the early 2000s, Tunisia, similar to other North African states, began to adopt the EU's logic of securitized migration politics in signaling their willingness to cooperate. In 2003, for example, the country ratified the UN Convention on Transnational Organized Crime and the accompanying Protocol to Prevent Suppress and Punish Trafficking of Persons, in Particular Women and Children. In 2004, the regime of Ben Ali enacted a law that criminalized unauthorized emigration that was once tolerated (Planes-Boissac 2010, 8).[11]

The principal actor in Tunisian migration politics at that time was the Ministry of Interior, especially its Border Department, which was known for its security-oriented agenda. In the context of a fragile civil society and hegemonic security-oriented, centralized state apparatus, legislation protecting migrants' rights, including access to asylum procedures, was absent, however. Although Tunisia had signed the UN Geneva Convention of 1951, its 1967 Protocol, and the 1969 Organization for Africa Unity (OAU) Convention for Refugees in Africa, it continued to lack a national legislative and institutional framework for handling refugees and asylum seekers, whose status was left to be determined by the UNHCR (Baba 2013). That same dynamic characterized most North African states at the time, despite the EU and UNHCR's active advocacy for protection schemes.

In response, motivated by economic concerns and the will to maintain ties with its emigrant communities abroad, Tunisia developed some of its own policies concerning 'regular emigration.' As for most North African countries, "transforming expatriates into actors in the development of their nation of origin, attracting their money, making use of their skills, and tapping their business networks became a stake" for the Tunisian government in the late 1980s (Fargues 2013, 17). Political institutions, including the Office of Tunisians Abroad (Office des Tunisiens à l'Étranger, OTE), founded in 1988, and the High Council of Tunisians Abroad (Haut Conseil des Tunisiens à l'Étranger), founded in 1990, aimed at maintaining good relations with citizens of Tunisia living abroad. In sum, though Tunisia elaborated its own emigration politics, no policies or institutional frameworks were designed to address the question of immigration and asylum under the Ben Ali regime (Di Bartolomeo, Fakhoury, and Perrin 2010, 7). Regarding the implementation of European policies on irregularized migration, Tunisia seemed to follow the securitized logic of migration control as much as necessary, but not more, in order to satisfy the EU and its member states.

Compared with Tunisia, Morocco played an active but also more ambivalent role during early negotiations in trans-Mediterranean migration politics. The country had long refused to cooperate on migration with the EU and its member states and, perhaps most remarkably, had resisted pressure to sign new, aggravated readmission agreements after having signed an Association Agreement in 1996. In the Agreement, Morocco consented to readmit its citizens but no foreign nationals who had entered the EU via Moroccan territory. Moreover, the country's bilateral readmission agreements with EU member states were never fully implemented on the Moroccan side (Cassarino 2010). Authorities declared that they had expected to gain more from cooperation and were opposed to becoming the "gendarme of Europe" (Belguendouz 2005). Even so, the state continued encouraging its citizens to emigrate for economic reasons (de Haas 2005).

In 2004, however, Morocco began cooperating on certain issues of international migration and adapted some of the most restrictive measures concerning transit migration in North Africa (Belguendouz 2005). In the country's highly centralized political system, the leading actor in the emerging field of migration politics was, as in Tunisia, the Ministry of Interior, which, with the king's support, became the gatekeeper in migration control. Although having effectively blocked EU–Moroccan cooperation between 1998 and 2005, the Ministry agreed to cooperate and, in turn, saw its funding from the EU balloon from 40 million to 67 million euros. With implementation executed according to Moroccan priorities and without being monitored by the EU, the Ministry's position as the central actor in migration politics in Morocco was strengthened with the help of EU money (Wunderlich 2010).

In exchange, the EU expected Morocco to elaborate a national strategy on migration and to become its "policeman" in North Africa (de Haas 2005). A major step in that process was the enactment of Law 02/03 regulating the entry and stay of foreigners, emigration, and immigration. The law was introduced in combination with another law combating terrorism and mostly copied from French legislation (Elmadmad 2007, 35). Among other things, it criminalized actors who facilitated 'irregular migration' and intended to establish detention centers in Morocco (ibid.). Similar to the Tunisian law of 2004, it also aimed to control and obstruct irregular entry into the country and sanction actors assisting it.

Despite the securitization of its migration politics, Morocco had ratified several international conventions concerning the rights of migrants and refugees.[12] Those paradoxical moves were fostered by gaps between existing legal measures and their practical application, especially regarding immigration and asylum (EMHRN 2012b). Although Morocco neither officially declared itself to be a country of immigration nor developed an explicit policy in the field, it nevertheless had to respond to the growing immigrant community in its territory, which it proceeded to do hesitantly and inconsistently. It established an office for refugees and stateless persons in 2004 (the Bureau des Réfugiés et Apatrides) that did not begin operations until 2014, thereby leaving control over increasingly sought asylum procedures to the UNHCR (La Cimade 2004), whose determination of status and drafting of an asylum system in Morocco were funded by the EU. However, the Moroccan state neither acknowledged the outcome of asylum procedures by the UNHCR nor guaranteed legal or social rights for asylum seekers or recognized refugees (Valluy 2007). Such inconsistent moves by Morocco in the early 2000s may have had different rationales. On the one hand, the increased number of Sub-Saharan immigrants discouraged Morocco from implementing protection schemes (Wunderlich 2010). On the other, Spain and the EU continued to pressure Morocco to cooperate with the EU by offering development aid and improving the status of migrants in Europe (Heck 2008). As a consequence, Morocco seized the opportunity to distinguish itself as the strongest partner in 'fighting irregular migration' and to strengthen its position in international negotiations in other fields of policy (El Qadim 2007).

As those developments in Tunisia and Morocco show, the externalization of migration policies has been "tricky and not entirely within Europe's control" (Gaibazzi, Bellagamba, and Dünnwald 2017, 4) and their implementation far from "straightforward and coherent" or "linear and smooth" (ibid., 7–9). Jean-Pierre Cassarino and Sandra Lavenex (2012) have argued that migration control gained importance as a bargaining tool and tactical resource for sending and transit countries in multi- and bilateral political negotiations in the early 2000s. During that time, Morocco and Tunisia became more interested in cooperating with the EU on migration (Aubarell and Aragall 2005; Casas-Cortes, Cobarrubias, and Pickles 2013). Due to their geographical location on major migration routes to Europe, both countries play key roles in the externalization of the EU's migration control. As such, they have gained enhanced negotiating powers and "a certain, albeit so far limited, space of manoeuvre in their relations to the EU" (Del Sarto and Steindler 2015, 373). However, despite their increasing bargaining power, Morocco and Tunisia have been unable to represent their interests in an optimal way (Adepoju, van Noorloos, and Zoomers 2010, 65). Due to their relatively weak economic and political position, they have been obliged to address migration as a security problem and to adopt the militarized measures of the EU. As a consequence, whereas "cooperation with the EU has allowed access to new technological instruments and resulted in the weakening of EU criticism of acts of repression in the short term," according to Pinar Bilgin and Ali Bilgiç (2011, 7), "it has further alienated civil society from the regimes, thus feeding into their insecurity in the long run." That empowerment-oriented perspective therefore questions prevailing perceptions of externalization as a smooth, top-down exportation of European discourses, regulations, instruments, and values. Albeit offering less Eurocentric explanations for the expansion of European migration policies, they remain focused on state-level interactions as the driving forces for developments in international migration politics.

With reference to the concept of the *European border regime* and the theory of the *Autonomy of Migration*, this book suggests an alternative view on the developments of trans-Mediterranean migration politics. It refers to a wide range of actors, including both IOs and migration movements, and regards the instability and contestedness of expanded migration control as inherent in its development (De Genova 2017, 5). Its unstable, contested nature became and continues to become particularly visible in recurring moments of so-called migration crises (Jeandesboz and Pallister-Wilkins 2014; Kasparek and Tsianos 2015; Vaughan-Williams 2015). In that sense, the collective fence climbing into Ceuta and Melilla in 2005 and collective crossings of the Mediterranean Sea from Tunisian in 2011 alerted the EU and its member states "to the idea that the securitarian approach to migration had its limitations and that it stimulated human rights violations" (Wunderlich 2010, 14). Those events, among others, have urged the EU and its member states to reorient their restrictive security-oriented migration policies, mobilize new approaches, and open space for new actors to emerge in international migration politics.

2.3 Shifting discourses, practices, and actors in trans-Mediterranean migration management

The context of the so-called Moroccan migration crisis in 2005 provided an opportunity for Spain to take the lead in European migration politics and advocate a new programmatic orientation in the European Council. The resulting "Global Approach to Migration: Priority Actions Focusing on Africa and the Mediterranean" set out a "balanced, global and coherent approach, covering policies to combat illegal immigration, and, in cooperation with third countries, harnessing the benefits of legal migration" (European Council 2006, 2). The GAM was designed to establish partnerships with sending and transit countries that reflected mutual interests by addressing development as well as security concerns. It placed stronger emphasis on cooperation in labor migration, human rights, and development, than previous initiatives but also restated the importance of cooperation in border control and readmission. Cooperation with sending and transit countries thus remained at the GAM's core, thereby shifting responsibility for access to asylum and the deterrence of migrants to North Africa and creating a buffer zone around EU territory (Del Sarto 2010).

The GAM was influenced by a new global policy discourse surrounding international migration management. The discourse promised a comprehensive approach that could turn migration into a win-win-win process from which all parties involved would benefit: receiving and sending states as well as migrants themselves (Geiger and Pécoud 2010a). European migration policies under the GAM framework shifted, at least programmatically, from promoting exclusively restrictive, security-oriented forms of control to a more (neo)liberal programmatic of border and migration management that no longer aimed to prevent or hinder migration but focused on its positive impacts instead (European Council 2006; Commission of the European Communities 2008). In the years that followed, the GAM became the programmatic backbone of European migration politics, especially concerning Africa. The GAM thus exemplifies an overall trend in European migration policies, in which focus has shifted from stopping people along the EU's external borders to steering them into an orderly, predictable, manageable process (Georgi 2009; Geiger and Pécoud 2010b; Kalm 2010).

The GAM was also a programmatic watershed in trans-Mediterranean migration politics by introducing the concept of migration management as a new approach to comprehensively governing the international movement of people beyond EU territory. The final part of this chapter thus outlines the discursive, practical, and institutional rearrangements under that paradigm and discusses the shifting power relations between multiple actors in the emerging *trans-Mediterranean field of migration management*. As such, it provides a historical context for the IOM's emerging interventions in North Africa.

The term *migration management* had gained prominence before finding its way into EU documents in the early 2000s. In international politics, it was introduced in 1993 by Bimal Ghosh in a report to the UN Commission on Global Governance, in which Gosh called for comprehensive, proactive migration policies that would make migration a more orderly, predictable, manageable process from which all stakeholders would benefit.

Although reactions to the proposal were "not very positive" at the time (Gosh 2012, 26), two decades later the term no longer seemed to be a "dirty word" (ibid., 30). According to Geiger and Pécoud (2010a, 3), the term migration management currently

> functions as a kind of empty shell, a convenient umbrella under which very different activities can be regrouped and given an apparent coherence, thus also facilitating cooperation between actors who would otherwise have little in common.

Many reports, policy papers, and semi-scientific publications have addressed (promises of) international migration management by institutions promoting the concept or by authors working for those institutions, many of them for the IOM. Those publications usually focus on what migration management should entail. Few independent studies examine what policies on the topic in fact address (e.g., Oelgemüller 2017). Among them, Geiger and Pécoud (2010b) have argued that migration management relies on a set of discourses, refers to a range of practices, and is mobilized by multiple actors, all of whom share one overall concern: the orderly management of migration.

In the international *discourse* on migration, a decisive break occurred in the early 2000s: Although migration had predominantly been viewed as a security threat throughout the 1990s, the managerial language began presenting migration as a permanent, normal, potentially positive, and thus economically productive process (Kalm 2012, 58). The emerging global policy discourse began describing migrants in entrepreneurial, sometimes even heroic, terms, which praised their adventurous character, willingness to invest in their human capital, and strong sense of responsibility for the development of their countries (ibid. 2010, 35; 2012, 62). Such argumentation builds on the same win-win-win logic, according to which migration can benefit sending states, receiving states, and migrants all at once. Thus, the top question was no longer how migration could be prevented or stopped but instead managed in order to maximize or optimize its impact for those three parties.

The impact of efforts toward that end has usually been measured in economic terms (Geiger and Pécoud 2010a, 12). If international migration management is to be compatible with an emerging global labor market, in which border controls facilitate and guide the circulation of workers, then migration management policies need to strategically channel the movement of people based on labor market demands (Mezzadra and Neilson 2013). According to Sandro Mezzadra (2007, 179), borders play a decisive role in producing the heterogeneous space and time of the global capitalist order that is open to flows of capital and commodities but closed to the movement of people. Because the commodity of labor power is traded on global markets, borders are necessary to regulate their mobility by governing the flows of migration between highly differentiated sites and temporal zones of the heterogeneous landscape of global capitalism. In that sense, "borders in the contemporary global order serve not simply as devices of exclusion but as technologies of differential inclusion" (Mezzadra and Neilson 2008). From that perspective, the productivity of border and migration control requires the regulation of labor mobility and its surplus (Mezzadra 2007, 183). In that sense, international migration management does not aim to stop migrants but to selectively and differentially include them, meaning that they are regulated in numbers and assigned a subordinated status conferring social and political rights on a conditional basis (Cuttitta 2010, 28f.). The aim is "not to hermeneutically close the borders of 'rich countries' but to build up a system of barriers" (Mezzadra 2007, 183, translation IB) that, according to Nicholas De Genova, serves to produce an "active process of inclusion of migrant work through their clandestinization" (quoted in ibid.). Accordingly, borders no longer function exclusively as geopolitical lines between sovereign states that justify excluding migrants from national territory. On the contrary, they are characterized as having a highly technologized, knowledge-based filtering function that regulates the differentiation of economically desirable from economically undesirable forms of mobility and expands globally along routes of migration (Mezzadra and Neilson 2013; see also Walters 2002, 2006). From that political–economic perspective, the neoliberal logic of differential inclusion seeks to sort and govern migratory movements predominantly according to their economic desirability and the demands of European labor markets.

The management paradigm thus breaks with the negative view that migration must be prevented and borders closed by all means. Instead, it promotes the more positive, managerial perspective that migration can and must be regulated to the (economic) 'benefit of all.' In terms of *practice*, the top political concern has therefore become designing appropriate programs, forums for cooperation and consultation, and a working mix of incentives and control. According to the report of the First Meeting of the Global Forum on Migration and Development (2007, 4),

> the real challenge lies in how best to structure a policy that allows for proper enforcement of immigration laws while letting immigration continue as a positive force for economic prosperity.

That statement underscores a belief in the capacity of migration policies to maximize the positive effects and limit the negative consequences of migration by steering human mobility. The EU's migration management affirms the belief that migration can be handled with policies and brought under the effective authority of states. Sara Kalm (2012, 67) has observed a

> great confidence that if the knowledge about migration is increased by the collection and dissemination of timely and accurate data, if

migration officials get more professional training, if national administrative capacity is enhanced by increased resources and expertise, and if interstate cooperation is promoted [...] then, migration policy can be used as an effective tool.

In practice, such migration management policies seek to govern subjects "at a distance," by "steering and guiding individuals' free actions and stimulating forms of responsibilization and self-regulation" (ibid. 2010, 40). They address migrants as economic actors and agents of development in order to make them neoliberal subjects and support their "migrant self-management" (Bakker 2010, 290). In the literature, practices of migration management are often conceptualized as governing techniques informed by economic rationales and understood as the effects of neoliberal discourses that materialize in different contexts of implementation (Andrijasevic and Walters 2010; Scheel and Ratfisch 2014; Schwertl 2015).

At the same time, migration management can be located within a broader neoliberal tendency to limit the state's role and government interventions. From that perspective, practices of migration management are employed by states that in new, inventive ways aim to preserve their power, ability, and legitimacy to productively channel migratory movements within and beyond their territories. With the economization of migration governance, the *actors* involved in governing migration have multiplied and been diversified via processes of outsourcing, privatization, and transnationalization (Lahav 2003; Betts 2011; Gammeltoft-Hansen and Nyberg-Sørensen 2013). Although states continue to be viewed as the most relevant actors in international migration politics, they have transferred specific functions to an increasing number of non-state and international actors (Lahav 2003). As a result, various multifaceted, sometimes conflicting, actors have gained influence in the transnationalized fields of border and migration control (Betts 2011). New forums have been created at the regional and global levels (Wihtol de Wenden 2012), while IOs, NGOs, newly established agencies, and private institutions have been delegated tasks formerly performed by states. Accordingly, the migration management paradigm accommodates a neoliberal logic characterized by the outsourcing of state functions and responsibilities. Inspired by the paradigm of new public management, the institutional architecture of neoliberal governance aims to reduce the role of states and make more room for market forces and competition. The marketization and privatization of migration control have opened space for a "migration industry" (Gammeltoft-Hansen and Nyberg-Sørensen 2013) and the "business of bordering Europe" (Andersson 2014) to emerge in and beyond Europe. A large, lucrative market has thus developed that offers all kinds of services demanded in the field of migration politics (ibid., 8ff). That economization of migration governance increasingly turns it into an object of commodification and competitive exchange (Betts 2013, 45).

From the perspective of states, the outsourcing of migration-related tasks seems to be a convenient way to enhance the effectiveness and efficiency of their policies while lowering costs (Lahav 2003). Moreover, it enables governments to go "venue shopping," so to speak, and select which issues should be addressed through which forms of cooperation or subcontracting (Guiraudon 2000). For example, European states can discuss migration from a developmental and human rights perspective at the UN while mandating Frontex to enforce their border control policies in the Mediterranean. The "migration industry" therefore helps states to maintain and even extend their "migration management apparatus" (Menz 2013, 110). While markets of migration control services are not a new phenomenon,

> the pervasiveness of neoliberal governance paradigms and the resulting out-sourcing and privatization of anything from guest worker schemes to running asylum centers and carrying out forced deportations mean that governments today actively sustain and fund large parts of the migration industry themselves.
> (Nyberg-Sørensen and Gammeltoft-Hansen 2013, 8)

The growing migration industry is not expected to supplant states in controlling migration but to bring about new modes and logics in the field. Transnational fields of migration politics are increasingly regulated by competitive logic, market forces, and relations between different contractors and their economic interests, which may or may not act on the exclusive and direct behalf of states. As a consequence, actors with little democratic legitimacy play an increasingly important role in international migration management. Operating beyond democratic control, they instead represent neutrality and expertise (Geiger and Pécoud 2010a; Georgi 2010). In sum, the marketization and commercialization of migration governance do not necessarily cause the loss of state control and sovereignty but instead prompt reconfigurations in governing practices, networks, expertise, and power relations. In literature on the politics of migration management, those functions are mostly characterized as neoliberal.

In North Africa, the privatization, transnationalization, and even "NGOization" (Hess and Karakayalı 2007, 53) of migration politics has brought new actors to the scene but also drawn on existing institutional structures, including governmental offices and ministries, police and military forces, international experts, private companies, IOs, and NGOs. Those actors have been subject to scientific investigation to sharply different degrees, especially regarding their practical work. Surprisingly little research has been done on the particular role of IOs in the trans-Mediterranean management of migration,[13] even though they have emerged as central actors in the field (Geiger and Pécoud 2014). Although most IOs are highly active in the production of scientific knowledge about issues related to their work, their activities in North Africa have rarely been the subject to systematic scrutiny by external observers. Their agendas and their influence on and interactions with sending and transit countries, non-state actors, and migrants are rarely taken into account in literature on the externalization of migration control. Moreover, the routines, values, structures, and struggles among and within those bureaucracies remain widely underresearched.

To conclude, the emerging politics of international migration management meant changes in discourses, practices, and actor constellations. Examining those changes predominantly from the perspective of political economy or discourse and governmentality studies, most of the literature focuses on structural developments in migration politics and their effects. Those perspectives alone risk overemphasizing economic, especially neoliberal, rationales that seem to enjoy unimpeded spread around the world by structuring and organizing people's actions via diverse "malleable and mutable" governing techniques (Wacquant 2012, 69f.). Conceptualizing management practices as neoliberal governing techniques offers fruitful perspectives on the discourse and governance programs surrounding migration as well as their emergence, combination, and depoliticizing effects. However, such trends may result in overly linear, Eurocentric narratives and predictable analyses (cf. Walters 2010, 2015; Garelli and Tazzioli 2013). In that respect, migration management may appear as a totalizing imperialist and neoliberal governance project with little room for the struggles occurring in historical and geographical situations and the essential role that migration movements play therein.

Against that background, this book turns to the practices and negotiations of implementing international politics of migration management in specific contexts. It examines the contested processes in which one collective actor, the IOM, with its internal dynamics, strategies, and stakes, turns the management approach into practice. The following chapters examine what is *at stake* for different actors involved in the elaboration and implementation of migration management, also in terms other than economic gains. They scrutinize the *implicit knowledge* and *embodied routines* that make the spread of the migration management paradigm possible, and they question why actors addressed by new governing techniques participate in their management or abstain. They reveal how neoliberal logic combines, resonates, and struggles with other logics in the field of trans-Mediterranean migration politics. As such, the following chapters are interested not only in new modes and institutional procedures of governing migration but also in their content, meanings, values, and moral convictions. To address those concerns, the chapters zoom into the micropolitics of international migration management implemented by the IOM in Tunisia and Morocco, where the EU and member states have sought new ways to expand the control of migration.

Notes

1 For an official history of the IOM, see Ducasse-Rogier (2001); for the evolution of the IOM from the Intergovernmental Committee for European Migration to the IOM, see Perruchoud (1989); for the development and detailed activities of the IOM since the end of the Cold War, see IOM (2011).

78 *IOM in the field of migration management*

2 See the IOM's website: https://www.iom.int/members-and-observers for most recent numbers [16.04.2021].
3 For further case studies in Sub-Saharan Africa and Asia, see the special issue "Researching the International Organization for Migration" in the *Journal of Ethnic and Migration Studies* (2018) Vol. 44 Issue 10.
4 For a comprehensive historical overview of migration from and to North African countries, see Fargues (2013).
5 According to the Consular Affairs Branch of the Foreign Ministry and OTE, about 1.2 million Tunisians lived abroad in 2011 (11% of its total population), mostly in Europe (quoted in EMHRN 2012a, 38). For Morocco, the number of citizens living abroad varies, depending on the source, from 2.9 to 4 million people (quoted in Khachani 2011, 8).
6 See Article 7 of the Schengen Agreement (1985): http://eur-lex.europa.eu/legal-content/EN/TXT/?uri=CELEX%3A42000A0922%2802%29 [16.04.2021].
7 For overviews on the formation of European border and migration policies since the 1980s, see Feldman (2011).
8 The Treaty of Maastricht (1992) established migration as an explicit object of intergovernmental regulation by introducing the "Third Pillar on Justice and Home Affairs." Those elements were communitarized in the Treaty of Amsterdam (1997).
9 For example, see the Declaration of the Summit of Laeken (2001), the EU Security Strategy (2003), and the EU Neighbourhood Strategy Action Plans (2004 and 2005).
10 For a detailed history of the externalization of migration policies, see Boswell (2003).
11 See Law No. 1975-40 of May 14, 1975, modified in 1998, 2004, and 2008.
12 Morocco was one of the first countries to sign the Geneva Convention of 1951 and the OAU Convention of 1969.
13 For exceptions to the UNHCR, see Valluy (2007); Scheel and Ratfisch (2014). For exceptions to the IOM, see Caillault (2012); Brachet (2016); Bartels (2017); Maâ (2020).

Literature cited

Adepoju, Aderanti, Femke van Noorloos, and Annelies Zoomers. 2010. "Europe's Migration Agreements with Migrant-Sending Countries in the Global South: A Critical Review." *International Migration* 48 (3): 42–75. doi:10.1111/j.1468-2435.2009.00529.x.

Andersson, Ruben. 2014. *Illegality, Inc. Clandestine Migration and the Business of Bordering Europe*. Oakland: University of California Press. doi:10.1525/9780520958289.

Andrijasevic, Rutvica, and William Walters. 2010. "The International Organization for Migration and the International Government of Borders." *Environment and Planning D: Society and Space* 28 (6): 977–999. doi:10.1068/d1509.

Ashutosh, Ishan, and Alison Mountz. 2011. "Migration Management for the Benefit of Whom? Interrogating the Work of the International Organization for Migration." *Citizenship Studies* 15 (1): 21–38. doi:10.1080/13621025.2011.534914.

Aubarell, Gemma, and Xavier Aragall. 2005. *Immigration and the Euro-Mediterranean Area: Keys to Policy and Trends*. EuroMeSco Papers 47. Lisbon: EuroMeSCo.

Baba, Wafa. 2013. *Investigation in First Asylum Country Tunisia/Shousha Camp*. KNOW RESET Research Report 2013/02. Florence: EUI.

Bakker, Matt. 2010. "From 'The Whole Enchilada' to Financialization: Shifting Discourses of Migration Management in North America." In *The Politics of International Migration Management*, edited by Martin Geiger and Antoine Pécoud, 271–294. Basingstoke: Palgrave Macmillan. doi:10.1057/9780230294882_13.

Bartels, Inken. 2017. "'We Must Do It Gently.' The Contested Implementation of the IOM's Migration Management in Morocco." *Migration Studies* 5 (3): 315–336. doi:10.1093/migration/mnx054.

Bartels, Inken. 2018. "Practices and Power of Knowledge Dissemination." *Movements. Journal for Critical Migration and Border Regime Studies* 4 (1): 47–66. https://movements-journal.org/issues/06.wissen/03.bartels--practices-and-power-of-knowledge-dissemination-international-organizations-in-the-externalization-of-migration-management-in-morocco-and-tunisia.html [16.04.2021].

Belguendouz, Abdelkrim. 2005. "Expansion et Sous-Traitance des Logiques d'Enfermement de l'Union Européenne: L'Exemple du Maroc." *Cultures & Conflits* 57: 155–219. doi:10.4000/conflits.1754.

Betts, Alexander. 2008. *Global Migration Governance*. GEG Working Paper 2008/43. https://www.geg.ox.ac.uk/sites/geg.bsg.ox.ac.uk/files/Betts_GEG%20WP%202008_43.pdf [16.04.2021].

Betts, Alexander. 2011. *Global Migration Governance*. Oxford: Oxford University Press. doi:10.1093/acprof:oso/9780199600458.001.0001.

Betts, Alexander. 2013. "The Migration Industry in Global Migration Governance." In *The Migration Industry and the Commercialization of International Migration*, edited by Thomas Gammeltoft-Hansen and Ninna Nyberg-Sørensen, 45–63. London: Routledge. doi:10.4324/9780203082737-12.

Bigo, Didier. 1998. "Frontiers and Security in the European Union: The Illusion of Migration Control." In *The Frontiers of Europe*, edited by Malcolm Anderson and Eberhard Bort, 148–164. London and Washington, DC: Pinter.

Bigo, Didier. 2002. "Security and Immigration: Toward a Critique of the Governmentality of Unease." *Alternatives* 27 (Special Issue): 63–92. doi:10.1177/03043754020270S105.

Bilgin, Pinar, and Ali Bilgiç. 2011. *Consequences of European Security Practices in the Southern Mediterranean and Policy Implications for the EU*. INEX Policy Brief 11. Oslo: INEX.

Boswell, Christina. 2003. "The External Dimension of EU Immigration and Asylum Policy." *International Affairs* 79 (3): 619–638. doi:10.1111/1468-2346.00326.

Brachet, Julien. 2016. "Policing the Desert: The IOM in Libya Beyond War and Peace." *Antipode* 48 (2): 272–292. doi:10.1111/anti.12176.

Bradley, Megan. 2017. "The International Organization for Migration (IOM): Gaining Power in the Forced Migration Regime." *Refuge: Canada's Journal on Refugees* 33 (1): 97–106. doi:10.25071/1920-7336.40452.

Bradley, Megan. 2020. *The International Organization for Migration: Challenges, Commitments, Complexities*. Abingdon, VA and Oxon: Routledge.

Caillault, Clotilde. 2012. "The Implementation of Coherent Migration Management through IOM Programs in Morocco." *IMIS-Beiträge* 40: 133–156.

Casas-Cortes, Maribel, Sebastian Cobarrubias, and John Pickles. 2013. "Re-Bordering the Neighbourhood: Europe's Emerging Geographies of Non-Accession Integration." *European Urban and Regional Studies* 20 (1): 37–58. doi:10.1177/0969776411434848.

Cassarino, Jean-Pierre. 2010. "Dealing with Unbalanced Reciprocities: Cooperation on Readmission and Implications." In *Unbalanced Reciprocities: Cooperation on Readmission in the Euro-Mediterranean Area*, edited by Jean-Pierre Cassarino, 1–29. Washington, DC: Middle East Institute. doi:10.2139/ssrn.1730633.

Cassarino, Jean-Pierre, and Sandra Lavenex. 2012. "EU-Migration Governance in the Mediterranean Region: The Promise of (a Balanced) Partnership?" In *Mediterranean Yearbook*, edited by IEMed, 284–288. Barcelona: IEMed.

Commission of the European Communities. 2008. *Communication from the Commission to the European Parliament, the Council, the European Economic and Social Committee and the Committee of the Regions: Strengthening the Global Approach to Migration, Increasing Coordination, Coherence and Synergies*. COM (2008) 611 final. Brussels: Commission of the European Communities.

Cuttitta, Paolo. 2010. "Das europäische Grenzregime: Dynamiken und Wechselwirkungen." In *Grenzregime. Diskurse, Praktiken, Institutionen in Europa*, edited by Sabine Hess and Bernd Kasparek, 23–42. Berlin and Hamburg: Assoziation A.

De Genova, Nicholas. 2017. "Introduction. The Borders of 'Europe' and the European Question." In *The Borders of 'Europe'. Autonomy of Migration, Tactics of Bordering*, edited by Nicholas De Genova, 1–36. Durham, NC and London: Duke University Press. doi:10.2307/j.ctv11smr05.4.

de Haas, Hein. 2005. "Morocco: From Emigration Country to Africa's Migration Passage to Europe." *Migrationpolicy.Org*. https://www.migrationpolicy.org/article/morocco-emigration-country-africas-migration-passage-europe [16.04.2021].

Del Sarto, Raffaella. 2010. "Borderlands: The Middle East and North Africa as the EU's Southern Bufferzone." In *Mediterranean Frontiers: Borders, Conflict and Memory in a Transnational World*, edited by Dimitar Bechev and Kalypso Nicolaidis, 149–165. London: Tauris Academic Studies. doi:10.5040/9780755620586.ch-008.

Del Sarto, Raffaella, and Tobias Schumacher. 2005. "From EMP to ENP: What's at Stake with the European Neighbourhood Policy towards the Southern Mediterranean?" *European Foreign Affairs Review* 10 (1): 17–38.

Del Sarto, Raffaella, and Chiara Steindler. 2015. "Uncertainties at the European Union's Southern Borders: Actors, Policies, and Legal Frameworks." *European Security* 24 (3): 369–380. doi:10.1080/09662839.2015.1028184.

Di Bartolomeo, Anna, Tamirace Fakhoury, and Delphine Perrin. 2010. *CARIM – Migration Profile Tunisia*. CARIM Migration Profiles. Florence: EUI.

Ducasse-Rogier, Marianne. 2001. *The International Organization for Migration, 1951–2001*. Geneva: IOM.

El Qadim, Nora. 2007. *"Gérer Les Migrations": Renouveau d'un Objet de Négociations Entre le Maroc et les Pays Européens*. Geneva: Institut Universitaire de Hautes Études Internationales.

Elmadmad, Khadija. 2007. *La Gestion Des Frontières*. 2007/04. CARIM Research Report. Florence: EUI.

EMHRN (Euro-Mediterranean Human Rights Network). 2012a. *Asylum and Migration in the Maghreb. Country Fact Sheet Tunisia*. Copenhagen: EMHRN.

EMHRN (Euro-Mediterranean Human Rights Network). 2012b. *Asylum and Migration in the Maghreb. Country Fact Sheet: Morocco*. Copenhagen: EMHRN.

European Commission. 2004. *European Neighbourhood Policy: Strategy Paper*. COM (2004) 373 final. Brussels: European Commission.

European Council. 2001. *Presidency Conclusions*. SN 300/1/01 REV 1. Laeken: European Council.
European Council. 2002. *Presidency Conclusions*. SN 200/1/02 REV 1. Seville: European Council.
European Council. 2003. *A Secure Europe in a Better World. A European Security Strategy*. Brussels: European Council.
European Council. 2006. *Presidency Conclusions of the Brussels European Council of 15 and 16 December*. SN 15914/01/05. Brussels: European Council.
Fargues, Philippe. 2006. "Arab Migration to Europe: Trends and Policies." *International Migration Review* 38 (4): 1348–1371. doi:10.1111/j.1747-7379.2004.tb00240.x.
Fargues, Philippe. 2011. *Voice after Exit: Revolution and Migration in the Arab World*. 2011/05. Migration Information Source. Washington, DC: Migration Policy Institute.
Fargues, Philippe. 2012. "Demography, Migration, and Revolt in the Southern Mediterranean." In *Arab Society in Revolt. The West's Mediterranean Challenge*, edited by Cesare Merlini and Olivier Roy, 17–46. Washington, DC: Brookings Institution Press.
Fargues, Philippe. 2013. "International Migration and the Nation State in Arab Countries." *Middle East Law and Governance* 5 (1–2): 5–35. doi:10.1163/18763375-00501001.
Feldman, Gregory. 2011. *The Migration Apparatus: Security, Labor, and Policymaking in the European Union*. Stanford, CA: Stanford University Press. doi:10.1515/9780804779128.
Fine, Shoshana. 2017. "Liaisons, Labelling and Laws: International Organization for Migration Bordercratic Interventions in Turkey." *Journal of Ethnic and Migration Studies* 44 (10): 1743–1755. doi:10.1080/1369183X.2017.1354073.
Gaibazzi, Paolo, Alice Bellagamba, and Stephan Dünnwald. 2017. "Introduction: An Afro-Europeanist Perspective on EurAfrican Borders." In *EurAfrican Borders and Migration Management. Political Cultures, Contested Spaces, and Ordinary Lives*, edited by Paolo Gaibazzi, Alice Bellagamba, and Stephan Dünnwald, 3–28. Basingstoke: Palgrave Macmillan. doi:10.1057/978-1-349-94972-4_1.
Gammeltoft-Hansen, Thomas, and Ninna Nyberg-Sørensen. 2013. *The Migration Industry and the Commercialization of International Migration*. New York: Routledge. doi:10.4324/9780203082737.
Garelli, Glenda, and Martina Tazzioli. 2013. "Challenging the Discipline of Migration: Militant Research in Migration Studies, an Introduction." *Postcolonial Studies* 16 (3): 245–249. doi:10.1080/13688790.2013.850041.
Geiger, Martin. 2010. "Mobility, Development, Protection, EU-Integration! The IOM's National Migration Strategy for Albania." In *The Politics of International Migration Management*, edited by Martin Geiger and Antoine Pécoud, 141–159. Basingstoke: Palgrave Macmillan. doi:10.1057/9780230294882_7.
Geiger, Martin. 2012. "Weltorganisationen in der Gestaltung globaler und regionaler Migrationspolitik: Die International Organization for Migration (IOM)." In *Weltorganisationen*, edited by Martin Koch, 129–151. Wiesbaden: VS Verlag für Sozialwissenschaften. doi:10.1007/978-3-531-18977-2_6.
Geiger, Martin. 2013. "The Transformation of Migration Politics." In *Disciplining the Transnational Mobility of People*, 15–40. Basingstoke: Palgrave Macmillan. doi:10.1057/9781137263070.0005.

Geiger, Martin. 2014. "The Production of a Safe Neighborhood and the Disciplining of International Mobility." In *Territoriality and Migration in the E.U. Neighbourhood: Spilling over the Wall*, edited by Margaret Walton-Roberts and Jenna Hennebry, 225–243. Dordrecht: Springer. doi:10.1007/978-94-007-6745-4_14.

Geiger, Martin, and Antoine Pécoud. 2010a. "The Politics of International Migration Management." In *The Politics of International Migration Management*, edited by Martin Geiger and Antoine Pécoud, 1–20. Basingstoke: Palgrave Macmillan. doi:10.1057/9780230294882_1.

Geiger, Martin, and Antoine Pécoud. 2010b. *The Politics of International Migration Management*. Basingstoke: Palgrave Macmillan. doi:10.1057/9780230294882.

Geiger, Martin, and Antoine Pécoud. 2014. "International Organisations and the Politics of Migration." *Journal of Ethnic and Migration Studies* 40 (6): 865–887. doi:10.1080/1369183x.2013.855071.

Geiger, Martin, and Antoine Pécoud. 2020. *The International Organization for Migration: The New 'UN Migration Agency' in Critical Perspective*. Basingstoke: Palgrave Macmillan. doi:10.1007/978-3-030-32976-1.

Georgi, Fabian. 2009. "Kritik des Migrationsmanagements. Historische Einordnung eines politischen Projekts." *Juridikum. Zeitschrift für Politik/Recht/Gesellschaft* 2: 81–84.

Georgi, Fabian. 2010. "For the Benefit of Some: The International Organization for Migration (IOM) and Its Global Migration Management." In *The Politics of International Migration Management*, edited by Martin Geiger and Antoine Pécoud, 45–72. Basingstoke: Palgrave Macmillan. doi:10.1057/9780230294882_3.

Georgi, Fabian. 2019. *Managing Migration? Eine kritische Geschichte der Internationalen Organisation für Migration (IOM)*. Berlin: Bertz + Fischer.

GFMD (Global Forum on Migration and Development). 2007. *Report for the First Meeting of the Global Forum on Migration and Development*. Brussels.

Gosh, Bimal. 1993. "Movements of People. The Search for a New International Regime." Presented at the Commission on Global Governance, Geneva.

Gosh, Bimal. 2012. "A Snapshot of Reflections on Migration Management. Is Migration Management a Dirty Word?" *IMIS-Beiträge* 40: 25–32.

Guild, Elspeth, Stefanie Grant, and Kees Groenendijk. 2017. *IOM and the UN: Unfinished Business*. SSRN Scholarly Paper ID 2927414. Rochester, NY: Social Science Research Network.

Guiraudon, Virginie. 2000. "European Integration and Migration Policy: Vertical Policy-Making as Venue Shopping." *Journal of Common Market Studies* 38 (2): 251–271. doi:10.1111/1468-5965.00219.

Heck, Gerda. 2008. "'Managing Migration' vor den Grenzen Europas: Das Beispiel Marokko." *COMCAD Arbeitspapiere – Working Papers 45*. Bielefeld.

Hess, Sabine, and Serhat Karakayalı. 2007. "New Governance oder die imperiale Kunst des Regierens. Asyldiskurs und Menschenrechtsdispositiv im neuen EU-Migrationsmanagement." In *Turbulente Ränder. Neue Perspektiven auf Migration an den Grenzen Europas*, edited by Transit Migration Forschungsgruppe, 39–56. Bielefeld: transcript. doi:10.14361/9783839407813-002.

Huysmans, Jef. 2000. "The European Union and the Securitization of Migration." *Journal of Common Market Studies* 38 (5): 751–777. doi:10.1111/1468-5965.00263.

IOM. 2011. "The International Organization for Migration: Renewal and Growth since the End of the Cold War." In *World Migration Report*, edited by IOM, 93–121. Geneva: IOM.

Jeandesboz, Julien. 2007. "Labelling the 'Neighbourhood': Towards a Genesis of the European Neighbourhood Policy." *Journal of International Relations and Development* 10 (4): 387–416. doi:10.1057/palgrave.jird.1800138.

Jeandesboz, Julien, and Polly Pallister-Wilkins. 2014. "Crisis, Enforcement and Control at the EU Borders." In *Crisis and Migration. Critical Perspectives*, edited by Anna Lindley, 115–135. London: Routledge. doi:10.4324/9780203078846-6.

Joffé, George. 2008. "The European Union, Democracy and Counter-Terrorism in the Maghreb." *JCMS – Journal of Common Market Studies* 46 (1): 147–171. doi:10.1111/j.1468–5965.2007.00771.x.

Kalm, Sara. 2010. "Liberalizing Movement? The Political Rationality of Global Migration Management." In *The Politics of International Migration Management*, edited by Martin Geiger and Antoine Pécoud, 21–44. Basingstoke: Palgrave Macmillan. doi:10.1057/9780230294882_2.

Kalm, Sara. 2012. "Global Migration Management, Order and Access to Mobility." *IMIS-Beiträge* 40: 49–74.

Kasparek, Bernd, and Vasilis Tsianos. 2015. "Back to the Future. Blair-Schily Reloaded." *Movements. Journal for Critical Migration and Border Regime Studies* 1 (1). http://movements-journal.org/issues/01.grenzregime/03.kasparek,tsianos--back-to-the-future-blair-schily-reloaded.html [16.04.2021].

Khachani, Mohamed. 2011. *La Question Migratoire au Maroc: Données Récentes*. CARIM Notes d'Analyse et de Synthèse 2011/71. Florence: EUI.

Koch, Anne. 2014. "The Politics and Discourse of Migrant Return: The Role of UNHCR and IOM in the Governance of Return." *Journal of Ethnic and Migration Studies* 40 (6): 905–923. doi:10.1080/1369183X.2013.855073.

Korneev, Oleg. 2014. "Exchanging Knowledge, Enhancing Capacities, Developing Mechanisms: IOM's Role in the Implementation of the EU–Russia Readmission Agreement." *Journal of Ethnic and Migration Studies* 40 (6): 888–904. doi:10.1080/1369183X.2013.855072.

La Cimade. 2004. *La Situation Alarmante des Migrants Subsahariens en Transit au Maroc et les Conséquences des Politiques de l'Union Européenne*. Paris: La Cimade.

Lahav, Gallya. 2003. "The Rise of Non-State Actors in Migration Regulation in the United States and Europe: Changing the Gate-Keepers or Bringing Back in the State?" In *Immigration Research for a New Century: Multidisciplinary Perspectives*, edited by Nanca Foner, Rubén G. Rumbaut, and Steven J. Gold, 215–241. New York: Russell Sage Foundation.

Lahlou, Mehdi. 2006. "The Current State and Recent Trends in Migration between Maghreb States and the European Union." In *Mediterranean Transit Migration*, edited by Ninna Nyberg-Sørensen, 109–128. Copenhagen: Danish Institute for International Studies.

Lavenex, Sandra. 2004. "EU External Governance in 'Wider Europe.'" *Journal of European Public Policy* 11 (4), 680–700. doi:10.1080/1350176042000248098.

Lavenex, Sandra. 2007. "The External Face of Europeanization: Third Countries and International Organizations." In *The Europeanization of National Policies and Politics of Immigration. Between Autonomy and the European Union*, edited by Thomas Faist and Andreas Ette, 246–264. Basingstoke: Palgrave Macmillan. doi:10.1057/9780230800717_12.

Lavenex, Sandra, and Rachel Kunz. 2008. "The Migration–Development Nexus in EU External Relations." *European Integration* 30 (3): 439–457. doi:10.1080/07036330802142152.

Lemberg-Pedersen, Martin. 2013. "Private Security Companies and the European Borderscapes." In *The Migration Industry and the Commercialization of International Migration*, edited by Thomas Gammeltoft-Hansen and Ninna Nyberg-Sørensen, 152–172. London: Routledge. doi:10.4324/9780203082737-17.

Maâ, Anissa. 2020. "Manufacturing Collaboration in the Deportation Field: Intermediation and the Institutionalisation of the International Organisation for Migration's 'Voluntary Return' Programmes in Morocco." *The Journal of North African Studies* 0 (0): 1–22. doi:10.1080/13629387.2020.1800210.

McKinley, Brunson. 2004. *Managing Migration: The "Four-Box Chart."* Geneva: IOM.

Menz, Georg. 2013. "The Neoliberalized State and the Growth of the Migration Industry." In *The Migration Industry and the Commercialization of International Migration*, edited by Thomas Gammeltoft-Hansen and Ninna Nyberg-Sørensen, 108–127. London: Routledge. doi:10.4324/9780203082737-15.

Mezzadra, Sandro. 2007. "Kapitalismus, Migrationen, soziale Kämpfe. Vorbemerkungen zu einer Theorie der Autonomie der Migration." In *Empire und die biopolitische Wende. Die internationale Diskussion im Anschluss an Hardt und Negri*, edited by Marianne Pieper, Thomas Atzert, Serhat Karakayalı, and Vassilis Tsianos, 179–191. Frankfurt aM: Campus.

Mezzadra, Sandro, and Brett Neilson. 2008. "Border as Method, or, the Multiplication of Labor." *Transversal Texts* June 2008. https://transversal.at/transversal/0608/mezzadra-neilson/en [16.04.2021].

Mezzadra, Sandro, and Brett Neilson. 2013. *Border as Method, or, the Multiplication of Labor.* Durham, NC and London: Duke University Press. doi:10.1215/9780822377542.

Nyberg-Sørensen, Ninna, and Thomas Gammeltoft-Hansen. 2013. "Introduction." In *The Migration Industry and the Commercialization of International Migration*, edited by Thomas Gammeltoft-Hansen and Ninna Nyberg Sørensen, 1–23. London: Routledge. doi:10.4324/9780203082737-10.

Oelgemüller, Christina. 2017. *The Evolution of Migration Management in the Global North.* London and New York: Routledge. doi:10.4324/9781315644547.

Pécoud, Antoine. 2010. "Informing Migrants to Manage Migration? An Analysis of IOM's Information Campaigns." In *The Politics of International Migration Management*, edited by Martin Geiger and Antoine Pécoud, 184–201. Basingstoke: Palgrave Macmillan. doi:10.1057/9780230294882_9.

Pécoud, Antoine. 2012. "Que Sait-on de l'Organisation Internationale Pour les Migrations?" In *Atlas des Migrants en Europe*, edited by Migreurop, 76–77. Paris: Armand Colin.

Pécoud, Antoine. 2018. "What Do We Know about the International Organization for Migration?" *Journal of Ethnic and Migration Studies* 44 (10): 1621–1638. doi:10.1080/1369183X.2017.1354028.

Pécoud, Antoine. 2020. "Introduction: The International Organization for Migration as the New 'UN Migration Agency.'" In *The International Organization for Migration. The New 'UN Migration Agency' in Critical Perspective*, edited by Martin Geiger and Antoine Pécoud, 1–27. Cham: Springer International Publishing. doi:10.1007/978-3-030-32976-1_1.

Perruchoud, Richard. 1989. "From the Intergovernmental Committee for European Migration to the International Organization for Migration." *International Journal for Refugee Law* 1 (4): 501–517. doi:10.1093/ijrl/1.4.501.

Planes-Boissac, Véronique. 2010. *Study on Migration and Asylum in Arab Countries*. Copenhagen: Euro-Mediterranean Human Rights Network (EMHRN).
Potaux, Claire. 2011. "The Current Role of the International Organization for Migration in Developing and Implementing Migration and Mobility Partnerships" In *Multilayered Migration Governance. The Promise of Partnerships*, edited by Rachel Kunz, Sandra Lavenex, and Marion Panizzon, 183–204. London: Routledge. doi:10.4324/9780203827833-16.
Prodi, Romano. 2003. "A Wider EUrope – A Proximity Policy as the Key to Stability." Presented at the Sixth ECSA-World Conference "Peace, Security and Stability – International Dialogue and the Role of the EU." Brussels.
Rumford, Chris. 2006. "Rethinking European Spaces: Territory, Borders, Governance." *Comparative European Politics* 4 (2–3): 127–140. doi:10.1057/palgrave.cep.6110089.
Sadiqi, Fatima. 2007. *Intentions, Causes, and Consequences of Moroccan Migration*. 2007/04. Analytic and Synthetic Notes. Florence: EUI.
Schatral, Susanne. 2011. "Categorisation and Instruction: IOM's Role in Preventing Human Trafficking in the Russian Federation." In *Perpetual Motion? Transformation and Transition in Central and Eastern Europe & Russia*, edited by Tul'si Bhambry, Clare Griffin, Titus Hjelm, Christopher Nicholson, and Olga G. Voronina, 2–15. London: School of Slavonic and East European Studies, UCL.
Scheel, Stephan, and Philipp Ratfisch. 2014. "Refugee Protection Meets Migration Management: UNHCR as a Global Police of Populations." *Journal of Ethnic and Migration Studies* 40 (6): 924–941. doi:10.1080/1369183X.2013.855074.
Schwertl, Maria. 2015. "Wissen, (Selbst)Management, (Re)Territorialisierung. Die drei Achsen des aktuellen Diskurses um Migration & Entwicklung." *Movements. Journal for Critical Migration and Border Regime Studies* 1 (1). http://movements-journal.org/issues/01.grenzregime/09.schwertl--wissen-selbstmanagement-reterritorialisierung-migration-entwicklung.html [16.04.2021].
Speer, Marc. 2014. "Die IOM in der Ukraine: Wissensproduzentin und Dienstleisterin von Migrationsmanagement." In *Grenzregime II. Migration, Kontrolle, Wissen, transnationale Perspektiven*, edited by Lisa-Marie Heimeshoff, Sabine Hess, Stefanie Kron, Helen Schwenken, and Miriam Trzeciak, 152–161. Berlin and Hamburg: Assoziation A.
Tocci, Nathalie, and Jean-Pierre Cassarino. 2011. *Rethinking the EU's Mediterranean Policies Post-9/11*. IAI Working Papers 11/06. Rome: Instituto Affari Internazionali.
Turner, Simon, Jairo Munive Rincon, and Ninna Nyberg-Sørensen. 2006. "European Attitudes and Policies towards the Migration/Development Issue." In *Mediterranean Transit Migration*, edited by Ninna Nyberg-Sørensen, 67–100. Copenhagen: Danish Institute for International Studies.
Valluy, Jerome. 2007. *Contribution à une Sociologie Politique du HCR: Le Cas des Politiques Européennes et du HCR au Maroc*. Mai 2007. Collection 'Etudes.' Recueil Alexandries. http://www.reseau-terra.eu/article571.html [16.04.2021].
Vaughan-Williams, Nick. 2009. *Border Politics: The Limits of Sovereign Power*. Edinburgh: Edinburgh University Press. doi:10.3366/edinburgh/9780748637324.001.0001.
Vaughan-Williams, Nick. 2015. *Europe's Border Crisis: Biopolitical Security and Beyond*. Oxford: Oxford University Press. doi:10.1093/acprof:oso/9780198747024.001.0001.

Wacquant, Loïc. 2012. "Three Steps to a Historical Anthropology of Actually Existing Neoliberalism." *Social Anthropology* 20 (1): 66–79. doi:10.1111/j.1469-8676.2011.00189.x.

Walters, William. 2002. "Mapping Schengenland: Denaturalizing the Border." *Environment and Planning D: Society and Space* 20 (5): 561–580. doi:10.1068/d274t.

Walters, William. 2006. "Border/Control." *European Journal of Social Theory* 9 (2): 187–203. doi:10.1177/1368431006063332.

Walters, William. 2010. "Foucault and Frontiers: Notes on the Birth of the Humanitarian Border." In *Governmentality: Current Issues and Future Challenges*, edited by Ulrich Bröckling, Susanne Krasmann, and Thomas Lemke, 138–164. London: Routledge.

Walters, William. 2015. "Reflections on Migration and Governmentality." *Movements. Journal for Critical Migration and Border Regime Studies* 1 (1). https://movements-journal.org/issues/01.grenzregime/04.walters--migration.governmentality.html [16.04.2021].

Wihtol de Wenden, Catherine. 2012. "Globalization and International Migration Governance." *IMIS-Beiträge* 40: 75–88.

Wunderlich, Daniel. 2010. "Differentiation and Policy Convergence against Long Odds: Lessons from Implementing EU Migration Policy in Morocco." *Mediterranean Politics* 15 (2): 249–272. doi:10.1080/13629395.2010.485052.

3 Information campaigns

Migration management as a global duty for education

> It was the most important work in the long term, to bring together the civil society and the authorities to work together in the most disadvantaged zones—the zones where there is a risk, let's say, there is an important impact of youth migration—and to understand if we can do something *before* the risky decision is taken.
>
> (Interview with IOM staff member, Tun. 2015)

This was how an International Organization for Migration (IOM) staff member reported one of their major fields of action in Tunisia during an interview in 2015—leaving it open to my knowledge and imagination what the Tunisian youth from "the most disadvantaged zones" should be prevented from doing. "Voila, 'I take a boat because there is not much to do,'" she added after a moment of silence, summarizing the decision many young Tunisians have made since 2011. Speaking about "risks" was one of the main topics in the interviews I conducted with IOM staff in the following years. From the IOM's perspective, managing migration in terms of minimizing risks means intervening "before the child, the young teenager decides to leave school" (ibid.). It means to spread information, promote education, and develop individual empowerment projects. As my interview partner emphasized, "it is not the law" that would prevent young Tunisians from becoming potential migrants (ibid.). Therefore, the IOM would develop "more appropriate solutions" to convince those "at risk of migration" to stay in Tunisia (ibid.). Framing its work in terms of risk management legitimates the organization to offer proactive management of an anticipated problem.

These explanations of the IOM's individually tailored approach to preventing irregularized migration sounded very similar to what I had heard about IOM information campaigns in Morocco: the same problem definitions of a "marginalized youth" in "disadvantaged zones" identified as "risks of irregular migration" that cannot be stopped by laws,

DOI: 10.4324/9781003204169-4

but through proactive instruments, such as information, education, and empowerment.

> Rather than saying "Me, as IOM, I do not want to work with Mohammed and his problems," it is to work in the field and that therefore have better access to the population. And often it is through civil society that is closer to the local community than the authorities.
>
> (Ibid.)

Emphasizing the IOM's intermediate and facilitating position in the field, its staff distinguished its practical work and expertise in prevention from state politics.

> There is no young person that knocks at the door of the Ministry of Social Affairs to say, "I have a problem; it is not working with my family." No, you find them in the streets beginning to deal, and sometimes if there is no option, you lose these children. So, the question is, how can we work *beforehand*?

The IOM staff member further illustrated the organization's problem perception and strategies to prevent irregularized migration from North Africa (ibid.). In this chapter, I reconstruct the IOM's "work beforehand" by tracing transnational information campaigns implemented in Morocco and Tunisia between 2010 and 2015. I analyze the practices, logic, and assumptions driving these projects in a context that was merely perceived as being shaped by traditions and dynamics of emigration.

Preventive approaches were introduced in international migration politics in the late 1990s. According to Christina Boswell (2003, 624), they aimed to "influence the factors forcing migration or encouraging migrants and refugees to travel to the EU" through "more targeted development assistance, trade, foreign direct investment or foreign policy instruments" on the one hand, and so-called reception in the region on the other. This so-called root causes approach should offer potential migrants and refugees "a real possibility of staying in their place of origin" (ibid., 625). At the European level, preventive policies became prominent within the multilateral framework of the Global Approach to Migration (GAM) in 2005. They profited from a rising political interest in preventing conflicts and crises through externalizing protection and assistance to other parts of the world (see Chapter 2). However, the implementation of preventive policies largely focused on restrictive measures to contain migrants in their region rather than addressing structural causes of their displacement (Lavenex and Kunz 2008, 453).

Initially, North African states with strong traditions of emigration to Europe were not pleased by the unilateral proposals of the European Union (EU) to make people stay in their territory. The Moroccan government, for example, refused to sign a corresponding action plan which promised development activities to reduce emigration.[1] One consequence of the tough negotiations with Moroccan state authorities was to include external actors in the implementation of preventive measures in the country. The IOM became one of the main beneficiaries of this outsourcing.

In line with the international "migration and development hype" (Schwertl 2015), the IOM initially framed its preventive work as a matter of *migration and development*. To comply with the ambitions of North African governments to strengthen state relations with their diaspora and profit from their resources, projects implemented under this label indeed promoted *(more) migration for (more) development*. They addressed the Moroccans Living Abroad (Marocains Résidants à l'Étranger, MRE) and Tunisians Living Abroad (Tunisiens Résidants à l'Étranger, TRE) and facilitated their contribution to the development of their countries of origin. While Moroccan and Tunisian governments welcomed these projects, European donors were more prone to fund activities that would contribute to their 'fight against irregular migration' in North Africa. While the IOM depends on the consent of its host countries' governments, it is also necessary for the organization to serve donor interests in order to raise sufficient funding for its projects. Mediating between the positions of the sending and receiving states, the IOM reoriented its preventive projects toward a *more development for less migration* approach. With the implementation of information campaigns, the IOM thus intervened in *symbolic and material struggles* about which forms of migration are wanted and facilitated and which forms should be stopped and prevented in the North African borderlands.

The IOM projects analyzed in this chapter are constitutive for this *more development for less migration* approach. While they seek to convince young Moroccans and Tunisians to voluntarily stay and engage in developing their countries of origin, they do not address the motivations for migration in a structural sense. Rather, they regard development as an individual matter of self-improvement and self-discipline. In this chapter, I examine how the IOM employs this neoliberal logic in relation to potential migrants and their communities. I reveal how migration is governed through soft measures that rely on the participation of potential migrants in their own management through individual incentives, self-discipline, and outsourcing of responsibility—rather than through repression and coercion. While existing literature describes such techniques as modes of neoliberal governing at a distance (Rose and Miller 2010), through freedom (Ong 2007) and responsibilization (Ferguson and Gupta 2002), I am interested in the concrete practices and meanings of prevention to consider why those who are supposed to be managed would (not) participate in programs of neoliberal governance. I argue that the *symbolic power* of the IOM's education and social work addresses morals, emotions, and beliefs to make entrepreneurial subjects participate in their own management. This way, the chapter shows how the IOM extends the boundaries of the field of international migration management to include new themes, tools, and target groups. It concludes that these practices of neoliberal risk management are based on an understanding of the IOM's work as that of a *global duty for education* (see also Bartels 2017). In this way, it also indicates how projects of international migration management echo colonial relations: based on a self-understanding as a global expert, the IOM feels competent to intervene in countries outside Europe in the name of educating their apparently backward societies. The organization seeks to educate marginalized youth in the North African borderlands about their place in an asymmetrically structured field of international mobility rights and change their behavior. Thereby, it contributes to spread neoliberal logic and values to North African politics and societies.

3.1 Preventing populations at risk of migration in Morocco

Prevention in Morocco means to "do projects to make them stay" (conversation with former IOM staff, Mor. 2014). Similar to their colleagues in Tunisia, for the IOM staff in Morocco, managing migration in terms of prevention meant to identify potential migrants and "make them stay" so they would not leave for Europe. Realizing that—despite the continuously rising levels of repression—migrants continued to challenge borders and other forms of restriction through their permanent unauthorized crossings, the IOM suggested softer interventions that aim to convince what the IOM assesses to be 'youth with high emigration risks' to voluntarily restrain from their plans, projects, and dreams of migration. According to Antoine Pécoud (2012, 197), these new modes of governing migration stem from the acknowledgment that "people cannot be successfully controlled in their displacement" and, therefore, "need to be convinced to adopt the right behavior by themselves and to comply with migration politics." Instead of repressive means and physical force, the IOM's preventive measures aim to make potential migrants participate in their own control because they believe in its merits. In this sense, IOM's information campaigns

> aim at promoting patterns of self-government among would-be migrants, who are supposed to renounce leaving their home not because they fear the punishment measures elaborated to stop them, but because they believe that irregular migration is a dangerous endeavor that is not worth risking.
>
> (Ibid., 196)

In the early 2000s, the IOM began to raise funds to implement such campaigns in Morocco. Southern European states, in which most of the Moroccans who clandestinely crossed the Mediterranean arrived at that time, were especially interested in preventing Moroccan youth from searching for a better life on the northern shores. In this respect, Spain and Italy provided funding for different projects to prevent Moroccans from leaving the country. In 2011, these "stay-at-home activities" made up two-thirds of the

Moroccan mission's overall budget (Caillault 2012, 149). Analyzing the implementation of one prominent prevention project in Morocco, the first part of the chapter sheds light on the symbolic power and violence employed by the IOM to influence individual decision-making and responsible behavior of potential migrants and their communities.

3.1.1 Practices and meanings of prevention: The SALEM project in Morocco

The IOM's most prominent prevention project implemented in Morocco was called Solidarity with the Children in Morocco (SALEM). Implemented in cooperation with the Moroccan Ministry of National Education, the Ministry of Youth and Sports, and local associations, it started in 2008, targeting youth in well-known emigration regions. It aimed to reduce irregularized migration from Morocco's Central region, known for its 'high emigration risk' to Europe in general and Italy in particular. According to a representative of the project's main donor, the Italian Development Cooperation (IDC), activities focused on the region of Khouribga since it is "where most of the Moroccans living in Italy come from" (interview with repr. of IDC, Mor. 2014). In addition to the Italian strategy to minimize the 'risks of irregular immigration,' the SALEM project was designed in accordance with the Moroccan government's ambition to strengthen the capacity of the national development agency Entraide Nationale and enhance administrative competences in the protection of minors and families in this region (IOM 2008, 1).

Expressing deep conviction, the IOM staff presented the project idea during an interview:

> The idea was to support the youth at risk of migration, basically to find new opportunities at the local level or to help them to resolve a bit the problems that they had in the field, to better direct them and help them to understand also the risks of migration ...
> (Interview with former IOM project staff, Mor. 2014)

In order to address these "risks of migration" on a local, individual level, the SALEM project aimed to "target the marginalized Moroccan youth" and

> provide alternatives to prevent irregular migration, to sensitize them for what irregular migration might mean and that the whole idea that the Eldorado is just 14 km across the Strait of Gibraltar is maybe a little too short-sighted.
> (Interview with IOM staff, Mor. 2014)

With the term "marginalized Moroccan youth," the IOM refers to young men with underclass backgrounds and poor education who live in the "disadvantaged zones" in the cities of the Moroccan hinterland. From the organization's point of view, this group lacks prospects in Morocco. Their false perceptions of and attitudes put them "at risk of migration." In IOM publications, the image of this Moroccan youth is visually represented by groups of young adults wearing sunglasses, baseball caps, and hip-hop clothes, posing as dangerous gangsters for the IOM's camera. This CD cover-esque arrangement gives a telling impression of the images and ideas of a misguided, underprivileged North African youth that guide IOM interventions in this field. They are presented as strong, proud, irrepressible groups of young men. The *symbolic violence* of the IOM's discourse constructs and categorizes them as a risk that needs to be minimized and prevented from spreading, especially to Europe. The IOM's preventive campaigns are justified by an imperative to anticipate the risks of irregularized migration embodied by young Moroccans and Tunisians and prevent them from leaving in the name of their own protection. Migrants are simultaneously conceptualized as vulnerable and dangerous being *at* risk and *a* risk themselves in relation to a third party, usually Europe (see Frowd 2018).

These youths are the main target group of IOM activities, whose imperative is to inform and educate them, so they understand that irregularized migration is not the solution to their problems. Members of this target group are expected to need better knowledge, more information, and individual empowerment provided by international experts, such as the IOM, in order to realize their projects in Morocco. Alternatives to the prospects of migration are provided in terms of individual training and other forms of self-optimization that seek to enhance their *cultural capital* and thus their chances to succeed in life and gain social recognition in their country. It is a shared *illusio* among IOM staff that more information and better education would change people's migration plans.

The 'disadvantaged neighborhoods' the IOM has classified as the main target zones of intervention are located in regions with long traditions and shared experiences of emigration to Europe. According to the IOM staff, these neighborhoods are "where you find clearly the highest rate of people with migration risks" (ibid.). "So, we try to do the two things at the same time," which one IOM staff member in the SALEM project summed up as protecting and preventing an apparently misguided Moroccan youth from their "false dreams and paths of emigration" and Europe from the "danger of irregular immigration" (interview with former IOM project staff, Mor. 2014). The "generalized suspicion" (Sayad 2010, 197) concerning this group legitimizes the IOM to implement its information campaigns.

In this sense, two meanings of risk merge in the IOM's preventive practices: the management of migration as a collective risk for Europe is implemented through the classification of so-called groups at risk and their individual protection and containment. According to Didier Bigo (2006, 88f.), managing migration through managing risks means "monitoring them, even without their knowledge, [and] following or anticipating their traces," their future movements and actions. Implementing prevention through risk management "aims to take care of individuals by continuous surveillance in the name of love" (ibid., 97). In Morocco, the IOM observed, classified, and evaluated young people in the name of their own protection.

3.1.2 The symbolic violence of constructing and infantilizing risk groups

"You cannot directly address the problem of border governance [...] if you do not understand what are the reasons that make people leave," a former project staff of the IOM said, pointing to the essential function of knowledge production for realizing the project (interview with former IOM project staff, Mor. 2014). The IOM produced data to describe and explain the behavior of young Moroccans and predict their behavior with regard to migration. An "Index of the preparedness for migration among Moroccan youth" (IOM 2010, translation IB), for example, explains emigration aspirations of young Moroccans as the result of rational thinking, individual decision-making, and cost–benefit analysis of existing opportunities on the one hand, and their feelings of social marginalization, experienced rejection, and lack of self-esteem on the other (ibid.). Taking potential migrants as rational-acting, sensitive but capable subjects, the index indicates that their emigration is not passive or inevitable, but always the result of an active decision for one option among others (ibid., 48). Symbolic elements, such as happiness related to the freedom of movement and the acquisition of postmodern competences, are goals for today's youth. These elements make Moroccan minors potential citizens of an interconnected world who are ready to migrate "at any costs" (ibid., 7, translation IB). In this respect, they differ from the generation that migrated primarily to ensure economic well-being for themselves and their families. In conclusion, the IOM suggests managing their migratory aspirations on an emotional, moral, and cognitive level.

According to the organization's staff in Morocco, the problem of these cosmopolite youngsters with postmodern values is that they grow up with

> disrupted family lives, abusive parents, drug abuse, and domestic violence. [Therefore,] they can't take an informed decision. Because, if you stand on the shore of Tangier and you look across, you think you can just swim to Spain and life is going to be easy!
> (Interview with IOM staff, Mor. 2014)

Living in such a "zone of malaise" (IOM 2010, 51, translation IB), which is defined throughout IOM publications by all kinds of problematic behavior, would make young people vulnerable to make what the IOM regards as wrong and irresponsible decisions. According to Loïc Wacquant (2009, 297), these knowledge practices of classification and selection operate "along sharp gradients of class, ethnicity, and place" to "divide populations and to differentiate categories according to established conceptions of

94 *Information campaigns*

moral worth." The classifications on which the IOM defines its target groups are linked to implicit expectations about moral capacities and intellectual dispositions to live a responsible life. According to Etienne Balibar (1991, 26f.), such post-racist selection practices lead to a form of social prophylaxis through the categorization and definition of risk groups based on individualized dispositions. By classifying groups at risk, evaluating their future chances, and monitoring their behavior, the IOM exercises a symbolic violence on young Moroccans that remains widely *misrecognized*.

The IOM defines its target group by two characteristics: their youth, which depicts their aspirations to migrate as an act of innocent immaturity, and their social background, which explains their "naively uninformed" behavior (Geiger 2013, 32) as a matter of lacking education, social marginalization, and backward-oriented societies. Their lack of *cultural and social capital* enables the IOM to construct young Moroccans as inferior to its expertise—which is supported by its staff's positions as White Europeans, highly educated, with middle-class backgrounds. As a result, those who implement information campaigns for the ones 'at risk of migration' often assume that they have the right, or even the duty, to educate others with their apparently universal expertise regarding what is morally right and intellectually rational to do. In this way, they actualize paternalistic power relations in the field of migration management introduced by Europe's colonial interventions on the African continent. In this sense, managing migration becomes a global duty to educate marginalized and apparently backward-oriented poor people in the Global South.

3.1.3 *The symbolic power of informing and forming responsible individuals*

The production of data is a main resource for the IOM to position itself in the field of international migration management. Based on the knowledge produced about young Moroccans from disfavored regions, the organization was able to enlarge its expertise to include marginalized groups of Moroccan society into the target group of its work. This way, the IOM practically enlarges the boundaries of the field, stretching them from the core issues of migration control toward social and pedagogic work directed at marginalized groups in society more generally.

In order to change the apparently problematic behavior of this group, the IOM employs information campaigns. These campaigns seek to influence those who were perceived as misguided young people and change their mystified conception of Europe. According to the IOM's definition, information campaigns

> aim at helping potential migrants make well-informed decisions regarding migration. Experience has shown that the most credible information is a balanced and neutral one that offers facts on the possibilities and

advantages of regular migration, as well as on the disadvantages of irregular departures.

(Quoted in Nieuwenhuys and Pécoud 2007, 1677)

Analyzing the IOM's information campaigns, Pécoud (2012, 184) notes that they are based on the assumption that irregularized migration results from a lack of appropriate information. Therefore, they would need to "address such disinformation which generates irrational behaviors and thus jeopardizes some of the positive outcomes expected from 'properly managed migration'" (ibid.). In this respect, potential migrants are expected to be "unaware of the rules governing the entry of non-nationals in destination states and that, if properly informed, they would renounce unlawful migration projects" (ibid., 186). In short, such campaigns rest on the belief that "if people leave, it is because they do not know what awaits them; if they know, they will not leave" (Nieuwenhuys and Pécoud 2007, 1683). This implies "first, that migrants lack information on migration; second, that their behavior is based on available information; and third, that information on migration is dark enough to discourage them from leaving" (ibid.). The "darkness of irregular migration," meaning the dangers and suffering that await migrants in destination countries, is a common feature of information campaigns (ibid., 1684). However, the IOM campaigns in Morocco sought to educate young people about the dangers of irregularized migration *and* enhance their emotional ties, personal capacities, and life skills to succeed in Morocco (IOM 2010).

From the IOM's perspective, young Moroccans who have not (yet) had the chance to receive an adequate education are nevertheless expected to be capable and willing to learn, work, and optimize themselves to follow their dreams. In this respect, young Moroccans shall "become themselves young autonomous and responsible adults who have the spirit of taking initiative and are conscious of their environment" (Hall, Massey, and Rustin 2013, 13). They are addressed as responsible for the success of their projects. Structural barriers are not considered in this neoliberal narrative which, according to Sara Kalm (2010, 31), promotes "entrepreneurialism and efficiency in institutions as well as in individuals, who are encouraged to maximize their 'human capital.'" In this perspective, the marginalization of young Moroccans appears as a natural fact—or even a personal defeat. Accordingly, the need for change is exclusively located within individuals and can be targeted by the IOM through information and education.

> Of course, if they want to migrate, we are the last to say, "you can't!" It is up to everybody to decide that on his own. However, what we also see is that it is important for people to have a good understanding in order to make an informed decision.
>
> (Interview with IOM staff, Mor. 2014)

96 *Information campaigns*

As pointed out by the IOM staff, information campaigns are not based on obligations and prohibitions but rather on proactive intervention into the way marginalized Moroccan youth believe in their capacities, perceive their choices, and take action in the future. The IOM does not condemn migration—if well planned and orderly conducted—but presents apparently neutral "objective" and "reliable" expert information (Coopération Italienne au Maroc 2008, 60, translation IB) to enable young people to make a responsible, "informed decision" about their future (Nieuwenhuys and Pécoud 2007, 1684). According to the main donor of the IOM's information campaigns, the IDC, these seek to

> convert a project of migrating abroad into a project of integrating into the local economic, educative, and social systems in order to relieve the pressure of expectations and emotional and material investments of families into the migratory projects of their children and instead offer them a realistic perspective.
> (Coopération Italienne au Maroc 2008, 60, translation IB)

The IOM campaigns aim to inform youth about their unlikely feasibility and want their target groups to internalize a more "realistic" perspective, which is defined by the IOM. Making "informed decisions" refers to information that is provided by apparently neutral international experts, such as the IOM perceives itself.

"This is particularly in light of the fact that in 2014, it was found that smugglers were one of the primary information sources in this regard," a study commissioned by the IOM points out (Altai Consulting 2015, 115). The shared knowledge and collective experience circulating among (potential) migrants and their networks are generally dismissed within these struggles about the morally right way to live, migrate, or stay. With regard to the international migration and development discourse, Maria Schwertl (2015, 12) highlights that not all forms of knowledge and expertise are of equal value. (Potential) migrants themselves are not regarded as knowing and well-informed subjects; instead, they appear as uneducated minors who are misguided by business-seeking smugglers. Therefore, they need to become enlightened by the foreign experts of IOs. While the IOM does not regard (potential) migrants as equal actors, the organization competes with smugglers in the field. On the transnational market of migration knowledge, the IOM positions itself in competition with smugglers regarding whose information counts among the Moroccan youth. In opposition to the misleading promises spread by smugglers, the organization holds its apparently neutral information as normatively superior and carves out its global moral expertise. Engaging in the *symbolic struggles* about which knowledge and whose expertise counts among (potential) migrants, the IOM has to make itself known and credible among the recipients of its services in order to be recognized as a trustworthy actor.

"They do education, education to help people to have a better job, other things, not to think about migration," a former IOM staff member in Morocco explained (conversation with former IOM staff, Mor. 2014). To stimulate changes in behavior, information campaigns are combined with social or cultural activities. In the framework of the SALEM project, the IOM offered professional trainings, support for rescholarization and employment reintegration, and psychosocial assistance (IOM 2008). These activities are based on an individualized approach to enhance people's capacities to master a path that is framed by the international state system and its restricted mobility rights. Within this unquestioned frame, the IOM takes on the task of educating and training people to optimize their chances to succeed in the competitive environment of scarce resources and opportunities. To implement these activities, the IOM cooperates with "associations in neighborhoods that are particularly marginalized and poor" (interview with IOM staff, Mor. 2014). These implementing partners would ensure that "children are going back to school, that children stay in school or get vocational training opportunities" (ibid.). In this context, they are informed about "HIV and AIDS, on irregular migration, on drug abuse, on all kinds of things. [...] it is a larger development project with information on migration, on opportunities, and on what alternatives can look like" (ibid.). In the beginning, the IOM worked with

> social workers who worked in the field and tried to approach the youth, to find the beneficiaries for the project ... We mostly did this through the empowerment activities. We organized football tournaments, theater plays ... these were the entry points,

a former project member explained (interview with former IOM project member, Mor. 2014). One of the most prominent empowerment activities was a rap music festival in Khouribga called Droubna ("Our Neighborhoods" in Arabic).[2] A youth association, founded by the SALEM project, organized concerts, break-dance workshops, and theater plays. These participatory methods aimed to recruit beneficiaries for the project.

The IOM's social work also achieved significant visibility through a project in which young Moroccans recorded a music video with a famous Moroccan rapper. The video was called Khouribga Mdate ("Khouribga has started" in Arabic). "It was a moment to give confidence to the young people and their capacity," a former project assistant recalled during an interview (ibid.). He concluded that "in these neighborhoods, I think that we have a good result, especially because we had a direct cooperation with the youth that also participated in these activities" (ibid.). Highlighting the "good results" because the youth "also participated" indicates that this was not self-evident but a real achievement for the IOM staff. The participation of the Moroccan youth was a key element for the IOM to distinguish its proactive, participatory approach from other activities in the field. However, it seemed to be one of the most challenging tasks for the IOM to recruit young people who actually wanted to be empowered by its activities.

The IOM's preventive practices of risk management do not seek to stop the potential emigration of young Moroccans through fences or impossible

98 *Information campaigns*

visa requirements but to steer their future behavior through symbolic power. This power works through practices of information and education about what is a morally good, legal, and orderly way to live and migrate and to empower them accordingly. Preventive migration management has been interpreted as disciplining and self-disciplining subjects before they even migrate (Geiger and Pécoud 2013). Through indirect or soft activating mechanisms and incentives of (self)control and personal fulfillment, it demands the individual's informed decision to behave orderly and responsibly and to contribute to a well-managed migration process because it seems in one's own interest. According to James Ferguson and Akhil Gupta (2002, 989), it employs mechanisms that seem to "work 'all by themselves' to bring about governmental results through the devolution of risk onto the 'enterprise' or the individual [...] and the 'responsibilization' of subjects who are increasingly 'empowered' to discipline themselves." In this sense, the IOM's preventive interventions address potential migrants as young, immature, and uneducated but rational thinking and capable subjects who can be held responsible for their irregular or unproductive behavior (Geiger 2013; Pécoud 2013). The IOM's information campaigns are not only about informing but also about forming people. Therefore, they intervene in local negotiations about the morally right behavior of young Moroccans. The IOM sees itself in the position to make them well-informed, responsible subjects who can be expected to behave according to the rules of the international state system and stay in the place that is designated for them.

Material support and structural changes, in contrast, are not considered in this neoliberal understanding of prevention (see Bartels 2017). 'Irregular migration' is diagnosed as the rational choice of young people, but the social, political, and economic conditions under which these decisions were made are not questioned or targeted. The IOM information campaigns seek to empower individuals, disregarding the structural conditions that make them prone to emigrate. The organization turns the international management of migration into the private matter of potential migrants' individual responsibility, personal decisions, and intellectual capacities. Its symbolic power aims to change individual behavior, not in the European border regime. However, what is rarely considered in studies about this neoliberal governing logic is that in order to be effectively implemented, the exercise of symbolic power and violence depends on the migrants' tacit acceptance and active participation in a project.

3.1.4 "But they know it is dangerous"—contradictions and contestations in the field

Through talking about the day-to-day work with one of the staff members of the SALEM project and a representative of its main donor, the IDC, it became clear that the IOM's strong belief in the project is neither shared by

Moroccan implementing partners nor by the young people who should be educated and empowered:

> At the level of implementation, it is not always easy to realize. Especially for the participation of youth, it is not easy to gain their confidence. I think it was really the most difficult task to find associations capable and available to do it.
> (Interview with former IOM project staff, Mor. 2014)

Contrary to the public presentation of smooth, top-down processes of such migration and development projects, the implementation of the SALEM project seemed a challenging process for the IOM in Morocco. "We must do it bit by bit and not arrive and say, 'we will change everything!'" the organization's staff explained its strategy vis-à-vis Moroccan partners (ibid.). "No, we must do it gently," a representative of the IDC agreed, emphasizing that IOM's interventions would need to bring about change softly (ibid.). One way the IOM adapted to the difficulties of finding participants was through the creation of youth organizations to approach, recruit, and bind young people to the project. Building its own local IO-dependent structures of street work, these structures helped the organization make itself known among new target groups and new spheres of action. In this respect, it turned subversive practices of marginalized youth culture into tools of migration management. Appropriating the creativity of its participants, the IOM publicly distinguished its innovative role and up-to-date performativity from other actors in the field.

In the first years of implementation, Moroccan authorities and European donors welcomed and praised the new educative and empowering forms of migration management from which young, disadvantaged Moroccans were to benefit. According to a representative of the Spanish Agency for International Development Cooperation (AECID), the IOM became widely known as the "institution to help Morocco fix the Moroccan population so they do not leave" (interview with repr. of AECID, Mor. 2014). He emphasized the Spanish interest in funding a project to

> establish education centers for minors, unaccompanied minors. But for *Moroccans*, I insist. These are Moroccans who are displaced. They had to displace themselves from rural areas toward Tangier or Nador. There, we implemented centers to support them, to give them the possibility to train themselves and to receive professional training.
> (Ibid.)

Despite this mutual beneficial reputation, the meager (measurable) impact on reducing unauthorized crossings led to skeptical voices and controversial discussions among donors. Some criticized the information campaigns as a new tool invented by the IOM to enlarge its portfolio and questioned its expertise in this field of social–pedagogic street work. Others complained about the missing official evaluations of the project. The IDC even withdrew its financial support after the first phase of the project.

Moroccan implementation partners of the IOM's campaigns differed in their judgment: some saw the project as useful support for their own work with street children (see IOM 2013a, 4). Others openly questioned the impact of these 'stay-at-home activities,' arguing that young Moroccans would already know that irregularized migration is dangerous. But they would nevertheless take the risk because of the desperation in the country and the striking disparities abroad (interview with activist, Mor. 2014). The IOM would underestimate migrants' *illusio* in the possibility of making it to Europe, deemed necessary to effectively risk the crossing. According to Glenda Garelli (2013, 78),

> these travel desires, these careful assessments about the radius of one's options, the ground beneath one's feet one starts to feel (or not), the choices as to whom to join in Europe, and the evaluations on where one may or may not cross,

can hardly be unsettled by such information campaigns. Nieuwenhuys and Pécoud (2007, 1685) argue that these campaigns ignore "the embeddedness of such decisions in collective strategies and social structures." Too strong is the common perception of lacking alternatives, the necessary adherence to the dream about Europe as the Eldorado that would solve one's problems, and the belief in the practical possibility to follow friends and family members who have already crossed. Moroccan actors mostly shared the view that young Moroccans know the dangers of crossing the Mediterranean but would continue to try it anyway. For the IOM's preventive work, this means migrants cannot be expected to participate in a project because it would seem rational for them to do so. Instead, their participation needs to be regarded as a social and emotional negotiation process whose outcome depends on the stakes migrants see for themselves in this game.

The IOM's position was unclear and ambivalent in this regard. In contrast to Pécoud and Nieuwenhuys' findings in Eastern Europe, IOM staff in Morocco seemed very convinced and even enthusiastic when talking about information campaigns. Showing a strong belief in education as an effective means of migration management, they proudly spoke about "enormous improvements in school retention rates" (interview with IOM staff, Mor. 2014). One of my interview partners repeated this phrase several times before specifying:

> We are seeing enormous improvements in getting children to go back to school. In particular, adolescents who then say "Hey, actually my education will get me somewhere and I will actually have a chance to do something else."
>
> (Ibid.)

They also emphasized that "a lot of beneficiaries" had reintegrated into schools or restarted their studies (interview with former IOM project staff, Mor. 2014). Secondly, integration into the local labor market figured as an important indicator of success. IOM staff proudly reported about cooperation

> with the large companies like Renault or others up in the north, where they then can get transferred for vocational trainings or internships. And we had the first ones being recruited. So, they actually get a proper job in a decent working environment, making a proper salary in Morocco. I think it is pretty cool!
> (Interview with IOM staff, Mor. 2014)

Most IOM projects have not undergone any independent evaluation. In contrast to these personal accounts, measurable results—the widely accepted currency of presenting evidence in the field—convey a different picture. For example, the IOM's official publications refer to 500 young Moroccans who were personally assisted between 2010 and 2012, including 35 children who were rescholarized after dropping out of school and 35 young Moroccans who received professional training in that period (IOM 2012, 1). Compared to the numbers of 80,000–95,000 young people with emigration risks in Khouribga that had been defined by the IOM as the target group (Coopération Italienne au Maroc 2008, 61), these numbers imply that the IOM only reaches out to a few potential migrants.

Such contradictions and shortcomings have not remained unnoticed by the IOM. While its staff in Morocco showed an enduring *illusio* in its educative mission, recent publications and official statements by high officials in the organization indicate a growing skepticism and the organization's willingness to adapt to rising criticism. The IOM-commissioned study "Migration Trends Across the Mediterranean" (Altai Consulting 2015, 114), for example, acknowledges that while "previous studies have demonstrated that information is circulating amongst migrants, [...] learning about the risks of the journey does not necessarily deter them." In 2014, the IOM's Director General (Swing 2014) warned:

> Don't let yourselves be fooled. The migrants know the dangers they pass through. They know that they risk their lives. But they do it by despair, because you have to be desperate to accept putting your wife and your children on such boats.

On the one hand, the IOM is aware of the moderate impact of its prevention strategies. On the other, projects such as SALEM are expanded to other countries in the North African borderlands. The IOM's symbolic power and violence to influence young Moroccan's beliefs, decisions, and behaviors in order to channel their movements and maintain the global order of unequal

102 *Information campaigns*

mobility rights was still a welcomed way for the EU and its member states to interfere in North African migration politics from a distance. Funding IOM information campaigns resonated well with their agenda to stabilize the border regime in the central Mediterranean without depending on the fragile and temporary political structures in postrevolutionary Tunisia. New campaigns were introduced in the country in 2011 to curb the rising number of unauthorized border crossings.

3.2 Participatory migration management in Tunisia

In Tunisia, the IOM had implemented various migration and development projects since the early 2000s. As in Morocco, these aimed at strengthening the institutional capacities and economic infrastructures that enable social and economic investments of the Tunisian diaspora in the country. Prevention became a key practice with the transnational extension of the SALEM project, now renamed SALEMM (Solidarity with the Children of the Maghreb and the Mashriq), and the START project (Stabilizing At-Risk Communities and Reinforcing Migration Management to Enable Smooth Transitions in Egypt, Tunisia and Libya). These projects were introduced in post-Arab Spring Tunisia at a time when the country received extraordinary international attention. European countries were highly interested in reestablishing stability and enhancing security in North Africa after the upheavals in Tunisia and Libya in 2011. Tunisia advanced quickly to the preferred focal point for European initiatives while other parts of the region were perceived as being taken over by political chaos and ongoing conflicts. In Libya, international cooperation became almost impossible since the central government was weak and unable to govern the country effectively. Since the defeat of the Gadhafi regime in 2011, numerous rival groups have fought about the authority over economic resources and political power. Perceived as the model country of the Arab Spring, Tunisia became the main field of interventions aiming to stabilize national orders and existing borders in North Africa.

However, more militarization of the sea and higher fences at the borders did not bring about the expected results in terms of effectively stopping migration movements. Rather, they increased deaths, suffering, and critical voices. Against this background, funding of information campaigns became a method of choice for European donors. The German Minister of Interior, for example, suggested that the

> measures taken by the EU and its member states need to be supported by balanced information campaigns in countries of transit and origin, which educate about the risks of irregular migration by crossing the Mediterranean.[3]

The IOM in Tunisia faced many European demands at that time (interview with IOM staff, Tun. 2015). As a result, information campaigns became an integral part of the IOM's work in the years after the revolution. As in Morocco, they resonated well with Tunisian expectations about migration management initiatives to provide services for citizens rather than immigrants. Tunisian authorities insisted on legal migration as their political priority when redesigning migration policies and institutional infrastructures. Analyzing the implementation of two projects in Tunisia, I demonstrate in the following section how the practices and meanings of prevention were renegotiated in a context of political transition and economic instabilities. I discuss the IOM's preventive interventions as part of a state-building project that spread neoliberal logic to Tunisian politics and society.

3.2.1 *Communicating opportunities to the benefit of all? The START project*

The EU's aim in funding the START program was "to stabilize at-risk communities and enhance migration management" in regions facing "complex migration challenges while also giving rise to new migration-related opportunities" (IOM 2013b, translation IB). The project should not only educate individuals to prevent them from irregularized migration but also "stabilize" entire "communities at risk" and enable their "smooth transition" (ibid.). Within this framework, the IOM implemented three pilot projects in the regions it identified as disadvantaged: El-Kef, Gafsa, and Tunis. In 2013, the organization opened Migration Resource Centers in these cities in cooperation with the National Agency for Employment and Independent Work (Agence Nationale pour l'Emploi et le Travail Indépendant) and the Office for Tunisians Living Abroad (Office des Tunisiens à l'Étranger, OTE). According to the project's online platform, the centers aim to "prevent irregular migration, facilitate legal migration, protect regular and irregular migrants, promote sustainable returns, and reinforce the links between migration and development."[4] It indicates the IOM's effort to satisfy different actors' ambitions with one project.

The Migration Resource Centers offer services to both Tunisian migrants and immigrants in the country (IOM 2014a). They provide "access to a certain number of opportunities for migration, notably for students and workers, but also a rich base of information about a certain number of destination countries."[5] This way, their goal is to provide migrants "the means to take informed decisions regarding their migration projects, minimizing the risks and maximizing the benefits of the migratory experience" (ibid.). The projects address individuals as rational, capable, and entrepreneurial subjects who seek to optimize their life projects through the enterprise of migration, for which they should also bear the risk. In practice, this meant the IOM should "well-communicate the opportunities" to migrate legally, even though these are known to be few for young Tunisians in the restrictive logic of the international migration regime (interview with IOM staff, Tun. 2015).

104 *Information campaigns*

"We were asked to communicate better, to work with the Tunisians who wanted to leave for a work experience of labor migration," the IOM staff member stressed that the founding of these centers was initially based on a demand by the Tunisian state (ibid.). In contrast to the Tunisian hesitation to cooperate with the IOM in other projects, the interim authorities had concrete stakes in this game. For the Tunisian authorities, it was most important that the Migration Resource Centers were not only for immigrants but offered services to all migrants, including those who return. For the IOM, in turn, immigrants in Tunisia were the primary target group of the project (ibid.). Finally, the IOM succeeded in getting the Tunisian partner to agree on a comprehensive target group for the program.

When the Migration Resource Centers were integrated into the Tunisian state structure of OTE, it became the first official service addressing immigrants in the country. The symbolic struggles about what migration means and whom migration policies are supposed to address were connected to very material struggles about creating and funding national institutions. While the long-standing Tunisian institution OTE sought to ensure its place in postrevolutionary Tunisian migration politics, the IOM looked for Tunisian partners that could care for TREs and be made responsible for immigrants in the country.

The OTE was founded in the late 1980s under the Tunisian Ministry for Social Affairs. The institution is well known in the country as a state service for TREs. My interview partner from the institution described it as a technical, apolitical structure that provides information and assistance for transnational development initiatives (interview with repr. of OTE, Tun. 2014). It also supports those who return to Tunisia in their administrative steps and social reintegration. In addition, the OTE offers cultural and political activities to connect TREs to the country. For a representative of OTE (ibid.), cooperating with IOM on the Migration Resource Centers was different from other projects because "this time we have added other target groups to our primary commitment." The cooperation with IOM was attractive for OTE as a "resource we can exploit to diversify our programs and reinforce our capacities" (ibid.). In the moment of reorganization of national migration politics after the revolution, the social capital OTE could gain by cooperating with IOM was helpful for the institution to foster its position in the field.

In conversations with OTE staff members, the cooperation with IOM sounded like a calculated extension rather than a fundamental shift in what migration means in Tunisia and who should be addressed by policies the new government designs in this field. The hierarchy between the different target groups was cemented by the architectural representation of their support structures: OTE's service for TREs is hosted in a highly visible building in the city center of Tunis. The building provides a famous monument of the importance of the Tunisian diaspora for the country. According to the IOM's website,[6] one of the Migration Resource Centers, which opened in December 2013, can be found inside this building. However, only a tiny sign at the top of the stairs leading to the colossal entrance door indicates its existence. Inside the ten-story office building, the uninformed visitor needs some patience and dedication to spot the center. Within the Kafkaesque building, it seemed impossible to find one's way through its winding corridors, floors, and staircases with numerous narrow passages without the assistance of one of the gatekeepers standing around. During my visit in 2015, I wondered how accessible and welcoming this secret place of advice in the heart of the OTE was for immigrants in Tunisia.

The hidden place within the long-standing service structure for TREs indicates that the two implementing partners—the IOM and the OTE—had found their ways and reasons to agree on addressing both potential Tunisian migrants and immigrants in the context of the START project. Tunisian state actors participate in projects designed by the IOM according to its objectives and target groups. However, in the moment of political rupture and change, the cooperation with international actors was of strategic importance for OTE to ensure and improve its position in the field.

In practice, immigrants in Tunisia hardly made use of the new service but rather turned to civil society actors that emerged in the country at the same time. At the Migration Resource Centers, "there are mostly Tunisians that look for opportunities for regular migration," the IOM staff reported after more than a year of implementation (interview with IOM staff, Tun. 2015). Even though examples of successful legal migration are rare, "there are some cases that exist, I think there are exchanges. For the businessmen, it is easy to obtain a visa; for students, it depends," she evaluated the limited possibilities the project can effectively offer to few exclusive groups, but not for most Tunisians (ibid.). "Afterwards, if they realize that there are not many ways for regular migration, many also take a boat" the IOM acknowledged the limited legal possibilities to migrate and the need to offer alternatives (ibid.).

"It is true that even during the information on irregular migration, in one moment, you also have to provide alternatives. If not, you can say 'be careful!' But so what?" the IOM staff questioned the effects of their own project (interview with IOM staff, Tun. 2015). The IOM staff working in Tunisia seemed to be aware of the limited impact of its projects. Tunisian migrants would too often come to a conclusion that "between dying here, because in fact, here is nothing, and trying to search elsewhere, I try. And if it does not work, at least I have tried" (ibid). She suggested that Tunisia needs a "strategic, economic development that would permit certain people not to make a choice that is almost obligatory to go abroad" (ibid.). The ambitions of young people to show that they "can make it elsewhere" seemed comprehensible to her. In the view of the IOM staff, the choice to migrate irregularly was not only a matter of global disparities, economic (under)development, or social marginalization but "also a spirit" (ibid.). Generally, the IOM seems in favor of young adventurous subjects who look for new opportunities and take initiative (see Kalm 2010, 35). Their "spirit" resonates well with the organization's mission to make migration an economically productive process for all stakeholders, including migrants. Voluntary initiatives and individual projects are preferred over governmental interventions and repression. In practice, however, it is difficult for the IOM to support these entrepreneurial subjects in a geopolitical context of intended scarce opportunities to migrate legally.

Since promoting possibilities and advantages of 'regular migration' is little promising in this context, the IOM focused on alternatives in Tunisia that should prevent the youth from leaving irregularly. However, the organization did not engage in structural changes. Its information campaigns aimed to foster the ties of young Tunisians to their country and family—socially, emotionally, and morally. In this respect, the IOM's work also contributed to the rebuilding of the Tunisian state, in institutional terms as well as symbolically and emotionally.

3.2.2 The symbolic power of the IOM's cinematography: The SALEMM project

The implementation of the SALEMM program in Tunisia was cofunded by the European Commission, Italy, and Switzerland. Focusing on the same disfavored regions identified for the START project, different interventions aimed

> to reduce the vulnerability of minors and young Tunisians regarding the risks of irregular migration and to reinforce their socio-economic integration and their entrenchment in their country of origin.
> (Ambassade de Suisse en Tunisie 2015, 4, translation IB)

Beyond the common discourse on preventing marginalized youth with high emigration risks from leaving North Africa, the SALEMM project paid particular attention to the endangered "entrenchment" of young Tunisians. According to the IOM's assessment (IOM 2014b), they have lost confidence in the temporary institutions and their apparently participatory democratic procedures. Since 2011, "youth have changed their vision on migration because a lot of Tunisians are going, thinking they can find the Eldorado," a representative of the International Labor Organization (ILO) explained regarding the situation in Tunisia (interview with ILO staff, Tun. 2015). While the main reason to emigrate from the country "used to be political, it is no more political now" (ibid.). From her point of view, it is not an economic motivation but the symbolic meaning of the "forbidden" that would attract many young people to leave:

> It is the forbidden thing, that you *can't* [...] For example, for students, it is normal that they want to travel; they want to discover other countries. But it is so difficult for them to get a visa [...] But because they are

students, they want to change their life, and if it is forbidden, that means it is better. They know it, and they keep doing it.

(Ibid.)

Acknowledging that there are too few legal migration opportunities to communicate, the SALEMM project aimed to "create sustainable alternatives for the youth" in Tunisia. However, this was not in terms of structural improvements of their living conditions and prospects in a world marked by unequal opportunities for people of different nationalities, but in terms of personal development, social integration, and emotional ties to the place designated for them within this system.[7] Therefore, the project focused on the social, moral, and emotional ties of young people in their environment. This way, it sought to turn the initiative of ambitious young Tunisians 'to make it elsewhere' into valuable projects for their country and community. The IOM defines the value of such initiatives.

> It is not "be careful, don't do it!" It is really to have a project here before giving up everything. Because often you arrive at the decision that the only solution is to leave, because you have explored everything, you do not identify with your community. So, you leave ... And one part of it is with the videos, with the social media,

the IOM staff pointed the innovative approach of the Tunisian SALEMM project (interview with IOM staff, Tun. 2015). For a national information campaign titled "20 young Tunisians, 20 views on migration," the IOM selected so-called ambassadors to produce short videos to inform their less-educated peers about the risks of irregularized migration (IOM 2014c, translation IB). In a first step, the IOM selected those it expected to become young leaders of Tunisian society to present a strong sense of responsibility toward their country and become "development agents" (Kalm 2010, 38). In this way, the IOM externalized the education of Tunisian youth. It outsourced the direct interaction and communication to a local elite who would act as translators of its mission and enhance its street credibility. In contrast to other programs, it was not vulnerability but leadership, talent, and innovative ideas that needed to be demonstrated with integrity and credibility to pass the competitive selection for the project. The IOM looked for reliable and creative implementing partners who were accepted in the local context and able to credibly spread the organization's mission through their own messages. The 20 most promising candidates were taught how to make a film. Trained in information technologies, communication, and media, the young Tunisians were expected to become

> ambassadors of their proper messages, active and responsible citizens who contribute with their stories, their creativity, and talents to inform and inspire other young people of their age about local alternatives of participation and dialogue.[8]

Neoliberal values such as creativity and talent qualified the role models for the mission to educate their peers about the risks of leaving and the merits of staying and productively engaging with their country and community.

The resulting videos were released in December 2014. The trailer promotes the project by calling upon the "shared responsibility" of young Tunisians to think about their families, their mothers, and their country before making the "irresponsible" decision to leave clandestinely.[9] In the end, it directs the attention to "create alternatives" (ibid.). Foot-tapping music underlines quickly moving pictures about the training, which the young "ambassadors" seem to enjoy, and their enthusiasm in producing the films. "People, wake up!" a bright voice repeatedly demands. It is an inviting and motivating call to become part of the morally good side that is shared by most of the videos. Instead of prohibition, punishment, and penalties, the trailer addresses young Tunisians as rational, moral, and emotional subjects who need believable incentives and reasons to stay in their country. They do so by focusing on the grief and pain of those left behind, especially families and friends. Mothers are prominent figures throughout the videos, confronting the viewer not only with the emotional ties but also with the moral burden loaded on such a project. Leaving your country means not only betraying those you love but also the national project of reconstructing postrevolutionary Tunisia. Feelings and values of patriotism, solidarity, and friendship can prevent young Tunisians from leaving. The symbolic power of the videos seeks to evoke the responsibility of young Tunisians to participate in the state-building project and, as such, their complicity in the prevention of irregularized migration.

The videos produced by the IOM ambassadors can be grouped into six thematic categories: death, grief, moral burden, solidarity and friendship, patriotism, and paradise. The death of young people who tried to migrate is the first powerful theme running through a group of videos. "Decide another path to be your own," a short artistic video called *Traces* urges the viewer. Soft music and breaking waves provide the background for the plaintive words that follow: "Think about every step ahead before it is too late… traces remember all those who left across the sea in search of—an often illusory—better life."[10] The video *Cafe Echatt* presents a similar message from the perspective of Tunisian men who survived the dangerous trip across the sea. Esthetic, calm images prime interviews with the returnees. According to their statements, they did not believe the stories about the deaths at sea, the dangers and discrimination they would have to experience in Europe before they took the boat to cross the Mediterranean. Once returned to Tunisia, they are happy to have survived the adventurous trip.

Focusing on the grief and pain of those left behind, a second theme explores the emotional consequences in perceptible and imaginable ways. They bring life to the concept of a selfish, immature, and irresponsible decision to leave. In an abstract way, *L'Absence* spreads the message that family and friends are the first victims of "the absence" caused by irregularized migration. The video reminds the viewer to think about those who count and incites them to consider family and friends before leaving in an irresponsible manner. *Espoire* pictures young people giving advice to believe in and do something with your life, but not to forget your home, family, and friends. A young woman challenges the viewer to "watch yourself in the mirror before leaving" to justify your departure in front of your mirror image and check if your conscience will let you go. For the protagonist of *Souffrance cachée*, this guidance to discipline yourself comes too late. In the video, a young man struggling not to drown regrets having left and apologizes to his mother (country) that shares the "hidden suffering" of so many. "I am terribly sorry, mom, please forgive me!" he puts the message shared by many of the SALEMM productions in a nutshell. The young people who are taking the boats at the Tunisian shores "do not think enough about their mothers that abandoned to their despair once they realize the deadly drama, unfortunately very frequently the case in the context of irregular migration." The film *Horga* also chooses a mother as the central figure; she is desperately and angrily crying because her son did not take her picture on his journey. This figure represents the feeling of loss and betrayal as well as the emotional link to the state.

Moreover, many videos address the moral burden loaded on such a project. *Hayet* is the only film that tells the story of a female protagonist. It conveys the particularly vulnerable position of women migrating, which is disregarded by the other videos. In the context of anti-trafficking campaigns, women are primarily pictured as "naive and defenseless victims of cruel male traffickers; being ignorant, they are unaware of what awaits them and therefore vulnerable" (Nieuwenhuys and Pécoud 2007, 1684). Having "experienced the horrors of trafficking and managed to escape," they are "to convince fellow young women of not leaving" (ibid.). Far from an empowering story, the video focuses on the family, especially the mother's worries for her.

A fourth theme, on the contrary, puts forward values of solidarity and friendship. "It is important to stay steady and believe in your dreams and ambitions without taking the easiest solutions that can turn out dramatic," warns a fashionable and catchy video called *3ich enti – Vivi tu*. Too late for his own departure, a boy arrives at the shore to discover his dead friends. "An impressively artistic and professional appeal to solidary and patriotism," the IOM's sleeve notes comment on the video. With about 1,000 clicks on YouTube, it is the most watched among the 20 productions. Patriotism, solidarity, and friendship are the underlying themes of several sketches performed against the background of the Mediterranean Sea, which represents a disturbing force to these values. In *El Gouna,* for example, a group of young men ready to depart hides in a deserted house at the coast when they receive the news about the revolution breaking out Tunisia. They debate whether to go and fight for their dreams or leave the country out of order. "The feeling of patriotism becomes stronger so that they decide to participate in the new collective adventure that begins in their country. A message of hope," the official IOM commentary describes.

The fifth theme the videos seek to get across is that staying in Tunisia and advancing your life also makes you happy. *Tiamo Hbiba – Ti amo* shows a football match between two teams of young Tunisians with opposing views on the question of migration. The promigration team dreams of more money, individual adventures, and personal development. Those who prefer to stay promote it as a matter of solidarity with their friends and families, as well as their commitment to their country and its development. The viewer is left with the impression that leaving Tunisia means betraying the national project. The decision to leave or to stay is also the focus of *La port du choix*. In the style of an advertising film, a well-dressed young man in front of two doors representing options "to migrate irregularly" or "to stay in your country" is torn by the decision about his future. He is pressured by voices from off the camera and troubled by dreams about expensive cars and other symbols of prosperity. The decision becomes a psychological struggle until he finally opens the door to stay. Bright light and soft music appear—a paradise metaphor used in many films. Taking his son by the hand, he walks down the road toward a school that welcomes them with the Tunisian national flag. "I will fight for a future in my country!" he is quoted in the credits. According to its brief description, the film shows that the question to leave or to stay blocks young people in constructing their lives and can cost them much time and energy. Once they decide to stay and participate in the (re)construction of Tunisia, however, they can rediscover their cheerfulness and advance in their lives.

A last theme presents return as the ultimate dream and real paradise for those who are unwilling to learn but decide to migrate anyway. *Looking for Paradiso* shows interviews with successful young people who manage their lives, studies, and work supported by their parents. They migrated legally to Europe and indeed returned to Tunisia. Their happiness is not demonstrated by their money but in terms of emotional and social ties. Legal migration is presented as an acceptable option, as long as it does not mean risking your life and disturbing the social and emotional peace in Tunisia and Europe. In this respect, the short documentary underlines the determining role of families in their children's choices. In the SALEMM project, the IOM discovered families as a central concept of its information campaigns. In this sense, the announcement of *Al Harka Horka* also warns: "The young people who are attracted by the idea of irregular migration escape their country and leave behind the burning hearts of their families." The emphatic reference to a paradise used in several films contrasts with the metaphor of hell and burning. The commentary continues:

> Unfortunately, leaving under these conditions is only a path to hell. Without being conscious of the dangers awaiting them, these young people destroy their passports for a future that they believe to be better and expose themselves to the arms of death.

The video shows burning pictures of friends and families, an analogy to the 'Harraga,' a Tunisian term for those who burn passports and borders, respectively. 'Irregular migration,' the video suggests, not only means burning passports but also memories and relations, which is a form of devastation for the migrant (Sayad 2004).

Analyzing the IOM's information campaigns in Eastern Europe, Nieuwenhuys and Pécoud (2007, 1684) observe that the "diversity of experiences and the possibility of 'making it' are seldom mentioned, and only one migratory experience exists, leading to failure, misfortune, and exploitation." In contrast to the warning tone dominating earlier campaigns (see also Heller 2014), most of the SALEMM videos focus on the pain and grief caused by leaving and being left behind. While some videos picture the loneliness, rejection, and failure young people experience abroad, most of them focus on feelings of shame and remorse of all those who leave instead of engaging in the development of what is supposed to be *their* country. The decision to migrate irregularly is presented as an ignorant and egoistic adventurous trip of mostly young men who betray their family, community, and country. Tunisia is presented as one large family with a common project for the future, which requires everyone's effort and solidarity. Its reconstruction and development are supposed to be the project of every young individual and the desired alternative to migration. Those who leave are regarded as cheating this national state-building project. If irregularized migration cannot be cured, at least it can be prevented from spreading further and infecting more young Tunisians through friendship, care, solidarity, and patriotism. Its management extends rational decisions that can be influenced through better education to intervene in the sphere of morals and emotions.

While the IOM is keen to leave it an individual decision whether one should stay or go, its advice to think wisely and responsibly about the consequences for oneself and one's family is emotionally strong and morally imperative. Metaphors of an awaiting paradise for those who stay (or at least return) versus hell for those who leave enhance the symbolic power of a morally charged, patriotic discourse. Mothers have become central figures to stand for the emotional ties to a 'mother country' that is left behind, disappointed and desperate about the 'irresponsible choice' of young migrants. The main message of the videos produced during the SALEMM project is simple: do not believe in the stories about Europe as an Eldorado but think and feel about your country, your family, or your mother before you make the foolish decision that is mostly only implied by the metaphor of taking a boat. Even if not visible from what is termed the misguided view of young Tunisians, the IOM ensures that there are always alternatives to "construct the project of a responsible life, far from the dangerous routes of irregular migration" (IOM 2015, translation IB).

Participatory migration management in Tunisia no longer focused on the actual risks of irregularized migration but on the "personal aspirations, values, and intimacy" of young Tunisians (Pécoud 2013, 5). According

112 *Information campaigns*

to Didier Bigo (2006, 92), it seeks to manage the risks of migration in the "name of love." The IOM's prevention thereby introduces a distinction between those who fit the IOM's expectations in the behavior of modern, rational, and responsible subjects on the one hand, and those who appear too 'uneducated' and 'backward' to be convinced by rational means. This symbolic violence of the IOM's classification of people echoes a colonial gaze that categorizes apparently backward people according to their (ir) rationality. While the Moroccan project demonstrated the organization's belief in the possibility to educate and train 'misguided' individuals, its information campaigns in Tunisia mobilize symbolic, moral, and emotional values to change a society.

> And some of [the movies], if you watch them, they are really tough. But that is how they [the young Tunisians] are. It is interesting because it is not me who comes from above and says what is going on, but it is them who present them like they wanted to.
> (Interview with IOM staff, Tun. 2015)

Instead of education "from above" by international experts who "say what's going on," the SALEMM project videos unfold their symbolic power through horizontal and digital dissemination in networks of the Tunisian youth. The distinction between "me who comes from above" and "them who present them like they wanted to" underlines clearly distinguished positions in the field: "above" indicates the position of the international expert who has the resources and sets the rules of the game. "Below" are the young and creative Tunisian elites who can participate in the game according to these rules and profit from the distribution of resources and recognition through the project. They are involved in the prevention campaign through the freedom to produce the movies "like they wanted to." Supported by the IOM, they are supposed to bring their skills, creativity, and credibility into play in order to convince their peers.

Participatory methods of virtual peer-to-peer education have not only been employed in the production of the SALEMM videos but also as tools of their dissemination. They seek to profit from the trend that Western observers have called the Facebook generation. As a Tunisian blogger (Heni 2013, 40) points out,

> the West generally loves [...] speaking of the Tunisian revolution as the "Facebook revolution", because it is sort of cultural success; and this digital culture which started in the U.S., in Europe, and in Japan, that, is considered in the West as able to change countries without the use of force—as if it as possible to change the regime with Facebook. Before, it was necessary to make an attack, with bombs and parachutists, while now, according to the West, this would not be necessary anymore, and this would be a success.

Information campaigns 113

To change movements of migration, the IOM's information campaigns exercise a similar symbolic power. Drawing on the "success" of the "Facebook revolution," the IOM demonstrated its *feel for the game,* using social media to bring about changes among disappointed young Tunisian postrevolutionaries.

According to Martin Geiger (2012, 140), this kind of virtual storytelling is employed to directly address the individuals, their bodies, and behavior and means to shape a certain lifestyle and society. The stories and images used in the IOM's information campaigns are based on the distinction of good, law-abiding, well-informed, and responsible migrants on the one hand and bad, dangerous, uninformed, and irresponsible, illegalized migrants on the other. This dichotomy is imposed on Tunisian society through the symbolic power of the movies. Against this moralized dichotomy, potential migrants are advised on how to behave in an orderly way and contribute not only to the development of their country but also to the objective of a well-managed migration process. In this respect, the IOM's information campaigns in Tunisia reflect "how not only migrants but also all those who could possibly think of crossing international borders and migrating are tentatively instructed to think and behave in a specific fashion" (Pécoud 2013, 4). In this sense, the IOM's migration management goes beyond the sheer issue of migration to address all people—whether mobile or not—as well as their future choices (ibid., 5). With the help of participatory methods such as the SALEMM videos, this instruction is no longer implemented through educational practices by international experts but externalized to a local elite of "ambassadors" who are expected to transmit the messages in more credible ways. In this context, irregularized migration is no longer tackled as a rational decision but as a question of emotional ties and moral conviction.

3.2.3 *"If the people were really convinced, they would not have left"—the doubtful impact of virtual migration management*

Throughout the IOM's publications, the film-making project stands out as one of the organization's most visible interventions in Tunisia. How the Tunisian youth actually perceived these interventions is a different question. Initially, the videos were made for educational work in schools, festivals, and other public events. While they were also shared via the IOM's website, Facebook,[11] and YouTube,[12] the videos did not receive much resonance on these platforms. The 20 videos have hardly been shared or liked on Facebook—with a maximum of four times—and received a quite moderate number of clicks on YouTube—about 900 maximum.[13] From these numbers, it remains doubtful whether these instruments can effectively reach Tunisia's so-called Facebook generation. Moreover, even if the messages would make it through to their attention, there is still the question of whether they would have any impact on their decisions, feelings, and behavior.

114 *Information campaigns*

Tunisian state and non-state actors were rather skeptical about the impact of the IOM's information campaigns. "With the IOM, there was theater. And afterwards, in 2011, we had an explosion" of migration to Italy, a representative of the Red Crescent in Tunisia recalled of the beginning of IOM's campaigning in 2010 (interview with Red Crescent staff, Tun. 2015). "So, if the people were really convinced, they would not have left," he argued (ibid.). According to his experience, the IOM's prevention efforts

> never resulted in anything. It has not diminished, and it has not slowed [down migration movements]. The solution is not information campaigns to convince people not to migrate. It is useless! They know it. They know that it is dangerous. They know about the problems with unemployment in Europe. They know about the global economic crisis. They know they will be deported. They know that there is exploitation on the way, but they continue to migrate.
>
> (Ibid.)

From the perspective of this humanitarian organization with long experience in the field, attempts to prevent irregularized migration through education and social work miss the point since it is not the lack of information but the lack of alternatives that make young Tunisians leave. Equally skeptical, a representative of one of the Tunisian ministries that cooperates with the IOM suggested to "formalize that irregularity" instead of campaigning against irregularized migration (interview with repr. of MDIC, Tun. 2015). She compared irregularized migration to the informal economy to explicate her point: "You cannot abolish the informal economy but only try to formalize the informal that means to push for that transition from the informal toward the formal in the field of migration" (ibid.). For the new representatives of the Tunisian state, the political priority was to enhance the possibilities for legal migration. Dealing with irregularized migration, in turn, was left to international actors and their projects in the early years after the revolution.

International organizations (IOs) competing with the IOM over spheres of action and influence also uttered their doubts about the impact of information campaigns. According to a representative of the ILO, the money for the SALEMM project was not well spent: "It is a lot of time and resources invested in one person while maybe you could help a whole region by building something different that would make them stay" (interview with ILO staff, Tun. 2015). She directed attention to the structural conditions of individualized prevention activities. In the south of Tunisia, "they don't even have a shopping center or a cinema or a swimming pool! They have nothing. Those youth, of course they want to leave that place" (ibid.). For her, covering basic needs was not sufficient to address the "root causes of migration":

> It is not only a question of being fed every day. It is more than that; it is a question of having a sense to their life. If your life is boring in

your region and you are not interested in anything, and then you have the television, and all day, every day you watch other cultures that are beautiful.

(Ibid.)

Without adequate alternatives being developed in Tunisia that would give "a sense to their life" (ibid.)—in her view, shopping centers, swimming pools, and cinemas were relevant indicators in this regard—she could understand that young people would decide to take the risk to leave.

These skeptical voices uttered by different actors in the field contradict and challenge the IOM's conviction that informing individuals can effectively make a difference within the structural conditions of an overall unjust system of growing global disparities. As long as young Tunisians are disadvantaged by the unequal global distribution of social rights and political freedoms and experience the continuously enforced differences in individual opportunities to move or to stay and live a decent life in Tunisia, it is hard to imagine that they would change their minds after watching a two-minute video clip on YouTube.

Nonetheless, the IOM staff seemed to uphold an illusioic belief in the general usefulness of its preventive management tools. Despite the doubtfulness of their impact, they helped the organization carve out its unique service provision. European donors indeed rewarded the IOM's soft tools to 'fight irregular migration' and extended their funding. With its information campaigns, the IOM proved its feel for the game and established a new product on the international market of migration management services which met an increasing donor demand despite its questionable results. The *symbolic capital* the IOM gained through the implementation of participatory projects helped the organization extend its influence within the *trans-Mediterranean field of migration management* beyond the sheer issue of migration and move the boundaries of the very field itself to include new target groups, tools, and temporalities.

3.3 The symbolic power of neoliberal risk management: why potential migrants would (not) participate in their own management

This chapter has demonstrated the IOM's stakes in implementing so-called migration and development activities. The organization did not respond to the call for *(more) migration for (more) development* proposed by North African governments. Instead, the IOM implemented projects that drew on a *more development for less migration* approach, which is in line with European donor priorities 'to fight irregular migration.' The organization neither opened possibilities for legal migration nor addressed structural causes of migration, such as global social inequalities or unjust international political and economic relations. Rather, it implemented information campaigns aiming to change the individual behavior of those deemed to be 'at risk of irregular migration.' These proactive tools of individualized risk management address the thoughts, feelings, and actions of potential migrants to make them stay in their countries of origin.

The literature has discussed such neoliberal modes of migration management as governing at a distance or through freedom, outsourcing, or discipline. What receives less attention is the question of why those targeted by such campaigns would actually participate in their own management. In this chapter, I have mobilized the concepts of symbolic power and symbolic violence to answer this question. These concepts help direct attention to the content of the politics of prevention and the perspectives of those who are to be governed by them.

The IOM's preventive practices build on the belief in the rationality of a well-managed migration reality. Within this reality, irregularized migration means a risk for potential migrants and the sending, transit, and destination countries. Depending on the funding of the latter, the IOM proposed to manage this risk on the southern side of the Mediterranean and prevent it from spreading further north. Such "calculations are introduced as exceptions to the prevailing political system, separating some groups for special attention, and carving out special zones" that represent a particularly high risk of migration, which in turn legitimates the IOM's interventions in the name of their own protection (Ong 2007, 6). Profiling such risk groups and targeting their members with disciplinary techniques, the IOM exercises a symbolic violence that seeks to individualize and externalize the responsibility for migration control to potential migrants and their communities. Through the classification of people and regions into rational and irrational, informed and uninformed, favored and disfavored, etc., the IOM intervenes in the symbolic orders and hierarchies of North African societies. While these symbolic interventions often remain misrecognized among those addressed, they affect the moral orders of who needs to be educated and whose behavior is acceptable.

The target group of preventive interventions in Morocco and Tunisia is defined as the 'marginalized youth' from regions 'with high emigration risk.' In Morocco, the IOM identified irregularized migration as the rational choice of immature, uneducated young people from disfavored regions. The circumstances under which this individual decision is made are not questioned or targeted by the organization. The projects hardly consider the social, political, and economic conditions that put these young people in despair to migrate irregularly. The IOM seeks to empower individuals, disregarding the structural conditions that put them at risk of leaving. Its aim is to change individual behavior, not the international system of unequally distributed mobility rights.

The IOM implements prevention through a mix of information, education, and empowerment. Based on the illusioic belief that more information and better education will change young Moroccans' ambitions to migrate, the IOM projects seek to enable them to make an 'informed decision' and 'behave responsibly'—which, for the IOM, ultimately means staying in Morocco. The symbolic power of this neoliberal prevention works through individual incentives and self-discipline rather than through prohibition and repression. While defined as misguided and immature, the target group is regarded as entrepreneurial subjects willing and capable of working on their self-optimization in order to live a successful life. Success, the IOM implies, is not achieved through migration but through hard work and self-discipline that contribute to the development in Morocco. For the IOM, it seems to be a moral duty to support them in this process and channel their energy, creativity, and ambitions toward productive projects in the country. This self-proclaimed duty to educate 'others' about what the organization regards as orderly behavior and valuable projects underlines the organization's progressive self-understanding as a global expert of neoliberal values.

Conscious of the fact that White foreign 'internationals' are not the most trustworthy and credible teachers for young Moroccans and Tunisians, the organization developed participatory methods of peer-to-peer education. Through these horizontal forms of knowledge dissemination, the IOM sought to exercise indirect influence through social networks and digital means of communication. In seeking to manage young people's dreams and aspirations through social work and media, the IOM aimed to inform them about the risks of irregularized migration and form their future behavior and choices.

The information campaigns in Tunisia moreover build on the belief in the morality of well-managed migration reality. They include emotional techniques and moral values in the management of irregularized migration. Potential migrants, their families, and communities have all become agents of migration control. Once they are well informed, educated, and trained, they are expected to participate in their own management and contribute to an orderly migration process and the stabilization of their communities. In contrast to IOM campaigns conducted in other regions, information campaigns in North Africa merely aim to communicate the positive effects of staying and engaging in the country of origin, rather than spreading a negative image of migration to Europe. They focus on the personal development, social integration, and emotional ties of potential migrants to their families, communities, and national societies. While patriotism and the commitment to a national project were important for Tunisian campaigns, advancing individual projects through hard work, self-reliance, and patience—also against obstacles and traditional conventions of society—were key themes in campaigns for Morocco. In both countries, the IOM aims to turn young people's "entrepreneurial spirit" (Kalm 2010, 34) into valuable, economically productive, and morally right projects. Activating individuals in the name of their rational interest, moral responsibility, or emotional well-being, the IOM's campaigns seek to voluntarily engage young people in the management of international migration and national development. Yet,

118 *Information campaigns*

from the perspective of those who are to be involved in the projects' implementation, their impact remains doubtful and contested.

Nevertheless, the IOM gained much symbolic capital through its design of participatory methods of migration management. This reputation allowed the organization to extend its influence to new spheres of action and foster its position as a relevant actor in the trans-Mediterranean field of migration management. Through its practical work, the organization extended the meaning of migration management toward new forms of social prophylaxes and thereby stretched the very boundaries of the field itself. There are (at least) four effects of the IOM's information campaigns on the expanding border regime in North Africa and beyond.

First, despite their feel-good image, they resonated well with the European-sponsored 'fight against irregular migration.' While effective border control measures remained high on the agenda for many donors, they also showed an increasing interest in new modes of governing migration that draw on the mobilization, participation, and responsibilization of potential migrants rather than prohibition, coercion, and repression. Employing softer instruments to prevent potential migrants from leaving is in line with European attempts to extract themselves from the accountability and avoid unpleasant implementation of repressive forms of direct interaction with migrants at their external borders. Preventing potential migrants through education by international experts promises less (openly) violent ways to stabilize the border regime than its militarization. The educative and empowering interventions were acceptable to Moroccan and Tunisian authorities and welcomed by European donors alike.

Second, the risks and responsibilities of irregularized migration are turned into a matter of individual behavior of potential migrants, not restrictive policies of the European border regime or persisting global disparities in people's rights of free movement. The IOM's information campaigns do not address structural changes but take global social disparities, the state-centric system, and its capitalist order for granted. To avoid potential protest and disobedient, unproductive behavior, the IOM's interventions provide social work and personal skill trainings to make potential migrants better fit in the "national order of things" (Malkki 1995). They engage their hopes and dreams, channeling them in productive but controllable ways. The symbolic power of disciplining human mobility thus contributes to the (re)installation of authority and order over irregularized migration. Differentiating people and their legitimate plans and aspirations, the individualized techniques of risk management create and reinforce global social inequalities. Information campaigns select certain people and populations to be fixed in place—ironically, often by highly mobile international or expat staff of IOs. For European donors financing information campaigns in North Africa, this soft and pedagogic way of upholding global social inequalities in people's rights to mobility is comparatively harmless and innocent.

Third, the preventive approach provides the organization with an opportunity to distinguish itself through participatory methods and to expand its work into new social, pedagogic areas, no longer directly linked to migration. Practices of prevention extended the field of migration management to include new stakes, strategies, and struggles. Notably, the extension of the IOM's work in terms of education and social work opened new sources of funding for the organization. Pécoud (2012, 189) argues that the organization's preventive interventions provide tools for "Western states [to practically achieve their] aim at erecting in people's minds the borders they fail to control between states. They do so by promoting a 'culture of immobility.'" In this regard, the IOM's information campaigns transmit the neoliberal logic of international migration management to immaterial and individual grounds. The IOM thereby fosters an image and self-understanding as a global moral expert that softly brings about progressive (neo)liberal changes in the Global South. It actualizes a colonial history of external interventions on the African continent in the name of better education.

Finally, Moroccan and Tunisian actors, and especially the young people who were to be addressed by the information campaigns, did not seem too enthusiastic and convinced about them. Moroccan and Tunisian state actors preferred to enhance legal possibilities for their citizens. Nevertheless, they strategically cooperated with the IOM in order to gain social and economic capital that would help them foster or improve their own positions in the field. Non-state actors participated for similar reasons but uttered their doubts about the individualized approach of the IOM projects more openly. Despite widespread doubts and skepticism regarding the impact of the information campaigns, the IOM was able to organize the participants needed to implement its participatory projects. Using its symbolic capital as an international expert, the IOM can succeed in conveying rationalities and moral values of international migration management even among potential migrants. This means young Moroccans and Tunisians would follow the recommendations of the IOM, apparently voluntarily, because they recognize its position and respect not only the organization but the international state system, which seems natural and unquestionable. The IOM's prevention practices contribute to the stabilization of this order and its *doxic* effect. Since there is a lot *at stake* for potential migrants, it is more common to evade management attempts than to openly question them. However, with every border crossing, they challenge this order and require state actors to make it explicit. This is where repression comes into play.

Notes

1 The Moroccan Action Plan of the High Level Working Group in the EU's Council of Ministers was one of eleven action plans for implementing the EU's external dimension of migration policies in selected countries of origin and transit in the late 1990s.

120 Information campaigns

2 See the project's Facebook page: https://www.facebook.com/FESTIVAL. DROUBNA4/ [17.03.2021].
3 Letter from German Minister of Interior, Thomas De Maizière, to EU Commissioner Cecilia Malmström, September 9th, 2014.
4 See the IOM project website: http://www.centresmigrants.tn/fr/presentation [17.03.2021, translation IB].
5 Quoted from IOM project website (see FN 4).
6 See the IOM project website in FN 4.
7 See the project description on the IOM Tunisia website: https://tunisia.iom.int/activities/%C2%AB-solidarit%C3%A9-avec-les-enfants-du-maghreb-et-du-mashreq-%C2%BB-salemm-en-tunisie [17.03.2021].
8 Quoted on the IOM's project website: http://www.salemm.org/fr/fr-campagne [translation IB] that was last accessed on January 30th, 2018. All videos can still be viewed on YouTube: https://www.youtube.com/channel/UCXCT8RZL3Ku-e3yDBKRpICg/feed [17.03.2021].
9 See the IOM project website www.salemm.org that was last accessed on January 30th, 2018.
10 All videos can be viewed on YouTube: https://www.youtube.com/channel/UCXCT8RZL3Ku-e3yDBKRpICg/feed[17.03.2021]
11 See the IOM project's Facebook page: https://www.facebook.com/salemmtunisie?fref=ts [17.03.2021].
12 See films on YouTube: https://www.youtube.com/channel/UCXCT8RZL3Ku-e3yDBKRpICg/feed [17.03.2021].
13 Last accessed on March 17th, 2021.

Literature cited

Altai Consulting. 2015. *Migration Trends across the Mediterranean: Connecting the Dots*. Cairo: IOM Mena Regional Office.
Ambassade de Suisse en Tunisie. 2015. *Domaine III: Migration et Protection. Fiches de Projets*. Tunis: Ambassade de Suisse en Tunisie, Division Coopération Internationale.
Balibar, Etienne. 1991. "Is There a 'Neo-Racism'?" In *Race, Nation, Class. Ambiguous Identities*, edited by Etienne Balibar and Immanuel Wallerstein, 17–28. London: Verso.
Bartels, Inken. 2017. "'We Must Do It Gently.' The Contested Implementation of the IOM's Migration Management in Morocco." *Migration Studies* 5 (3): 315–336. doi:10.1093/migration/mnx054.
Bigo, Didier. 2006. "Protection. Security, Territory and Population." In *The Politics of Protection. Sites of Insecurity and Political Agency*, edited by Jef Huysmans, Andrew Dobson, and Raia Prokhovnik, 84–100. London: Routledge. doi:10.4324/9780203002780-13.
Boswell, Christina. 2003. "The External Dimension of EU Immigration and Asylum Policy." *International Affairs* 79 (3): 619–638. doi:10.1111/1468-2346.00326.
Caillault, Clotilde. 2012. "The Implementation of Coherent Migration Management through IOM Programs in Morocco." *IMIS-Beiträge* 40: 133–156.
Charles Heller. 2014. "Perception Management – Deterring Potential Migrants through Information Campaigns." *Global Media and Communication* 10 (3): 303–318. doi:10.1177/1742766514552355.
Coopération Italienne au Maroc. 2008. *Coopération Italienne au Maroc*. Report 2008. Rabat: Bureau de la Coopération Italienne au Maroc.

Ferguson, James, and Akhil Gupta. 2002. "Spatializing States: Toward an Ethnography of Neoliberal Governmentality." *American Ethnologist* 29 (4): 981–1002. doi:10.1525/ae.2002.29.4.981.
Frowd, Philippe M. 2018. *Security at the Borders. Transnational Practices and Technologies in West Africa.* Cambridge: Cambridge University Press. doi:10.1017/9781108556095.
Garelli, Glenda. 2013. "Schengen Intermittences: The On/Off Switch of Free Circulation." In *Spaces in Migration. Postcards of a Revolution*, edited by Glenda Garelli, Federica Sossi, and Martina Tazzioli, 75–95. London: Pavement Books.
Geiger, Martin. 2012. "Weltorganisationen in der Gestaltung globaler und regionaler Migrationspolitik: Die International Organization for Migration (IOM)." In *Weltorganisationen*, edited by Martin Koch, 129–151. Wiesbaden: VS Verlag für Sozialwissenschaften. doi:10.1007/978-3-531-18977-2_6.
Geiger, Martin. 2013. "The Transformation of Migration Politics." In *Disciplining the Transnational Mobility of People*, edited by Martin Geiger and Antoine Pécoud, 15–40. Basingstoke: Palgrave Macmillan. doi:10.1057/9781137263070.0005.
Geiger, Martin, and Antoine Pécoud. 2013. *Disciplining the Transnational Mobility of People.* Basingstoke: Palgrave Macmillan. doi:10.1057/9781137263070.
Hall, Stuart, Doreen Massey, and Michael Rustin. 2013. "After Neoliberalism: Analysing the Present." *Soundings* 53 (April 2013): 8–22. doi:10.3898/136266213806045656.
Heni, Issam. 2013. "'A Tribute to the Anonymous People'. An Interview with Issam Heni." In *Spaces of Migration. Postcards of a Revolution*, edited by Glenda Garelli, Federica Sossi, and Martina Tazzioli, 27–40. London: Pavement Books.
IOM. 2008. *PROJET OIM/Ministère des Affaires Etrangers Italien: SALEM (Solidarité Avec les Enfants du Maroc).* Rabat: IOM Morocco.
IOM. 2010. *L'Attitude des Jeunes au Maroc à l'Égard de la Migration: Entre Modernité et Tradition. Réalisation d'un Index de Propension à la Migration (IPM).* Geneva: IOM.
IOM. 2012. *Lettre d'Information N°15.* Janvier 2012. Rabat: IOM Morocco.
IOM. 2013a. *Lettre d'Information N°18.* Rabat: IOM Morocco.
IOM. 2013b. *START. Stabilisation des Communautés à Risque et Renforcement de la Gestion des Migrations Afin d'Accompagner les Transitions en Égypte, Tunisie et Libye.* Cairo: IOM MENA Regional Office.
IOM. 2014a. *Centres de Ressources Pour les Migrants à Tunis, El Kef et Sfax. Note Informative Projet.* Tunis: IOM Tunisia.
IOM. 2014b. *L'Organisation Internationale Pour les Migrations & la Jeunesse en Tunisie.* Tunis: IOM Tunisia.
IOM. 2014c. *Communiqué de Presse: L'Organisation Internationale Pour les Migrations Célèbre l'Inauguration du Guichet d'Information sur les Migrations au Sein de l'Observatoire National de la Jeunesse à Tunis.* Tunis: IOM Tunisia.
IOM. 2015. *Communiqué de Presse: SALEMM Présente le 1er Forum des Opportunités. Mercredi 4 et Jeudi 5 Mars au Centre de Défense et d'Intégration Sociale (CDIS) de Melassine.* Tunis: IOM Tunisia.
Kalm, Sara. 2010. "Liberalizing Movement? The Political Rationality of Global Migration Management." In *The Politics of International Migration Management*, edited by Martin Geiger and Antoine Pécoud, 21–44. Basingstoke: Palgrave Macmillan. doi:10.1057/9780230294882_2.
Lavenex, Sandra, and Rachel Kunz. 2008. "The Migration–Development Nexus in EU External Relations." *European Integration* 30 (3): 439–457. doi:10.1080/07036330802142152.

Malkki, Liisa H. 1995. "Refugees and Exile: *From* 'Refugee Studies' to the National Order of Things." *Annual Review of Anthropology* 24 (1): 495–523. doi:10.1146/annurev.an.24.100195.002431.

Nieuwenhuys, Céline, and Antoine Pécoud. 2007. "Human Trafficking, Information Campaigns, and Strategies of Migration Control." *American Behavioral Scientist* 50 (12): 1674–1695. doi:10.1177/0002764207302474.

Ong, Aihwa. 2007. "Neoliberalism as a Mobile Technology." *Transactions of the Institute of British Geographers* 32 (1): 3–8. doi:10.1111/j.1475-5661.2007.00234.x.

Pécoud, Antoine. 2012. "Informing Migrants to Manage Migration? An Analysis of IOM's Information Campaigns." In *The Politics of International Migration Management*, edited by Martin Geiger and Antoine Pécoud, 184–201. Basingstoke: Palgrave Macmillan. doi:10.1057/9780230294882_9.

Pécoud, Antoine. 2013. "Introduction." In *Disciplining the Transnational Mobility of People*, edited by Martin Geiger and Antoine Pécoud, 1–14. Basingstoke: Palgrave Macmillan. doi:10.1057/9781137263070_1.

Rose, Nicholas, and Peter Miller. 2010. "Political Power beyond the State: Problematics of Government." *The British Journal of Sociology* 61 (1): 271–303. doi:10.1111/j.1468-4446.2009.01247.x.

Sayad, Abdelmalek. 2004. *The Suffering of the Immigrant*. Cambridge: Wiley.

Sayad, Abdelmalek. 2010. "Immigration and 'State Thought.'" In *Selected Studies in International Migration and Immigration Incorporation*, edited by Marco Martiniello and Jan Rath, 165–180. Amsterdam: Amsterdam University Press.

Schwertl, Maria. 2015. "Wissen, (Selbst)Management, (Re)Territorialisierung. Die drei Achsen des aktuellen Diskurses um Migration & Entwicklung." *Movements. Journal for Critical Migration and Border Regime Studies* 1 (1). http://movements-journal.org/issues/01.grenzregime/09.schwertl--wissen-selbstmanagement-reterritorialisierung-migration-entwicklung.html [17.03.2021].

Swing, Wiliam L. 2014. "Des Vies de Migrants Sont en Jeu, n'Attendons pas Trop Tard." Le Monde December 16th, 2014.

Wacquant, Loïc. 2009. *Punishing the Poor: The Neoliberal Government of Social Insecurity*. Durham, NC: Duke University Press. doi:10.2307/j.ctv11smrv3.

4 Voluntary return programs

Migration management as a moral responsibility to protect

"The IOM?" a migrant from West Africa responded to my question about his experiences with the organization, loudly stirring his coffee and taking his time before beginning his story:

> The IOM is an organization that takes care of immigrants here in Morocco, mostly those who do not want to stay here anymore, where there is poverty and where they do not have a voice. So, they will take care of you, they will pay your flight ticket...they will see you to your country, they will give you a bit of money to stay for some time with your family until you have the means to—how to say it?—you have the means to care for yourself.
> (Interview with migrant, Mor. 2014)

I met him in a cafe in downtown Rabat in summer 2014 to learn about his experiences participating in the International Organization for Migration's (IOM) voluntary return program. He recounted to me his long and exhausting journey spanning more than eight years and four countries. I was surely not the first to which he told (t)his story, as interviews with state officials and in international organizations (IOs) are an integral part of it. Still, perhaps I was the first to ask him about these specific encounters with IOM.

After he had arrived in Morocco through a Spanish pushback at sea in 2005, he stayed in the country for five years until he decided to return to West Africa. It was "in 2010, [that] I went to the IOM, in Rabat. Without documents here, you always have difficulties" (ibid.). He described his reasons to go back: the Moroccan police "will always take you to Oujda. [...] you show your passport and they take you, again and again" (ibid.). Because of recurring state repression and deportations to the Algerian border, he finally decided to return:

> It was too dangerous. I was risking dying there in the desert, because there are gangs; they have knives, very long knives. When they see an African, they think you carry money with you and they attack you. They start to hit you, they kick you, and if you try to escape they will

DOI: 10.4324/9781003204169-5

124 *Voluntary return programs*

undress you until you are naked. You are always escaping everywhere. So with this, I decided to return home.

(Ibid.)

In the context of the European Union's (EU) external borders becoming increasingly militarized, along with numerous racist attacks and repressive deterrence of Sub-Saharan migrants in the North African borderlands, many looked for options to change their routes and projects of migration. From their perspective, participating in the IOM's Assisted Voluntary Return and Reintegration (AVRR) program was a welcome alternative to dangerous, spontaneous returns, as well as to the state-enforced deportations at that time. As a result, the rising demand among migrants wishing to participate in the program made *voluntary return*[1] a flourishing business for the IOM in Morocco.

In the Global North, the IOM began to implement the AVRR program in the 1970s; in North Africa, it started to promote what is now its most prominent service in the early 2000s (IOM 2013). At that time, however, North African governments perceived themselves primarily as countries of emigration; as such, they showed little interest in projects that focused attention on the situation of transit migrants on their territories (see Chapter 3). It was in the context of the widely publicized 'Moroccan migration crisis' in 2005 (see the Introduction) that the IOM was able to convince the Moroccan government to accept the program's implementation.

In this chapter, I take the two prominent North African 'migration crises' that were proclaimed in Morocco in 2005 and in Tunisia in 2011 as an empirical starting point, analyzing how perspectives of migration and practices of its control in the two countries changed when IOs entered the field to manage what was perceived as the increasingly visible 'problem' of transit migration in the North African borderlands. The Moroccan case shows how the IOM promised more effective and less conflict-laden measures to deal with the presence of Sub-Saharan migrants than the repressive forms of migration control that prevailed at the time. Utilizing voluntary offers and individual incentives rather than physical force and state repression, the IOM seeks to motivate migrants to engage in their own return.

Examining the contested implementation of this new approach to governing transit migration, the first part of this chapter explores what is *at stake* for the different actors involved in the voluntary return business—namely IOs, European donors, Moroccan state authorities, civil society movements, and migrants. By analyzing the struggles that move, challenge, and co-opt the making of voluntary return, the chapter provides insights into the *rules*, *logic*, and *illusioic beliefs* involved in playing this *game*. Against this background, I argue that the *symbolic capital* gained by the IOM by implementing the AVRR program in Morocco permits the organization to establish itself in a profitable position in the emerging *trans-Mediterranean field of migration management*, which works according to neoliberal logic of marketization and competition among different service providers. I also demonstrate how—contrary to the IOM's promotion in public and political discourses—its practices of voluntary return are particularly successful when inherently intertwined with and influenced by a threat of deportation and detention, in a context marked by the repressive logic of state politics. Rather than increasing the systematic and effective return of all migrants in transit, the combination of different return instruments in this single emerging repatriation regime enhances migrants' *returnability* (see Bartels 2019)—and thus the demand for the IOM's assistance. At the same time, I also show how return practices based on active consent and participation provide various options for migrants to escape repatriation, to appropriate the AVRR program, or to collectively resist it.

The second part of the chapter explores how the IOM's practices of voluntary return acquired a new meaning and a new practical logic of aid and assistance in the context of the so-called humanitarian crisis at the Tunisian-Libyan border in 2011. I argue that, from the perspective of the IOM, migration management became an unquestioned moral responsibility, a practice of protecting certain groups of migrants from the dangers of moving on to Europe. This humanitarian recodification provided new forms of authority and legitimization for the organization, even beyond the emergency situation in 2011. It resonated in the symbolic production of new categories and hierarchies of migrants—which in turn had very material consequences for their access to protection, as it directly impacted the IOM's processes of sorting and reorienting migration trajectories in transit. By providing assistance to Sub-Saharan migrants, who were regarded as passive recipients of aid rather than individuals with rights to asylum (or individuals with potential who could be empowered), the IOM contributed to shifting logic in the field from a rights-based approach to humanitarian aid that also rearranged the *strategies, struggles,* and *stakes* of other actors in the field, including migrants. The IOM's particular *fit* in the trans-Mediterranean field of migration management—which is moved by a combination of repressive, neoliberal, and humanitarian logics—made it possible for the organization to emerge and establish itself in such an influential position.

4.1 The IOM's promise of a cost-effective and humane alternative to deportation

In Morocco, the IOM promoted the AVRR program primarily as an innovative response to the collective struggles of migration in 2005 (see the Introduction). Instead of promoting repressive means, the organization suggested softer techniques to deal with the increasingly visible and unwelcome presence of Sub-Saharan migrants. In contrast to state instruments, these tactics rely on the active cooperation of member states and of potential participants. Therefore, the IOM had to convince the various stakeholders of the benefits of its program. This involved gaining the trust of the Moroccan government and promoting voluntary return as a time-saving and "cost-effective, humane alternative [to the prevailing practice of deportation] that assists stranded migrants in destitution" (IOM 2013, 43). At the same time, the IOM also needed to ensure that the AVRR program was "perceived by both sending and receiving countries as a humane and dignified service" in order to prevent international conflicts around questions of readmission (ibid.). With respect to European donors, the organization stressed that implementing the AVRR program in Morocco would effectively contribute to "combating irregular migration" while better respecting human rights than existing practices of migration control (ibid., 13). In doing so, it responded to the rising European demand to control migration not only more effectively (in terms of time, costs, and numbers) but also in line with international human rights norms (such as the principle of non-refoulement), thus making it less prone to public criticism and European media attention (cf. Webber 2011; Dünnwald 2013; Loher 2020).

As the IOM's official discourse indicates, the IOM regards it as "essential" that AVRR is "conveyed as a positive alternative to forced return" (2013, 21). Its publications and outreach activities explicitly highlight "the individual's free and, therefore, voluntary decision," which is defined by the "absence of any physical or psychological pressure" and by an "informed decision, which requires the availability of enough accurate and objective information upon which to base such decisions" (ibid., 15). Emphasizing the *voluntariness* of returning through the IOM, the organization symbolically distinguishes its program from the services provided by other actors in the field.

In contrast to the widespread representation of migrants as passive objects of international migration management, the AVRR program expects them to actively engage in the successful and sustainable execution of their return. In this sense, it seeks to "empower them to become agents in their own development, as well as in the development of their own communities, ensuring durable solutions for each and every returnee" (ibid., 8). Administering return through seemingly voluntary, free, and informed decision-making thus aims to make migrants active, responsible, and capable subjects of international migration politics. By making use of the techniques of self-management and self-discipline, the IOM guides and motivates migrants who decide to return because it would be in their own interest and well-being (see Bartels 2017). Unlike practices of deportation, which can be enforced under (the threat of) state repression, the recruitment of participants for the AVRR program relies on individual incentives and the morally charged promise of a life 'in dignity' in the country of origin.

The reference to *dignity* is one of the keywords that the IOM appropriated from the demands of migrants and their support structures. In practice, 'to return in dignity' means, at a minimum, that migrants leave the airplane in their country of origin without being handcuffed. For a 'life in dignity,' the IOM provides approximately 500 euros in reintegration assistance. Through such material incentives and moral appeals, the organization aims to steer international migration into 'orderly' processes without (too much) government intervention. The term *orderly* indicates the IOM's unquestioned belief in the need and possibility to channel the movement of people according to the rules, principles, and categories of the international state system and without turbulences of migrants' resistance, the necessity of physical violence, or death. For the IOM, directing and maintaining migration movements according to orderly trajectories thus means to stop, hinder, return, and prevent unwanted and unproductive forms of migration while facilitating, promoting, and supporting other forms that are regarded as morally right and/or economically beneficial. In this way, the IOM's practices of voluntary return tacitly exercise a *symbolic violence* that contributes to maintaining order in the distribution of global mobility rights, one of the central stakes in the trans-Mediterranean field of migration management for many European countries.

From the IOM's perspective, these diverse objectives are in line with its general promise for its work to be "mutually beneficial to migrants, governments and other sectors of society affected by migration" (IOM 2013, 14). According to this comprehensive approach, effectively managed migration could and should be turned into a win-win-win process that benefits all parties involved: the receiving states, the transit states, the sending states, and the migrants themselves. The IOM's self-presentation and its discursive promotion of the voluntary return program use business language that indicates the IOM's self-understanding as an efficient but human rights-respecting service provider offering states innovative projects, best practices, and sustainable solutions. The program helps the IOM position itself in the expanding, competitive market of international migration management (Gammeltoft-Hansen and Nyberg-Sørensen 2013). This "business of bordering Europe" (Andersson 2014) is largely ruled by economic gains, employment opportunities, and professional project management; accordingly, the profitability of migration control services—including voluntary return—is another central stake in the field.

These fragments of the IOM's official discourse exemplify different elements of the neoliberal logic that conducts international migration management in (among other places) North Africa. To realize the AVRR program in Morocco, the IOM had to play by the rules of this internationalized and commercialized migration management business. As about 90% of its funding was project-based (Caillault 2012, 144), the IOM's mission in Morocco needed to promote the usefulness and uniqueness of its services among its member states—especially as distinct from other service providers, such as the United Nations High Commissioner for Refugees (UNHCR). At the same time, it had to make itself known and credible among Sub-Saharan migrants in the country in order to convince participants to 'voluntarily' participate in its program. As a consequence, even after the program was formally authorized by the Moroccan government through a Memorandum of Understanding in 2007, its implementation was not an "outcome of

128 *Voluntary return programs*

consistent planning" but continually left "repair work" for the IOM (Sciortino 2004, 32).

In what follows, I analyze the conflicting perspectives of the actors involved in the AVRR program and the stakes they have in this game. I argue that, despite the IOM's rhetoric of mutual benefit, the practical implementation of the program was largely conditioned by the IOM's need to satisfy its donors' priorities, rather than shaped by a commitment to migrants' needs. While the organization symbolically distanced its program from state practices of repression, detention, and deportation, I show how these instruments work together and influence each other within an overall context of restrictive politics on migration so as to persuade undesirable migrants to return to their countries of origin.

4.1.1 Competition in the voluntary return business

The IOM is neither the first nor the only international actor to engage in what has become a transnational business of assisting people in desperate situations by offering them a return to their country of origin. In Morocco, the French Office of Immigration and Integration (Office Français de l'Immigration et de l'Intégration) has provided assistance, including social and financial aid, to Moroccans returning from France for legal or humanitarian reasons, since the 1990s (MIIINDS 2008). Additionally, the UNHCR became involved in the return and reintegration of refugees at the end of that decade (Koch 2014). According to Jennifer Hyndman (2000, xxiv), this involvement was part of the UNHCR's general reorientation from a "refugee organization into a more broadly-based humanitarian agency." Since this reorganization led to conflicts with the IOM related to overlapping and competing spheres of action and influence, the two IOs redefined their roles and activities in a Memorandum of Understanding in 1997 (UNHCR 1997; see also Lavenex 2007; Valluy 2007). In this official agreement, they distinguished their areas of work based on the categorization of people on the move, sorting them into different target groups for their services. With reference to its mandate given by the Geneva Convention, the UNHCR claims responsibility for so-called persons of concern; formerly, these were only refugees and asylum seekers, but nowadays it also includes internally displaced people, returned refugees, and stateless persons (Hyndman 2000, xxvi). The IOM offers its assistance to other groups of returning migrants who are explicitly not part of the UNHCR's mandate.

For its return assistance work, the IOM coined the term Assisted Voluntary Return (AVR). According to Koch (2014, 911), this term not only serves to legitimate the organization's interventions but also to distinguish "a unique place for the institution within the overall migration management system." The IOM (2013, 2) broadly defines AVR as

> the administrative, logistical, financial and reintegration support to rejected asylum-seekers, victims of trafficking in human beings, stranded

migrants, qualified nationals and other migrants unable or unwilling to remain in the host country who volunteer to return to their countries of origin.

The list of such diverse potential beneficiaries indicates the broad and flexible target group that the IOM promises to take on. This can be contextually specified and adapted to the various interests that materialize in different contexts. The target group specified in the project guidelines provides the basis for the inclusion and exclusion of certain people in/from the organization's assistance and for the justification of the individual selections of its beneficiaries.

While the IOM presents itself as ambiguous and flexible in how it defines and delineates its clients, its distinction from the UNHCR's 'persons of concern' (notably refugees and asylum seekers) is definitive for its work. In this way, the IOM establishes its proper sphere of action and influence. While many governments see those recognized as refugees and asylum seekers as entitled to a certain legal status or social rights, people who fall under the purview of the IOM are only offered its assistance if the organization has raised sufficient funding among its donors to do so. Therefore, benefitting from the IOM's voluntary return program is not a legal right to be claimed by migrants in need, but an "act of mercy" (Fassin 2016) of an IO without normative mandate or democratic basis that is formally accountable only to its (financially strong) member states—not to the well-being of migrants (see Bartels 2017). As a consequence, access to protection and material services are justified neither by individual rights of migrants and refugees nor by their supposed economic use for destination countries (cf. Mezzadra and Neilson 2013), but on the basis of the mandate and funding requirements of an IO.

In this respect, the IOM contributes to changing the rules about access to international protection and assistance within the trans-Mediterranean field of migration management. As Johanna Neuhauser, Sabine Hess, and Helen Schwenken (2017, 34) point out, such flexible categorization practices create new hierarchies of people on the move. When IOs define new target groups for their services, they establish new symbolic (b)orders, with significant material effects on migrants' options and constraints related to moving on. Through these practices of classification and categorization, IOs exercise a symbolic violence that largely constrains migrants' life in transit. Constantly and repeatedly imposed by the dominant discourse of the IOM, their categories generate durable modes of thinking, so that they often appear self-evident and legitimate to other actors in the field and are rarely questioned (Sayad 2010, 168). For those concerned, they often remain opaque and hardly comprehensible.

4.1.2 Migrants' encounters with an international bureaucracy

"In the beginning, the IOM did not even manage to get people who wanted to return!" recalled a long-standing activist for migration issues in Morocco,

130 *Voluntary return programs*

remembering the IOM's initial attempts to recruit participants for its program in 2005 (interview with activist, Mor. 2014). While many migrants were interested in leaving Morocco, only a vague knowledge had been circulated among them about the IOM and its program at that time:

> You arrive at IOM. There are people who know IOM. They advise you to go there. It is them who will escort you. They will not go with you to the door, they will just show you from distance: "You see, that is IOM over there! You will explain to them your problem, your situation, how it is."
>
> (Interview with migrant, Mor. 2014)

Most of the potential returnees are guided by informants from their community who know where to find the organization. Its presence is only indicated by small sign on a huge blue iron gate somewhat blocking the view to its office, which is hidden behind high fences and palm trees that typically line the calm streets of Souissi, an affluent neighborhood in Rabat. Those who escort potential participants to the IOM also provide them with the necessary knowledge about how to pass the selection procedures. Equipped with these instructions, my interview partner arrived at the IOM's office. He recalled delivering his performance, hoping to meet the organizations requirements to qualify for their program:

> I explained my situation, how I feel bad here and that I want to return to my country. I do not want to stay like this. Here without documents, you are nothing, you suffer. Everything they [the Moroccans] will give you is tough. They will give it to you because you are without documents. After all that, I decided to return to my country.
>
> (Ibid.)

From their experiences with the performances and stories they are expected to give as a 'migrant in need' at the IOM's office, migrants and activists collected practical knowledge about the rules of the game, the categorizations and criteria forming the basis of access to the program. They also developed strategies to present an image of a migrant that meets the expectations of those working at the IOM. According to their observations, participation in the AVRR program primarily depended on migrants' origin: while West Africans were quickly processed, migrants from Central Africa often had to wait. In a conversation with a former employee of the IOM, she agreed that migrants were "very well informed among themselves" (conversation with former IOM staff, Mor. 2014). For example, they knew that

> this week there are many Malians[2] who leave and not Togolese. Because they have friends among themselves and there are many—for example,

there are three Malians who will leave; they are their friends. But there are many, for example, Togolese who have their dossiers that are waiting.

(Ibid.)

And when migrants with a "wrong nationality" applied for the AVRR program, she explained that "you tell them clearly that for the moment we do not have funds for the return" to their respective country, detailing the organization's selection procedures (ibid.). While the formal authority over defining specific target groups is a matter of donor priorities, the individual selection is performed by IOM.

When "I organize a return to Mali this week or next week. I will see the priorities. [...] we decide that this, this, and this person will leave" (ibid.). In order to determine priorities, the IOM staff interview potential returnees about their social, economic, and physical situation in Morocco. At the office in Rabat, it is primarily young, foreign staff who receive the migrants, interview them, fill out the documents, and organize the transfer to the embassy. They also prepare and organize the journey. According to the standardized procedures, they must explain the rules of AVRR to potential returnees as well as collect information for the person's administrative dossier during the first interview. They ask the migrants about their route, their civil and social status, and their motivation to go back. In a second interview, the potential returnee has to propose a reintegration project to be funded by the IOM, which will start six months upon return.

From a migrant's perspective, these routinized procedures appeared to be a long, opaque process full of undetermined waiting periods for decisions and bureaucratic steps to be suddenly made:

> They will take some hours to analyze everything. They will see your situation. It is there where it is decided if they will help you. Afterwards, they will call you: "We have accepted your request. We have decided to send you to your country. That day, be prepared! And do not forget that we give you a date. You must not forget that! Keep waiting until that day!"
>
> (Interview with migrant, Mor. 2014)

While the IOM handles administrative procedures—obtaining the travel documents from the embassy and the authorization to leave the country from the Moroccan government—the selected returnee is expected to be "prepared" for the sudden moment of return (IOM 2013, 40). The IOM defines the rules and procedures of each voluntary return. Its bureaucratic use of time, numbers, and papers assigns a passive position to migrants in these procedures. While the IOM decides, the migrant waits. Underlining the asymmetrical, paternalistic relationship between migrants and the IOM staff handling their cases, another staff member detailed that the IOM team is responsible "for keeping their travel documents, performing the

132 *Voluntary return programs*

formalities, and then giving them their money" (conversation with former IOM staff, Mor. 2014). She emphasized that it is only "at the airport that they get the money, not before! Because once they arrive, maybe they have to take a transport, have something to eat...We will not leave them in the wild" (ibid.). Using the word "wild" to describe the migrants' countries of origin, her statement distinguishes the IOM's 'civilized' position from the recipients of its programs. In this respect, the IOM's work actualizes the postcolonial relationships of European subjects coming to the African continent to help its 'uncivilized' inhabitants.

From the migrants' point of view, this "wild" means their country of origin, a context in which they are allowed to travel independently and supported with a small sum of money. After a few days, the migrant said, the IOM employees "call you to give you either money or they will buy you things from the shops, clothes, etc. It depends on you: if you have nothing, they will buy you things" (interview with migrant, Mor. 2014). What happens after a migrant has returned is conditional on their ability, creativity, and persuasiveness to create a project that the IOM is willing to fund:

> If you have a project, there is a sum that they will give you: 500 euros, or 600 euros, if you are lucky they will give you a million. If not, you can have 300 euros, 400 euros, like that, it depends. It depends on your project.
>
> (Ibid.)

While a wide range of possible amounts has circulated in the myths of AVRR among migrant communities, IOM publications precisely state the systematic financial reintegration assistance as 485 euros (IOM 2010).[3] However, this sum is not given unconditionally to every returning migrant but is "adapted to the specific needs of any particular migrant on a case-by-case basis" (ibid. 2013, 25). In contrast to the impression promoted by the IOM of systematic reintegration assistance, its material support is subject to an individualized negotiation with each returnee. Through the individualized practices of selecting returnees and negotiating their reintegration projects, the IOM gets to decide whether migrants are eligible to return and whether their reintegration projects are worthy of support. The organization values well-planned, economically sound projects that indicate the efficiency and sustainability of a migrant's return. Benefitting from reintegration assistance is thus conditional on migrants' performance and credibility in acting according to the IOM's assumptions about a (life) project that is worthy of being funded. Consequently, reintegration assistance is focused less on the migrants' needs than on active participation and individual competitiveness. While the IOM must act according to the rules set by European states, the organization is able to determine the rules for which migrants can participate in the program. This way, the organization tacitly transmits the competitive logic, keywords, and convictions of neoliberal project management to migrants' behaviors and future plans.

At the same time, the shared knowledge about the rules and procedures of AVRR empowers migrants to benefit from the program and achieve their desired return projects. However, such knowledge does not automatically prevent troubles, disappointments, and misunderstandings during the selection and return processes. Beyond their shared knowledge and out of reach of their influence, sponsored target groups and rules of participation in the program are continuously actualized based on the shifting of funding rationalities and more or less explicit donor preferences. Even though migrants developed profound knowledge about the procedures of the bureaucratic game and learned how to play by its rules, they were hardly able to change them. Their position in the trans-Mediterranean field of migration management is that of recipients of the IOM's services. In this "dominated position within the field of symbolic of power relations," they are not recognized as equal players (Sayad 2010, 175). They are involved in a game that they are not "well equipped to play" and that they cannot master; a game that they have not "chosen to play, which is always played on the home ground of the dominant, in their way, in accordance with their rules and with their weapons of choice" (ibid.). Still, even though migrants remain at marginal positions in the field, they are constitutive of its struggles, as there is simply no voluntary return business without migrants who agree to return.

4.1.3 Donor influence and the international play of funding (ir)rationalities

"40,000 people that were simply ignored by the Moroccan state," said a representative of one of the donors as they explained the decision of European governments to fund the program in 2006 (Discussion with representatives of German Consulate, Mor. 2014). Living without documents in Morocco, migrants

> were taken and brought to the Algerian border. The police did it. They kicked them out [of the country]. And [the migrants] had to cope with it to continue. Many came back on foot. Some tried to continue in Algeria. Some went to the north...But of course, this was not a reasonable way to deal with the problem.
>
> (Ibid.)

Since European states did not expect the Moroccan government to properly manage what they perceived as the "problem," they turned to IOs to provide "a reasonable way" to deal with the migrants at the external borders of Europe. Seeing the IOM as a "trustworthy service provider" in other countries (Korneev 2014, 894), they expected the organization to take care of transit migrants more diplomatically than Moroccan authorities. Funding the AVRR program was a way to present their own public "reasonable" solutions for the precarious situation of migrants, ones that were not based on violence and coercion. This way, they were able to demonstrate their capacity to act in response to the so-called Moroccan migration crisis. For the IOM, in turn, it was an opportunity to mobilize the networks it had in other countries to position itself in the emerging field of migration management in Morocco. This *social capital* and the *symbolic distinction* from repressive state politics were important assets to the IOM in order to gain funding for its services.

4.1.3.1 "Attracting realistic numbers of migrants": the need for participants

Only about 200,000 of the 15 million euros that the organization received from its European member states in 2005–2011 were regular membership fees (Caillault 2012, 144). The rest were designated for specific projects. For every project, the IOM must define activities that are bound by time and place and whose results can be measured and evaluated. Not only the objectives, timelines, and target groups, but also the costs for its staff, office, and equipment are laid out and negotiated anew for every project. This funding logic assigns the donors a powerful position over those who are working for the IOM, since the latter are directly accountable to and dependent on the willingness of donors to fund their work. In this way, European donors exercise implicit but important influence on the designs, objectives, and target groups of IOM projects.

This influence is exercised, for one, through the funding of services for specific groups of people from countries that are the sources of many immigrants to the donor countries. These unspoken priorities for certain nationalities are expressed in the selection criteria of participants of the AVRR program. However, the IOM is reluctant to publicly admit the political entanglements and external restrictions that come with each funding scheme. A former IOM employee explained, "sure, there were plans" for the selection of returnees (conversation with former IOM staff, Mor. 2014): "When you work [for the IOM], you understand in one way or another that no, we cannot return the Togolese. [Because] we have funding for the Malians, but not for the Togolese" (ibid.). Another former staff member revealed that sometimes students and "other profiles of migrants" asked to participate in the program, and even if they did not belong to the official target group, they ended up being accepted simply because they had "the nationality that [we] are supposed to accept, as this was the deal with the donors" (conversation with former IOM staff, Egypt 2015). While the IOM claims to assist all migrants in desperate situations, in practice, it is often the nationality of an applicant that is pivotal to the probability and rapidity of their return (cf. Maâ 2019).

The IOM designed outreach strategies to promote the program among migrants that would fit the target profile predefined by the funding schemes. Its staff are not supposed to attract anyone, but they are encouraged to "attract realistic numbers of migrants" who match the "eligibility criteria" that were predefined in the program's funding proposal (IOM 2013, 30). While the IOM generally establishes migrants' need as the main eligibility criteria of its program (ibid.), it could be observed in Morocco that participants were recruited according to their nationality. This tacit rule predetermined the selective recruitment by the IOM that needs to match the numbers and nationalities calculated and defined in its project fundraising portfolios.

In contrast to much of the IOM's rhetoric, the implementation of voluntary return is not primarily based on migrants' needs or desires to return but instead is driven by funding guidelines, specific target groups, precise timeframes, and measurable objectives to which potential participants need to be matched. Aware of its public performativity, the IOM's publicity aims to selectively increase the number of specific, nationally defined target groups while trying to regulate expectations and demands according to existing funding schemes. Its work is structurally conditioned by the rules that are set by its donors, but the organization has to implement them diplomatically—that is to say, without making them explicit because the perception of AVRR being a service for migrants in need gives the IOM a better reputation—and enhances it symbolic capital—than the perception of being a service to European states. Its adaptiveness to external criticism and its willingness to optimize its work is an important resource employed by the IOM in the competition over funding, reputation, and credibility.

Instead of directly interfering in Moroccan migration policies, European states prefer to pay IOs to provide migration control services outside Europe. While states outsource these services, they still seek to have a say in the content of the programs they finance. Governing migration by funding IOs thus makes it possible for them to practically influence the content of migration control without making their strategies explicit. The IOM's mutual benefit rhetoric and its neutral, apolitical working conviction resonate well with this situation: they provide a form of *cultural capital* that can be converted into *economic capital*, that is to say the funding for new projects. As a former IOM staff member explained in more detail:

> You finance a project: you want help the others, [but] you want to help yourself too. So, I can do both: I can help migrants return, but I can also help myself not receive migrants. It is just a matter of planning.
> (Conversation with former IOM staff, Mor. 2014)

For its donors, the funding of the AVRR program is rational when it serves to filter those who might irregularly move on to Europe and when it effectively returns them to their countries of origin without using physical violence. The IOM follows these unspoken rules of selecting beneficiaries according to the priorities of its donors in order to continue to receive funding. In this international play of funding (ir)rationalities, the IOM occupies the position of individually selecting those who fit the predefined target groups of European donors.

4.1.3.2 "The more people repatriated, the better the program": the need for numbers

According to its own statistics, the IOM returned approximately 6,800 people from Morocco to more than 30 different African countries in 2005–2016 (IOM 2016, 1). These returns were financed by Belgium, Germany, the United Kingdom, Italy, the Netherlands, Norway, Spain, the European Commission, and Switzerland (ibid. 2010, 1).[4] In light of these moderate numbers of about 600 returns per year, the IOM's actual contribution to the 'fight against irregular migration' that many European states sought to fund remains a controversial subject of debate. While official publications praised the program, representatives of European states shared doubts about the efficiency and sustainability of the program when I met them for interviews in the well-protected embassies in the wealthy neighborhoods of Rabat during my fieldwork. One of them lamented: "And even if the estimation of 40,000—but I think it is too high—let's say 30,000 illegals. If only 4,000 in a decade managed to go back, it is not a big success!" (interview with repr. of Belgian Embassy (BE), Mor. 2014). According to his experience of cooperation with the UNHCR and the IOM, their staff would always complain that they "have a lot of work, and it is complicated because there are six people that came…and then another twelve somewhere" (ibid.). Still, in his opinion, "it is never thousands of people. It is always a few…It is families of four or five or eight, and they make a big issue about it" (ibid.). Comparing the low numbers of "six" and "twelve" people that IOs handle with the supposed "thousands" of immigrants in Morocco, he expressed his doubts about the AVRR program as an efficient way to reduce the number of irregularized migrants in the country and to stop movement to Europe. Criticizing his colleagues working for IOs for making "a big issue about it," he made clear that what counts for donors are quantifiable results. When he said, "so, we responsibilize them [the IOM], and they have to present results of course," he explained the tacitly accepted rules and power relations in the trans-Mediterranean field of migration management, in which the IOM not only competes with other IOs but also with non-governmental organizations (NGOs) for European project funding (ibid.). As approximately 90% of its funding is project-based, it is essential for the IOM to please donors and to convince them of its projects' impact by proving the efficiency, sustainability, and accountability. As almost all funding for country offices and employees is secured through projects, its staff is busy in its efforts to "provide evidence that their money [is] being well spent" (Barnett 2005, 730). This evidence is mostly expressed in terms of numbers and statistics.

Through the "appearance of scientific rigor," Michel Agier (2011, 33) argues, statistics are able to "produce truth effects that are seemingly beyond discussion" in international migration politics. Since they are recognized as scientific, they enhance the *symbolic power* "to act upon the world by acting upon the representation of the world" (Bourdieu and Wacquant 1992, 148).

Due to their scientific authority, they provide an important currency that converts an image of the IOM's past practices into new projects and thus into renewed funding for its mission in a particular country. Statistics are the raw material for the IOM to manage its reputation and to make a profit (see Mau 2017, 11). Consequently, numbers are as crucial for constructing a problem and for legitimizing international interventions as they are for evaluating interventions' effectiveness, sustainability, and funding worthiness. Numbers enable comparisons of different interventions, putting them in a hierarchical relation (ibid., 49ff). In this way, they provide the basis for external evaluation and competition among services. However, the phenomenon of irregularized migration is, by definition, hard to quantify. While none of my interview partners was able to give exact numbers of how many foreigners are living on Moroccan territory without authorization, most estimated 25,000–40,000 migrants in the country, based on numbers published by the Moroccan Ministry of Interior in 2013.[5] Since then, these imprecise numbers have figured as a yardstick for the urgency, usefulness, and effectiveness of interventions in the field. Thus, numbers are powerful but contested resources in the *symbolic struggles* over irregularized migration and legitimate forms of action on its behalf.

Consequently, practices of knowledge and data production have become essential for the IOM, as they are inherently linked to propositions, implementations, and evaluations of its services. However, playing according to these shared rules and unquestioned beliefs of the field was a challenging task for the organization. In order to achieve the expected results, the IOM improvised its selection of participants. Aiming to meet donors' demands to return certain nationalities, the IOM increased success rates by recruiting participants who did not belong to its primary target group but who matched the nationalities of returnees funded (see previous section). According to a former employee, this enabled the IOM to "raise the numbers of returnees, which is considered indicative of success of the program" (conversation with former IOM staff, Egypt 2015). "The more people repatriated, the better the program," she stated, pinpointing one of the *doxic beliefs* in the field (ibid.). Regardless of if they are wildly guessed, cosmetically raised, or accurately counted, numbers are the preferred form of knowledge and central for negotiating impact in the trans-Mediterranean field of migration management. They are not only essential for the IOM to assess its services but also to legitimate the need for new ones. Numbers make it possible for the IOM to convert its expertise into new projects—or, in Bourdieu's terms, to convert its scientific or cultural authority into economic capital.

Where hard facts are missing, statistics are combined with different forms of virtual self-presentation. Newsletters and reports of the IOM's mission are illustrated with pictures of its busy staff—easily detectable by their white uniforms with the highly visible blue IOM logo—in action, directing, advising, catering, or otherwise caring for migrants. In contrast, migrants are mostly represented as traveling in large, less distinguishable groups, assisted with the widely recognizable IOM bags. These pictures convey the asymmetrical

138 *Voluntary return programs*

relationships between the active staff of IOs and the passive position of the migrants they take care of. Besides these anonymous crowds, another recurring format is portrayals of single smiling migrants presented next to individual stories celebrating successful returnees. These notable exceptions of individuals who were actively engaged in their return and reintegration projects are another medium to portray the IOM's success. The combination of different forms of representation is well tuned to convey a challenging but dynamic performance, supplementing its measurable results. Whether conveyed through numbers, pictures, or personal stories, the IOM's professional outward performance provides an important form of cultural capital for the organization that it uses to market its services in North Africa.

4.1.4 *Rising demand in the context of repressive state politics*

The IOM's continuing struggles with the need to secure funding was particularly obvious when the AVRR program stopped in 2010 and 2012 due to a lack of financial support. From the point of view of its staff members, the program ran out of funding because

> during the economic crisis governments were not really interested in financing this type of activity. They thought, "you know, it is Morocco towards Sub-Saharan-Africa, it is Morocco towards Asia, why should we pay for this, if Morocco itself does not get engaged?"
> (Interview with IOM staff, Mor. 2014)

In her perspective, it was not a lack in the IOM's efficiency but of European interest and (perceived) Moroccan responsibility. However, with recurring riots and repressions in 2011 and 2012, the situation for Sub-Saharan migrants remained very difficult—especially in northern Morocco, where a new era of Spanish-Moroccan cooperation had brutal effects (MSF 2013).

According to an activist from an association advocating for the rights of female migrants in Morocco, "the violence was really high at a certain time" (interview with activist, Mor. 2014). During a long conversation over coffee in downtown Rabat in summer 2014, she recounted many cases of deaths and racism: "There was one migrant assassinated on a bus, a Senegalese person. And afterwards, there was a Congolese person from Brazzaville who was chased in the forest of Gourougourou. And then, in Tangier, they chased someone" (ibid.). While she repeatedly assured herself that nobody would listen to our conversation, she reported a rising frequency of push-backs and everyday violence faced by migrants in Morocco, along with the difficulties of establishing a regular life and providing for one's basic needs. The everyday threat of arbitrary detentions, deportations, and forced displacements characterized the already-precarious living conditions of many migrants, and even those recognized as refugees and asylum seekers by the UNHCR were not shielded from state repression. Living in this constant state of legal uncertainty and *deportability* (De Genova 2002), some began to opt for a way back to their countries of origin. Offering an end to their uncertain status by providing a safe, legal way to escape the precarious and dangerous situation in northern Morocco, the AVRR program became a significant option for Sub-Saharan migrants.[6]

As I had heard during my first visit to the IOM's office in 2013, a growing number of migrants had created a waiting list of more than 1,000 people willing to return with the IOM (interview with IOM staff, Mor. 2013). The growing demand for voluntary return was directly linked to the racist violence, constant precarity, and advancing externalization of border control in Morocco. The IOM was able to establish the AVRR program as a profitable business in this environment of everyday insecurity produced by repressive state practices (Loher 2020, 119). Facing a constant threat of deportation encouraged migrants to return 'voluntarily,' thus enhancing their returnability (Bartels 2019). In this context, the IOM did not have to support deportations: it simply needed to anticipate them, in order to regain funding. The situation demonstrates how practices of voluntary return and deportation become especially productive in a reciprocal relationship: the offer to return 'voluntarily' legitimizes deportations as a last resort to enforce a state-ordered removal, while deportations are necessary to make the option of voluntary return attractive or acceptable to migrants (Dünnwald 2013, 233). Voluntary return thus operates against the backdrop of—and often hand-in-hand with—forced removal and other forms of repression. Thus, migrants' return can be enforced by different means, some of which appear more desirable than others, and from the IOM's perspective, voluntary returns are morally better than forced deportations (see Loher 2020, 121).

4.1.4.1 *"IOM! just return home without violence": protesting for a right to voluntary return*

While the IOM had widely promoted its assistance, the organization had to stop the AVRR program in 2012. In this context, civil society associations and even activist groups that had generally been rather skeptical of the IOM's services in Morocco supported the demands of migrants and organized for the program's continuation in times of increasing state repression against migrants. Together, they protested in front of the IOM's office in Rabat. "When the demand was high, [the IOM] drew back their offer," as my interview partner remembered of the situation that seemed to discredit the IOM's self-proclaimed role of aiding migrants in need (interview with activist, Mor. 2014).

> They said, "there is no money." I went there a million times to say that this will cause problems for certain migrants who wanted to return and they said that there was no budget. The migrants went there to riot. And that made it on TV!"
>
> (Ibid.)

140 *Voluntary return programs*

Expelled from the forests in the north and threatened with deportations by the Moroccan police, many migrants came to the IOM's office in Souissi, the capital's wealthy neighborhood. Carrying large pieces of cardboard demanding "IOM! Just return home without violence" and a "right to return voluntarily," a group of mostly underage migrants from various West African countries set themselves up on the pavement. "We are here because we want to return to our countries," said one of the migrants, as quoted by an activist who shared their situation and spread their voices (email conversation with migrant activist, Mor. 2016). "That is how we came here to the office of IOM, an international agency to help us return to our countries," as he explained the object of choice of their protest (ibid.). Their demands did not address the Moroccan authorities nor European states but the IOM, which was perceived as the highest institution of political power that was responsible for their "right to return."

In response, the IOM clarified that there is no "right to return voluntarily" but that the program was an offer made by the organization and that was no longer available due to a lack of funding. Its staff reacted rather indifferently and largely ignored the migrants camping in front of their windows. Their message was that without funding, they were not able to help. According to the migrants, the IOM staff

> would pass by in the morning and in the evening. They drove by in their huge cars and they were not interested in us. They did not even give us a simple blanket. We slept outside in the middle of the winter and sometimes the police came to chase us away. [...] We cannot understand how these people treat us. Europe says it does not want us and we would like to return to our countries, but [...] they do not want to help us return.
>
> (Ibid.)

Despite such disappointing encounters, the migrants still believed in the organization's capacity and authority to help them, and they continued their protest for two months. The observable discrepancy between the "huge cars" and "no funding" made them angry, but also confident in receiving help. Exhausted by the precarious situation that they experienced in Morocco, they showed a strong belief in the AVRR program that had become prominent in the country. They displayed their hardship in front of the IOM's office and phrased their demands using the IOs' own discourse. They called on the sense of compassion and responsibility of the IOM staff to recognize their suffering and help them. The use of the IOM's keywords shows that they knew how to play by the rules of international migration management; while they were not recognized as relevant actors in the field, they nevertheless developed strategies to appropriate its discourses and practices.

The international media attention for the migrants' protest was unintentionally very helpful for the IOM's search for funding. Given the publicly visible demand for its program, the organization was able to raise awareness and to reemphasize the necessity and urgency of its work in Morocco. In this respect, the IOM transformed the external pressure of the migrants' protest into a convincing argument for renewed funding. It took advantage of not only criticism from above but also collective protest from below by making subversive practices and unexpected alliances productive for its work. As a result, the migrants' protest did not discredit the organization but enhanced its symbolic capital as an "international agency to help us return to our countries," which was helpful for the IOM in regaining the economic capital needed to continue its work. This shows how much the organization's work relies on a context of permanent threat of coercion. To promote and legitimize the AVRR program, the IOM positions its practices in relation to forced deportations (see also Loher 2020, 114).

4.1.4.2 "A demand that came from Morocco too": negotiating ownership and responsibility

In fall 2013, the continuation of the program was finally ensured by a number of European donors under the condition that Morocco would also contribute financially.[7] A representative of a former donor country explained:

> I think for a long time now, maybe two or three years, the IOM is struggling with the government here. Because they made promises that they will co-fund part of it, for example through seats on the Royal Air Maroc flights. And the funding is not forthcoming, so they are waiting, waiting, waiting for a long time. On the other hand, all these illegal people here, it is very cheap labor for Moroccans,

detailing Morocco's inconsistent behavior, strategies, and calculations regarding the implementation of the AVRR program (interview with repr. of BE, Mor. 2014). While the program was generally well perceived in Morocco, its government had been reluctant to contribute to implementing or funding it until 2013. In 2013, however, Moroccan authorities suddenly agreed to finance the transport of 1,000 migrants returning to their countries of origin. This unexpected decision was part of the inconsistent developments that followed the announcement by the Moroccan king in September 2013 introducing a New Migration Policy (Berriane, De Haas, and Natter 2016).[8] Until then, Morocco had not officially recognized itself as an immigration or transit country nor had it developed an explicit policy in this field (see Chapter 2).

Following the report "Foreigners and Human Rights in Morocco: A Radically New Immigration and Asylum Policy" by the National Human Rights Council (Conseil National des Droits de l'Homme, CNDH), the king demanded that the government make suggestions for a new national migration and asylum policy. In the following year, the Moroccan state conducted a regularization campaign for specific groups of irregularized migrants, especially women and children. The king's decision redirected international attention from the donors and IOs back to Morocco, after the former had begun to focus their interventions on countries in which the Arab Spring promised new opportunities for their money and projects. Under the New Migration Policy, voluntary return became the official preferred strategy of the Moroccan state to return irregularized migrants to their countries of origin. In a presentation in front of representatives of the international community, a member of the newly founded Ministry in charge of Moroccans Living Abroad and Migration Affairs declared that it would

> encourage the voluntary return of illegal migrants, in collaboration with the embassies from their country, and under circumstances that respect their rights and dignity. We attempt to free them from the illegal immigration mafia and return them to their country of origin under safe conditions.
> (Debbarh 2014)

This presentation exemplified how Moroccan government officials symbolically appropriated and eloquently replicated the keywords of international migration management. Playing by the rules of this game, they employed the symbolic power of the IOM's wording to gain recognition as a rights-respecting country and to reposition themselves in international negotiations.

The new symbolic as well as material Moroccan ownership of the AVRR program was welcomed among European donors. Among others, the new Moroccan stewardship motivated the Spanish Development Agency AECID to renew its funding. While the IOM had asked

> for a very long time, [before] 2013 we did not want to fund it. It was not a priority for us. But since Morocco started to also ask for it, and since the demand was Moroccan and from the IOM at the same time, at this moment we decided to give the funding. Because it was a demand that came from Morocco too.
> (Interview with repr. of AECID, Mor. 2014)

For the donors, this was a positive sign that the Moroccan government would take responsibility for the 'fight against irregular migration' and would understand transit migration as its own problem. By funding the AVRR program, they expected to indirectly influence the content of Moroccan migration politics and to keep the country accountable for governing irregularized movements in the future. Embedded in the colonial history of European influence on African countries, European states see themselves in the position to encourage and support North African governments to learn how to efficiently and diplomatically solve what they perceive as the 'problem of irregular migration.' In contrast to the deportations for which the Moroccan state was known, its government's cooperation in the AVRR program was praised by the donors, as it was compatible with human rights standards and therefore less prone to provoking criticism from civil society. The cooperation and complicity of the Ministry in charge of Moroccans Living Abroad and Migration Affairs (instead of the Ministry of Interior) provided a new basis for the IOM's long-term involvement in the country. From the perspective of North African governments, projects implemented by the IOM, an intermediary actor, were easier to accept than direct European interventions.

However, in the aftermath of the king's announcement of the New Migration Policy in September 2013, Moroccan authorities acted inconsistently. While the government decided to support the AVRR program, increasing raids and repression against Sub-Saharan migrants made their situation ever more dangerous and precarious. This hostile environment influenced the IOM's work and again increased the demand for its voluntary return service. At the same time, however, rising criticism among civil society actors accompanied the program's relaunch within the context of the Arab Spring, which had also left its mark on Morocco's politics and society. Strengthened civil society actors accused the IOM's program of being "forced voluntary return" (interview with activist, Mor. 2014). As Moroccan activists became aware of the program's inconsistent political entanglements, they pointed to the connections between the rising demand and the increasing raids and forced displacements that put migrants in a constant state of returnability. According to the independent activists' association No Borders Morocco (2015), it was doubtful

> whether regularization achieves anything but making it easier for the state to control clandestine migrants slipping through their surveillance network. The inhumane and degrading treatment of migrants at the external(ized) border of the European Union exposes what is behind the human rights façade—a racist and unequal war waged against undesired migrants until they die or accept "voluntary" return.

The activists criticized how the AVRR program was offered to migrants who had been arrested and detained for their irregular status in Morocco and who were not questioned about their wish to return. They pointed out how much the program's demand was driven and shaped by the increasing repression, rather than being based on voluntary decisions:

> Voluntary return—in quotation marks—is [the IOM's] main thing. They offer it to everyone [who] is really fucked. There are no detention centers here, but with all the raids, chases, and pushbacks, it was not supportable. There were people returning by their own means, but the IOM made a business out of it.
> (Conversation with activist, Mor. 2014)

The activists exposed the proclaimed voluntariness of the program as merely symbolic while also revealing how powerful and economically useful this symbolic capital was for the IOM. In their view, the IOM was a main beneficiary of the inconsistent moves in the migration politics of the Moroccan state. As a result, the "IOM is [in] with the service of the Ministry for Migration to make people return," one of them complained (interview with activist, Mor. 2014). She denounced the intensified cooperation between the IOM and the Moroccan state as enhancing the returnability of migrants "who are not profitable for Morocco" (ibid.). In case migrants refused to participate, the IOM would offer them

> an absurd amount so that they will return. [...] The IOM wants to be at the hub of playing this role. The European Union will finance it. IOM is at all the sources now. When the Ministry intervenes, IOM prepares!

she concluded, detailing her impressions about the IOM's ambitions to claim a central position in Moroccan migration politics (ibid.). The IOM aims to be accepted as a relevant actor by the higher levels of the Moroccan state and to gain influence beyond mere provision of logistical support and social assistance, becoming able to influence future directions of its migration policies. Consequently, the IOM was hesitant to officially distance itself from the repressive backlash in 2014.

As a consequence of the rising doubts about the voluntary character of the AVRR program, prominent civil society organizations (such as Caritas) quit the voluntary return business in Morocco. "Often, these were people who had difficulties," and they were "not returned voluntary, [they were] sometimes forced," a representative explained during an interview (interview with repr. of Caritas, Mor. 2014). "They are told: either you accept return or tomorrow you are in prison" (ibid.). Similarly, a staff member of the Red Crescent in North Africa also expressed his concern that it is

> not really voluntary return, because there is no third alternative. They cannot stay. There is only the case of "return" [...] that is to say, the program of AVRR is not always well perceived. It has a different face

that is closely linked to state repression and deportation (interview with Red Crescent staff, Tun. 2015). These humanitarian non-state organizations feared that the label of voluntary return would lose—or even reverse—its symbolic power. Questioning the program's voluntariness blurred the distinction from repressive state politics. In this case, cooperation was no longer reasonable or lucrative for actors who had a humanitarian reputation to lose.

The inconsistent behavior of Moroccan state actors required the IOM to flexibly maneuver between its need to maintain and foster good relations with its host country and to accumulate social capital on the one hand while symbolically distancing its practices from the repressive state practices of migration control on the other hand. In the short term, the rising level of violence against migrants made voluntary return a profitable business. In the long term, the IOM's new partnership with the Moroccan state made possible for the organization to position itself at the hub of the trans-Mediterranean field of migration management. Thus, its work in the North African borderlands is not only conditioned by the rules set by its donors but also by the strategies of state authorities.

4.1.5 The IOM as a travel agency: practices of appropriation and repair

Facing such precarious conditions in Morocco, migrants developed strategies to appropriate the AVRR program for their own aims and plans. They used the program to temporarily return to get their administrative affairs in order, to earn money through the reintegration assistance, or to meet family and friends (Maâ 2019, 18).

> Yes, I did something when I returned. I made a shop to sell things with my mother. I made money to get a passport, to come back here [to Morocco]. Like this, I spent my time. Because here, there were Moroccans who said, "If you have a passport we can give you work." So, when I returned home, I did everything: I opened the shop there where my mother now sells the things. Me, I decided to come back to work to make my life here,

recounted the migrant with whom I talked over a coffee in Rabat, concluding the story about his experience with the IOM (interview with migrant, Mor. 2014). As confirmed by a staff member of the Red Crescent, migrants know very well how to "play the game. And after having started the [reintegration] project, they sell everything, all the material, all the equipment, and they return" to North Africa (interview with Red Crescent staff, Tun. 2015).

Despite being expected to stay in their countries and allowed to participate in the AVRR program only once, migrants developed various strategies to make use of the program as a temporary return and circulation service in North and West Africa. As migrants and their supporters explained to me, some would change their name before traveling back to Morocco; others would return in somebody else's name. Those who sign up for the program but then find work, often pass their "ticket" on to "their countrymen to return in their place" (interview migrant, Mor. 2014). One sees "many cases where people do not give their real identity," an activist confirmed (interview activist, Mor. 2014). The respective embassy does not seriously check, simply issuing a passport. On this basis, the IOM will "give them a ticket, they will return home, they take the small sum that will be given to them, they return" (ibid.). Within the limits of the overall migrant-unfriendly context, migrants shared knowledge and developed strategies to appropriate the AVRR program for their own needs and aims.

146 *Voluntary return programs*

In response to such subversive practices and reinterpretations, the IOM felt compelled to remedy the program. A former staff member gave insights into relevant symbols and embodied performances she experienced during the selection processes of participants:

> It is difficult to know it. Sometimes you can understand, for example when you do an interview and you see that this man, he is very sophisticated in what he is doing, for example you see the sneakers that he wears with the T-shirt with the jeans, but he simply wants to have a free ride.
> (Conversation with former IOM staff, Mor. 2014)

Focusing on the "body, his physical appearance and those forms of external appearance," the IOM staff look for "symbolic attributes or meanings" of migrants' conditions (Sayad 2010, 174) to select those who would (not) be "worthy of compassion" (Ticktin 2011, 13). Migrants informed about the rules of the IOM's selection procedures tried to perform the appearance of 'a migrant in need' they expected would convince the staff. Performing vulnerability became an important resource in the hands of migrants for accelerating opaque bureaucratic procedures (cf. Maâ 2019, 13). With this "conspicuous mimicry" (Sayad 2010, 174), they expected to pass the selection in order to gain what became known among migrants and others as a "free ride." Besides a credible performance of misery, migrants were expected to tell their story honestly and in detail in order to receive assistance. On this basis, the IOM staff determined whose "suffering is recognizable" and worthy of its support (Ticktin 2014, 411).

According to a former staff member of the organization, "passing as another person" at the embassy and at the IOM was possible for migrants whose identity was difficult to verify due to living "in difficult situations" (conversation former IOM staff, Mor. 2014). "You are different than in relaxed situations. Even the face is different, it is nice, it is good," she explained, as she detailed the pitfalls and loopholes of the IOM's selection procedures (ibid.). While migrants were supposed to pass through only one time, she affirmed from her personal experience that

> one or two years later, he came back. And then, there was another who I met again also. Because if you work with migrants, every time when you see them in the street they come to talk to you. And afterwards, when I left the IOM, I understood that they left twice!
> (Ibid.)

By growing "a beard" or otherwise altering their appearance—migrants could successfully use different names and pictures to apply for different travel documents (ibid.). While the IOM would introduce biometrical data collection in later years, at the time "there were no finger prints. Because they had confidence in the embassy. […] But well, even at the embassy they cannot handle everything. It is a population that is not identifiable!" she shared, excusing an imagined collective of international bureaucrats who she believed work to their best of their abilities (ibid.). From the perspective of mostly White international aid workers, Sub-Saharan applicants appear as a "population that is not identifiable"; they are perceived as anonymous crowds rather than individuals who can be recognized. However, it remains questionable whether diplomats of African embassies suffer from the same postcolonial blindness.

After some time, the IOM became aware of migrants' appropriations of its services, and it tried to adopt its procedures. A decade ago, as a migrant recalled during an interview,

> migrants left and came back. They liked to see their families, they left, they gave them the euros there and they stayed a week, two weeks and [then] came back again. There were people who did this, they continued to do so until the IOM discovered all that. You see, we had a system.

He summarized the collective practices used in the past to appropriate the AVRR program, practices that obliged the IOM to fix and improve its own system (interview migrant, Mor. 2014). When the IOM realizes that a migrant is applying for the second time, the organization rejects the demand, mobilizing the moral authority of helping migrants in need. Quoting the IOM staff, he shared:

> You told us that you have enough of staying here, always in misery, you left, you came back, and now you are again sitting on the bench of the IOM. But no, a second time, we cannot help you. You have lied.
>
> (Ibid.)

As this example demonstrates, the implementation of the AVRR program has involved constant repair work for the IOM in Morocco, not least because migrants themselves learned how to play by the rules of the game of international migration management and to appropriate its services. While the constant threat of repression faced by migrants in transit urged many to return 'voluntarily,' these practices indicate that it is not their only motivation for applying to the program. The strategic appropriation of the IOM's services provides a rare possibility for them to travel legally and safely. Viewing the AVRR program from the perspective of migration emphasizes the agency of migrants that is often ignored in the field of migration management. In this asymmetrically structured field, migrants are mostly addressed as objects of management and aid. While the IOM believes in the capacity of individual, entrepreneurial subjects to manage their own return and reintegration, this neoliberal perspective of the autonomous individual does not mean that migrants are considered as relevant actors in this field.

148 *Voluntary return programs*

As the Moroccan case has shown, the IOM had to adapt to turbulences in migration in order to ensure that the program was implemented according to the terms that were set and funded by its donors. Even though the representatives of European donors seemed aware of the program's limited impact, they renewed their funding for it. What counts in the voluntary return business is not only the actual number of successful repatriations but also the presentation of a reasonable solution and the demonstration of taking action concerning the critical situation at the external borders of the EU. For the IOM, what is mostly at stake is a credible and professional performance in the competitive field of trans-Mediterranean migration management. In this regard, the AVRR program made it possible for the IOM to gain material and personal resources, establish transnational social relations, and build a reputation as a reliable and diplomatic provider of migration control services. Accumulating these different sorts of capital, the organization was able to gain recognition among many actors, not only within the country but also beyond it.

4.2 Voluntary return as humanitarian crisis management in Tunisia

> It meant to rent airplanes, boats [...] There were enormous arrivals! It meant medical assistance, it meant unaccompanied minors, it meant many migrants in very little time from about 110 countries! So, it was enormous. It was a lot of work.
>
> (Interview with IOM staff, Tun. 2015)

Thus did a staff member of the IOM describe the beginning of its mission in Tunisia in 2011, highlighting how extraordinary it was in scale, urgency, and intensity compared to the work that the organization had done in North Africa in previous years. The IOM had been tolerated under the Ben Ali regime and had occasionally implemented information campaigns since 2004 but had operated outside of public attention in this period (see Chapter 3). This changed after the revolution in 2011, notably in the context of what the IOM called "one of the largest migration crisis in modern history" (2011a, 2; see also the Introduction). With this dramatic tone, many IOM publications highlighted the singularity and unpredictability of this "Tunisian migration crisis," which

> generated a massive influx of migrants and refugees in Tunisia [...] and presented several new challenges to the humanitarian community. While the huge magnitude of the flows was not unprecedented, nothing approaching that scale had ever happened in the Mediterranean. The whole international community was taken by surprise, particularly in Tunisia which had never been affected by any substantial influx of refugees or displaced persons.
>
> (Ibid.)

Accompanied by a superlative-laden discourse that defined the Tunisian-Libyan border as a zone of crisis and emergency, the IOM became part of a joint international intervention that aimed to provide immediate relief to migrants fleeing the civil war in Libya. In 2011, more than 350,000 people—including 10,000 migrants from diverse African countries, in addition to 100,000 returning Tunisians and many more Libyans—entered southern Tunisia via its land border with Libya (IOM 2011b). In this situation, many governments requested the IOM's assistance to "ensure the safe and timely return of their nationals" (ibid., 2). Together with the UNHCR and transnationally operating NGOs, the IOM installed camps in the border region between Tunisia and Libya. Within these camps, the IOM was in charge of providing food, water, and shelter for arriving migrants (ibid., 16). In addition, the organization was also responsible for the selection procedures at the border as well as for the transport of migrants to the camps, ports, and airports from which they were returned, resettled, or handed over to other organizations. In the course of what the IOM called a massive evacuation operation, it offered different kinds of assistance to more than 150,000 migrants mostly coming from Algeria, Chad, Egypt, Sudan, and Tunisia. About 6,000 of them were assisted in voluntary return to their countries of origin (ibid. 2011a, 2).

Thus, in Tunisia the AVRR program became known as part of an international humanitarian intervention in its southern border region. Introduced in the name of humanitarianism, the program was no longer promoted as an offer of individual empowerment for migrants who decide to return, but rather as an exceptional instrument for governing so-called mixed migration movements in transit. The organization promised to bring the emergency in Tunisia under control and to prevent the 'humanitarian crisis' from spreading further. While the IOM was already well known at the time as a reliable service provider in the global market of migration management, the organization was able to also position itself as a relevant actor in international crisis management. As I demonstrate in the following sections, the IOM contributed to and profited from a change in the rules and stakes in the trans-Mediterranean field of migration management by recoding its work as humanitarian.

4.2.1 The symbolic production of a humanitarian crisis at the Tunisian-Libyan border

Framing the situation at the Tunisian-Libyan border as an emergency, the IOM contributed to a symbolic production that entailed the need for external intervention. Without playing down the precarious situation for many migrants at the external borders of Europe—who were fleeing wars, conflicts, and desperate economic situations elsewhere and who were facing raids, repression, and racism in transit—the IOM's proactive naming politics indicate how the definition of a crisis, along with the responses promoted in its name, are subject to symbolic and material struggles among different actors seeking to improve their position in the field. Virtual self-presentation and demonstrative performativity (often written in an advertising style and illustrated by movie poster-like imagery) are some of the instruments employed by IOs to enhance their symbolic power when they launched their interventions in 2011. The IOM took a leading role in this self-eventization of humanitarian work, producing three monthly reports (IOM 2011a, 2011b, 2011c), sending out newsletters (ibid. 2011d), and setting up a website allowing visitors to interactively follow its intervention in real time.[9] For the IOM, the virtual presentation of its activities became an important form of cultural capital that helped the organization claim expertise and make itself known as a humanitarian service provider.

Production and dissemination of knowledge are powerful practices in this process. Based on screenings of people crossing the border and the registration of personal information, the IOM produced statistics, visualizations, maps, and profiles of migrants' movements, needs, and future aspirations (IOM 2011b, 16). The combination of these formats created the reality of the 'Tunisian migration crisis' and transmitted it to the global public and European politics. In addition, the organization compiled reports on evacuation operations, supplemented with colorful tables, graphs, and photos and often concluding with a final section that "gives a human face to the crisis" through the personal accounts of migrants who benefited from its assistance (ibid., 3). Overly positive discourses, touching illustrations, detailed statistics, and interactive maps round out the tools that the IOM employed to brand its activities in the field. These demonstrate the organization's capacity to act and solve problems in a setting otherwise marked by passivity and chaos.

Didier Fassin (2007a, 512) argues that the knowledge produced by IOs in the context of humanitarian interventions risks essentializing migrants as victims: "against the thickness of biographies and the complexity of history, it draws a figure to which humanitarian aid is directed." In this process, migrants' multiple and nuanced voices disappear from the glossy noise of IOs' collective success stories. Often too busy with self-marketing and distinguished performativity, IOs hardly take into account the perspectives of those who are supposed to be managed and helped by their services. The postcolonial relations and patriarchal logic in IOs' discourses of humanitarian crisis management primarily position migrants as passive, undefined masses of people to be cared for by international experts.[10] The staff of IOs, in contrast, figure as active heroes, saving not only migrants but also Tunisia from the crisis and chaos threatening to spill over from Libya (IOM 2011b, 1).

The visual and discursive production of knowledge assigns different roles to the actors and defines their relations in this international game of humanitarian crisis management, in which aid is "always directed from above to below, from the more powerful to the weaker, the more fragile, the more vulnerable" (Fassin 2012, 4). The symbolic production of a humanitarian crisis at the Tunisian-Libyan border thus actualizes postcolonial discourses about Western subjects who intervene in the Global South in order to help passive, powerless populations. Disseminated by the powerfully positioned IOM, which is equipped with the symbolic capital of a recognized international expert, such discourses gain wide and unquestioned acceptance, stabilizing the asymmetrical relations in the field and contributing to the *symbolic domination* of international actors over the lives of people on the move on the African continent.

At the same time, the IOM's constant concern with the public presentation of its services underlines how the logics of competition and self-marketing are integral parts of such crisis management. Declared as exceptional compared to existing politics and as limited by time, place, and target groups, the IOM launched a specific "moral imperative" to act (Ticktin 2011, 2). The humanitarian presentation of its work furnished the organization with a new moral authority that helped distinguish itself from other service providers. Moreover, this humanitarian turn legitimated its intervention vis-à-vis Tunisian actors: since the crisis was believed to be "too big to be handled by the directly affected," it seemed to require "extraordinary measures" and "outside interventions" (Hilhorst 2013, 6). The power to contribute to the symbolic making of a humanitarian crisis allowed the IOM to create an urgent, unquestioned demand for its services and to expand its activities into new spheres of action. While symbolic, the production of knowledge provides a powerful resource for the IOM to employ in the trans-Mediterranean field of migration management, driven as it is by the competition among IOs around spheres of influence, distinguished expertise, and secured funding. This power is based on resources, relations, and recognition that the IOM gained in previous struggles in the field, notably in its work in Morocco. Its symbolic capital as a somewhat objective, international expert made the symbolic power that the IOM exercises through its discourses difficult for other actors to recognize. As a result, the IOM's discourse of humanitarian crisis management remained largely unquestioned and gained wide acceptance.

Against this backdrop, the following sections examine the implementation of the IOM's voluntary return program in the name of humanitarianism. Initially, the program was marked by cooperation rather than competition with other actors in the field. However, once international actors called their humanitarian mission completed, voluntary return became the only solution offered to those in the Choucha camp near the Libyan border whose requests for asylum were rejected. Consequently, open conflicts and criticisms challenged the IOs' presence in Tunisia. The struggles of Choucha manifest the contested meanings of voluntary return within an emerging repatriation regime that has been installed by various actors in the country. Despite the unresolved situation in southern Tunisia and the fading demand for the organization's services in 2013, I show how the IOM gained recognition as a humanitarian actor and advanced its expert position in the trans-Mediterranean field of migration management. I argue that from this position, the IOM contributed to a shift in the practical logic of the field, which also motivated other actors to rearrange their strategies and stakes.

4.2.2 Practices of divide, rule, and return in the North African borderlands

> It was the first time that it was not [only] a population fleeing from their own war and needing assistance in terms of refugees. Most of those leaving Libya were asylum seekers and refugees and therefore in need of international protection. The rest was definitely protection of human beings, but they were people who needed assistance to return to their countries of origin. So, they were migrants.
> (Interview with IOM staff, Tun. 2015)

This statement from a member of the IOM staff underlines the central distinction in international migration politics between "refugees"—who fear persecution in their country and are usually "fleeing their own wars"—and others, referred to as "migrants." This distinction was the basis on which the IOM and UNHCR also organized their joint intervention in Tunisia. The IOM was awarded a central role in categorizing the people arriving at the Tunisian-Libyan border, sorting them according into the target groups of the different organizations. Essentially, those who were originally from countries that European states and IOs classified as unsafe were expected to have well-founded claims of asylum. These persons were directed to the UNHCR to individually prove their situation. Persons from countries that are safe according to European states and IOs' assessment, and who escaped Libya but not a war in their country, were offered assistance by the IOM.

While the relation of the IOM and the UNHCR was marked by competition rather than cooperation in Morocco (see Section 4.1.1), their joint crisis management in Tunisia reads as a success story of harmony. As a Policy Development and Evaluation Officer of the UNHCR pointed out:

> there was an early strategic decision at the highest levels of HCR and IOM's leadership to cooperate closely within a flexible interpretation of their mandates (for refugees, and for migrants more generally, respectively). This strategic cooperation was the key to the success of the operation.
> (Ambroso 2012, 6)

In the Memorandum of Understanding that the two organizations reached in 1997, the UNHCR invited the IOM to contribute to the "coordinated United Nations emergency contingency planning" and to "participate in planning for possible refugee influxes" (UNHCR 1997). The IOM was asked to "review with national counterparts and UNHCR ways in which its ongoing country operations may quickly be adjusted to enable the IOM to provide emergency assistance" (ibid.). Within this framework, the two organizations established a joint IOM-UNHCR Humanitarian Evacuation Cell, hosted by the IOM and cooperating with diverse actors—including Tunisian authorities (especially the Ministry of Interior and the Ministry of Social Affairs), transnational NGOs (e.g., the Tunisian Red Crescent and the Islamic Relief), and the Tunisian army (IOM 2011c, 3)—to classify incoming "mixed migration flows" according to the target groups of the participating actors (ibid. 2015, 9).

Formally, the responsibility for determining the individual statuses of refugees in Tunisia and resettling them remained under the authority of the UNHCR, as mandated by the Geneva Convention.[11] Practically, however, the IOM was primarily in charge of the registration and screening procedures, camp logistics, transportation, and medical care. In this context, the IOM was able to gain additional funding from the United States (US), Sweden, Norway, Canada, Germany, and Spain for a special AVRR program called Promoting the Return and Reintegration of Rejected Asylum Seekers (PRIRAC) (ibid. 2011c, 11). As indicated by its name, the initiative was meant for those whose claims of asylum were rejected by the UNHCR. It offered transportation to the country of origin as well as juridical assistance, medical aid, cultural orientation, and skill and language training before leaving Tunisia. Labeling a certain category of refugees as "rejected" indicates how the increasingly moralized politics of recognition grant protection to those who seem to deserve it while excluding others as non-deserving (Fassin 2016, 7f.). These politics of recognition are accompanied by shifting moral economies, from compassion for innocent victims—in this case, those who were accepted by the UNHCR and resettled to another country—to a mistrust and suspicion of those who are undesirable and who thus remain in the desert in southern Tunisia. By categorizing migrants in transit, the IOM draws a "line between those considered to belong, and enjoy specific protections, and those outside the moral community that a bureaucratic ethic is concerned with" (Eckert, 2020, 23). However, the category of refugees and asylum seekers was almost impossible to employ for most migrants who were fleeing the conflict in Libya but not what IOs called "their own war."

Among these migrants, the concept of vulnerability became the most decisive sorting criterion on which inclusion in and exclusion from the IOM's program was based (IOM 2011c, 11). In order to earn the support of the IOM, migrants not only had to tell a convincing story but also "to prove their pathology" (Fassin 2007b, 151). The IOM's return assistance for these apparently helpless individuals became a matter of empathy and goodwill. In contrast to the widespread image of migrants as a 'risk for Europe' (see Chapter 3), these migrants were regarded as potential 'victims of criminal networks of smugglers and traffickers.' Through their voluntary return, they would be protected by being prevented from the dangerous crossing of the

Mediterranean and any exploitation during transit. According to this humanitarian logic, voluntary return became a *moral responsibility to protect migrants in need*. The priority given to support women, children, sick, and elderly people as well as 'victims of human trafficking' (see also Chapter 5) led to new hierarchies in the chances and legitimacy of various claims for protection in transit. This humanitarian reconfiguration and the consequent focus on the unbearable suffering of migrants were instrumental not only in securing funding but also in providing a new moral legitimization for the expansion of migration control services in transit countries.

In practice, the IOM was directly implicated in sorting such 'mixed migration flows' in the North African borderlands into different groups, to be governed by different actors and under different standards of international migration politics. While those recognized as refugees and (potential) asylum seekers were offered consular services and were taken care of by the UNHCR, others were directed to the IOM and—if credibly in need— promised to leave Tunisia "in dignity" (IOM 2012a). This sorting was not only organized according to international norms like the Geneva Convention but was also based on more fluid categories of international migration management. This fostered the international trend of offering protection to flexibly defined target groups as an act of benevolent charity, rather than granting rights of asylum that can be claimed by individuals (see Fassin 2016). This divide, rule, and return approach according to humanitarian principles added to the production of what Agier (2011, 213) called new "hierarchies of misfortune" among people on the move. These had very material consequences for the migrants concerned, as it differentiated their options to stay and their directions to move on. The IOM's intervention in southern Tunisia thus contributed to new forms of differentiation of mobility rights and to the production of inequalities in transit.

4.2.3 *In the camp: postcolonial relations and patriarchal logic*

By the end of 2011, more than 4,000 people were recognized as refugees and resettled to other countries by the UNHCR in the context of a widely advertised Global Resettlement Solidarity Initiative (Al-Jamai 2013). In the same time period, the IOM assisted 6,000 people in their voluntary return. Many more left Tunisia on their own. However, about 1,000 people remained without legal status because they were not recognized by the UNHCR as refugees and because Tunisia lacks a functioning asylum system to regularize their situation (Crépeau 2012). Most of them remained in the Choucha camp along the Tunisian-Libyan border, waiting for what IOs call a 'durable solution' (Boubakri 2013).

The Choucha camp is the first refugee camp to be opened in Tunisia since the Algerian war in 1962. It was the biggest and longest-operating of four camps that were set up in southern Tunisia in February 2011. Located on the Tunisian side about 9 km from the Libyan border, it was directed by the UNHCR and jointly managed by the IOM and the Danish Refugee Council, a large humanitarian NGO that provides assistance to "conflict affected communities and persons."[12] The camp had been designed to accommodate a few thousand people, but about 20,000 people lived there at its peak; it became overcrowded and lacked food, water, and medical supplies, with tensions between different communities rising (CeTuMa 2013).

From the perspective of those working for IOs, it was a "luxury camp," built with new materials and generous donations from Europe and the Gulf region (conversation with Tun. Researcher 1, Tun. 2015). Fearing that conflicts and crises could spread from Libya to what was perceived as the model country of the Arab Spring, international actors were desperate for the IOs' intervention to become a success story. Under the spotlight of cameras and the eyes of numerous journalists, a number of international VIPs,[13] politicians,[14] and high-ranking officials of IOs[15] wandered through the camps at the Tunisian-Libyan border. Between long rows of quickly installed tents, they expressed the international community's compassion and commitment to find 'durable solutions' for their desperate inhabitants. Under intense international attention and political pressure, international staff and their temporary Tunisian colleagues working in the camps were urged to quickly process requests for asylum and to speed up resettlement procedures. They shared an understanding of their work as not partisan or political but humanitarian, along with an impatience to help desperate people with urgent needs. Highly motivated and very dedicated, many young, sometimes unexperienced aid workers underwent quick training and had to conduct their work by referring to international guidance manuals for humanitarian crisis management. "We learnt on the job!" one of them proudly explained.[16] Despite a strong sense of identification with their work and a rather unquestioning belief in the benefits of the mission, the individual *habitus* of these young aid workers can be characterized as highly career-oriented, mobile, and motivated to move on to the next crisis once that they accomplished their mission in southern Tunisia.

Most workers in higher positions were so-called internationals coming from the Global North. Most of them were Western and White, many of them with an Italian nationality. Agier (2011, 186) characterizes them as "young men and women who have come from their pleasant countries in Europe, the United States or Australia to spend a few months in the 'heart of darkness' and take part in the great movement of international humanitarian aid." From the perspective of the camps' Sub-Saharan inhabitants, these staff worked hard to make a successful career in the international community, but they often lacked knowledge about the places and their histories they were supposed to support with their expertise. A few Tunisians also worked in the camp, which was marked by asymmetrical power relations between the IO staff and the migrants under their care, reflecting postcolonial continuities and patriarchal logic that largely inform humanitarian interventions in the Global South.

At the Choucha camp, no employees from Sub-Sahara Africa were part of the IO staff. According to an activist who himself immigrated from a West African country to Tunisia,

> the real problem of Choucha was the problem between the people of Choucha and the IOM and UNHCR! [While] IOM works for the immigrants of whom the majority are Sub-Saharan Africans, in its staff in Tunisia there are no [Sub-Saharan] Africans. Zero.
> (Interview with activist, Tun. 2015)

For this reason, he argued during our interview, a lot of misunderstandings and miscommunications occurred in the camp. For one thing, the majority of the people working for IOs spoke only English, French, and Arabic. "But those people arriving from Libya, did they understand these languages? Why were there no employees speaking Wolof, or other African languages?" (ibid.). Furthermore, he criticized how the IO staff did not know anything about the backgrounds and cultures of the migrants. As a result,

> those working for the IOM and the UNHCR did not know much about the situation of the migrants, because for many it was the first time working in the field. It was their first time meeting and talking with people from another culture.
> (Ibid.)

This lack of experience, cultural sensitivity, and mutual trust led to a situation in which the staff were supposed to assist people about whom they knew little and who they did not understand very well. Consequently, the migrants did not trust the staff who were supposed to care for them. In terms of the categorizations, decisions, and material assistance, the inhabitants of the Choucha camp wondered about the aid workers' predefined procedures and strange questions, but they were not able to question or avoid them. Most of the time, migrants had to wait for the next step to be determined by the organization to which they were assigned. While migrants were expected to be patient and gratefully receive aid, those working for IOs acted as the experts who made decisions about their needs for protection and their possibilities for moving on. In the camp, the staff were in the position to define and implement the rules according to which the migrants had to live.

4.2.4 In the office: The illusio of humanitarian migration management

> We were not there to determine the question of refugees. We had a project that supported those who wanted to return. Because, at a certain time in 2011 [and] in the beginning of 2012, some remained; those people who wanted to return, they had all returned. And there were asylum

seekers and their requests, they were evaluated ... and in the end, there was a negative answer to their requests for asylum,

said an IOM's representative in Tunisia, describing the organization's role during an interview in 2015 (interview with IOM staff, Tun. 2015). I met her in the IOM's main office in one of the suburbs of Tunis, where many foreign embassies and international institutions are located. It seemed that mostly young women worked at the office, many of them Italian. The woman at the reception offered me some tea and directed me to an office on the first floor, where a large window offered a direct view over a small square with European-style coffee shops and boutiques. The office was decorated with official IOM flags and symbols. We took seats in heavy armchairs. She willingly responded to my questions in detail, showing no hurry to finish or cut off our conversation.

"We had a project: if you want to return to your country, we can help you, but it is voluntary return. So, if you do not want to return, we don't do anything—we cannot, you see?" she explained, specifying the organization's working ethos centered around the voluntariness of its clients (ibid.). She emphasized that by offering voluntary return to the remaining inhabitants at the Choucha camp, the IOM was not responsible for the determination of their refugee status and their resettlement; it was only concerned with those who explicitly "want to return" to their countries of origin. However, her report failed to address the issues of how their willingness was enhanced by the lack of alternatives and the precarious living conditions in the Tunisian desert.

In 2012, the AVRR program was the only (legal) option available to these migrants, and its demand was directly conditioned by the lack of alternative solutions. Her conviction that the IOM would "not do anything" if someone did not want to return contradicts observations of the organization's continuous efforts to encourage the migrants remaining in the desert to participate in the program. As in other contexts, the IOM's staff in Tunisia seemed aware that repressive state politics are indispensable for the AVRR program's efficient function. Distancing her work from these practices, she reiterated the IOM's principle to only be "consultants, independently and objectively informing their clients—i.e., the migrants—about their rights, duties, constraints and opportunities" (Loher 2020, 114). At the same time, when talking about migrants' desperate situations, the IOM staff sincerely expressed their personal and emotional concern for these people. They are in close contact with the migrants they help. For them, they work compassionately and try to find the best possible solutions. Nevertheless, the criteria and categorizations of those who are worthy of their assistance—and those who are not—seem deeply internalized and rarely questioned. During my interviews, it was obvious that the IOM staff preferred to talk about the "suffering and compassion rather than interests and justice" that motivates them (Fassin 2012, 3). Showing a strong belief in the moral value of their

158 *Voluntary return programs*

work, they rarely questioned the rules, assumptions, and routinized procedures that define their mission. In this respect, the IOM's professionals were not only committed to their clients but also to their office (Loher 2020, 128).

'Migration needs to be controlled' was an assumption expressed in almost every conversation with the global bureaucrats working for the IOM. While they were very quick to refer to the external constraints on their interventions by their mandate, capacity, or resources, I heard little about these members' attempts to provoke change in international politics. Many of them take the job as a distinctively called international for a global, powerful IO that provides them with a good salary and status in a country where they benefit from many privileges. When they manage the projects, which they had to design and promote themselves among potential donors, the problems and ambiguities that they encounter on the ground disappear during their marketization. Those employed at an *international* organization indirectly work for the governments of its member states. There is no democratic control, but they are accountable to the states that finance their services in order to efficiently and diplomatically control migration. Accepting these rules of the international state system and its selectively restrictive mobility, they perceive their own interventions (especially those in the name of humanitarianism) as alleviating the suffering of migrants under these conditions. With this conviction, the IOM's staff proudly told me how the organization satisfactorily fulfilled its mission to manage the humanitarian crisis at the Tunisian-Libyan border. The growing protests by those still waiting in the desert for an acceptable solution, in turn, were placed beyond her office's responsibility and sphere of influence.

4.2.5 *Making invisible: Tunisia's Local Integration Program and IOs' retreat from the field*

At the same time, Tunisian authorities in partnership with the Red Crescent offered a Local Integration Program to those waiting in the Choucha camp for a solution. Germany funded the provision of basic services for participants. Geographically, these services were bound to the south of Tunisia, so that their distribution ensured that the recipients would stay in this region if they want to take advantage of the services. This way, the program confined the mobility of migrants and prevented them from moving to the north, beyond an imaginary geographical border stretching between Gafsa in the west to the coastal city of Gabès in the east (Choucha Delegation 2014). By offering assistance only in the south, the Tunisian government compelled migrants to stay there, making it possible to control their mobility and potentially restrict it. In this respect, such migrants' exclusion from IOs' concern did not entail exclusion from state control (Tazzioli 2014, 3).

The funding that migrants received through the Local Integration Program proved to be insufficient to cover living costs in Tunisia.[17] Consequently, many migrants moved on to the cities at the coast anyways, in

Voluntary return programs 159

order to search for work and support. On their way, they frequently faced controls, arrests, and forced returns.[18] Moreover, the Tunisian government, which had promised to regularize (at least temporarily) the migrants remaining in Choucha, never delivered residence permits, de facto illegalizing their stay in the country and institutionally barring their integration (ibid.). Those who did not want to or could not return to their countries of origin thus found themselves in a precarious situation of lawlessness, criminalization, and discrimination in Tunisia. "Each time we go to Tunis to complain, we are arrested and forcibly returned to the camp," a migrant reported (quoted in Guguen and Bensaied 2014). They had the choice between staying illegally in a country whose migration policy punished irregular entry/stay with a one-month to one-year prison sentence and a 6–120 dinar fine (3–60 euros) (Ledrisi 2015), or taking the 1,500 dinars (about 750 euros) offered by the Local Integration Program to start a project in the south of Tunisia—coincidentally, the exact amount that was needed for a place on a boat from Libya to Italy at that time, thus allowing an attempt to cross the Mediterranean Sea (Potot 2014).

The Local Integration Program combined humanitarian assistance with repressive control. It conducted what Agier (2011, 47) describes as a strategy "to break or reorient the trajectories" of those migrants remaining in Tunisia and "to control them more closely, rather than make them absolutely impossible." The strategy to keep migrants away from the coast and from public attention also involved an important symbolic dimension: it made it possible for the Tunisian government to demonstrate to its citizens and donors that the country did not face a 'migration problem' and was able to control its northern sea borders. At the same time, migrants were allowed to move freely in the south and to cross the land borders with Libya and Algeria. Aware that migrants would either leave the country or serve as cheap labor in the south, Tunisian authorities hoped to discharge the 'problem' through locally bound humanitarian assistance and selective border controls. This Tunisian way of addressing transit migration showed that its authorities were able to play by the rules of the humanitarian game of migration management, even without investing much money.

When the urgency of the 'Tunisian migration crisis' disappeared from the international agenda in 2012, none of the actors that was involved in crisis management in 2011 felt responsible for the precarious situation of those who remained in the desert.[19] The blame was pushed back and forth between government and IO actors; Tunisian authorities repeatedly claimed that they did not have the capacity to offer any other solutions to these migrants, referring them to the IOM (cf. IOM 2012b). A representative of the Tunisian Ministry for Development and International Cooperation declared during a later interview:

> We have neither the resources nor nothing, really. We have done everything possible but now we have no more anything. But I think that

it is the UNHCR that is responsible. And the IOM also, they also intervened in this area.

(Interview with repr. of MDIC, Tun. 2015)

In response, the IOM pulled back to occupy the position of being responsible only for those willing to return to their countries of origin (see the previous section), and the UNHCR saw its mission as completed. According to the UNHCR's representative in Tunisia, those whose claims to participate in the Global Resettlement Solidarity Initiative were rejected, were

not people of our concern anymore. So it's not our problem what they do with their lives. They are not vulnerable or at risk, it is their life, we are not responsible for them and it's not our fault if they die going to Italy by boat.

(Quoted in Tazzioli 2014, 2)

From the UNHCR's point of view, those who were not recognized as refugees or asylum seekers fell outside of its mandate and therefore its concern. The flight from the war in Libya was not sufficient for their protection by the UNHCR; instead, they had to prove well-founded fears of personal persecution in their countries of origin.[20] Moreover, staff members of the UNHCR repeatedly stressed that even for those recognized as refugees, participation in its resettlement initiative "is not a right of every refugee" and that there is no "obligation of a country to accept them for reinstallation" (discussion with UNHCR staff, Mor. 2014). In cases where no country would receive them, refugees were directed to the IOM's AVRR program.

The clear lack of alternatives increasingly called into question the voluntary character of the AVRR program. Despite their precarious situations and their lack of legal alternatives, many migrants did not regard voluntary return as an acceptable solution, and they refused to participate in the program. It obviously served as the last option before their impending illegality. Those who faced the repressive consequences of the selective migration politics became increasingly skeptical of IOs' humanitarian crisis management. In this context, categorizing people into different organizations' spheres of concern not only served the IOs by legitimating their work and dividing their spheres of influence, authority, and expertise: differentiation into specific target groups of divide, rule, and return was also helpful in diffusing and discharging responsibility as criticism and protest against their unfinished mission rose. Voluntary return was part of a joint humanitarian mission that offered protection to selected migrants while aiming to efficiently and smoothly return all others. It was based on the assumption that those migrants who are actually recognized as being eligible for asylum can only be granted international protection if others are consistently encouraged to return. Thus, participation in neither the IOM's AVRR program nor in the UNHCR's resettlement initiative are rights to be claimed by migrants; such participation is subject to the symbolic violence exercised through the seemingly natural and legitimate categorizations by IOs as well as to the mercy of donors funding these programs.

When the Choucha camp was closed after four years, IOs and their donors celebrated the closure and called their mission complete. Consequently, the widely published success story of a "humanitarian emergency response to the Libyan crisis" (IOM 2011c) eventually disappeared from the international gaze. However, those people who were left out of the IOs' concern did not accept the offered solutions and questioned what they perceived as arbitrary practices of categorization and charity (see the next section).

When most of the international action and attention waned, practices of invisibilization occurred from 2013 on. "Choucha does not exist anymore. Those who are still there are only nomads in the desert," a staff member of an IO was quoted as saying in 2014 (Statewatch 2014). During their operations, the IOM and UNHCR had been busy collecting precise data and accurate numbers about the people under their concern in order to raise awareness, to propose 'durable solutions,' and to quantify their success in the beginning; however, once that they began to remove themselves from what they perceived as the problem of Choucha, they cared remarkably little about "just a few persons in the desert."[21] The practices of divide, rule, and return led to an "incessant production of differentiated migration profiles," so that in the end the few people who could not be integrated remained (ibid.). Accordingly, no humanitarian concern needed to take these "uncountable few" into account (ibid.). Through their symbolic violence—categorizing and dividing the inhabitants of Choucha into governable and returnable groups, without further justification—IOs and the Tunisian state tried to minimize the issue and finally agreed on the non-existence of the camp. Condemned as "nomads in the desert," those rejected by the UNHCR seemed to have "failed in some important moral way," and thus no one felt responsible for their suffering anymore (Ticktin 2011, 23). In contrast to the right to asylum, international protection according to humanitarian rules of migration management depends on IOs taking responsibility and raising sufficient funding.

When the widely promoted humanitarian crisis management threatened to turn into a permanent struggle with those whose demands for protection were rejected, most international actors left the border region after two years of "spectacularly effective" crisis management (Andersson 2014, 17). While dozens of local and international organizations worked in and around the Choucha camp when it opened in 2011, one by one they left as international attention and funding options moved to other crises in the region, mostly in the direction of Syria. As much as the 'migration crisis' at the Libyan-Tunisian border alarmed the international community and urged their joint humanitarian intervention, it was abandoned just as quickly when action was more urgently needed elsewhere from 2013 on. The support for migrants in Tunisia not only depended on the moral convictions of IOs but was also conditioned by the rules and rhythms of the international aid economy.

Already beginning in October 2011, the UNHCR regularly decreased its food and medical supplies, totally ceasing in November 2012. In April 2013, the organization cut the electricity and reduced the amount of drinking water in order to persuade those who were not accepted into the resettlement program to participate in the IOM's voluntary return program (Tringham 2013). Those who still remained in the so-called "ghost town" camp reported that IOM staff repeatedly visited the camp in order to convince people to return (Guguen and Bensaied 2014). "They came and offered us voluntary return. But they know themselves that it is not a solution," one of the remaining inhabitants of the camp shared in a conversation two years later (conversation with refugee from Choucha, Tun. 2015). Activist groups supporting those who identified themselves as the Rejected Refugees of Choucha expressed doubts about the voluntariness of this offer, observing how inhabitants of the camp were pressured to accept either local integration in Tunisia or voluntary return to their countries of origin, with no other legal options (email conversation with activists' collective, Tun. 2015).

The IOM's repeated offer for migrants to return voluntarily was part of the joint effort by IOs to classify the remaining inhabitants into even smaller groups by treating every case individually and dispersing them among different cities in southern Tunisia (Statewatch 2014). This way, the IOs expected that the 'problem of Choucha' would become invisible and that collective protest would be impossible. When European states feared that Choucha could become a focal point for migrants who were rescued at sea by the Tunisian navy and for refugees independently heading there from Libya, the UNHCR ultimately abandoned its former model camp with all the praised new material. However, those who had already waited for years in the desert did not easily accept a return option, even when offered a refund of their travel expenses and some US dollars.[22]

Finally, only the Tunisian army remained present at Choucha, waiting to turn the space into a military zone (see Article 13 2013). In the end, the IOM and the Tunisian Red Crescent announced the camp's definite closure and eviction of the remaining inhabitants within two weeks (Massy 2014). As criticism arose, all international actors that had been involved in managing the camp denied any responsibility for the eviction: instead, they referred to a decision by the Tunisian authorities. The latter justified the eviction as a matter of "reasons of security" and the need to concentrate "on real problems," such as terrorism and elections (ibid.). While the situation in the desert remained unsolved and precarious, IOs and the EU publicly celebrated their humanitarian crisis management as success. As the objectives agreed on in the project guidelines had been achieved, the temporary staff was moved to other crises in the region.

When it was no longer framed in terms of emergency and crisis management, the situation at the Choucha camp disappeared from agendas and became a "permanent condition of being dismissed from any humanitarian gaze, the junk of the Libyan war."[23] In this respect, international attention renders certain forms of suffering visible while turning a blind eye to other forms of suffering. What matters is not necessarily experiences of violence and injustice, but crises and vulnerabilities as defined and promoted by IOs with a *feel for the game* of humanitarian crisis management. Situations that are no longer strategic for their interventions and funding applications, or that even risk a loss of their control, are erased from the international map of migration crises and are both physically and symbolically rendered invisible for the global public (cf. Wacquant 2009, 288). This symbolic power to discursively *make* and *unmake* crises is one of the most powerful resources that IOs employ in the trans-Mediterranean field of migration management.

4.2.6 "At least Choucha is free": a space of rumors and hope

Once it was outside the immediate control of IOs, the Choucha camp became a place of rumors and hope for all those discharged from the international politics of protection. The self-organized space developed its own rules and political dynamics that challenged the moral foundations and routinized practices of humanitarian crisis management through its sheer persistence: "I even knew people who arrived in Tunisia at the airport, who took a car to go to Choucha. Because they were told that in Choucha you will get a visa," reported an activist, discussing the illusio(n) spreading among migrants in the North African borderlands (interview with activist, Tun. 2015). While the experience of those abandoned in the desert proved these rumors wrong, hopes and beliefs that an acceptable solution would come remained strong among the Rejected Refugees. "In the beginning, the UNHCR promised us everything, that they would 'find us a country,'" shared one of the refugees who had been rejected by the organization, illustrating its politics of hope, but "since 2013, we have been completely abandoned" (quoted in Guguen and Bensaied 2014). From the perspective of those living in Choucha, the supposed success of international crisis management being promoted in the glossy brochures of IOs appeared in a different light. When the IOs' 'persons of concern' left the country, a heterogeneous group of people outside the concern of the international community remained in the Choucha camp, protesting against the rejection of their claims and hoping for an acceptable solution.

"The camp is *not* closed. We are still living there!" emphasized a Rejected Refugee (conversation with refugee from Choucha, Tun. 2015), correcting the dominant narrative. In contrast to the 'Choucha does not exist' consensus and the 'ghost town' rhetoric shared by IOs and the Tunisian authorities, those labeled as rejected revolted against their classification. They started to fight for their own visibility and for Choucha as a space of their unfinished struggle, seeking international recognition and protection. For this reason, they preferred to stay in—or even returned to—the now self-organized camp in the desert. "At least Choucha is free, the desert is free!" they said, justifying their refusal to leave the place (quoted in Chennaoui

2014). In the southern Tunisian cities in which they were supposed to be locally integrated, they experienced racist discrimination and were unable to find either formal jobs or affordable sleeping places (Choucha Delegation 2014)—despite the individual success stories that promote IOs in their public relations material. Thus, even some of those who had moved to Tunisian cities under the Local Integration Program came back to the former camp, where they felt safer and better protected by their community (ibid.). They preferred the indefinite wait under extreme challenging conditions of intense sunshine and sandstorms, only protected by worn-out, sundried tents that were left behind by the UNHCR and only supported by the cars passing by on their way to the Libyan border (see Chennaoui 2014; Potot 2014). Still lacking acceptable alternatives, they became used to waiting in this buffer zone of international migration politics. From their perspective, the only way out seemed to be either finding work in unstable Libya or securing a place on a boat to Italy (see Choucha Delegation 2014).

Despite their lack of legal alternatives, they did not consider the IOM's AVRR program an acceptable option; consequently, the demand for the program decreased by the end of 2013. While it had been widely welcomed and applauded in its immediate response to the 'Tunisian migration crisis' in 2011, the IOM faced increasing difficulties in recruiting beneficiaries and thus in meeting expected numbers of returnees in the subsequent years. Instead of waiting for assistance, the Rejected Refugees of Choucha organized themselves to claim their rights and to fight for their needs. In this respect, migrants' encounters with IOs in the camps in southern Tunisia were less a story of the appropriation of the IOM's services (as seen in the Moroccan case) but were instead a story in which interactions were characterized by open conflicts with and contestation of the IOs' practices of care and control, classification and charity. While migrants are not able to change the rules of the field, they can refuse to play by them—which causes existential problems for the AVRR program, as it depends on their 'voluntary' participation. When the IOs left Choucha, migrants began to set their own rules for the self-organized space.

Despite the unsolved situation in Choucha, the IOM established itself as a humanitarian actor that was not the principal addressee of rising criticism and protest. While the UNHCR, the EU, and the Tunisian government were criticized for their politics of containment and their discharge of 'undesirables' in the Tunisian desert, the IOM's seemingly unpolitical practices of governing migration by offering technical and logistical assistance to migrants in need proved to be immune to increasingly organized forms of protest. The Rejected Refugees saw the UNHCR as duty-bound to help them with their right to resettlement. Having internalized the official division of labor among IOs, the Rejected Refugees did not expect much from the IOM, whose only offer remained voluntary return to the country of origin. Still, the contested but symbolically powerful offer of voluntary return made the organization not only known to migrants but also to many actors operating in the Tunisian field of migration management. The recognition of its work as humanitarian thus provided the IOM with an important form of symbolic capital that could be reemployed at other sites in the field.

4.2.7 Voluntary return within cycles of criminalization and illegalization

When the PRIRAC initiative expired in December 2013 (see Section 4.2.2), the IOM took a new approach to continue and adjust its services. The organization designed a new program to offer assistance to those rescued at sea and detained in Ouardia, Tunisia's most prominent "reception center" for irregularized migrants, on the outskirts of Tunis.[24] Redefining the target group for its voluntary return services, the IOM was able to benefit from renewed funding from the Swiss Development Cooperation (SDC) in 2014 for a project called Humanitarian Assistance and Voluntary Return for Vulnerable Migrants Rescued on the High Seas. The SDC redirected funds that had not been spent implementing the PRIRAC initiative, since the demand for voluntary return had not met the numbers calculated by IOs and their donors.[25] As in Morocco, Swiss funding was not only conditional on a Tunisian commitment to cofinance migrants returning to their countries of origin but was also motivated by the Swiss self-perception as humanitarian donors. Unlike the funding ambitions of other European donors, the funding was presented as a neutral, impartial, and selfless offer of protection for migrants in need. However, the SDC did not cover the entire costs of the program, in order to stimulate Tunisian actors to cooperate in and contribute to its implementation (Ambassade de Suisse en Tunisie 2015). Moreover, the SDC canceled the reintegration component, arguing that a monetary incentive was not deemed necessary for returnees who were detained in Ouardia with an impossible charge to buy themselves out of the prison. Thus, in the years after the revolution, voluntary return became ever more interlinked with and shaped by increasingly arbitrary and repressive Tunisian state politics and their economies of division, detention, and deportation.

While many migrants made it to Europe, those who had been 'rescued' from the Mediterranean Sea by the Tunisian navy were brought to Ben Guerdane, a city in southern Tunisia. Additionally, those who were intercepted by the European border agency Frontex in the civil-military operation Hermes found themselves returned to Tunisia.[26] For those arriving at the Tunisian coast, the Red Crescent registered asylum claims, as the UNHCR was no longer directly accessible to its 'persons of concern' (Chennaoui 2014). In 2013, the UNHCR's budget for emergency operation in the region was halved (UNHCR 2013), and in the summer of 2014, the majority of its staff left the office in the nearby coastal town of Zarzis before the organization's major presence in southern Tunisia was completely closed. Its remaining office—located within walking distance of the IOM's headquarters in a suburb of Tunis—became equally difficult to access, as the organization not only removed its door sign but also stopped picking up the phone and responding to its official email address (as I myself discovered during my efforts to request an interview with one of its representatives in 2015).

As a result of the UNHCR's retreat from the field, only the Tunisian Red Crescent remained present in southern Tunisia and was therefore responsible for separating arrivals into different governable groups (Chennaoui 2014). Those who were recognized as asylum seekers were offered sleeping places for a maximum of 21 days in overcrowded, substandard buildings in the neighboring city of Medenine, where the UNHCR and the Red Crescent had moved their (much less noticeable) operations (Statewatch 2014). The majority of the rescued migrants were rejected because they had confirmed that they were "migrants" when questioned by the IOs upon their arrival (ibid.). For many Sub-Saharan migrants, it seemed impossible to disagree with the statement, after having traveled for years before being rescued to Tunisia. Consequently, they were either detained in Ben Guerdane or imprisoned in Ouardia (GDP 2015). If they had been recognized as refugees or asylum seekers in another country before their departure, they lost their status (Chennaoui 2014). In addition, many were charged for their (failed) attempts to illegally leave the country. In the aftermath of the Tunisian revolution, the prominent law regulating "the entry and stay of foreign nationals in Tunisia" since 2004 was practically no longer applied; still, it was never officially abandoned, and so unauthorized border crossings could still be punished with detention (Crépeau 2012). For the migrants who were returned or rescued to Tunisia, the law was still applied in an arbitrary manner.

However, since the Tunisian state lacked the money for deportations, it employed a special instrument, so-called penalties: a fee for every month of 'illegal stay' in Tunisia required to be paid by detained migrants, in addition to their own return ticket to self-deport themselves to their countries of origin. Those migrants unable to pay the quickly rising sums were threatened with deportations to the deserts in Libya and Algeria (Garelli, Sossi, and Tazzioli 2015). Through this process of criminalization and illegalization, the Tunisian state not only discharged itself of the remaining people in the desert but even found a way to profit from their precarious presence. Framed as an open-door policy toward its neighboring countries and complementary with the Local Integration Program in the south (see Section 4.2.5), the Tunisian state provided migrants with the financial means to silently leave for Libya and to go by sea to Europe. If they were returned to Tunisia, they were detained for 'illegally leaving the country' and had to pay both their return ticket and the penalties. Otherwise, they might be deported to the desert. While migrants' deportability was mainly used as an incentive to make them pay the money, some were indeed displaced on an arbitrary basis. In this way, the Tunisian politics of detention and deportation added to the returnability of migrants rescued to the country, which in turn boosted the demand for the IOM's assistance.

Tunisia became a buffer zone in the immediate European neighborhood for people who were escaping wars and conflicts and for those who, if rescued, were jailed, deported, or even sent back at their own expense. While the Moroccan government symbolically and materially supported the AVRR program from 2013 on, Tunisian authorities sought to profit from it; both states developed their own strategies of playing the game of humanitarian migration management in order to gain social, symbolic, or economic capital. Despite their skillfully appropriated humanitarian discourses, their control practices remained rather repressive.

Nevertheless, their obvious disrespect of international protection standards was hardly criticized by international actors. European donors viewed the Tunisian approach of taking ownership and responsibility for transit migration favorably, since it resonated well with their ambitions to establish Tunisia as a key country of the central Mediterranean border regime to which people seeking to reach Europe could also legally be rescued and returned in the future. Even when they were well informed about the arbitrary practices of detention and (self-)deportation of the Tunisian authorities, IOs remained equally uncritical of them. Instead of distancing themselves from repressive practices, their diplomatic responses allowed them to develop and maintain stable relations with Tunisian government representatives. As the case of the Tunisian penalties shows, the IOM's work in North Africa not only depends on migrants willing to return and on European states willing to provide funding but also on state authorities willing to cooperate. For the IOM, it was essential to develop a long-term partnership with Tunisian state actors in order to gain a relevant position in the field of emerging migration politics. While the organization does not have to support their politics of deportation and detention, these politics provide a necessary condition for effective implementation of the AVRR program. Repressive practices make its supposedly voluntary service particularly profitable, since migrants have few other legal and safe options for leaving the unbearable situations they face at the external borders of the EU.

4.2.8 Struggles for durable solutions: beyond charity and "associative things"

Even though they suffered under precarious conditions in Tunisia, those who collectively organized as the Rejected Refugees of Choucha refused the IOM's repeated offer to return; instead, they took their struggle to another level and raised further reaching demands. Whether housed in Medenine, detained in Ouardia, or deported to Algeria, many migrants returned to the tolerated, self-organized space in the desert where they found a place to live self-determined lives and to organize their ongoing struggle for a decent life. Refusing to be divided and made invisible by the IOs, the Rejected Refugees started a nationwide protest in May 2011 that raised international attention and transnational solidarity in subsequent years.

168 *Voluntary return programs*

"We are rejected asylum seekers, abandoned in the Choucha camp since 2011. We demand a durable solution."[27] The major demands of the Rejected Refugees of Choucha were to be granted asylum and provided international protection in a safe country, which for them meant an effective system of protection. Tunisia did not satisfy these criteria; therefore, they demanded that everyone in the Choucha camp should be resettled—not returned.[28] Aware of the keywords and the mechanisms of the international politics of protection, the Rejected Refugees strategically employed the vocabulary and concepts of IOs to criticize their management. They proclaimed that these organizations negated the human rights of people and their ability to reconstruct their lives in dignity.[29] Addressing these actors with their own jargon, the Rejected Refugees pointed out that

> we want you to understand that we are *not migrants*. We sincerely have our fears that prevent us from returning to our countries of origin. But unfortunately, we were not understood and no one cares to understand us. If we were just *travelers* or *economic migrants*, we should all be in Italy by now, many have gone across already but those of us writing this letter are not after travelling for greener land, we are genuinely unable to return to our countries of origin and beg of you to consider our situation and grant us international protection.[30]

The Rejected Refugees thus engaged in the symbolic struggles of international migration management. While they took on the categorical differentiation between "economic migrants" and "genuine refugees" in order to advance their claims for international protection, they denounced the "partitioning system" that sorts between refugees, Rejected Refugees, and non-resettled refugees and divides their struggles (Chennaoui 2014). Instead, they focused on their common experience of escaping the war in Libya as a reason to be granted international protection, coming from countries involved in war (ibid.). "We are also *refugees*. We are also fleeing from war, just not in our home countries. But what difference does it make?" they strategically asked the international community.[31] "We cannot go back there, but neither can we stay here, as we are experiencing discrimination in Tunisia every day. [...] So, the only solution is to cross the Mediterranean," they argued, distancing "normal" routes and forms of traveling from dangerous, "clandestine" attempts to cross the Mediterranean (ibid.). "We entered Tunisia legally, at the border post of Ras Jedir, just normal with a stamp on our passports" (ibid.). These claims show their cultural capital that enables them to strategically articulate themselves according to the rules of international migration management, asserting that the common experiences of suffering in Libya and facing vulnerability in Tunisia entitle them to international protection. With this illusioic perspective, IOs were expected to assist and ultimately free them from their desperate situations.

These symbolic struggles in Choucha were accompanied by very physical forms of protest and repression. After numerous demonstrations on the streets around the camp in May 2012, 50 people traveled to Tunis one year later to conduct a hunger strike in front of the UNHCR's head office. At first, their protest primarily focused on the UNHCR, which was perceived as the responsible actor in terms of their demands for international protection and resettlement.[32] The "UNHCR is not a travel agency," a representative of the UNHCR commented at a press conference defending its position (quoted from AEI 2013, translation IB). "In one way or another, its inhabitants must have benefited from the situation, otherwise they would not have stayed there to suffer without any reason," another employee concluded at the same conference (ibid.).

Between February and April 2013, the Rejected Refugees of Choucha organized sit-ins in front of the office of the EU Delegation and in front of European embassies in Tunis. They demanded them to "finish their job" and to "stand up to their responsibilities, not turning deaf ears to the situation" but allowing them admission into their countries.[33] Finally, they went to the Tunisian government to call for an end to the Local Integration Program (Choucha Solidarity Network 2013). None of the addressed actors felt responsible, only calling the police and sending protestors to jail.[34] Frustrated by the stalling tactics and the demoralizing and divisive politics of temporariness practiced by IOs, the EU, and its member states, the Rejected Refugees searched for new local and transnational alliances.

In 2013, the World Social Forum (WSF) took place in Tunisia for the first time. The Rejected Refugees of Choucha intended to use it as a broader platform for their demands, calling on Tunisian and foreign activists for support (Bartels 2013); however, on their way to the capital, their bus was stopped by the police and returned to the Choucha camp. Official support from the organizing committee of the WSF was missing. Despite these setbacks, a few activists from Choucha made it to the Forum individually by public transportation. Their presence and the banners of their demands at the gates, at numerous workshops, and at demonstrations during the five days of the Forum made their struggles one of the most visible and debated issues of the WSF 2013. As a result, Tunisian associations and transnational networks put the rights of the refugees from the Choucha camp high on their agenda (ibid. 2014); they organized conferences and published press releases to draw attention to the obligations of the Tunisian government, the UNHCR, and the European states that were involved in the war in Libya. While civil society organizations and networks from Europe collected funds and raised awareness about the situation in Choucha, the UNHCR used the growing activism as an excuse to retreat from its services and to deny responsibility.[35] The former organized press conferences, debates, film screenings, and demonstrations—not only in Tunisia but also in many European cities. At these events, an image was promoted that did not present the Rejected Refugees as victims or as objects of humanitarian aid, but as actors of resistance who were articulating their demands for political and social rights. While this transnational solidarity did not resolve the desperate situation in southern Tunisia, it enhanced their social and economic capital and encouraged them to continue their struggle.

Since the WSF in 2013 was not able to achieve a successful result for the collective struggle of Choucha, those always persevering in the camp returned to Tunis for the next global meeting two years later. Equipped with the cultural capital of old and new banners, flyers, and slogans, Rejected Refugees' reestablished presence at the front gates as well as in the new Migration Space was even more noticeable than before. Disappointed by the previous meeting, they demanded that "this time, we need to bring our forces together to start fighting,"[36] and they complained that "we are not here for decoration only!" (observation at WSF, Tun. 2015). Frustrated with the persistent well-intentioned calls by foreign activists for financial and material donations, they stressed the need for "real solidarity" and joint political struggle beyond selective acts of charity. Displaying large banners decorating the crowded rooms of the El Manar University buildings, they stressed that all kind of support should be in service to their only aim: "resettlement to a safe third country with effective refugee/asylum protection" (ibid.). "Any further help (material, medical, basic needs) [would only] be an individual choice but not a long-term and effective political solution."[37] In this respect, the Rejected Refugees continued to question and reject humanitarian logic and to concentrate on political demands for a right to resettlement. In other words, they demanded to be treated by different rules.

Similarly, the demands written on large cardboard signs lining the road to the Libyan border explicitly rejected the cry for humanitarian aid: "No visits of the media and the Tunisian Red Crescent. [...] We do not forget our suffering without reinstallation" (quoted in Potot 2013). This clearly articulates their impression of being immobilized by the charity of IOs and the incomplete stories of impatient, sensationalist journalists as explaining why their political demands remain unheard. At a visible spot on the road, they reaffirmed their prominent slogan: "We demand the rights of all who fled the Libyan crisis in 2011. No one in the Choucha camp is illegal" (observation, Tun. 2015). Empowered and inspired by their exchanges with social movements from around the world, the remaining group of 60 men with diverse backgrounds and statuses stressed their independence—not just from international politics but also from the expanding civil society sector in post-revolution Tunisia that was increasingly funded by European states and foundations. They were very explicit that they did not want to be another of the quickly growing "associative things" (as a Tunisian activist called the numerous NGOs popping up everywhere in Tunisia after 2011) that made protest movements addressable and fundable for international donors but also precluded fundamental criticism and political demands, thereby disempowering ongoing struggles.

It is remarkable how, throughout these struggles of Choucha, the IOM managed to stay out of the main line of protest and criticism. While the organization had publicly prided itself on its humanitarian crisis management in 2011, it was quick to deny any responsibility for the increasingly precarious situation of those remaining in Choucha once critical voices and open protest gained ground. The IOM argued that it cannot do more than offer its voluntary and supposedly apolitical return service to those rejected by the UNHCR, since the ultimate responsibility and authority for decisions about asylum and resettlement was left to the UNHCR and to potential countries of resettlement. While in practice the IOM was in charge of the screening procedures that were decisive in categorizing people into the groups of concern of the different IOs, the UNHCR and European states were perceived as the main responsible actors for guaranteeing protection and resettlement to those who had escaped the Libyan war. As a result, the IOM remained in good standing among donors and humanitarian actors alike, even while Tunisian activists and transnational groups supporting the Rejected Refugees denounced the AVRR program as a pseudo-voluntary instrument of the externalized European border regime.

4.3 The humanitarian politics of return: revisiting strategies, struggles, and stakes in the field of international migration management

> The IOM became the primary institution to deal with Sub-Saharan migrants in Morocco; to give answers to the influx of Sub-Saharan migrants. IOM began to establish techniques which did not exist before.
> (Interview with repr. of AECID, Mor. 2014)

These new "techniques" of managing migration through voluntary return were introduced in reaction to struggles of migration in Morocco in 2005. The AVRR program promises to effectively manage migration—not only in terms of saving costs, having a sustainable impact, and presenting measurable numbers but also in ways that attract less criticism and public attention. Instead of forcing migrants to return by repressive means, it offers incentives for them to actively participate in creating what are presumed to be orderly processes of migration. The program promotes a seemingly voluntary decision for personal protection, economic empowerment, and a dignified life in their country of origin. In this way, the IOM presents its services as mutually beneficial for states (origin, transit, and destination) and migrants alike.

In practice, however, migrants' wish to return is often only evoked by their precarious and desperate situations in transit, due to the militarization of European borders and the conjunctures of state repression in the North African borderlands. Analyzing the perspectives of different actors

172 *Voluntary return programs*

in the field and the sense they make of the AVRR program, this chapter has demonstrated how the program's implementation was largely driven by competition among IOs over funding, reputation, and relations, as well as by the need to satisfy their donors' priorities rather than to meet the needs of migrants in transit. However, it also became clear that the IOM depends on cooperation with Moroccan and Tunisian state authorities to effectively execute the program. Paying particular attention to the experiences and knowledge of migrants, this chapter has moreover highlighted how their struggles challenge, appropriate, and resonate with shifting techniques and (ir)rationalities of migration management.

While donor priorities significantly impact the practices, rules, and logic of the voluntary return business, they are neither static nor homogenous, nor are they the only issues negotiated during implementation. IOs improvise within these constraints and suggest new spheres of action by defining new target groups or intervention sites; Moroccan and Tunisian state actors participate with regard to their own strategies and stakes, such as the prospect of international reputation or funding; and migrants learn how to play by the rules of the game of international migration management in order to realize their returns. While it would be misleading to regard the implementation of voluntary return as a smooth process of externalizing European policies, it nevertheless happens in an asymmetrically structured field of power relations. The positions, the relations, and even the boundaries of this field are subject to constant negotiation, and actors have to be recognized by others in order to enter the field and participate in its struggles. International and state actors do not recognize migrants as equal actors but regard them as objects of their management, care, or control. However, especially the struggles of Choucha indicate how migrants organize to make themselves heard in the field and can challenge the discourses, rules, and assumptions.

In this respect, the IOM had to make itself known and gain the necessary capital to become recognized as a relevant actor in the field. The implementation of the AVRR program in Morocco shows how the organization experimented with its migration management tools in the context of transit: it involved constant repair work for the IOM. In Tunisia, the organization could take advantage of the symbolic capital it had accumulated through its work in Morocco. Its reputation as a reliable service provider and an international expert was pivotal to its quick acceptance. In the postrevolutionary situation in 2011, the program was introduced as part of a joint international intervention of humanitarian crisis management. The urgency and exceptionalism that this discourse implies symbolically produced a humanitarian emergency, which legitimated extraordinary measures by external actors. At the same time, the perception of Tunisia as the model country of democratic transition in a region of growing uncertainty made it impossible for the mission to fail. In this context, the stabilization of the Tunisian state and its future as a reliable partner in international migration politics were important stakes for European donors.

To achieve its mission, the IOM also depends on North African state authorities as well as migrants to believe and cooperate in this game. While donors define and sometimes change the rules, the IOM implements them vis-à-vis other actors—often without making them explicit. This symbolic violence of the IOM in introducing and spreading concepts, categories, and criteria of international migration management within transit countries remains widely unrecognized. In this way, the organization holds a powerful position that means it cannot be reduced to an instrument of European states, even though the organization depends on their funding.

Responding to a European demand for less brutal techniques of migration control within countries of transit and origin, the IOM increasingly promoted the AVRR program as a humanitarian alternative to repressive state politics. Codifying the program according to humanitarian logic helped the IOM gain symbolic capital and organize the participation of many actors in the trans-Mediterranean field of migration management, even beyond the urgency of the exceptional crisis management situation in 2011. However, its humanitarian pivot cannot fully be explained by the organization's ambition to fulfill external expectations: in my observations, it was also driven by a *practical sense* and a shared *illusio* of those working in the field that offering voluntary return to suffering migrants excluded at the external borders of the EU is the morally right thing to do.

> Inequality is replaced by exclusion, domination is transformed into misfortune, injustice is articulated as suffering, violence is expressed in terms of trauma....This novel account of the world has largely been taken for granted,

Fassin (2012, 6) concludes in the introduction to "Humanitarian Reason." Thus, the proliferation and institutionalization of humanitarianism in the field comes at a time when the meaning of humanitarianism itself has been significantly expanded and transformed. According to Michael Barnett (2005, 723),

> [h]umanitarian action was formerly recognized as a separate sphere of activity, defined by the impartial relief to victims of manmade and natural disasters; now the term, according to many, includes human rights, access to medicine, economic development, democracy promotion, and even building responsible states.

While the concept of humanitarianism still conveys a meaning of temporarily providing impartial, independent, and neutral relief to those in immediate harm—setting it explicitly in opposition to politics (ibid., 724; see also Agier 2011, 202)—recent academic discussions about its use in different fields of international politics have focused on its political entanglements and effects. In these discussions, border and migration scholars widely refer to Fassin's

(2007b, 151) analytics of a "humanitarian government," which he broadly defines as "the administration of human collectivities in the name of a higher moral principle which sees the preservation of life and the alleviation of suffering as the highest value of action." Referring to Fassin's (2007a) and Ticktin's (2014) work on the politics of humanitarianism, many scholars argue that by being recoded as humanitarian aid and moral sentiment for vulnerable victims, the European border regime is able to distract attention away from its cruel effects (e.g., Walters 2010; Kasparek 2015; Cuttitta 2017). Normalizing suffering and placating struggles, the border regime gains new legitimacy and is able to stabilize and expand, particularly in times of crises and emergencies.

In this way, the IOM actively contributes to the externalization of the "humanitarian border" (Walters 2010) to countries of transit and origin. Acting in the name of humanitarianism, the IOM's interventions gain new forms of authority and legitimacy (Scheel and Ratfisch 2014). Still, in line with shifts in international funding rationalities and donor expectations, the recodification of its program as humanitarian is not only motivated by strategic interests and situational cooperation but also fits its staff's self-understanding and identification as humanitarian aid workers. With a combination of institutional tactics and personal compassion, they focus their work on relieving migrants' suffering and misfortunes, rather than on the violence and injustice that such migrants face in transit. Instead of addressing and changing inequalities, exploitation, and discrimination, IOM staff perceive that the moral imperative to care and the responsibility to protect migrants from suffering provide a powerful, unquestioned *illusio* for their work. This moral justification of international interventions opens new sites of authority and action but also leads to political contradictions and (un)intended effects in the field (Fassin 2007b, 151). In what follows, I point out four effects of the IOM's humanitarian politics of return.

First, the AVRR program is implemented by humanitarian bureaucrats who are mobile, flexible, and very committed to hopping from one crisis to the next in order to alleviate migrants' suffering. Even though they often perform well-intended and compassionate work, IOM staff get tangled up in the inevitable contradictions of humanitarian work, actualizing postcolonial power relations between mostly Western and White subjects who rescue vulnerable 'victims' from the Global South (Cuttitta 2017). These asymmetrical relations between subject positions of victims and their saviors are reproduced through paternalistic care practices (Fassin 2012, 4). As subjects of "sympathy or pity," passive and "innocent victims" have become well-known figures represented throughout the IOM's publications (Ticktin 2014, 412). Consequently, the symbolic power of its discourses and its paternalistic care practices establish a powerful position for the organization and an asymmetrical relation between the IOM and migrants. In this way, they draw on and actualize colonial hierarchies in the field.

Second, with the introduction of humanitarian logic, the concept of vulnerability has become a powerful category for differentiating and governing migrants in transit. The concept produces new forms of differential inclusion and new hierarchies between migrants that sort and reorient their movements before they reach the external borders of the EU in terms of humanitarianism, rather than in terms of individual rights to asylum. By offering assistance to a deserving few and discharging responsibility for the undeserving rest, this sorting process breaks up and mollifies collective struggles of migration. Giving specific meaning and value to the vulnerable, the suffering, and its visible evidence, the IOM's humanitarian selection criteria make the AVRR program part of what Fassin (2007a) has called a "politics of life." The concept refers to those techniques of evaluating human life to determine who should be helped, saved, or protected—and who should not. It leads to new hierarchies in the legitimacy of claims to move and to stay; hierarchies that are connected to the values assigned to those who articulate them. Driven by the practical sense of humanitarian actors, the IOM staff seek to save migrants' lives without questioning the conditions that are responsible for their suffering; thus, the staff contribute to the stabilization of such conditions. It is their vocation and conviction to select and save those eligible for protection while mistrusting and rejecting any others. Acting in the name of humanitarianism, IOM staff become experts who "decide whose lives are grievable and whose suffering is recognizable" (Ticktin 2011, 411). Since the recruitment and selection procedures for the AVRR program often "incorporate personal testimony and eyewitness accounts from migrants" (Walters 2010, 152), migrants need the capacity to credibly perform their vulnerability as well as to appropriate and strategically employ this factor to benefit from services (Fassin 2007a, 515ff). According to William Walters (2010, 150), the focus on the production of biopolitical knowledge concerning migration "problematizes the border as a site of suffering, violence and death, and not a political zone of injustice and oppression."

Third, the IOM's humanitarian work is promoted as cost-effective and efficient and is thus part of an expanding neoliberal aid economy (Barnett 2005, 730). To implement AVRR, the IOM needs to constantly compete with other actors in the field over funding for its project. Therefore, the organization needs to prove the efficiency and sustainability of its projects, which is preferably done by presenting measurable results. The IOM profits from the desperate situation of migrants at the external borders of the EU, which itself fosters their individual desire to return. Different forms of state repression and removal create their precarious situation and maintain demand for the IOM's assistance. In this respect, practices of forced deportation and voluntary return often work hand in hand to enhance migrants' returnabilty; together, they seek to remove the unwanted presence of migrants from transit countries while international protection is offered to a select few. Thus, the success of the IOM's mission in North Africa is conditioned and directly rewarded by some of the violent practices of the border regime, neutralizing and normalizing the brutal effects of the latter.

Fourth and finally, the IOM's symbolic power of categorization and care is misrecognized by many actors who participate in implementing AVRR for their own reasons and due to their own beliefs. Encouraging participation by North African state actors who seek to benefit from international cooperation, the program made it possible to expand humanitarian standards and procedures of international migration management to Morocco and Tunisia. Spread by IOM projects, these standards and procedures are easier for the governments to accept than direct European interventions, which more openly display the colonial continuities of such interactions. The IOM, along with its implementing partners and donors, widely perceive and evaluate humanitarian logic as apolitical, neutral, and selfless (Barnett 2005; Fassin 2007a). However, they do not consider or question the social and political conditions that put migrants in vulnerable situations without alternatives (Walters 2010): for them, it is not a result of international politics but is represented as the migrants' fate or even the migrants' own fault. Moreover, the power to decide who is worthy of help and according to which criteria has remained largely opaque and absent from public debates (Fassin 2007b). In this sense, while humanitarian practices of voluntary return provide a less brutal alternative to forced deportations, they are part of the same border regime that aims to control undesired, unproductive movements of migration from the Global South. They are thus "palliative" (Barnett 2005, 733) and "restorative" (Ticktin 2011, 20), upholding the global inequality in mobility rights.

While the humanitarian logic has helped to regain (at least the impression of) control over unauthorized movements of migration and thus stabilization of the Europe border regime in times of crisis, this control remains fragile and contested. Notably, the Moroccan case demonstrates how migrants develop their own knowledge and strategies to take advantage of the IOM's services for their own projects, needs, and dreams of migration. Additionally, the struggles of Choucha was a moment in which migrants collectively rejected the categorization and charity of IOs. Thus, the total control of migration remains an unattainable *illusio*, and its management persists as a project under permanent (re)construction. Despite the symbolic power of humanitarianism to give new meanings to international interventions, humanitarian practices of care do not smoothly legitimize repressive practices of control. From a relational perspective, struggles of migration are not external to humanitarian government but an integral part of it— challenging, co-opting, and actualizing the practices of migration management, thereby leading to its redefinition and further development. In sum, this chapter has shown how in the trans-Mediterranean field of migration management, restrictive, security-oriented logics are combined with neoliberal rationalities—which manifest most notably in the marketization of migration control services; in the governing of migration through offers, incentives, and skills training that assume the responsibility of the individuals to cooperate in their own management; and in the high flexibility, mobility, and responsibility of IO staff. The IOM's work in Tunisia has further demonstrated how the IOM put forth a humanitarian logic that turned migration management into an unquestioned moral responsibility to protect (certain) migrants in transit. Through the flexible (re)combination and distinction of these three logics, the IOM's practices of voluntary return have helped the European border regime reinvent and even expand itself in times of fading legitimization of existing control practices; and the organization to establish itself in a powerful, influential position in the field.

Notes

1 For a critical discussion of the term, see Dünnwald (2010) and Webber (2011). In questioning the voluntary nature of such programs and to point out their connection with other forms of return, the European Council on Refugees and Exiles (2003) uses the term "ordered return," Anne Koch (2014) proposes speaking of "state-induced return," and Stephan Dünnwald (2013) distinguishes between forms of "simple," "voluntary," and "forced" returns. In this chapter, I examine state-enforced deportations and the IOM's program of voluntary return as different repatriation practices that are mutually dependent and that interact in one transnational return regime. I view the discursive emphasis on the voluntary character of the AVRR as part of the return policy to be analyzed. Therefore, the extent to which the program is considered voluntary by migrants themselves is not determined a priori but is the subject of my analysis.
2 All countries and nationalities have been changed.
3 One of the widespread myths about the AVRR is that the IOM does not give out cash but provides material assistance for reintegration projects. However, its handbook qualifies that "in rural areas, receipts and documentation usually necessary to record budget expense are not readily available. In such cases, the only option available may be to provide cash support upon return" (IOM 2013e, 51).
4 At the same time, the IOM was involved in the AVRR of Moroccans returning mostly from European countries.
5 Civil society actors refer to lower numbers: the transnational NGO Doctors without Borders (Médecins Sans Frontières, MSF), for example, speaks of 500–1,000 irregularized migrants in Oujda and about 500–1,000 in Nador (quoted in HRW 2013, 3).
6 The only alternative was to return spontaneously (GADEM 2013); however, this option was almost impossible for migrants without documents, since an authorization from the police to leave the country was required in order to quit the country by legal means. This administrative encounter required a migrant to present a valid passport. Moreover, even those who had managed to go through the bureaucratic procedures were sometimes blocked between the Moroccan and Mauritanian border, where Mauritanian authorities demanded visas for third-country nationals to pass the territory.
7 See the article "Maroc: 35 subsahariens ont bénéficié du programme de retour volontaire en 2 mois." November 8th, 2011. https://www.yabiladi.com/articles/details/20785/maroc-subsahariens-beneficie-programme-retour.html [04.08.2020].
8 During my visit to Morocco in September 2013, various interview partners expressed their surprise about the king's announcement. While most of them welcomed the new policy, they were skeptical about its implementation. Their explanations included pressure from civil society actors for more humane immigration and asylum politics, the king's ambitions to position Morocco as a leader

178 *Voluntary return programs*

       on the African continent, and European pressure to cooperate in migration issues in exchange for (financial) aid in other policy areas.
9 See the IOM's website: www.migration-crisis.com/libya/ that was last accessed on December 15th, 2013 but is no longer online.
10 This contrasts with the Moroccan context, where migrants were primarily presented as entrepreneurial agents of their own return projects and their communities' development.
11 "Pending the creation of a national asylum system, the UNHCR is the sole entity conducting refugee status determination in Tunisia. A main focus of UNHCR's protection work is to ensure that persons of concern are registered with UNHCR, and issued with UNHCR certificates to protect them against arbitrary arrest, detention or expulsion. So far, UNHCR registered 444 persons. UNHCR's overall objective in the country is to support the creation of a comprehensive national protection system, most notably by commenting on the draft asylum law shared by the Ministry of Justice, organizing targeted seminars and offering refugee law training opportunities to relevant officials" (UNHCR 2014).
12 Quoted from the website of the Danish Refugee Council: https://drc.ngo/where-we-work/middle-east-and-north-africa/tunisia [06.08.2020].
13 For Angelina Jolie's visit to the camps, see the UNHCR's website: "More aid for Libya, Côte d'Ivoire exodus, urges Angelina Jolie." April 5th, 2011. http://www.unhcr.org/news/latest/2011/4/4d9b3a0e6/aid-libya-cote-divoire-exodus-urges-angelina-jolie.html [06.08.2020].
14 See the article on http://www.tunivisions.net/39085/223/149/une-commission-interministerielle-tunisienne-rend-visite-aux-residents-du-camp-de-choucha.html that was last accessed on October 10th, 2013 but is no longer online.
15 For the visit of Antonio Gueterres, UNHCR's then-High Commissioner, see the UNHCR's website: "UNHCR chief returns to Tunisia to meet refugees from Libya." June 17th, 2011. http://www.unhcr.org/news/latest/2011/6/4dfb43b09/unhcr-chief-returns-tunisia-meet-refugees-libya.html [06.08.2020].
16 Originally quoted from the website of the International Red Croix/Red Crescent: "Chronology of a new transit camp on the Tunisian border." 2011. https://reliefweb.int/report/libya/chronology-new-transit-camp-tunisian-border [06.08.2020].
17 Those who participated in the Local Integration Program, which was cofinanced by European countries, were offered 90 dinars (about 45 euros) to rent a house somewhere nearby in Ben Guerdane (Tringham 2013). Due to this impossible task and the racial discrimination experienced while trying to do so, more than 50% refused to participate in the program (see the article "Choucha Refugee Camp to Close, Leaving Hundreds of Residents in Limbo." June 28th, 2013. https://familienundfreundinnengegenabschiebung.wordpress.com/2013/07/05/choucha-refugee-camp-to-close-leaving-hundreds-of-residents-in-limbo/ [06.08.2020]).
18 See the article in Courrier de l'Atlas "Tunisie. Fermer le camp de Choucha et après?" October 8th, 2014.
19 See the blog entry on April 23rd, 2014, on voiceofchoucha: https://voiceofchoucha.wordpress.com/2014/04/23/arrest-of-rejected-asylum-seekers-during-protest-in-front-of-the-e-u-delegation-building/ [06.08.2020].
20 See further information in FN 11.
21 Quoted from report "Choucha, that space still exists." August 22nd, 2014. FFM – Forschungsgesellschaft Flucht & Migration e.V. http://ffm-online.org/2014/08/22/tunesien-fluechtlingslager-choucha-aktuelle-reportage/ [30.01.2018].
22 See the open letter by Choucha refugees, July 28th, 2014. FFM – Forschungsgesellschaft Flucht & Migration e.V. http://ffm-online.org/2014/07/28/choucha-offener-brief-fluechtlinge-tunesien/ [30.01.2018].

23 Quoted from report "Choucha, that space still exists." August 22nd, 2014. FFM – Forschungsgesellschaft Flucht & Migration e.V. http://ffm online.org/2014/08/22/tunesien-fluechtlingslager-choucha-aktuelle-reportage/ [30.01.2018].
24 See the blog: http://closethecamps.org/ [06.08.2020].
25 Compared to the significant number of 116,000 migrants who (according to the IOM 2015) benefited from the AVRR program in Tunisia in 2011, the official numbers published by the Swiss Embassy are extremely low: only 311 people had effectively been returned with this initiative by the IOM by the end of 2013. Nineteen of them were rejected asylum seekers from Choucha; otherwise, the program had 37 rejected asylum seekers from Tunis, 123 migrants rescued at sea in 2013, and 132 stranded migrants picked up elsewhere in Tunisia (Ambassade de Suisse en Tunisie 2015).
26 Even though no official agreement with the Tunisian government mandates the agency to do so, in practice, Frontex sometimes hands rescued migrants over to the Tunisian navy at sea (Bundestagsdrucksache 2011).
27 Quoted from article on the FFM website, March 19th, 2014. http://ffm-online.org/2014/03/19/tunis-choucha-protest-vor-eu-delegation/ [30.01.2018].
28 See the blog of Choucha refugees: http://voiceofchoucha.wordpress.com/ [06.08.2020].
29 See the open letter by Choucha refugees (FN 24).
30 Quoted from article on the FFM website, emphasis IB (FN 30).
31 Quoted from *Boza*, a film by Walid Fellah, emphasis IB.
32 See the article in Jungle World, April 14th, 2013.
33 Quoted from "Protest declaration." February 2nd, 2013. http://voiceofchoucha.wordpress.com/ [06.08.2020].
34 See Communique de presse "La prison ou l'expulsion pour les réfugiés de Choucha?" February 9th, 2014. http://ffm-online.org/2014/02/09/tunis-20-protestierende-choucha-fluechtlinge-vor-eu-delegation-verhaftet/#more-18439 [30.01.2018].
35 Regional Public Information Officer for the UNHCR in Tunisia, quoted in "Choucha Refugee Camp to Close, Leaving Hundreds of Residents in Limbo." June 28th, 2013. https://familienundfreundinnengegenabschiebung.wordpress.com/2013/07/05/choucha-refugee-camp-to-close-leaving-hundreds-of-residents-in-limbo/ [06.08.2020].
36 Quoted from "Declaration of the Choucha Refugees from the 2015 World Social Forum." April 9th, 2015. https://voiceofchoucha.wordpress.com/2015/04/09/declaration-of-the-choucha-refugees-from-the-2015-world-social-forum/ [06.08.2020].
37 Quoted from "June 15 # Choucha Refugees Debate/Statement for the Discussion@ FTDES." June 18th, 2015. https://voiceofchoucha.wordpress.com/2015/06/18/june-15-%e2%80%aa%e2%80%8echoucha-refugees-debatestatement-for-the-discussionftdes/ [06.08.2020].

Literature cited

AEI (Afrique-Europe-Interact). 2013. "Vergessen in der tunesischen Wüste? Solidarität mit allen Flüchtlingen aus dem Lager Choucha und dem Hungerstreik vor dem UNHCR in Tunis!" April 9th, 2013. Press Release. AEI.

Agier, Michel. 2011. *Managing the Undesirables. Refugee Camps and Humanitarian Government*. Cambridge: Wiley.

Al-Jamai, M. 2013. "A Refuge No More. Camp Choucha Officially Closed on June 30 but Some Refugees Are Refusing to Go." July 1st, 2013. http://www.correspondents.org/node/2946 [15.12.2013].

Ambassade de Suisse en Tunisie. 2015. *Domaine III: Migration et Protection. Fiches de Projets*. Tunis: Ambassade de Suisse en Tunisie, Division Coopération Internationale.

Ambroso, Guido. 2012. "Bordering on a Crisis." *Forced Migration Review* 39: 6–7.

Andersson, Ruben. 2014. *Illegality, Inc. Clandestine Migration and the Business of Bordering Europe*. Oakland: University of California Press. doi:10.1525/9780520958289.

Article 13. 2013. "Rapport de la situation des réfugiés du camp de Choucha: Visite du 13 au 15 julliet 2013." July 31st, 2013. http://blechvisa.blogspot.de/ [06.08.2020].

Barnett, Michael. 2005. "Humanitarianism Transformed." *Perspectives on Politics* 3 (4): 723–740. doi:10.1017/S1537592705050401.

Bartels, Inken. 2013. "We Are the Youth In-between Two Periods." Young Tunisian Activists' Perspectives on the WSF 2013. Berlin: Mittelmeer Institut Berlin. https://www.sowi.hu-berlin.de/de/forschung/forschungsschwerpunkte/mib/worldsocial-forum-2013 [06.08.2020].

Bartels, Inken. 2014. "Die Neuordnung der tunesischen Migrationspolitik nach dem 'Arabischen Frühling.'" *Berliner Debatte Initial* 25 (4): 48–64.

Bartels, Inken. 2017. "'We Must Do It Gently.' The Contested Implementation of the IOM's Migration Management in Morocco." *Migration Studies* 5 (3): 315–336. doi:10.1093/migration/mnx054.

Bartels, Inken. 2019. "'Rückführbarkeit fördern.' Das Zusammenwirken von freiwilliger Rückkehr und Abschiebungen in Nordafrika." *Peripherie* 39 (156): 343–368. doi:10.3224/peripherie.v39i3.02.

Berriane, Mohammed, Hein de Haas, and Katharina Natter. 2016. *Revisiting Moroccan Migrations*. Milton Park and New York: Routledge. doi:10.4324/9781315619897.

Boubakri, Hassan. 2013. *Revolution and International Migration in Tunisia. 2013/04*. MPC Research Report. Florence: EUI.

Bourdieu, Pierre, and Loïc Wacquant. 1992. *An Invitation to Reflexive Sociology*. Chicago, IL: University of Chicago Press.

Bundestagsdrucksache. 2011. *Situation der Sub-Saharischen Flüchtlinge in Libyen und Tunesien*. 17/7270. Berlin: Deutscher Bundestag.

Caillault, Clotilde. 2012. "The Implementation of Coherent Migration Management through IOM Programs in Morocco." *IMIS-Beiträge* 40: 133–156.

CeTuMa (Centre de Tunis pour la Migration et l'Asile). 2013. *Special Feature: Report on the Rejected Asylum Seekers of Choucha Refugee Camp*. Tunis: CeTuMa.

Chennaoui, Henda. 2014. "Reportage: Tunisie–Libye, aux frontières de la guerre at de l'oubli." August 19th, 2014. http://nawaat.org/portail/2014/08/19/reportage-tunisie-libye-aux-frontieres-de-la-guerre-et-de-loubli/ [06.08.2020].

Choucha Delegation. 2014. "Report Choucha Delegation vom 18. Januar bis zum 26. Januar 2014." Borderline Europe. http://www.borderline-europe.de/sites/default/files/features/Report_Deutsch_Endversion-3.pdf [30.01.2018].

Choucha Solidarity Network. 2013. "Protest für Flüchtlingsrechte vor der EU-Delegation in Tunis, Tunesien." April 23rd, 2013. Press Release. chouchaprotest.noblogs.org [06.08.2020].

Crépeau, François. 2012. *Le Rapporteur Spécial des Nations Unies pour les Droits de l'Homme des Migrants conclut sa première Visite de Pays dans son Étude régionale des Droits de l'Homme des Migrants aux Frontières de l'Union Européenne: Visite en Tunisie*. Geneva: Office of the High Commissioner for Human Rights.

Cuttitta, Paolo. 2017. "Zwischen De- und Repolitisierung. Nichtstaatliche Search and Rescue-Akteure an der EU Mittelmeergrenze." In *Der lange Sommer der Migration. Grenzregime III*, edited by Sabine Hess, Bernd Kasparek, Stefanie Kron, Mathias Rodatz, Maria Schwertl, and Simon Sontowski, 115–125. Berlin and Hamburg: Assoziation A.

Debbarh, Jaafar. 2014. "The New Immigration and Asylum Policy for the Kingdom of Morocco." Presented at UNFPA Workshop La CIPD+20 et l'agenda de développement post-2015, Rabat.

De Genova, Nicholas. 2002. "Migrant 'Illegality' and Deportability in Every-Day Life." *Annual Review of Anthropology* 31 (1): 419–447. doi:10.1146/annurev. anthro.31.040402.085432.

Dünnwald, Stephan. 2010. "Politiken der 'freiwilligen' Rückkehr." In *Grenzregime. Diskurse, Praktiken, Institutionen in Europa*, edited by Sabine Hess and Bernd Kasparek, 179–200. Berlin and Hamburg: Assoziation A.

Dünnwald, Stephan. 2013. "Voluntary Return." In *Disciplining the Transnational Mobility of People*, edited by Martin Geiger and Antoine Pécoud, 228–249. Basingstoke: Palgrave Macmillan. doi:10.1057/9781137263070_12.

Eckert, Julia M. 2020. "The Office: Ethos and Ethics in Migration Bureaucracies." In *The Bureaucratic Production of Difference*, edited by Julia M. Eckert, 7–26. Bielefeld: transcript. doi:10.14361/9783839451045-001.

ECRE (European Council on Refugees and Exiles). 2003. Position on Return. PO1/10/2003/Ext/MP. ECRE. https://www.unhcr.org/4d948adf9.pdf [06.08.2020].

Fassin, Didier. 2007a. "Humanitarianism as a Politics of Life." *Public Culture* 19 (3): 499–520. doi:10.1215/08992363-2007-007.

Fassin, Didier. 2007b. "Humanitarianism, a Non-Governmental Government." In *Nongovernmental Politics*, edited by Michel Feher, Gaëlle Krikorian, and Yates McKee, 149–159. New York: Zone Books.

Fassin, Didier. 2012. *Humanitarian Reason. A Moral History of the Present*. Berkeley and Los Angeles: University of California Press.

Fassin, Didier. 2016. "Vom Rechtsanspruch zum Gunsterweis. Zur moralischen Ökonomie der Asylvergabepraxis im heutigen Europa." *Mittelweg 36* 25 (1): 62–78.

GADEM (Groupe Antiraciste de Défense et d'Accompagnement des Étrangers et Migrants). 2013. *Report on Morocco's Implementation of the International Convention on the Protection of the Rights of all Migrant Workers and Members of their Families*. Rabat: GADEM.

Gammeltoft-Hansen, Thomas, and Ninna Nyberg-Sørensen. 2013. *The Migration Industry and the Commercialization of International Migration*. New York: Routledge. doi:10.4324/9780203082737.

Garelli, Glenda, Federica Sossi, and Martina Tazzioli. 2015. "Migrants in Tunisia: Detained and Deported." Storiemigranti. http://www.storiemigranti.org/spip.php?article1080 [06.08.2020].

GDP (Global Detention Project). 2015. *The Detention of Asylum Seekers in the Mediterranean Region*. Geneva: GDP.

Guguen, Guillaume, and Imed Bensaied. 2014. "Stranded in Tunisia, the Forgotten Refugees of Libya's 2011 Conflict." August 5th, 2014. France 24. http://www.france24.com/en/20140804-stranded-tunisia-forgotten-refugees-libya-2011-conflict [06.08.2020].

Hilhorst, Dorothea. 2013. "Disaster, Conflict and Society in Crises: Everyday Politics of Crisis Response." In *Disaster, Conflict and Society in Crises. Everyday Politics of Crisis Response*, edited by Dorothea Hilhorst, 1–15. London and New York: Routledge. doi:10.4324/9780203082461.

HRW (Human Rights Watch). 2013. Abused and Expelled. Ill-Treatment of Sub-Saharan African Migrants in Morocco. HRW. https://www.hrw.org/report/2014/02/10/abused-and-expelled/ill-treatment-sub-saharan-african-migrants-morocco [06.08.2020].

Hyndman, Jennifer. 2000. *Managing Displacement. Refugees and the Politics of Humanitarianism*. Minneapolis: University of Minnesota Press.

IOM. 2010. *Programme de Retour Volontaire Assisté de Migrants en Situation irrégulière au Maroc et de Réinsertion dans leur Pays d'Origine (AVRR)*. Rabat: IOM.

IOM. 2011a. *Humanitarian Response to the Crisis in Libya*. February to December 2011. December 2011. Geneva: IOM.

IOM. 2011b. *Humanitarian Evacuation on the Libyan Border. Three Monthly Report on IOM's Response*. March 2011. Geneva: IOM.

IOM. 2011c. *Humanitarian Emergency Response to the Libyan Crisis. Seven-Month Report on IOM's Response*. September 2011. Geneva: IOM.

IOM. 2011d. *Newsletter Juillet 2011*. Tunis: IOM.

IOM. 2012a. *Une Commission interministérielle Tunisienne rend Visite aux Résidents du Camp de Choucha*. Geneva: IOM.

IOM. 2012b. *Camp de Transit de Choucha: Plus de 2 600 Réfugiés réinstallés dans un Pays tiers*. Geneva: IOM.

IOM. 2013. *Assisted Voluntary Return and Reintegration Handbook for the North African Region*. Geneva: IOM.

IOM. 2015. *Migration in Egypt, Morocco and Tunisia. Overview of the Complex Migratory Flows in the Region*. Cairo: IOM MENA Regional Office.

IOM. 2016. *AVRR Depuis Le Maroc: Aide Au Retour Volontaire et à la Réintégration*. Rabat: IOM Morocco.

Kasparek, Bernd. 2015. "Was war Mare Nostrum? Dokumentation einer Debatte um die italienische Marineoperation." *Movements. Journal for Critical Migration and Border Regime Studies* 1 (1). https://movements-journal.org/issues/01.grenzregime/11.kasparek--mare-nostrum-debatte.pdf [06.08.2020].

Koch, Anne. 2014. "The Politics and Discourse of Migrant Return: The Role of UNHCR and IOM in the Governance of Return." *Journal of Ethnic and Migration Studies* 40 (6): 905–923. doi:10.1080/1369183X.2013.855073.

Korneev, Oleg. 2014. "Exchanging Knowledge, Enhancing Capacities, Developing Mechanisms: IOM's Role in the Implementation of the EU–Russia Readmission Agreement." *Journal of Ethnic and Migration Studies* 40 (6): 888–904. doi:10.1080/1369183X.2013.855072.

Lavenex, Sandra. 2007. "The External Face of Europeanization: Third Countries and International Organizations." In *The Europeanization of National Policies and Politics of Immigration: Between Autonomy and the European Union*, edited by Thomas Faist and Andreas Ette, 246–264. Basingstoke: Palgrave Macmillan. doi:10.1057/9780230800717_12.

Ledrisi. Lamia. 2015. "Tunisia, the Humanitarian Emergency of the Choucha Refugee Camp." June 18th, 2015. Forschungsstelle Flucht und Migration (FFM). https://ffm-online.org/2015/06/18/tunesien-choucha-lager-uebersichtsartikel/ [30.01.2018].

Loher, David. 2020. "Governing the Boundaries of the Commonwealth: The Case of So-Called Assisted Voluntary Return Migration." In *The Bureaucratic Production of Difference. Ethos and Ethics in Migration Administrations*, edited by Julia M. Eckert, 113–134. Bielefeld: transcript. doi:10.14361/9783839451045-005.

Maâ, Anissa. 2019. "Signer la déportation. Agencéité migrante et retours volontaires depuis le Maroc." Terrain. Anthropologie & sciences humaines (Novembre). http://journals.openedition.org/terrain/18653 [06.08.2020]. doi:10.4000/terrain.18653.

Massy, Perrine. 2014. "Le ministère de la Défense tunisien confirme l'évacuation imminente de 114 réfugiés du camp de Choucha." October 14th, 2014. http://www.webdo.tn/2014/10/14/ministere-defense-evacuation-choucha-refugies/ [06.08.2020].

Mau, Steffen. 2017. *Das metrische Wir. Über die Quantifizierung des Sozialen*. Berlin: Suhrkamp.

Mezzadra, Sandro, and Brett Neilson. 2013. *Border as Method, or, the Multiplication of Labor*. Durham, NC and London: Duke University Press. doi:10.1215/9780822377542.

MIINDS. 2008. Fonds Européens pour le Retour. Programme Pluriannuel 2008–13. Annexe 1. Ministère de l'Immigration. https://www.immigration.interieur.gouv.fr/Info-ressources/Fonds-europeens/Le-Fonds-europeen-pour-le-retour-FR/Textes-de-reference-FR [06.08.2020].

MSF. 2013. Violence, Vulnerability and Migration: Trapped at the Gates of Europe. MSF. https://www.doctorswithoutborders.org/sites/usa/files/Trapped_at_the_Gates_of_Europe.pdf [06.08.2020].

Neuhauser, Johanna, Sabine Hess, and Helen Schwenken. 2017. "Unter- oder überbelichtet: Die Kategorie Geschlecht in medialen und wissenschaftlichen Diskursen zu Flucht." In *Der lange Sommer der Migration. Grenzregime III*, edited by Sabine Hess, Bernd Kasparek, Stefanie Kron, Mathias Rodatz, Maria Schwertl, and Simon Sontowski, 176–195. Berlin and Hamburg: Assoziation A.

No Borders Morocco. 2015. "Update III on Detentions and Deportations of Sub-Saharan Migrants in Morocco." February 25th, 2015. https://beatingborders.wordpress.com/2015/02/23/update-iii-on-detentions-and-deportations-of-sub-saharan-migrants-in-morocco/ [30.01.2018].

Potot, Swanie. 2014. "Migrants de Choucha (Tunisie): Pris en étau entre désert et grande bleue. Témoignage." June 14th, 2014. https://blogs.mediapart.fr/swpotot/blog/270614/migrants-de-choucha-tunisie-pris-en-etau-entre-desert-et-grande-bleue-temoignage [06.08.2020].

Sayad, Abdelmalek. 2010. "Immigration and 'State Thought.'" In *Selected Studies in International Migration and Immigration Incorporation*, edited by Marco Martiniello and Jan Rath, 165–180. Amsterdam: Amsterdam University Press.

Scheel, Stephan, and Philipp Ratfisch. 2014. "Refugee Protection Meets Migration Management: UNHCR as a Global Police of Populations." *Journal of Ethnic and Migration Studies* 40 (6): 924–941. doi:10.1080/1369183X.2013.855074.

Sciortino, Giuseppe. 2004. "Between Phantoms and Necessary Evils. Some Critical Points in the Study of Irregular Migrations to Western Europe." *IMIS-Beiträge* 24: 17–43.

Statewatch. 2014. "Tunisian Authorities Undertake Border Control for Italy." August 12th, 2014. Statewatch. https://www.statewatch.org/news/2014/august/italy-tunisia-tunisian-authorities-undertake-border-control-for-italy/ [06.08.2020].

Tazzioli, Martina. 2014. "'People No of Our Concern.' Rejected Refugees in Tunisia." *Radical Philosophy* 184. https://www.radicalphilosophy.com/commentary/people-not-of-our-concern [06.08.2020].

Ticktin, Miriam. 2011. *Casualties of Care. Immigration and the Politics of Humanitarianism in France*. Berkeley and Los Angeles: University of California Press. doi:10.1525/9780520950535.

Ticktin, Miriam. 2014. "Humanitarianism as Planetary Politics." In *At the Limits of Justice. Women of Colour on Terror*, edited by Suvendrini Perera and Sherene Razack, 406–422. Toronto: University of Toronto Press. doi:10.3138/9781442616455-025.

Tringham, Oliver. 2013. Stuck at Choucha. Rights in Exile. Fahamu Refugee Legal Aid Newsletter. https://rightsinexile.tumblr.com/post/51870473319/stuck-at-choucha [06.08.2020].

UNHCR. 1997. Memorandum of Understanding between the United Nations High Commissioner for Refugees and the International Organization for Migration. UNHCR. https://www.unhcr.org/4aa7a3ed9.pdf [06.08.2020].

UNHCR. 2013. "Aperçu opérationnel sous régional 2013 – Afrique du Nord." UNHCR. http://www.unhcr.fr/cgi-bin/texis/vtx/page?page=4aae621d58f&submit=GO [06.08.2020].

UNHCR. 2014. *Factsheet UNHCR Tunisia*. September 2014. Tunis: UNHCR.

Valluy, Jerome. 2007. Contribution à une Sociologie Politique du HCR: Le Cas des Politiques Européennes et du HCR au Maroc. Collection 'Etudes.' Recueil Alexandries. http://www.reseau-terra.eu/article571.html [06.08.2020].

Wacquant, Loïc. 2009. *Punishing the Poor: The Neoliberal Government of Social Insecurity*. Durham, NC: Duke University Press. doi:10.2307/j.ctv11smrv3.

Walters, William. 2010. "Foucault and Frontiers: Notes on the Birth of the Humanitarian Border." In *Governmentality: Current Issues and Future Challenges*, edited by Ulrich Bröckling, Susanne Krasmann, and Thomas Lemke, 138–164. London: Routledge.

Webber, Frances. 2011. "How Voluntary Are Voluntary Returns?" *Race & Class* 52 (4): 98–107. doi:10.1177/0306396810396606.

5 Anti-trafficking politics

Migration management as a struggle for hard facts and soft influence

"To integrate the question of migration into the national dynamics of each country," answered the International Organization for Migration (IOM) staff member, summarizing the long-term objective of its work in North Africa (interview with IOM staff, Tun. 2015). She insisted, however, that it is not "just copy and paste" (ibid.); instead, the IOM would closely "observe the things" and if "there are certain questions where we think that it would be good to work together," the IOM would offer its expertise (ibid.). "If there is a need for assistance, we look how we can support the needs. We listen," she explained, indicating the organization's seemingly disinterested services. Through these symbolic forms of influence, the IOM introduces, spreads, and implements international norms, global concepts, and standardized procedures of migration management in contexts in which state actors have not been interested in governing human trafficking for a long time. The organization presents its services as objective and apolitical expertise for Moroccan and Tunisian actors that is not imposed by force but rather offered to partners.

In times of political transition, the organization extended its work beyond assistance to immigrants and potential migrants (see Chapters 3 and 4) and became increasingly involved in direct government consultation and the elaboration of laws and policies. In terms of content, the IOM expanded its portfolio of interventions by engaging in the politics of anti-trafficking. By informing, recommending, setting agendas, and building capacities in this field, the IOM influences national migration politics through a *symbolic power* that goes largely unrecognized. Reorienting its mandate and sphere of action helped the organization foster its position in the *trans-Mediterranean field of migration management* and (re)ensure the need of its services.

The case of anti-trafficking enables reconstruction of the IOM's mainstreaming of a global phenomenon into the scientific debates, political discourses, and institutional-legal structures of countries in the Global South. The concept of anti-trafficking emerged in public and political debates in the beginning of the 1990s. For many years of campaigning, feminist and human rights groups had struggled for the political recognition of the issue as an international problem (Sullivan 2010). They promoted an understanding of sex

DOI: 10.4324/9781003204169-6

trafficking as a form of modern slavery. Especially in the United States (US), a "remarkable diverse group of social activists and policy makers," including abolitionists, feminists, evangelical Christians, and conservative and liberal government officials joined these struggles in the 1990s (Bernstein 2010, 45), demanding national legislation and international action. In post-Cold War Europe, political interest in the issue grew within a context of rising concerns about irregularized migration and transnationally organized crime that were expected to spread from Eastern Europe.

When the United Nations (UN) adopted an anti-trafficking protocol in 2000, it was celebrated as a sign of international acceptance and a breakthrough for the topic in international politics. The Protocol to Prevent, Suppress and Punish Trafficking of Persons, in particular Women and Children, which has become known as part of the Palermo Protocols, defines human trafficking as a process that occurs over time and that is organized for the purpose of exploitation.[1] Going beyond concerns about sex trafficking, the protocol deals with subjecting people to any kind of exploitation and is not limited to issues of prostitution (O'Connell Davidson 2016). It establishes the *trafficking of persons* as a distinct crime from the *smuggling of people*. Attached to the Convention against Transnational Organized Crime, the Palermo Protocols do not address human trafficking as a human rights issue but as a criminal justice issue (Kapur 2005).

"Unlike many UN declarations and agreements, the ones addressing trafficking and smuggling have been integrated into many national states' policies" (Sharma 2003, 58). The policies that have been "designed to prevent trafficking, prosecute traffickers, and protect victims" around the world no longer focus exclusively on sex trafficking (Sullivan 2010, 89). Still, special concern with the exploitation and protection of women and children persists. Within the expanding international policy discourses, human trafficking is predominantly framed as a problem of international criminal networks, illegal prostitution, and border security. These problems invoke the need for enhancing transnational prosecution, the protection of women, and more restrictive migration controls. Thus, by the end of the 20th century, anti-trafficking became a hot topic in international border and migration politics (Hess 2012, 131).

The IOM has participated in anti-trafficking politics since the mid-1990s. The organization quickly emerged as a major player in this field, actively shaping the perceptions, knowledge, and political strategies around human trafficking in many countries as an "extreme form of irregular migration and a severe violation of human rights" (Schatral 2011, 3). In accordance with the Palermo Protocols, the IOM developed a global strategy that makes anti-trafficking an essential part of migration management. The strategy combines the provision of direct assistance to Victims of Trafficking (VoTs) with capacity building for governments to motivate them to provide such assistance themselves; moreover, it involves training civil society and raising public awareness on the issue, and it aims to strengthen regional partnerships and international cooperation among diverse actors. Initially, the IOM's anti-trafficking campaigns focused on sex trafficking in and from Eastern Europe (Andrijasevic 2007). Subsequently, the IOM extended the gendered focus and geographical scale of its interventions (Schatral 2010). According to Eva Bahl, Marina Ginal, and Sabine Hess (2010, 168), the IOM's anti-trafficking campaigning has significantly contributed to the organization's prominent position in the field of international migration politics.

In North Africa, human trafficking became a relevant issue in the early 2000s, when the sealing of the European Union's (EU) external borders led to rising numbers of deaths in the Mediterranean Sea, since migrants had to take riskier routes to illicitly cross the sea. Confronted with increasing criticism concerning the deadly consequences of its fortification, the EU propagated a discourse that made the transnational business of smugglers and traffickers responsible for the increasing number of tragedies in the Mediterranean. Reproduced across a wide range of European politicians and journalists, this discourse directed attention away from the cruel effects of the militarization of European borders. The IOM actively promoted the dominant narrative of evil smugglers and cultivated a discursive link to the rising phenomenon of human trafficking. Moreover, the organization responded to European migration policies by offering to implement anti-trafficking projects in countries of transit and origin. Through its implementation of information campaigns and humanitarian assistance, the IOM has become recognized as a reliable partner for international cooperation and a credible and diplomatic actor in Morocco and Tunisia. Based on the *symbolic capital* that it has gained through this operational work, the IOM made its way into national fields of migration politics.

To the IOM, mainstreaming its anti-trafficking expertise into North African migration politics meant "not to see migration as a problem but to promote its management," as a staff member of the IOM explained their work in Tunisia in 2015. "And there is a support that we can offer" (ibid.). "We" refers to the IOM staff, which had steadily grown in number since the revolution in order to support the country in its transition toward a stable and reliable partner in international migration management. The staff member emphasized that it was "strategic" for the IOM to intervene in Tunisia under these conditions (ibid.).

Focusing on the case of anti-trafficking, this chapter analyzes the IOM's long-term, strategic engagement in North Africa. I examine practices of knowledge production and dissemination, capacity building, law, and policy-making to show how the IOM mainstreams its own vision of international migration management into politics and societies in moments of reconfiguration and change. I reconstruct how the IOM contributed to the understanding of human trafficking as a problem of transnationally organized crime that is linked to international migration. Moreover, the chapter demonstrates how the organization proposed solutions to manage this problem as per its own expertise and services. It reveals how the IOM mobilizes state actors to introduce new categories of protection for VoTs, along with criminal persecution for smuggling and trafficking. Focusing on the IOM's relation to state actors, the chapter points to contested processes of negotiation and institutionalization and discusses why these actors would participate in the IOM's 'fight against human trafficking.' Against this backdrop, I conclude that the IOM took on the position of a recognized expert for anti-trafficking and is able to influence *doxic beliefs* and to broaden the *boundaries* of the field for new issues, measures, and actors. As a result, the IOM's anti-trafficking projects contribute to making Morocco and Tunisia 'safe countries'—not only for refugees and transit migrants but also for VoTs—as well as to establishing a system of criminal justice that punishes all other forms of irregularized migration. In this way, the chapter shows how anti-trafficking politics in North Africa foster a restrictive but humanitarian border regime and strengthen the IOM's position in the field as a humanitarian actor and as a liberal advocate for women's rights.

5.1 Mainstreaming migration politics in times of transition

> All external programs of the EU in third countries have to be used in order to support police and custom institutions as well as coast guards in their fight against these phenomena [human trafficking and migrant smuggling] which are destabilizing these countries themselves.[2]

This statement by the German Interior Minister in 2014 indicates how anti-trafficking has become an integral part of the externalization of European border and migration policies. The IOM's global expansion of anti-trafficking campaigns resonated well with the objective of the EU and its member states, which aimed to integrate anti-trafficking measures into their cooperation with sending and transit countries. Since 2008, the IOM has profited from a new European funding scheme that was introduced under the Convention of the European Council for the Fight against Human Trafficking.[3] In line with European policy guidelines and funding opportunities, the IOM designs projects for North Africa, drawing on its experience in Eastern Europe (Andrijasevic 2007; Schatral 2010).

In 2008, Morocco was the first North African country that the IOM supported in national policy-making on anti-trafficking (IOM 2009, 12). At that time, the Moroccan government—notably the Department of Migration and Border Surveillance under the Ministry of Interior—was concentrating its efforts on establishing a National Strategy Against Smuggling of Human Beings, which had been initiated in the context of the increasing securitization of borders and the criminalization of migration in the early 2000s. The issue of human trafficking, in contrast, was only of marginal concern for Moroccan politicians; the IOM observed a general lack of public interest, specific policies, and national legislation in this field (ibid., 67). In the following years, the situation in Morocco changed: while the Moroccan government did not sign the Palermo Protocols until 2011, international debates and the European promotion of anti-trafficking left its mark on national politics. In this context, the Moroccan government initiated an "integrated and transversal strategy" to combat both the trafficking and the smuggling of human beings (ibid., 12). In Moroccan policies, the issue of human trafficking was closely connected to questions of migrant smuggling. Thus, from the beginning, anti-trafficking politics were understood and negotiated as a matter of border and migration control.

Tunisia had signed the Palermo Protocols in 2003; however, it only started implementation in 2009, through an ad hoc interdepartmental group that was headed by the Tunisian Ministry of Justice. Its mission was to draft a national law against trafficking in persons. At the same time, the Ministry of Interior also began to deal with the issue, focusing on the criminalization of human trafficking (IOM 2013a, 9). As in Morocco, Tunisian national laws on migration were passed under European pressure at the beginning of the century. These laws focused on the control and criminalization of the irregular entry, stay, and exit of people. The Tunisian government's concern with human trafficking was merely to signal to European states that it fulfilled international commitments by adopting law-and-order measures; practical procedures to identify victims were not implemented at that time.

Despite its rhetorical commitment to 'fight human trafficking,' the Tunisian state provided assistance to neither Tunisian nor foreign victims. For foreign victims, the only legal solution remained repatriation to their countries of origin, in which they often feared becoming revictimized as they would face continuous threats and retaliation. Moreover, hardly any civil society structures took care of victims at that time (ibid., 70). Prerevolutionary anti-trafficking politics in Tunisia focused only on the criminalization of transnationally organized trafficking and smuggling networks. "In recent years little has been done specifically against trafficking in Tunisia," pointed out the IOM in its pioneering study on the issue, published in 2013 (ibid., 24). At the same time, it praised Tunisia's great potential (ibid., 67). According to the IOM, actors from the growing independent civil society scene were increasingly interested in the issue but lacked profound knowledge.[4] With this diagnosis of a lack of know-how but a willingness to act among various actors, anti-trafficking became one of the organization's main fields of intervention in postrevolutionary Tunisia.

The following section shows how the IOM introduced anti-trafficking in North Africa as a distinct issue that was nevertheless closely related to the smuggling of migrants. This conceptual framing and institutional connection allowed the organization to incorporate anti-trafficking into its general mission of migration management and to position itself as an expert on the issue.

5.1.1 Producing knowledge on human trafficking

> Borders? No, not at all. They [IOM staff] do research at the level of trafficking, that yes! And that's why they sometimes go there and do investigations to see the networks of trafficking that are managed by the Sub-Saharans. But even then, normally, they try to identify the bad guys of the groups, the person who manages, who are the chiefs of the trafficking of human beings. But at the level of the border, in fact there, it is Europe.
> (Interview with repr. of AECID, Morocco 2014)

As a representative of the Spanish Development Cooperation in Morocco explained, the IOM's interventions did not take place at the external borders where European actors, such as Frontex, would intervene. Instead, the IOM's work is located at different semantic and cognitive sites of knowledge production and dissemination, such as information brochures, training manuals, and international conferences. The North African countries whose national fields of migration politics were under transition provided the IOM with favorable conditions to intervene as an expert and to introduce its predefined concepts and ready-made tools (see Bartels 2018).

Research is an integral part of the IOM's work (not only) in North Africa (IOM 2010; IOM and ADB 2012; Altai Consulting 2015; IOM 2015a). Producing knowledge about migration provides the basis for developing strategies to manage it. With its prominent publications, the organization dominates certain issues and frames their meaning. Such studies centralize and professionalize the data and views on a certain phenomenon in the hands of the IOM (Heller and Pécoud 2020). Through this "world-making," the IOM exercises a form of symbolic power (Bourdieu 1992, 150, original in English). Producing knowledge of human trafficking in North Africa, the IOM intervenes in the *symbolic struggles* over the enactment of a legitimate view on the mobility of people and over the reproduction of supposedly natural distinctions and hierarchies between different groups of people on the move.

The IOM's attempt to mainstream anti-trafficking into national migration policies depicts this *struggle for hard facts and soft influence*. In Morocco, the IOM started to intervene in this field with its publication of "Transnational Trafficking of Persons: State of the Art and Analysis of Responses in Morocco" in 2009 (IOM 2009, translation IB). This groundbreaking 100-page study contributed to establishing the existence of the phenomenon and its need to be governed by IOM project devices. The study played a decisive role in introducing international concepts and terminology to the Moroccan context, such as the distinction between *smuggling* and *trafficking* and the links between transnationally organized crime and international migration. With regard to the existing Moroccan National Strategy Against Smuggling of Human Beings, the authors complained that the term "smuggling of human beings" does not exist in the language of international relations, confusing the semantic system that relies on a clear distinction between the "smuggling of migrants" and the "trafficking of human beings" (ibid., 66, translation IB). They observed "much confusion between the notions of trafficking in persons and smuggling of migrants, even though they are different juridical categories which entail different levels of protection" (ibid., 10). As for the terms and standards that are used in international conventions and organizations, the study sought to theoretically disentangle the two phenomena while keeping them empirically linked. Working with the "fuzzy boundaries" of smuggling and trafficking (O'Connell Davidson 2016, 62), the IOM turned them into productive categories for its overall mission of migration management.

Since the two terms are not defined by specific law in Morocco, the IOM suggested basing political action on the definitions given by the two Additional Protocols of the UN Convention on Transnational Organized Crime: the Protocol to Prevent, Suppress and Punish Trafficking of Persons, in particular Women and Children, and the Protocol on the Smuggling of Migrants by Land, Sea and Air—better known as Palermo Protocols. They define human trafficking as

> the recruitment, transportation, transfer, harboring or receipt of persons by means of threats or use of force or other forms of coercion, abduction, fraud, deception, abuse of power or of a position of vulnerability or the giving or receiving of payments or benefits to achieve the consent of a person having control over another person, for the purpose of exploitation. Exploitation shall include, at a minimum, the exploitation of the prostitution of others or other forms of sexual exploitation, forced labor or services, slavery or practices similar to slavery, servitude or the removal of organs.
> (UN 2000, 32)

According to this definition, trafficking in persons includes at least three components: the act(s) (what is done), the means (how is it done), and the purpose(s) (why is it done). Moreover, it makes explicit reference to morally charged issues, including prostitution and modern slavery.

While none of these issues is necessarily linked to international migration, the IOM introduced the concept of human trafficking as delineated from the well-known concept of migrant smuggling in Morocco. The IOM's study dedicated much room to the categorical distinction of the two phenomena: in the case of smuggling, there is no intention of exploitation in the moment of recruitment, while in the case of trafficking, the exploitation of the victim is an explicit aim (IOM 2009, 11); therefore, it is a criminal act. For the IOM, the main difference lies in the consent of the person: in the case of smuggling, the migrant who wants to cross an international border by irregular means has given valid consent, while in the case of trafficking, the victim is forced and exploited. In the case of smuggling, it is the state that is the victim, not the migrant. Therefore, the IOM's study came to the conclusion that while migrant smuggling involves organizing someone's unauthorized crossing of an international border in exchange for money or something else, human trafficking is about exploiting someone, whether nationally or internationally. In contrast to consensual smuggling, the concept of trafficking necessitates designing policies that aim to prosecute criminal traffickers and to protect their victims. According to this conceptualization, the trafficking of human beings can be national or international and is thus not per se linked to migration. However, as the 'migration agency,' the IOM stresses the empirical link between migration and its "pathological form" of human trafficking by discursively connecting both concepts to the smuggling of migrants and transnationally organized crime (ibid., 72). Through this participation in the symbolic struggles over legitimate forms of mobility, the IOM disseminates a certain reality and mandates itself to intervene in this expanding field of anti-trafficking.

In postrevolutionary Tunisia, the IOM published a "Baseline study on Trafficking in Persons in Tunisia: Assessing the scope and manifestations" in 2013 (IOM 2013a). The 200-page book has an English and a French version. The light blue IOM-colored paperback, covered with Oriental ornamental design and pictures of sad-looking women, stands on almost every shelf in the offices of Tunisian ministries, non-governmental organizations (NGOs), and other important actors in the field of migration politics. During my fieldwork, the book was repeatedly offered to me when I started conversations about the IOM. In my observations, it seemed that IOM reports on human trafficking have very influential readers. These practices of knowledge production and dissemination have contributed to its reputation as an expert of anti-trafficking. They made it possible for the organization to gain symbolic capital, which fostered its position within the symbolic struggles over dominant meanings and categorizations of migration.

Only six pages of the study are dedicated to the issue of international trafficking and thus are potentially related to questions of international migration. In order to stress the link between migration and human trafficking, the study reassembled the concepts of human trafficking and migrant smuggling through empirical observations. As in Morocco, the Tunisian study did so through a focus on transnationally organized crime. It highlighted the empirical links between trafficking, smuggling, and migration in the sense that

> smuggling networks are often used by criminals who offer to help individuals during smuggling processes with the intention of exploiting them at the end. In other cases, smugglers and traffickers form a network, which requires the migrant wishing to cross the border irregularly, to repay their debt by submitting themselves to one or more forms of exploitation during the migration process and on arrival. Finally,

irregular migrants are particularly vulnerable to various forms of exploitation, including human trafficking.

(Ibid., 13)

Drawing on such empirical observations, the study concluded that "trafficking and migration are intrinsically linked" (ibid.). By establishing a collective understanding of human trafficking as unquestionably linked to migration, this conclusion legitimizes the IOM's intervention in the field of anti-trafficking.

With the production and dissemination of these studies, the IOM introduced a convincing link between trafficking and migration to political discourses in North Africa. However, the organization was confronted with the difficulty of proving the empirical relevance of human trafficking in the region. Phenomena such as irregularized migration and human trafficking are, by their clandestine nature, difficult to research and quantify. Potential victims are often ashamed to tell their story and are reluctant to share their experiences with unknown interviewers (cf. IOM 2009, 93; 2013a, 26). Moreover, not only were networks of smugglers and traffickers annoyed by international researchers snooping around and collecting data: Moroccan authorities also restricted international organizations' (IOs) access to those regions in which they did not want to be observed dealing with irregularized migrants.[5]

Despite these difficulties in generating empirical data on human trafficking, the IOM "guestimates" (Sullivan 2010, 93) that "every year there are 800,000 victims of cross-border trafficking" (IOM 2013a, 8). For North Africa, the IOM did not have any "mythic" numbers to present,[6] but it was eager to meet the demands for measurable statements and precise numbers. In Morocco, the number of VoTs seemed of little quantitative significance (IOM 2009, 7): the IOM's newsletter reported four young women who had been assisted in returning voluntarily from Morocco to Nigeria in 2013 (ibid. 2013a, 2), and seven had benefited from its support, including housing, medical, and psychosocial aid (ibid.). The IOM in Tunisia detected nine Nigerian women among 1,414 migrants being assisted after their rescue at sea (ibid. 2015a, 81). According to its database, the number of VoTs assisted by the IOM as of 2015 included 61 people in Morocco and 14 people in Tunisia. While every victim freed and helped is important, the low number of actually detected cases of human trafficking provided a weak empirical basis for the IOM to promote its political relevance and the need for its international interventions.

Instead of questioning the use of numbers and statistics in this situation, however, the IOM played with its presentation of small numbers so that human trafficking would appear as a large, dangerous, and politically relevant phenomenon. First, while absolute numbers of VoTs were extremely low, they were turned into percentages so the IOM would be able to make impressive statements. For example, out of the 61 VoTs assisted in Morocco, the IOM showed that 94% were female Nigerian migrants who had been trafficked by transnationally operating networks of prostitution (ibid., 81). In Tunisia, the IOM directed attention to the majority (54%) of victims from the Ivory Coast (IOM 2015b); in absolute terms, however, only 45 VoTs had been detected, with 25 of them from the Ivory Coast. Through this scheme, IOM publications turned moderate absolute numbers into exorbitant percentages. This euphemistic use of data, in terms of high percentages for more and less relevant categories, has become a major rhetorical device in the IOM's politics of representation: visualized through simplified charts and graphs, such edited data reduces contradictions, complexities, and variations in experiences to high numbers and colorful flesh (O'Connell Davidson 2016, 62). For the IOM, this provides a form of *cultural capital* that can be utilized to illustrate the relevance of human trafficking and the need to take action.

Another trick used for this purpose presents low empirical numbers in the shadow of vague predictions and colossal estimations. "The number of identified victims can seem low, however, there are some factors that lead us to think that the situation could get worse," the IOM's study on Morocco vaguely concluded (IOM 2009, 95, translation IB). While actually "only one Asian woman (from The Philippines) has been detected in Tunisia in recent years," the IOM highlighted that "there could be thousands of migrant Asian women in domestic servitude in Tunisia" (ibid. 2015a, 86). Producing such trends helps the IOM justify its work and its mandate. According to critical observers, the organization has been "instrumental in making a 'trend' out of occurrences which may also be seen as isolated incidents" (Baird, Spijkerboer, and Cuttitta 2015). Many of the empirical, methodological, and ethical challenges to researching human trafficking are obscured by the IOM's exaggerated statements that emphasize its political relevance. The IOM's alarming discourse contributes to a "moral panic" around human trafficking (Bernstein 2010, 49). While the IOM was not able to deliver results in the preferred currency of numbers and statistics, it was able to promote its expertise and to expand its activities. It is not the hard facts that account for the IOM's position but rather the soft influence that it is able to exercise through its credible performance as an international expert. Producing knowledge thus helped the IOM emerge in a central position in the field of anti-trafficking politics.

Engaging in the politics of anti-trafficking, the IOM extends its core business of international migration management to generating knowledge, setting standards, and proposing procedures in new spheres of action and expertise—often disregarding existing local perspectives and practices. The Tunisian study, for example, addressed the employment of children in domestic work and criticized its widespread acceptance (IOM 2013a, 52). While the problem of child labor has little to do with international migration, the IOM recommended that "café owners who see children strolling all day long in front of their terrace could also deliver valuable information, and the same for taxi drivers" (ibid., 75, translation IB). The example shows how IOM's belief in its duty to educate supposedly backward societies and developing countries goes beyond the issue of migration. This mission also expands well beyond the political actors involved in this field. The production of knowledge on human trafficking thus enables the organization to cultivate new areas of influence, thereby renewing the need for its services. For the IOM, anti-trafficking campaigns are a promising way to tap new sources of funding and to accumulate *economic capital*, which is necessary for the organization to ensure its self-preservation in the competitive field of international migration management.

The next section examines the negotiations between the IOM and the actors who accept, reject, and appropriate its knowledge. Zooming in on the micropolitics of anti-trafficking, it pays particular attention to the symbolic power that the IOM exercises through dissemination of definitions, standards, and methods of anti-trafficking.

5.1.2 The play of international conferences

One of the main objectives of the IOM's anti-trafficking work in North Africa is to mainstream certain ways of understanding and governing human trafficking into political processes and social structures. The IOM sought to disseminate its knowledge about anti-trafficking among important actors in national fields of migration politics; therefore, the organization advised governments to develop National Action Plans to institutionalize anti-trafficking in their policies and legislations (IOM 2009, 99; 2013a, 80). In addition, the IOM introduced a standardized way to understand and govern the phenomenon in the Moroccan and Tunisian administrations and their official statistics. Therefore, the organization supported actors in both countries in establishing standardized procedures of data collection and processing (ibid. 2009, 99; 2013a, 90). On a practical level, the IOM also offered trainings in international standards, legal frameworks, and 'best practices for identifying and protecting VoTs, targeting various actors working in the field (ibid. 2009, 74; 2013a, 70).

Offering such trainings and consultations, "the IOM was keen on creating a trust-based relationship" with state authorities and other actors in the field, in order to make them its "partners in fighting against irregular migration and human trafficking" (conversation with former IOM staff, Mor. 2014). Through the rhetoric of partnership, the IOM implied that it would cooperate with equals, yet, the IOM's practices of knowledge dissemination reflect the superior position that the IOM claims in relation to North African state officials, administration members, security forces, representatives of NGOs, and the media. Teaching 'best practices' and 'international standards,' the IOM established and maintained a hierarchical relationship with Moroccan and Tunisian actors. Despite being framed by discourses of mutual exchange and partnership, these practices actualized colonial relations involving European experts who intervene in the Global South to educate and train local elites to govern populations according to their pre-defined rules. Still, these symbolic interventions seem easier for state actors to accept than legally binding commitments (see Pécoud 2015). They provide low-level points of access for state actors to show their willingness and commitment to becoming active in this new sphere of political action. The questions that follow are whether and why North African state and non-state actors indeed cooperate with the IOM on this issue.

"It seems that they are everywhere," a Moroccan researcher and long-standing observer commented on the IOM's expanding activities on anti-trafficking (conversation with researcher, Mor. 2014). "But in these dialogues in which they organize discussions between the ministries, it is where they include their vision, the content, the orientation, the philosophy!" he added, directing my attention to the importance of the numerous formats of so-called mutual exchange organized by IOs to share their knowledge with their North African 'partners' (ibid.). He invited me to join an international workshop organized by a UN sub-organization. While conferences, workshops, and seminars were not accessible to the greater public, they were open to international researchers.[7] Participating in these events provided me with the opportunity to observe the IOM staff in action—"forming and formatting people," as one of the participants put it—as well as to get an impression of the performances and cultures of discussion, of what is normal, and of what can be said and done in these constitutive situations of negotiating international migration politics. These situations made it possible for me to gain insights into the ambitions, strategies, and imitations *at stake* in the politics of anti-trafficking.

Waiting for the first session to begin, a Moroccan colleague pointed out in a low voice that the IOM's mission in Morocco was "well-informed about everything. They take everything" (ibid.). He went on to explain that currently "…ministries, when they do not know how to do something, they think that IOM can do everything. Or at least, that it has the technical know-how, so they approach [the] IOM" (ibid.). While IOs' activities were for a long time only tolerated in Morocco, the situation changed with the king's announcement of a New Migration Policy in September 2013 (see Chapter 4). Being part of a general democratic opening in response to the Arab Spring, Moroccan authorities increasingly called for international advice to implement the new policy in the following years. In this context, numerous politico-academic events have been organized on asylum, integration, and anti-trafficking.

As I noted in my field notes,

> these events are exhausting, even when accompanied with orange juice in a five-star hotel. While I can stick to my role as an observer, I suddenly find myself in the middle of the game called international migration politics: a long narrow conference hall with oversized comfortable chairs and

gold-framed Impressionist paintings on the walls, freezing air conditioning and overloaded PowerPoint presentations celebrating the New Moroccan Migration Policy. Thirty people, about half of them 'internationals,' sit in two rows around a long conference table for about five hours.
(Observations at UN Workshop, Mor. 2014)

At the center of attention, the IOM staff aim to deliver a professional performance. Most of the time, they are invited to comment on developments in the country as international experts and to propose solutions. They also act as moderators of various thematic seminars, working groups, and roundtables. This puts them in the position of summarizing the results or highlighting specific points that the organization regards as important while leaving out critical issues, deferring to the omnipresent sheer lack of time. Well equipped through its funding from European donors, the IOM is also able to organize such costly events. This economic capital enables the organization to set the agenda, invite speakers, and edit follow-up publications. Based on its comparative advantage in economic and symbolic capitals, the IOM is able to define and implement the rules of such events.

The events I observed resembled each other across countries and topics. Often, the same people representing a small number of governmental or international institutions meet in the capital's expensive hotels around overcrowded buffets, sharing experiences and 'best practices,' presenting extensive PowerPoint presentations to each other with blinking numbers and repeating the key words of international migration management. At first sight, Europe, the EU, and its member states do not seem to play a very prominent role; however, the discourses dominating such occasions indicate their symbolic influence. The global policy discourse of migration management throughout the presentations, discussions, and publications—predominantly articulated in French—is compatible with European conventions, standards, and definitions. For example, the Council of Europe's Convention on Action against Trafficking in Human Beings serves as a major point of reference for anti-trafficking. Beyond such explicit references, the discourse barely escapes the implicit assumptions of European-dominated international policies, such as the dominant dichotomies of legal vs. illegal migration, voluntary vs. forced displacements, or victims vs. criminals. Even when no representatives of the EU and its member states sit at the table, they are involved in the symbolic struggles over North African migration policies through the knowledge disseminated by IOs with the help of their funding. Consequently, discussions at such events often revolve around the same issues and key words of international migration management.

However, for relations and distinctions in the field, it makes a difference who is invited and who is not. For example, among government officials, formal invitations to international conferences and workshops serve as an important indicator of their political relevance. In Morocco, the newly founded Minister in charge of Moroccans Living Abroad and Migration Affairs was invited to such occasions, since he had taken the official lead on migration from the Ministry of Interior in 2013. Through their invitations, IOs enhanced the new ministry's *social capital* and strengthened its position in the national field of migration politics.

In Tunisia, postrevolutionary struggles over political positions and resources were still ongoing at the time of my fieldwork in 2015. Different ministries—mainly the Ministry of Social Affairs (MSA), the Ministry of Interior, the Ministry of Foreign Affairs, and the Ministry of Development and International Cooperation—dealt with different aspects of migration. Both nationally and internationally, they struggled for recognition and resources in order to carry out their different priorities. While many of them questioned cooperation with European states on restrictive migration control, cooperating with IOs was helpful in legitimizing certain policy changes at the national level (Korneev 2014, 900). The social capital and the cultural capital, in the form of networks, competences and know-how gained through interaction with IOs, could be reemployed in the national struggles over positions, resources, and recognition.

At international conferences and workshops, these strategies were not only noticeable among the officially invited speakers but also among civil society actors. In postrevolutionary Tunisia, they actively engaged in debates with representatives of the ministries, donors, and IOs, and they confronted them with their concerns and demands. Tunisian migration policies after the revolution developed in direct interaction with old and newly founded civil society groups and migrant (self)organizations (Bartels 2014). While temporary and interim solutions made protest difficult, many political changes were indeed initiated from below.

In Morocco, new policies were unilaterally decreed by the king, and policy-making was a hierarchically structured process. At official events, there was little room for oppositional forces or critical voices from below. At most, internationally established researchers took the floor and expressed their slightly opposed opinions. NGOs and migrant (self)organizations were widely missing at the tables and microphones; if present, they were designated a place in the audience, which was often limited to invitation only. In this way, the officially proclaimed participatory policymaking processes that were started in Morocco in 2013 were essentially turned into diplomatic exchanges between government officials and 'internationals'—usually highly qualified, Western and White professionals working in the "transnational galaxy" of IOs (Pandofli and McFalls 2010, 171). They were said to work particularly hard to make a successful career in the international community but often lacked knowledge about the place and its history, which they were supposed to support with their expertise.

As I noted in my field notes,

> the IOM staff play the game of international migration management very skillfully. Its team is well-positioned at the conference: it is present

with three members, the first to take a seat, keen and concentrated but also excited or nervous to start working. The team of the UNHCR joins them. Moreover, representatives of the main European donors take their seats at the table. In terms of content, a difference in their positions is hardly noticeable. They rather complement each other—in their colorful presentations that are full of complex charts and graphs as well as at the lunch table.

(Observations at UN workshop, Mor. 2014)

Usually, the staff of IOs stay for three months to three years in a country before they are replaced by a new, highly motivated team that is better qualified for the next project. While individuals working in this field compete for positions within the organizations, they often "develop similar dispositions" and a similar *individual habitus* that influences the *collective habitus* of an organization (Jackson 2009, 107). This "migrant and deterritorialized community" of early-career staff seemed themselves ready to move on, driven by the *illusio* that "there is still a lot to accomplish" (Pandofli and McFalls 2010, 183). They seem highly motivated and passionate about supporting the country that the organization has sent them to. The IOM staff in Morocco and Tunisia share a strong sense of identification with their organization and an unquestioned belief in the benefits of its mission. At the same time, however, their habitus is very career-oriented, mobile, and motivated to move on. They are focused on their personal mission to implement a particular project according to predefined procedures. Their motivation for technically correct implementation results from the need to prove their skills and expertise and to expand their networks in order to leave for the next mission with an excellent recommendation. Their work is driven as much by their embodied competition over individual stakes of cultural and social capital as by the illusioic belief in the benefits of international migration management.

Whether due to their little experience or their low position within the organization's hierarchy, such young professionals often avoided sharing personal opinions during interviews. They frequently stated that they could not report on certain issues and directed my question to someone else. While IO staff members referred to their mandates, representatives of donors pointed to European capitals as where politics are *made*. Working on the implementation side, both share a neutral view of themselves as being in a position that does not allow for political decisions and opinions; instead, they followed project guidelines, administrative rules, and the terms of references negotiated and decided on by the headquarters of their organizations, donors, and governments. However, for many of my interview partners, it was important to emphasize that 'nothing was imposed' but rather came from the demands of Moroccan and Tunisian authorities. This self-understanding reflects the collective habitus shared by many IOs in the trans-Mediterranean field of migration management.

Long-standing Moroccan experts in the field complained that it was difficult to build lasting partnerships with rotating young internationals. With every new international expert, they needed to start over in explaining and negotiating the same issues. In addition, they worried that the presence of representatives of international actors legitimized the supposed participatory processes that were announced by the Moroccan government in the context of the New Migration Policy. Indeed, in 2013, Moroccan government officials called for experts to create and implement new migration policies. Civil society activists and researchers who had worked on these issues for a long time without official authorization feared being subsumed by the expanding interventions of IOs. "Every time that there is a project, IOs take it. If there is a need expressed at the level of a ministry, they contact it and say: 'we take it', 'we will do it for you,'" a researcher complained during a workshop coffee break (conversation with researcher, Mor. 2014). However, "they do not have real expertise. They just take existing bibliographies, they use your work, but they never say it" (ibid.). From the perspective of Moroccan researchers, the government's rhetoric of participation in practice turned into an unsatisfactory process of international consultations and top-down information. Consequently, they criticized the involvement of IOs, as their proclaimed expert knowledge would legitimize the declared participatory processes announced by the Moroccan government.

This policy-making *à la Marocaine* illustrates the Moroccan *feel for the game* of international migration management. Moroccan authorities seemed to know how to play by the rules and to maneuver the country through the demands and challenges of international migration management, taking some progressive steps forward without making too many truly democratic concessions. Rhetorically, Moroccan government officials appropriated and eloquently replicated the dominant discourses spread by IOs. "Morocco stands for a global and integrated approach," a representative of the new Moroccan Ministry in charge of Moroccans Living Abroad and Migration Affairs announced at one of the workshops (Observations at UN workshop, Mor. 2014). On the same occasion, he explicitly demanded that IOs help Morocco "fight against human trafficking" through capacity building and trainings, and he thanked them for their support on law development (ibid.). According to his presentation, the new Moroccan laws on asylum, integration, and anti-trafficking entailed each a chapter on cooperation with the IOs. In this way, the IOM's position as an expert on human trafficking was institutionalized in Morocco. For the Moroccan authorities, this cooperation is not only helpful within national struggles over power and positions but also at the international level; through the appropriation of international discourses, they reemploy the cultural capital of migration management to obtain economic and social benefits in international negotiations.

Moreover, this complicity enabled Moroccan authorities to avoid struggles with Moroccan researchers. "They call for international experts, because those are more discreet. They are not so critical," one of the researchers observed (conversation with researcher, Mor. 2014). Representatives of IOs acted in accordance with their institution's mandate and diplomatic practice and therefore remained uncritical of state politics (see Korneev 2014, 898f.). In conferences and workshops, they did not openly criticize their member states but instead took moderating positions; open criticism was—if at all—only uttered by independent NGOs or migrant associations.

While the general tone was diplomatic and public criticism was hard to find in Morocco, critical stances were more openly articulated in Tunisia. For example, government officials self-confidently highlighted the need for long-term strategies instead of ever-more short-term projects implemented by IOs. They shared their doubts about the sustainability of projects after the departure of the international staff, and calling for their "national appropriation" and seeking to limit the influence of international actors (interview with repr. of MDIC, Tun. 2015). Civil society actors criticized the behavior of Tunisian government officials in international negotiations. In reference to negotiations with the EU about a Mobility Partnership, they complained that critical perspectives had not been taken into account. Their outspoken protest indicates their expectation of a democratic and inclusive approach. While cooperation with the EU was criticized by NGOs and researchers, cooperation with the IOM was easier to justify from the perspective of Tunisian state actors; as in Morocco, the organization was "not directly seen as a machinery and intermediary of the EU" (Korneev 2014, 901), and its entanglements in the externalization of European migration control were rarely denounced in Tunisian politics.

Many Moroccan and Tunisian actors—state and non-state—indeed tried to win IOs' trust and favor: during coffee breaks, the IOM staff were often surrounded by crowds of participants, distributing their cards and publications from large white plastic bags like advertisements for customers at a fair. In such situations of material and symbolic knowledge dissemination, it was difficult to find critical voices. "The IOM does many things; they published this study recently about trafficking, it is very well known," a participant told me during lunch at a conference in Tunisia (conversation with researcher 2, Tun. 2015). From his point of view, the IOM has nothing to do with the securitization and externalization of European migration control. "There are other associations that deal with it," he argued, referring to Frontex as an example (ibid.). In contrast to actors working at the border, the IOM is mostly perceived as a scientific actor, providing Moroccan and Tunisian actors with statistics and keywords rather than fences and radar equipment. Located on the seemingly good side of science, its services are increasingly demanded: "first we need statistics, numbers, facts, etc. in order to develop policies, measures, etc. afterwards" was a view shared by many participants. To achieve various implicit and explicit strategies and ambitions, many actors had internalized the knowledge disseminated by IOs and learned how to play by the rules of international migration management. Even though the boundaries of politics and science are blurred in this field, a doxic belief in the separation between supposedly neutral, useful science

202 *Anti-trafficking politics*

and mistrusted politics persists. This tacit acknowledgment of the structures and rules in the field helps obscure the symbolic power of the IOM to spread a legitimate way of dealing with migration (Bourdieu 1977, 167f.).

Organizing workshops and conferences to share international standards, 'best practices,' and 'lessons learned,' the IOM was able to establish anti-trafficking as a well-known discourse among state and non-state actors in North Africa. Appearing as neutral and objective experts, its staff sought to (in)form other actors in the field and to promote a global discourse and dominant understanding of human trafficking. The doxic belief in the objectivity of science and the neutrality of international expertise obscured the IOM's involvement in the politics of externalization and made it possible for the organization to export measures of migration control to North African politics and societies. While IOs were able set the rules of international workshops and conferences, other actors furthered their own stakes and ambitions at such events, including strategic cooperation with IOs or the imitation of their discourses and presentations. The social capital and cultural capital gained through this cooperation can be reemployed in national and international struggles over positions, resources, and recognition. The symbolic power of knowledge dissemination relies on the participation of Moroccan and Tunisian state and non-state actors; it is a powerful form of "violence which is exercised upon a social agent with his or her complicity" (Bourdieu and Wacquant 1992, 171). Consequently, the *symbolic violence* of introducing concepts, categories, and classification schemes to North African migration politics provides an efficient but often *misrecognized* mode for implementing politics of anti-trafficking and international migration management (see also Bartels 2018).

5.2 Victims of trafficking as a new target group of migration management

> Victims of trafficking don't fall into the UNHCR's mandate, unless they are refugees or potential asylum seekers. And here in Morocco, the vast majority comes from Nigeria. And Nigeria has 0% acceptance rate on asylum claims. So here, it is much more us,

an IOM staff member explained, meaning that the IOM would practically take care of VoTs (interview with IOM staff, Mor. 2014). The IOM's engagement in the field of anti-trafficking enables the organization to extend not only its expertise and authority but also its operational activities of social work and humanitarian assistance. By establishing VoTs as a new category of international migration management, the IOM established a new target group for its various services. Defining this new figure requiring protection and prevention built on its semantic work in creating profiles, statistics, and shared knowledge about the phenomenon. The discursive introduction and dissemination of anti-trafficking as a relevant political issue in North Africa helped the IOM delineate a new sphere of action and influence, including a proper 'protection mandate' for a specific category of persons that was distinct from the United Nations High Commissioner for Refugees' (UNHCR) concern with refugees and asylum seekers.

This new category is characterized by the vulnerability of female migrants in transit, whose suffering justifies international interventions in the name of their protection. Armed with representations of passive, innocent victims, the IOM intervenes in the "distinction and categorization games" of international migration politics (Bourdieu quoted in Adler-Nissen 2013, 6). By giving female migrants a certain position in the international struggles of migration, the organization actualizes asymmetrical power relations between the producer of such categories and the categorized—and in the case of the IOM's anti-trafficking campaigns, both positions are primarily occupied by women. The mostly European, female staff working for the IOM mandates itself to rescue female migrants in the North African borderlands from transnational criminal networks and prostitution, predominantly through their 'voluntary' return. By extending the focus to 'vulnerable groups at risk' of being trafficked, the organization also promotes its campaigns for prevention on their behalf.

The following sections analyze in detail how the IOM applies its tools of migration management to these new target groups. They reveal that anti-trafficking interventions are based on a gender-biased logic that distinguishes vulnerable female migrants who need to be protected (and preferably returned) from criminal traffickers who should be prosecuted.

5.2.1 Forced, sold, prostituted—defining VoTs through female suffering

According to the IOM's investigations in Morocco, the few victims who could be identified indicate that the phenomenon of human trafficking concerns the exploitation of Moroccan women in Gulf countries, as well as West African women in transit (IOM 2009, 7). While the IOM underlines that human trafficking is not exclusively limited to foreign women, these are the main figures in IOM discourses. Detailed narratives present the suffering of female victims throughout its publications. A recent study on the trends of migration in the Mediterranean reported that these women "suffer from physical and sexual abuses and other inhumane treatment. They are usually forced to prostitute themselves every day in devastating conditions that endanger their health and personal safety" (ibid. 2015, 85). They are

> retained in houses in Casablanca, Rabat or in the forest in Nador and Oujda, under the control of a chairman [...] who is the man in charge of their "protection" along the way, and essentially the guardian of the victim. [...] Women live in apartments of 30 or 40 people, waiting for the best moment to try to reach Europe or to be sold to other networks.
> (Ibid.)

According to another study commissioned by the IOM, these women are "often controlled by voodoo [black magic] and told by their exploiters that if they escape, voodoo will be used against their family at home" (Altai Consulting 2015, 24). The IOM's narratives present an image of women in passive, helpless positions, being *forced, controlled, sold, prostituted*, etc. by their traffickers but also *protected* and *taken care* of, by either the traffickers or those who save them from these criminals.

In Tunisia, human trafficking is chiefly associated with Nigerian women. During screenings of migrants who were rescued at sea by the Tunisian coast, the IOM detected few cases that shared a similar profile to those rescued in Morocco. Among these migrants, nine women were identified as former VoTs in domestic servitude in Libya who were supposed to be sent to Italy by transnationally operating networks for the purpose of prostitution (IOM 2015a, 81). Other cases detected in Tunisia include young Sub-Saharan girls who were exploited as domestic workers without passports or the possibility to leave their employer's house. In addition, a few cases of young Tunisian women who were sexually exploited in the Middle East were also reported (ibid., 4). According to the IOM's investigations, these women traveled in a regular way, but upon arrival their passports were confiscated to prevent them from escaping their exploiters (ibid., 81). In contrast to the widely shared perception of human trafficking as a phenomenon that is linked to irregularized migration, most victims detected by the IOM entered the countries of their exploitation by legal means.

The IOM's reports show how women's agency is omitted from the desperate stories of human suffering. Differentiations are only made along nationalities and modes of exploitations (e.g., in Altai Consulting 2015, 44). The IOM categorizes VoTs based on their trajectories of international mobility: Moroccans and Tunisians are exploited in other Arab countries; Moroccans and Tunisians are exploited in Europe; Nigerian women are exploited and transited through North Africa; Filipinas are also exploited in the region; and so on. International border crossing is critical for the IOM's profiling of different groups of VoTs (IOM 2009, 25). In this way, the IOM implicitly strengthens the link between human trafficking and international migration and underscores its authority to take care of the victims.

In addition, the IOM emphasizes the link between human trafficking and prostitution. The IOM depicts female migrants as victims in debt bondage due to their passage, which they must pay off afterwards—most commonly through prostitution. This view infantilizes migrant women. The IOM characterizes them as traveling alone, despite the observation that many women travel in groups with other (female) migrants; in this gender-biased view, alone means these women are not accompanied by a male partner, and other female migrants, friends, and children are not considered as relevant company in the IOM's view and classifying system. The few cases taking women's agency into account refer to their criminal activities:

> Upward mobility within the network and becoming a "madame" is one of the more common options opted by women after paying the debt.

They will start recruiting other women, changing their role from victim to trafficker, and perpetuating the existence of the network.

(Ibid. 2015, 85)

Stories and pictures of passive, helpless women and their suffering bodies are at the core of the IOM's discourse on anti-trafficking in North Africa. These elements call for humanitarian interventions to save women from their desperate situations. In terms of the Eastern European context, migration scholars have pointed out that the IOM's anti-trafficking discourse separates (potential) migrants into individual victims and cruel smugglers and traffickers (Bojadzijev and Karakayali 2007, 206; Karakayali 2008, 195). Continuing this logic, the IOM argues that in North Africa vulnerable migrants, primarily women and children, are forced by criminal networks on boats to cross the Mediterranean. Poor and helpless, they must pay for their journey through prostitution in transit or destination countries.

For many female migrants on their way to Europe, this is the sad and traumatizing reality; however, the stories and pictures promoted by the IOM offer a one-sided perspective on the struggles of migration, one that is informed by a gender-biased view that neglects the agency of women from the Global South. According to this narrative, "authentic victims" are only those who do not decide to migrate or earn money through sex work but are explicitly forced to do so (Cheng and Kim 2014, 12). Innocence and helplessness are required in order to deserve protection and rehabilitation by IOs from this "modern form of slavery" (Bernstein 2010, 49). In contrast, those who are regarded as responsible for their own predicament are punished by the criminal justice system or restrictive migration policies (Ticktin 2008, 868). Therefore, as Nandita Sharma (2003, 59) notes, for women who seek protection, it is important to present "one's self as a victim." For (female) migrants in Morocco and Tunisia, performing vulnerability is the condition to receive the IOM's assistance and to participate in its voluntary return program. If helped by the IOM, the only way out of their precarious condition in the North African borderlands is not a legalized safe passage to Europe but a return to their proper place "at home," which indicates their family, house, or nation (Andrijasevic 2007, 123ff). Protecting women from human trafficking became a common device of international migration management that helps gain control over the undesired movements of an increasingly female migration, through the protection and (voluntary) return of victims on the one hand and the criminalization and deportation of traffickers and their accomplices on the other.

5.2.2 Protecting vulnerable migrants

Despite the IOM's active lobbying, neither a systematic screening of migrants for potential VoTs nor a specific mechanism of assistance for VoTs were implemented in Morocco and Tunisia. In both countries, the UNHCR offers few possibilities in this regard. It intervenes if the victim holds a foreign nationality and can be accorded refugee status for a reason recognized by the organization (see IOM 2009, 83). However, refugee status is not provided for being identified as a VoT. As for Moroccan or Tunisian migrants who have been trafficked abroad, no mechanisms or special structures exist to ensure their return and reintegration (IOM 2013a, 73). Given these insufficient identification and protection measures and the lack of institutional support for VoTs, the IOM offered its assistance.

Through the anti-trafficking projects the IOM has implemented in Morocco and Tunisia, the organization proposed its Assisted Voluntary Return and Reintegration (AVRR) program (see Chapter 4) as the primary option of ensuring protection for VoTs.[8] To make the program an effective instrument for victim identification, protection, and assistance, the IOM suggested that screenings for VoTs should be integrated into the program's general procedures. Acknowledging that returning VoTs are particular vulnerable to the risk of being exploited again, the IOM collaborated with partner organizations in the countries of origin to reintegrate VoTs and to offer them psychosocial support.

Providing assistance to VoTs is in line with the organization's reorientation of its services to vulnerable migrants. The selection criteria for benefitting from IOM assistance has become framed mainly in terms of "vulnerabilities" (IOM 2015c, translation IB). According to the IOM staff in Morocco, migrants in "an extremely vulnerable situation enter some kind of a short track mechanism" to participate in the AVRR program (interview with IOM staff, Mor. 2014). In Tunisia, a staff member explained that support to migrants mainly

> depends on their vulnerability. It is no longer for everyone, but for those who become vulnerable. It is important to keep this humanitarian way open for assistance and to consider people's vulnerability.
> (Interview with IOM staff, Tun. 2015)

Managing migration in North Africa no longer aimed to filter potential refugees and asylum seekers from the "mixed flows" but instead to identify those who are particularly vulnerable (IOM 2015a, 11). The IOM staff pointed out that migrants "follow the same journeys, and are often in the hands of the same smugglers," but they do not have the same "need of international protection" that is laid out in the Geneva Convention (interview with IOM staff, Tun. 2015). However, the staff member highlighted that migrants "possess human rights that deserve to be protected, and there are a number of risks and vulnerabilities that arise out of the nature of the journey itself" (ibid.). Not all migrants who arrive in Tunisia can be considered as refugees and asylum seekers—and therefore be protected by the UNHCR—but many need international protection as long as the Tunisian state has not established the institutions necessary to care for them. For vulnerable migrants, this protection is provided through IOM services.

Anti-trafficking politics 207

This reorientation of the IOM's assistance to vulnerable groups is part of a larger trend in the international politics of protection, whose focus has shifted from a predominant concern with refugees and asylum seekers to interventions on behalf of vulnerable people (see Chapter 4). Critical migration scholars have argued that this development pits the protection of vulnerable groups against the individual right to asylum (Neuhauser, Hess, and Schwenken 2017, 198). The IOM's anti-trafficking projects contribute to spreading this humanitarian logic in the trans-Mediterranean field of migration management. While it makes North African countries safe(r) for those groups of people defined by IOs as vulnerable, it provides legitimacy to criminalize other groups of migrants transiting through North Africa.

5.2.3 The prevention of risk groups

Confronted with the difficulty of finding enough 'vulnerable migrants' willing to be protected by the IOM's services (see Section 5.1.1), the IOM redefined its target group to also include 'vulnerable groups at risk of trafficking.' As 'real victims' were not sufficiently detectable for the organization, the IOM (2013a, 62) argued that these "vulnerable groups should be at the heart of policies to fight human trafficking." In addition to female West African migrants, the new category included non-accompanied minors in irregular situations and children of Sub-Saharan migrants born in transit without a legal status (ibid. 2019, 7). According to the IOM, irregularized migrants can easily fall into the hands of smugglers and thereby enter a cycle of exploitation. Refugees were also considered a particular 'risk group,' since they were already victims in their country of origin or could be easily recruited by smugglers in the camps that are supposed to provide shelter. While the few VoTs identified by the IOM had migrated by legal means, the organization's identification procedures for these groups focused on irregularized migrants. Drawing on the construction of an individualized risk of being trafficked and a collective threat of criminal networks, the IOM mobilized the tools of risk management otherwise used to prevent irregularized migration (see Chapter 3). It called for better information and education of potential VoTs in the name of preventing vulnerable groups from the risks of human trafficking.

Designed for this purpose, the two-minute cartoon *The Story of Fatma* tells the story of a young woman who dreams about jobs and wealth in Europe.[9] She applies to an offer that she found on the internet and travels to Europe. Upon her arrival at an airport in a big European city, a sinister-looking man with a remarkable hooknose takes her passport away and drives her through the city to a dark place. Red contours against a black background indicate a potential brothel, but what actually happens after she is locked in a dungeon is only implied. "Beware of the promises of well-paying jobs on the internet" runs a message in huge white letters across the scene. The sinister trafficker sneers nastily in the background. "Human trafficking is a click away" warns the IOM on Tunisian Facebook. Published on YouTube in 2013, the short clip has received about 6,400 clicks.[10]

In contrast to the IOM's information campaigns in other countries, *The Story of Fatma* does not make use of eroticized pictures of naked, mistreated women. Instead, it presents an artistically designed manga-like cartoon in order "to turn risky subjects into *prudent* and careful persons, who avoid risks like irregular migration" (Schatral 2010, 256, emphasis in original). Moreover, it resorts

> to victimizing images of female bodies as a way of warning potential women migrants about the dangers of migration and prostitution, and as a means of empowering them to make informed choices concerning working and travelling abroad.
>
> (Andrijasevic 2007, 27)

Presenting young women as innocent and naïve, the IOM calls for their education as risk-conscious subjects (Schatral 2010, 254). Well in line with the IOM's global anti-trafficking campaign, the Tunisian video spreads the message that the safest option for young women from the Global South is to stay 'at home' (Sharma 2003; Andrijasevic 2007)—or, as Susanne Schatral (2010, 261) concludes in relation to the IOM's campaign in Russia: "The only means to obviate the risk suggested by the IOM's campaign is: If you can't follow the rules of the game, don't leave home." The rules of the game are defined by the IOM, which fosters an image of migration as an individual enterprise for which migrants have to bear the risks. Since the IOM doubts that female migrants fit the entrepreneurial, neoliberal subjects able to succeed in their individual migration projects, the organization seeks to prevent them from their supposedly hopeless experiments. Paradoxically, it is often the international, mobile female staff of the IOM who do this job. The unequal conditions under which different people enter and play this game are not considered by the organization. Its virtual anti-trafficking campaigns aim to change the behavior of (potential) female migrants who do not stay in their designated place 'at home' but dare to take the risk of moving across borders and challenging the international regime of restricted mobility rights for people from the Global South. In this way, the IOM's mission to save non-Western women from their men, families, and communities, as well as to prevent them from potential risks, is entangled in colonial schemes and patriarchal routines of governing migrants, especially Muslim women from the Global South (Ticktin 2008; Yurdakul 2010).

In sum, the IOM's operational interventions in the field of anti-trafficking rest on the discursive construction of human trafficking as a risk for vulnerable groups—VoTs or those at risk of becoming them—who are regarded as worthy of being saved and protected by the organization. From this perspective, anti-trafficking is part of its global moral mission to save innocent individuals—notably, non-Western female migrants—from evil criminal networks, if possible through neoliberal forms of risk management, but if not, through individual(ized) humanitarian solutions. In this respect, the IOM's anti-trafficking projects are "deeply rooted in the organization's culture" (Schatral 2010, 259). Its operational work focuses on publically exposing and denouncing individual, especially female, suffering and male violence, rather than calling for global social justice, gender equality, or equal rights to international mobility (Yurdakul 2010). Reproducing prominent gender stereotypes, they disempower women in the Global South from migrating and instead assign them a place 'at home,' which is apparently not associated with danger and exploitation (Berman 2003; Cheng and Kim 2014). While the IOM presents itself as working on behalf of the well-being of women, the organization establishes a patriarchal relationship with those whom it seeks to save or shield from the dangers of human trafficking, thereby distinguishing its Western, liberal identity from the criminal networks operating in non-Western countries. In this way, the IOM's practices of anti-trafficking also actualize racialized stereotypes, colonial hierarchies, and the persistence of unquestioned modes of domination in the field of migration management.

5.3 Building capacities and negotiating laws

Beyond its preventive and humanitarian and interventions on behalf of VoTs, the IOM also intensified and extended its direct influence on Moroccan and Tunisian state politics. After the revolution in 2011, many IOs offered their services to "develop governance capacities" to the new actors taking political power in North Africa (interview with ILO staff, Tun. 2015). In the field of migration, not only the IOM but also the International Labor Organization (ILO) and the International Centre for Migration Policy Development (ICMPD) began to implement projects framed by similar key words and employing the same tool box of international project management. As a representative of the ILO explained, they all proposed to build capacities and mechanisms of cooperation, "ultimately leading to a better governance of the migration issue" (ibid.). Within the joint international state-building project for Tunisia, the IOM mainly focused its capacity- and institution-building on anti-trafficking.

5.3.1 The symbolic power of law- and policy-making in Tunisia

> We work here with regard to the Palermo Protocols and the other things that Tunisia has signed. But what is missing is in fact a basis, a national law that on the one side could also facilitate the prosecution of smugglers, of traffickers and on the other side facilitate the protection of victims,

explained IOM staff in 2015 (interview with IOM staff, Tun. 2015). At that time, the organization supported the Tunisian government in developing legal measures and institutional structures to prosecute smugglers and traffickers. With meandering hand gestures, my interview partner described the negotiations with government officials: a little bit forward, a little bit backward, giving them time, asking again, giving them some more time, until they finally agreed and then promoted it as their own idea. In her words:

> We would suggest something, a project on migration and integration in Tunisia for example. They would say "No." We give more information, explain it better. Then we wait, and at some point, they would say "Yes." It is not a linear process, you need to be diplomatic and patient,

in order to convince Tunisian state actors about their objectives (ibid.). For IOM staff, it was always important to emphasize that they would "not impose anything" while they tried to gain political acceptance for international standards and policies (ibid.). Instead, the organization presented itself as a neutral expert that would only inform Tunisian actors about a "range of possible solutions" (Korneev 2014, 899). In this way, it was possible for the Tunisian actors to accept solutions suggested by IOs, conveyed with symbolic power, without the solutions appearing to be imposed by an external intervention.

Nevertheless, anti-trafficking policies and legislation implemented in cooperation with the IOM bear the trademark of international migration management. In Tunisia, the organization was directly involved in developing legislative measures. In the context of the SHARE (Support and Handover of Assistance and Referral mechanism as well as Exchange of practices in Anti-trafficking) project, for example, the IOM cooperated with actors from the government, civil society, and international institutions to prepare a law against trafficking, and it supported the implementation of a National Action Plan against Trafficking (IOM 2015d). Moreover, the organization instructed juridical staff on how to judge people in line with international standards in the absence of a national law (ibid. 2015b). As a result, international standards and definitions found their way into the adopted text of the law, which was enacted in 2015 (DCAF 2015). Accordingly, the law seeks to *prevent* all forms of exploitation to which people, notably women and children, are exposed and to combat against trafficking by *prosecuting* traffickers and *protecting* and assisting victims (ibid., 1, emphasis IB). It thus adopts the international definition of trafficking persons from the Palermo Protocols, with some extensions.[11] The law explicitly refers to national and transnational organized forms of trafficking, but it contains no link to international migration (ibid., 2). In terms of prosecution, the law establishes a penalty of up to ten years of imprisonment and a fine of 50,000 dinars (ibid., 3); however, the accused person can be exempted from prosecution if they identify the network of trafficking (ibid., 5). According to Sharron FitzGerald (2011, 167), this "name and shame" strategy gives the state further knowledge about tracking networks but also criminalizes irregularized migration and sex work. In addition, the strategy allows the government to present itself as the "rescuer" of suffering women (ibid.).

At the same time, the Tunisian law decriminalizes the acts committed by VoTs, regardless of their active consent. Tunisian law punishes illegal prostitution with six months to two years of imprisonment and a fine of 20–200 dinars (IOM 2013a, 40); however, the new law states that crimes committed as a victim are not to be punished. While criminalizing 'voluntary' sex work, the law decriminalizes 'forced' prostitution and offers protection to 'real,' innocent victims (Cheng and Kim 2014). According to Miriam Ticktin (2008, 868), such strategies

> divide women up into those who are seen as helpless, innocent victims who must be saved and those who are seen as responsible for their own predicament and therefore forfeit their right to state protection.

Protection is not provided unconditionally but depends on one's willingness to denounce others. "Useful victims" are regarded as helpful, both as witnesses in lawsuits and as informants about transnational criminal networks (Schatral 2011, 11). Those who seek protection are expected to deliver an honest story and a credible performance of suffering.

The enactment of the law was widely celebrated by IOM publications. They extensively quoted Tunisian government officials who expressed their thankfulness for the IOM's support: "With the support of the IOM in the context of the SHARE project, we have learned how to develop appropriate mechanisms and strategies in order to better face the problem" (IOM 2013b, translation IB). By including a quote that explicitly states that the Tunisian government has "learned" how to deal with the "problem" of human trafficking, the IOM points to its educative role and symbolic power in Tunisian policy- and law-making. In a similar tone, the IOM's newsletter quoted a member of the Tunisian government who explained that

> the IOM has provided us with fundamental and decisive support. All the official reports predating the Explorative Study on Trafficking of Human Beings, conducted by the IOM, did not indicate any phenomenon of trafficking in Tunisia before. Through this study, the trainings, media, and information campaigns, and the technical support in the development of a law in this field, the IOM has played a crucial role in supporting the Tunisian government.
>
> (IOM 2014c, 3, translation IB)

Referring to the IOM's pioneering study on human trafficking published in 2013, the quote supports the impression that the organization has enlightened the country. It highlights the "crucial role" that the IOM played, through its knowledge production and dissemination, to establish human trafficking as a relevant issue in Tunisian state politics. The government

212 *Anti-trafficking politics*

official's praise for the IOM's anti-trafficking work concluded by expressing the hope to

> benefit from the same support for trainings, debates, and conferences in the future in order to exchange good practices and strengthen our cooperation with our partners from abroad. Moreover, we hope to develop more specialized studies about issues related to different forms of trafficking.
>
> (Ibid.)

The statement expresses a continued demand for IOM services in the field of anti-trafficking, and it echoes the IOM's claim that, despite its noticeable influence, 'nothing is imposed' on the country. The process behind this law exemplifies how the IOM was able to influence concrete developments in Tunisian migration policy by using its symbolic power to achieve their desired results, which did not seem to be imposed from above but a product of genuine Tunisian politics.

"A successful project" was the first and quickest response of my interview partner from the Migration Department within the MSA, the main governmental actor in the field of migration, when I asked about the IOM's anti-trafficking campaigns (interview with repr. of the MSA, Tun. 2015). However, she emphasized that the implementation of anti-trafficking measures was "difficult for countries like Tunisia" (ibid.) "It is a lot of work," so she appreciated the IOM's "very active" support on "many things, all that is migration" (ibid.). She praised it and explicitly distinguished it from the UNHCR, which was only "occupied with refugees" (ibid.). As to the cooperation with the IOM on the anti-trafficking law, she seemed satisfied with the results, but pointed out that such processes are "always a compromise since you have to satisfy everyone with it" (ibid.).

According to a representative of the Red Crescent in Tunisia, the IOM should

> be serious [with the Tunisian actors]. They are not fools. If you do a seminar to convince them, they will say: "Well, we liked the hotel, we did the training, lunch and dinner was great—but we will not change our opinion. We take your trainings, your information, but we will not change our opinion." You have to be really serious with them, because otherwise you just disperse money without any impact.
>
> (Interview with Red Crescent staff, Tun. 2015)

His statement highlights the agency of Tunisian government officials, who carefully review services offered by IOs and select the ones in which they would get involved and possibly "change their opinion." They are not passive recipients of international services but decide whether these services will have an impact or not. It is less through material incentives, such as a "great hotel, lunch and dinner," and more through recognition as "serious" partners that Tunisian actors could be convinced by the trainings. Calling for international expertise can help them push their agenda on the national level. At the same time, my interview partner shared his doubts as to whether "the peak of the political pyramid of decision-making in the country has understood these aspects"—especially since they "came from a generation far off" (ibid.). For the new Migration Department within the MSA, which looks up to the Ministries of Interior and External Relations at the top of the country's political pyramid, complicity and cooperation with IOs was important to establishing its position and agenda within national politics. In Tunisia, the agenda of migration politics was still determined by the actors holding traditionally powerful positions, such as the Ministries of Interior and External Relations, and my interview partner from the Migration Department expressed the hope that "external pressure" would change these hierarchies (interview with repr. of MSA, Tun. 2015). By cooperating with IOs, she expected to strengthen the ministry's position and extend its influence within the changing field of migration politics.

Cooperation with IOs especially helped new political actors strengthen their authority and legitimize their projects within the government's internal struggles over power and positions (Korneev 2014, 900). Moreover, international projects would bring badly needed money to Tunisia. The concern of state actors was that if Tunisia did not cooperate on issues such as anti-trafficking, the country would not get European support and funding for other issues. From the perspective of a representative of the Tunisian MSA, this was not an option for Tunisia in 2015. In this respect, the decision to cooperate (or not) with IOs and European donors is also a question of financial resources and their distribution in Tunisian politics. Knowing that they generally do not have much room to maneuver in international negotiations, Tunisian state representatives tried to use cooperation with IOs for their own purposes—notably, economic gains and reliable networks of support.

In the years after the revolution, the EU was very willing to fund projects in Tunisia, since the country was perceived as the democratic hope in North Africa. European funding has generously been given to support civil society organizations, although direct funding for Tunisian state institutions has remained conditioned by political agreements that ensure European interests. From the perspective of the new Tunisian government, it seemed a relatively easy task to implement legislation and design institutions that would fulfill international standards and satisfy European expectations in the field of anti-trafficking. Nevertheless, the main priorities in postrevolutionary Tunisia appeared to be other issues.

In this respect, the representative of the MSA saw Tunisia as being in a different situation than Morocco, where migration has been an issue of public and political debate for a longer time. Tunisia does not even have a ministry that exclusively focuses on migration issues; it has neither an asylum system nor the legal framework, institutions, and resources to implement one in the near future. She argued that in postrevolutionary Tunisia, the priorities were different and the money, time, and energy were spent on more important aspects of its reconstruction. Being "a more stable country," she saw Morocco as further advanced in this process, where the New Migration Policy was decreed "from above" by the king (interview with repr. of MSA, Tun. 2015). But in Tunisia, she argued, a more active and powerful civil society was present that could put pressure on government institutions. "Politics are very different here," she concluded (ibid.). The different logics informing the national fields of migration politics shape IOM anti-trafficking interventions. In postrevolutionary Tunisia, new policies were designed as temporary solutions by intermediary institutions; in this context, IOM interventions were part of a larger state-building project. The newly founded Tunisian institutions cooperated with the IOM to gain recognition and resources that could be employed in the national struggles over power and positions.

The next section demonstrates how the IOM encountered self-confident, well-established actors in Morocco who knew how to use anti-trafficking for their own political purposes. Cooperating with the IOM on these issues was instrumental for the government to legitimize repressive means against irregularized migrants.

5.3.2 Repressive migration control in the name of anti-trafficking in Morocco

During my first encounter with the IOM in Morocco in summer 2013, I was told that the organization's attempts to "raise awareness from below" did not lead to expected results "because of the strong hierarchies" in its political system and culture (interview with IOM staff, Mor. 2013). One of the effects of the New Migration Policy announced by the Moroccan king later that year was that the IOM gained a position to support the implementation of policies decreed from above.

However, when I interviewed IOM staff again during a second visit in 2014, the situation for the IOM's capacity-building ambitions had not significantly improved. The organization still struggled with the determination of many actors to actually implement the announced policy changes. While the top of the political pyramid in Morocco announced new immigration and anti-trafficking policies, those designing and implementing such policies for the government and its administration were not necessarily convinced. Moreover, the IOM staff felt that "Moroccan society was not ready for it" (interview with IOM staff, Mor. 2015). In order to successfully introduce the new policy, my interview partner argued,

> you had to start with three targeted communication campaigns: the first "in your own shop," or "in your own government," the second one vis-a-vis the Moroccan society, and the third vis-a-vis migrants.
>
> (Ibid.)

In addition to the insufficient management of communication, the IOM staff complained that

> in the area of assistance for victims of trafficking we are still in a limbo, because today the victims still remain irregular migrants. There is no protection network available, there are no shelters, there is nothing in that regard. And the law hasn't been adopted, so we can't start working on establishing such networks, establishing such support mechanisms.
>
> (Ibid.)

After having organized numerous consultations, conferences, and trainings, the IOM acknowledged that these activities had not led to the desired results in terms of legal and institutional structures. Only after the King's announcement in 2013 did the Moroccan government start to work on the first explicit legislation dealing with asylum, immigration, and anti-trafficking. This announcement renewed the IOM's interest in directly cooperating with the Moroccan government, seizing a new opportunity to be heard by state authorities. Offering technical assistance and political advice to the government was seen by the IOM as an opportunity to mainstream the national migration policies according to international norms and standards. While the UNCHR had offered its assistance in developing a national asylum system, the IOM became the government's main advisor on anti-trafficking.

The IOM's direct influence on Moroccan policy- and law-making was particularly noticeable in the normative origins and discursive directions of the policy documents and legislative drafts.[12] With the linking of migration and anti-trafficking policies, the recommendations of the National Council for Human Rights bore witness to the influence of the IOM's discourse. In a statement released in September 2013, the National Human Rights Council (Conseil National des Droits de l'Homme, CNDH) dedicated about a quarter of its call for "a radically new immigration and asylum policy" to the "fight against the trafficking in persons" (CNDH 2013). The section explicitly credits the work of IOs as inspiration (ibid., 6). The text proposes introducing dispositions in the Moroccan penal code to suppress the recruitment, transport, transfer, accommodation, and reception of persons by threatening someone with force or using force or other means of constraints, etc. for the aim of exploitation. The definition of human trafficking and the subsequent specifications around the term exploitation are taken almost verbatim from the Palermo Protocols (ibid.). From their outset, Moroccan anti-trafficking politics have been part of migration politics, without further justification as to how and why the two phenomena should be related.

To put anti-trafficking policies into practice, the Moroccan government largely drew on instruments of border and migration control. In a presentation at a UN workshop in Morocco that I attended in 2014, a representative of the Ministry in charge of Moroccans Living Abroad and Migration Affairs proposed the following anti-trafficking measures: First, the planned activities for detecting criminal networks should be focused on the northeastern border region, in which most migrants wait to cross from Algeria to Morocco. Second, maritime surveillance should be increased to reduce the activities of criminal networks that offer transport to immigrants. Third, forests near the two Spanish enclaves of Ceuta and Melilla, typically used by immigrants as a refuge while they wait to cross, should be kept under better surveillance. Finally, he announced a genuine Moroccan plan to encourage the voluntary return of irregularized migrants. "We attempt to free them from the illegal immigration mafia and return them to their country of origin under safe conditions," he stressed (Observation at UN workshop, Mor. 2014). With these recommendations, the Ministry in charge of Moroccans Living Abroad and Migration Affairs sought to implement anti-trafficking policies through measures enhancing the surveillance of irregularized migrants blocked at the borders to Europe.

One year later, the Moroccan government started to raid the forests in the name of protecting potential VoTs. According to the activist collective No Borders Morocco (2015),

> 12 migrants were arrested during the Guruguru raid on 10th of February and taken to the police commissariat in Nador. [...] The authorities charged them with assassination, trafficking and drug abuse. [...] On 16th of February, 9 were taken from police custody to Kariat Arekmane and then transferred to Agadir, but the 3 remaining people continue to be imprisoned under trafficking accusations, and threatened with continued imprisonment or deportation.

When confronted in a press conference over mounting riots and repression, the Minister of Interior argued that these operations "permitted the liberation of many migrants, notably the women and children who had been forced to live in this forest by the networks of smugglers and traffickers of human beings" (quoted in Chambost 2015, translation IB). Moreover, he announced that a "similar operation will be conducted systematically in order to evacuate all the places squatted by migrants who plan to organize attempts of irregular migration" (ibid.). He proudly shared that 105 human trafficking networks were dismantled in 2014 (ibid.).

These repressive measures taken against irregularized migrants demonstrate how anti-trafficking politics were instrumentalized to legitimize repressive practices against migration. In the name of putting an end to the suffering and violation of women's rights, Moroccan state actors justified enhanced controls, increased identity checks, racially informed policing, and deportation. According to Julia O'Connell Davidson (2016, 69), such "emancipation propaganda" is based on vocabularies provided through the knowledge transfer and capacity-building activities of IOs. It "can be used by any powerful nation-state when it wishes to paint over the horrible things it has done in the brilliant brush strokes of the gift of freedom" (Wood quoted in ibid.). Appropriating the IOM's discourse, the Moroccan government openly announced its persecution of smugglers and traffickers in order to free and save vulnerable victims.

Independent civil society associations criticized this repressive initiative of the Moroccan government in February 2015. The No Borders Morocco collective (2015) argued against following the "European model" in its repressive and racist migration politics:

> Morocco justifies these inhuman and completely absurd actions with a human rights discourse which they have probably copied one-to-one from Europe [sic]. The eviction of the camps has the purpose of "liberating" the migrants from the grip of smugglers and traffickers. With this line of reasoning, Morocco is reproducing the stereotypes that we are being fed constantly from European governments and mainstream media: The people living in the Moroccan forests are a threat; Djihad, Ebola or Mafia, the reasons are exchangeable but the racism remains the same.

In a communication issued on the matter, the anti-racist association GADEM (2015) also called

> on the relevant authorities—who are detaining these individuals on the pretext of freeing them "from smuggling and trafficking networks"—to release them and return to the discussion table in order to peacefully finalize the new migration policy's implementation process.

The association had denounced the artificial link between the New Moroccan Migration Policy and anti-trafficking discourses since the beginning, in 2013. From an activist point of view, the phenomenon of human trafficking potentially concerns all Moroccans and foreigners and should therefore be treated as a broader issue (conversation with activists, Mor. 2014). In Morocco, however, it was misused as the justification of a repressive migration policy criminalizing migrants (ibid.). The transnational NGO Doctors without Borders called on Moroccan state actors to protect vulnerable migrants. According to an influential report it published on its experience in the northeast of Morocco, networks of smuggling and trafficking exploit irregularized migrants in Morocco who do not receive any kind of protection and who are criminalized by the state (MSF 2013). Moreover, migrants are obliged to pay smuggling networks in order to be able to enter Morocco, as the border to Algeria remains closed (ibid.). The report concluded that, despite the fact that Morocco has signed the Palermo Protocols in 2011, the government focused more on arresting and deporting potential traffickers instead of on identifying and assisting their victims (ibid., see also GADEM 2013). It further criticized the fact that IOs were not allowed to work in the northeast of Morocco, since the government did not want international observers in that disputed area (MSF 2013, 31).

218 *Anti-trafficking politics*

Despite the growing criticism, the IOM continued its interventions in Morocco that aimed to enhance the legal and institutional capacities of anti-trafficking. Traditionally, the IOM had exercised its symbolic violence through knowledge transfer, the exchange of experiences and 'best practices,' and participatory trainings and workshops. After the turn in Moroccan migration politics in 2013, the organization advocated more openly for concrete policies and legislative reforms. Some actors of the Moroccan government welcomed this international assistance; the newly founded Ministry in charge of Moroccans Living Abroad and Migration Affairs explicitly demanded the advice and technical support of IOs. In contrast, other parts of the Moroccan government, especially the Ministry of Interior, wanted to shake off international surveillance. They instrumentalized anti-trafficking policies to advance a more repressive agenda on irregularized migration in the name of protecting VoTs. The radicalism and brutality of the effects of the anti-trafficking politics depended on the state institutions that were responsible for their implementation. These institutions had learned how to play the game of anti-trafficking to their own advantage: while they insisted on their sovereignty and independence, they copied European laws, policies, and practices. The IOM taught them how to do this.

5.3.3 "They take everything!"—perceptions of the IOM's position and influence

Civil society organizations and migration scholars have not only criticized the Moroccan state for its instrumentalization of anti-trafficking policies; they have also expressed their skepticism of the expansive practices of the IOM in the country. From their point of view, IOM staff have become omnipresent since the announcement of the New Migration Policy:

> We always meet. I cannot pass two weeks without a meeting where the IOM is not present. In whatever meeting, even in very small meetings, trivial meetings, a representative of the IOM has to be present. They are "partners" now, "partners" with all the ministries,

observed a migrant activist concerning the IOM's new position and expanding influence (interview with activist, Mor. 2014). Given that "they also do the problem of trafficking, it is their new credo," she expressed her unease with the IOM's proactive expansion into new spheres of action (ibid.). "Maybe it is for the money, maybe it is a favor to the governments ..." she speculated, articulating the sorts of capital the IOM potentially gained through its interventions (ibid.). Hesitantly searching for words, she finally concluded, "they take everything," meaning all kinds of projects (ibid.).

> So, for now, it is trafficking. But trafficking, what is that? That is the [job of the] United Nations, because it is a very, very sensible issue, because you have to ensure the safety of the person who demands it,

Anti-trafficking politics 219

she explained, indicating that she did not expect the IOM to fulfill this task (ibid.). From her point of view, the IOM had a different mission: "Their principal objective is voluntary return. But that has nothing to do with trafficking!" (ibid.) In other spheres of action, such as anti-trafficking, she doubted its expertise and ability to ensure the victims' protection.

According to a Moroccan researcher, the IOM's expansion in the field was possible because the organization is "in close contact with the donors" (conversation with researcher, Mor. 2014). This advantage in social capital ensures the organization is "well-informed about available resources" and "can easily find funding" (ibid.). As a result, the IOM could "take everything" (ibid.). He explained: "If, for example, Spain wants to do a project in Tunisia, they propose that 'we can also do it in Morocco!'" (ibid.). They copied projects from one country and used it in another. "They have gained confidence and established a huge but superficial portfolio of projects," he stated, summarizing the IOM's powerful position in the field (ibid.). An activist for migrants' rights in Morocco held a similar view: anti-trafficking "is their new field of action where they offer their expertise, which they don't have— their study is bullshit!" he exclaimed, questioning the IOM's cultural capital (conversation with activist, Mor. 2014). "The UNHCR helps for asylum and IOM helps for trafficking. They are both recognized by the Moroccan state for their expertise. But they offer an expertise which they do not have, it is only a discourse," he went on, questioning IOs' increasing influence on emerging migration politics in Morocco (ibid.).

In contrast to the IOs, the expertise of NGOs that had worked in the country for a long time without official authorization was rarely invited to cooperate with the Moroccan state. The associations kept demanding to be included in the law-making processes at a stage when it was still possible to make substantial changes. In this respect, they feared that the active participation of IOs in law- and policy-making processes would prevent the government from engaging in 'real' participatory politics that included critical voices from independent associations. "The IOM takes the entire field and competes with other actors for funding that will get less than before, or only through redistribution by the IOM," a long-standing observer of Moroccan migration politics explained (conversation with former IOM staff, Mor. 2015). In Morocco, the political field is exclusive and isolated, with little openness to outsiders. State authorities have no desire to accept new actors in the field, especially if they promote the rights of immigrants. In contrast, the apolitical, technical interventions of IOs "that would always respect national policies" were welcomed (conversation with former IOM staff, Egypt 2015), as these signaled a cautious opening of national politics toward issues of immigration and asylum.

While Moroccan civil society and researchers described their relationship with IOM as marked by competition and mistrust, the IOM staff called it "a strong partnership" (interview with IOM staff, Mor. 2014).

> I think we also appreciate each other's strengths and see that we also have very complementary mandates. Often, the NGOs can say things

that we as a member state-based organization could never say. Even I am sometimes very envious that they can be so outspoken and I cannot,

she went on distinguishing the different roles (ibid.). "However, I also think that provides us with a more diplomatic leverage," she explained, establishing the advantages of the IOM's position (ibid.). "This is also a good point of IOM," agreed a former staff member, "it is our added value, because states trust us and because they have more open doors for us" (conversation with former IOM staff, Egypt 2015). Concerned with the public perception of their work, the IOM staff seemed quite aware of the ambivalent role that it plays in the field. The organization is not immune to criticism, but it presents itself as adaptive and able to maneuver among different expectations.

In Tunisia, IOs approached NGOs as new partners for implementing their projects when restrictions on international and non-state actors were loosened in 2011. Through their increased contacts and cooperation, NGOs became more interested in the IOM's mission. While independent associations and transnational networks remained skeptical about the IOM, others tried to profit from new possibilities of cooperation and funding. Just like government institutions, NGOs also used their involvement with and reference to international experts to lend weight to their own arguments and projects—especially in negotiations with state authorities.

5.4 Compassion and repression in mainstreaming anti-trafficking politics

After years of feminist and human rights groups campaigning against human trafficking in general and sex trafficking in particular, these issues gained widespread attention and recognition in international politics in the 1990s (Hess 2012). As a result of the growing international publicity, anti-trafficking became an integral part of European and international migration management in the beginning of the 2000s. While global anti-trafficking politics were primarily pushed and funded by the US and European states, the IOM became one of the main international advocates of these politics, implementing campaigns and promoting policies around the world.

This chapter has shown how the IOM expanded its standardized services to encompass combating human trafficking and spread these services to North African countries under transition. In contrast to its operational work on prevention and voluntary return, the IOM not only provides assistance to (potential) migrants or VoTs but also aims to directly advise government actors on how to develop national policies and legislation. This way, the organization strategically intervened in national policy fields. Its anti-trafficking interventions seek to make Morocco and Tunisia 'safe countries' for refugees, transit migrants, and VoTs, while they institutionalize a humanitarian but restrictive border regime beyond the external borders of the EU.

When the IOM started its anti-trafficking campaigns in North Africa, human trafficking was not regarded as a relevant issue or political problem in neither Moroccan nor Tunisian politics and societies. Due to the IOM's knowledge production and dissemination, agenda-setting, lobbying, and capacity building, both countries adopted anti-trafficking laws as part of their migration politics. Through its pioneering production and dissemination of expert knowledge, the IOM advanced a discourse that connects human trafficking to the smuggling of people, transnational crime, prostitution, and international migration. The organization actively contributed to the spread of a "moral panic" around human trafficking as a "modern form of slavery" (Bernstein 2010, 49). In the literature, the international, morally laden discourse of anti-trafficking is criticized as misrepresenting the contradictions, complexities, and varieties of experiences (cf. O'Connell Davidson 2016, 62), and many scholars point out that it neglects the agency of the victims (Berman 2003; Sharma 2003; Andrijasevic 2007; Sullivan 2010).

By holding workshops and organizing conferences to share international standards, 'best practices,' and 'lessons learned,' the IOM managed to establish human trafficking as a widely known concept in North African politics and societies. Appearing as international, neutral, technical, and therefore objective experts, the IOM staff (in)formed Moroccan and Tunisian actors about the transnational crime of human trafficking, assisted them in developing definitions and categories to detect the phenomenon, and thus promoted a certain transnational language and dominant understanding of international migration management.

The imperative to manage migration in the name of anti-trafficking calls for a fight against criminal traffickers and the protection of innocent victims, predominantly women. Victims' suffering due to trafficking, prostitution, and irregularized migration provides the legitimacy for the IOM to expand its activities and to intervene where national institutions and legal measures are absent. In terms of protection, the IOM promotes its voluntary return program as the preferred strategy to help VoTs. The term *return* implies that the person goes back to where they naturally belong (see Berman 2003, 60). Such assistance reproduces the "ideological connection between women and domesticity" (Cheng and Kim 2014, 14); moreover, it romanticizes home "as a place devoid of conflict, danger and exploitation" (Andrijasevic 2007, 31) and presents the international movement of women as inherently problematic and damaging (see also FitzGerald 2011). As Sharma notes (2003, 54), "exploitation 'away from home' is conceptualized as a separate problem from exploitative and/or untenable economic relations 'at home.'" In the context of anti-trafficking, it is the unauthorized international mobility of women from the Global South that attracts the most political attention.

Since only very few VoTs have actually been identified in North Africa, the IOM directed attention to the prevention of trafficking for 'risk groups.' Women are again presented as particularly vulnerable here. However, the extension of IOM projects to managing this new 'risk group' has been framed by a different moral imperative: while pity motivates the protection of the 'authentic victims' who are discovered, the majority of young female migrants traveling alone are viewed with growing mistrust and suspicion (see Fassin 2016). The IOM proposes information campaigns to educate them about 'appropriate behavior' that goes well beyond the question of migration. Designating a 'proper place' for them in terms of familial order, gender roles, and international labor markets, the IOM's interventions seek to reeducate them as "prudent subjects" (Schatral 2011, 6). Through individual risk management, IOM projects aim to reinstall social and gendered hierarchies in international mobility rights.

This gendered categorization of international migration management has been mainstreamed into national policies and legislations through the IOM's capacity- and institution-building. The organization supported Moroccan and Tunisian governments in institutionalizing anti-trafficking as a matter of criminal justice and of humanitarian protection. The resultant policies do not consider the "structural preconditions of exploited labor more generally" (Bernstein 2010, 49); nor do they account for the violations of women's rights in a broader sense nor for the restrictive European migration politics that make clandestine modes of traveling necessary in the first place (Andrijasevic 2007). O'Connell Davidson (2016, 67f.) argues that anti-trafficking policies are not employed to "eradicate exploitation, violence, suffering or restraints on freedom of movement or choice" but primarily help states in "shoring up their own monopoly over both violence and the control of mobility." In this context, the IOM encouraged Morocco and Tunisia to introduce new exceptional categories for humanitarian migration management and provided the discursive grounds to legitimize more restrictive migration control. While it is important to note that the various Moroccan and Tunisian actors involved in the IOM's anti-trafficking politics follow their own aspirations and ambitions, the dominant logic of these politics is compatible with the ongoing humanitarian externalization of the European border regime. Their implementation contributes to making them 'safe countries' for refugees, transit migrants, and VoTs, and it provides a powerful moral legitimation to expanding the 'fight against irregular migration' by pursuing and criminalizing transnational trafficking and smuggling networks in the name of saving innocent victims.

Since anti-trafficking discourses position traffickers "as responsible for everything from illegal immigration to moral chaos, a dangerous 'law unto themselves', infecting 'our' community with violence and disease" (Sharma 2003, 54f.), their networks are feared to threaten the central power of North African states and their ability to control their national territories and borders. In this respect, the IOM's anti-trafficking campaigns also serve to educate the two North African 'model states' in good governance and human rights standards. The predicted expansion of trafficking networks is regarded as a deviant, foreign practice threatening development in the region. In Tunisia, the state-building mission is observable in the support for its democratic transition and the restabilization of security. In Morocco, it is concerned with enhancing the rule of law and ensuring economic stability. Thus, the IOM's promotion of anti-trafficking policies and legislation is also about preserving and extending state powers and authority vis-à-vis transnational criminal networks and movements of unauthorized migration (O'Connell Davidson 2016, 59ff). From the European perspective, the introduction of legal measures to combat human trafficking makes Morocco and Tunisia more reliable partners for the European objectives of joint international migration management and of the expansion of border control along the routes of migration on the African continent. Ensuring the human rights of vulnerable people is regarded as an important criterion for potential practices for containing and returning migrants on their way to Europe. Criminalizing migrant smuggling and human trafficking allows states to legitimize police and military interventions in places of migrant shelter and solidarity.

Engaging in anti-trafficking politics helps the IOM distinguish its position in the field as a humanitarian actor; playing the humanitarian card makes possible for the organization to distance itself from European political interests in controlling migration in North Africa and the deadly consequences thereof. At the same time, the organization can distinguish itself from unstable North African states that nevertheless appear willing to learn from its international expertise. As to the latter, the IOM presents itself as a liberal advocate of women's rights. Gökce Yurdakul (2010) lays out the work of feminist postcolonial scholars who have revealed the typical entanglements of those who advocate women's rights in the Global South—and more recently among immigrant communities in the Global North—with colonial and racist politics (see also Neuhauser, Hess, and Schwenken 2017). Through its representation of female, often Muslim migrants as passive victims of the "barbaric and uncivilized" criminal networks on the African continent who need to be saved by international interventions (Ticktin 2008, 865), the IOM establishes for itself a progressive and enlightened Western identity and an unquestioned 'responsibility to protect.' Its anti-trafficking mission in North Africa resonates well with a logic of racial, cultural, and religious "otherness" and with "orientalist fantasies" about "Muslim cultures" being more traditional, patriarchal, and violent than Western ones (ibid., see also Yurdakul 2010, 116ff; Hess 2012, 146). According to Miriam Ticktin (2008, 865), neocolonial discourses about saving African, Arab, or Muslim women serve to perpetuate the global violence against women as "part of a larger nationalist and imperial project"—in this case, the international management of migration.

Remarkably, the majority of IOM staff working in the field are themselves young women, albeit mostly from the Global North and highly mobile due to their nationality, education, and class background. According to Elizabeth Bernstein (2010, 63), working in the field of anti-trafficking reinforces "their own perceived freedom and autonomy as Western women," imagining themselves

224 *Anti-trafficking politics*

as "more free and ethical than their 'sisters' from the developing world." The work provides them with a feminine "counterpart to the masculine politics of militaristic rescue" (ibid.). Relatedly, the IOM's influence is based on a symbolic power to streamline norms, discourses, and practices of political actors without exercising direct coercive power. Drawing on new forms of political and moral authority, the IOM strengthened its role as an international expert and gained direct influence in national fields of migration politics.

Notes

1 For the entire text, see: http://www.ohchr.org/EN/ProfessionalInterest/Pages/ProtocolTraffickingInPersons.aspx [01.04.2021].
2 Letter from German Minister of Interior Thomas De Maizière to the EU Commissioner for Home Affairs, September 9th, 2014, translation IB.
3 See the website "Action against Trafficking in Human Beings" of the Council of Europe: http://www.coe.int/en/web/anti-human-trafficking/home [01.04.2021].
4 See the project description on the IOM Tunisia website: http://tunisia.iom.int/activities/soutien-et-transfert-des-m%C3%A9canismes-d%E2%80%99assistance-d%E2%80%99orientation-et-d%E2%80%99%C3%A9change-d-%E2%80%99exp%C3%A9riences-en [01.04.2021].
5 See the news on AI website: "Amnesty International staff members expelled from Morocco." June 11th, 2015. https://www.amnesty.org/en/latest/news/2015/06/amnesty-international-staff-members-expelled-from-morocco/ [01.04.2021].
6 According to a report by the UNESCO, numbers and claims about the global spread of human trafficking are based more in myths that in facts (quoted in Cheng and Kim 2014, 4).
7 During my fieldwork, for example, I could assist the international seminar "The new migration politics in Morocco—which integration strategy?" organized by the IOM (IOM 2014a, 8, translation IB). With regard to human trafficking, the IOM has organized several big events in both countries. In Tunisia, for example, an international seminar was organized in 2012 with the support of the IOM office in Kuwait to support the exchange of good practices on trafficking in the region. Two years later, an international conference on Combating the Trafficking of Human Beings. A plural response to a phenomenon with multiple forms was also organized by the IOM (IOM 2014b, translation IB).
8 See the website of IOM International: https://www.iom.int/fr/lutte-contre-la-traite-des-personnes [30.01.2018].
9 See YouTube: https://www.youtube.com/watch?v=rKoKfU4zuMM [01.04.2021].
10 Last accessed April 1st, 2021.
11 The official text of the Tunisian law, with my emphasis on the parts going beyond the Palermo Protocols:

> La traite des personnes : Est considérée comme traite des personnes, le recrutement, le transport, le transfert, le détournement, le rapatriement, l'hébergement ou l'accueil de personnes, par le recours ou la menace de recours à la force *ou aux armes ou* à toutes autres formes de contrainte, ou d'enlèvement, de tromperie, d'abus d'autorité ou d'une situation de vulnérabilité ou par l'offre ou l'acceptation de paiements ou d'avantages pour obtenir le consentement d'une personne ayant autorité sur une autre aux fins d'exploitation, *quelle que soit la forme, que cette exploitation soit commise par l'auteur de ces faits ou en vue de mettre cette personne à la disposition d'un tiers.* L'exploitation comprend l'exploitation de la prostitution d'autrui ou

d'autres formes d'exploitation sexuelle, le travail ou les services forcés, l'esclavage ou les pratiques analogues à l'esclavage, la servitude ou la *mendicité, le prélèvement total ou partiel d'organes, de tissus, de cellules, de gamètes et de gènes ou toutes autres formes d'exploitation.*

(DCAF 2015, 1)

12 See, for example, the draft law on anti-trafficking approved by the Moroccan government in September 2015 (see the news on the website of UN Women: "New draft law to combat human trafficking brings hope in Morocco." September 9th, 2015. http://www.unwomen.org/en/news/stories/2015/9/new-draft-law-to-combat-human-trafficking-brings-hope-in-morocco [01.04.2021]).

Literature cited

Adler-Nissen, Rebecca. 2013. "Introduction. Bourdieu and International Relations Theory." In *Bourdieu in International Relations: Rethinking Key Concepts in IR*, edited by Rebecca Adler-Nissen, 1–23. New York: Routledge.

Altai Consulting. 2015. *Migration Trends across the Mediterranean: Connecting the Dots.* Cairo: IOM Mena Regional Office.

Andrijasevic, Rutvica. 2007. "Beautiful Dead Bodies: Gender, Migration and Representation in Anti-Trafficking Campaigns." *Feminist Review* 86 (1), 24–44. doi:10.1057/palgrave.fr.9400355.

Bahl, Eva, Marina Ginal, and Sabine Hess. 2010. "Unheimliche Arbeitsbündnisse. Zum Funktionieren des Anti-Trafficking-Diskurses auf lokaler und europäischer Ebene." In *Grenzregime. Diskurse, Praktiken, Institutionen in Europa*, edited by Sabine Hess and Bernd Kasparek, 161–178. Berlin and Hamburg: Assoziation A.

Baird, Theodore, Thomas Spijkerboer, and Paolo Cuttitta. 2015. "Spectral Vessel." *OpenDemocracy.* https://www.opendemocracy.net/en/can-europe-make-it/spectral-vessels/ [01.04.2021].

Bartels, Inken. 2014. "Die Neuordnung der tunesischen Migrationspolitik nach dem 'Arabischen Frühling.'" *Berliner Debatte Initial* 25 (4): 48–64.

Bartels, Inken. 2018. "Practices and Power of Knowledge Dissemination." *Movements. Journal for Critical Migration and Border Regime Studies* 4 (1): 47–66. https://movements-journal.org/issues/06.wissen/03.bartels--practices-and-power-of-knowledge-dissemination-international-organizations-in-the-externalization-of-migration-management-in-morocco-and-tunisia.html [16.04.2021].

Berman, Jacqueline. 2003. "(Un)Popular Strangers and Crises (Un)Bounded: Discourses of Sex-Trafficking, the European Political Community and the Panicked State of the Modern State." *European Journal of International Relations* 9 (1): 37–86. doi:10.1177/1354066103009001157.

Bernstein, Elizabeth. 2010. "Militarized Humanitarianism Meets Carceral Feminism: The Politics of Sex, Rights, and Freedom in Contemporary Antitrafficking Campaigns." *Signs: Journal of Women in Culture and Society* 36 (1): 45–71. doi:10.1086/652918.

Bojadzijev, Manuela, and Serhat Karakayali. 2007. "Autonomie der Migration. 10 Thesen zu einer Methode." In *Turbulente Ränder. Neue Perspektiven auf Migration an den Rändern Europas*, edited by Transit Migration Forschungsgruppe, 203–210. Bielefeld: transcript. doi:10.14361/9783839407813-011.

Bourdieu, Pierre. 1977. *Outline of a Theory of Practice.* Cambridge: Cambridge University Press. doi:10.1017/CBO9780511812507.

Bourdieu, Pierre. 1992. *Rede und Antwort*. Frankfurt aM: Suhrkamp.
Bourdieu, Pierre, and Loïc Wacquant. 1992. *An Invitation to Reflexive Sociology*. Chicago, IL: University of Chicago Press.
Chambost, Pauline. 2015. "L'Intérieur entame le démantèlement des camps de migrants." February 10th, 2015. TelQuel. https://telquel.ma/2015/02/10/linterieur-entame-demantelement-camps-migrants_1433918 [01.04.2021].
Cheng, Sealing, and Eunjung Kim. 2014. "The Paradoxes of Neoliberalism: Migrant Korean Sex Workers in the United States and 'Sex Trafficking.'" *Social Politics: International Studies in Gender, State & Society* 21 (3): 355–381. doi:10.1093/sp/jxu019.
CNDH. 2013. *Thematic Report on the Situation of Migrants and Refugees in Morocco. Foreigners and Human Rights in Morocco: For a Radically New Asylum and Migration Policy*. Rabat: CNDH.
DCAF (Centre pour le Contrôle Démocratique des Forces Armées). 2015. "Projet de Loi Organique Relatif à la Prévention et la Lutte Contre la Traite des Personnes." https://legislation-securite.tn/node/54205 [01.04.2021].
Fassin, Didier. 2015. "Vom Rechtsanspruch zum Gunsterweis. Zur moralischen Ökonomie der Asylvergabepraxis im heutigen Europa." *Mittelweg 36* 25 (1): 62–78.
FitzGerald, Sharron. 2011. "Vulnerability and Sex Trafficking in the United Kingdom." In *Regulating the International Movement of Women: From Protection to Control*, edited by Sharron FitzGerald, 158–174. London and New York: Routledge.
GADEM (Groupe Antiraciste de Défense et d'Accompagnement des Étrangers et Migrants). 2013. *Communication du GADEM au Comité sur les Droits des Travailleurs Migrants*. Rabat: GADEM.
GADEM (Groupe Antiraciste de Défense et d'Accompagnement des Étrangers et Migrants). 2015. *Morocco's Exceptional Program of Regularization Cut Short*. Rabat: GADEM.
Heller, Charles, and Antoine Pécoud. 2020. "Counting Migrants' Deaths at the Border: From Civil Society Counterstatistics to (Inter)Governmental Recuperation." *American Behavioral Scientist* 64 (4): 480–500. doi:10.1177/0002764219882996.
Hess, Sabine. 2012. "Das Anti-Trafficking Dispositiv. Gender in der europäischen Migrationspolitik." In *Biopolitik und Geschlecht. Zur Regulierung des Lebendigen*, edited by Eva Sänger and Malaika Rödel, 129–151. Münster: Westfälisches Dampfboot.
IOM. 2009. *Traite Transnationale des Personnes. Etat des Lieux et Analyse des Réponses au Maroc*. Rabat: IOM Morocco.
IOM. 2010. *Cartographie des Flux Migratoires des Marocains en Italie*. Geneva: IOM.
IOM. 2013a. *Baseline Study on Trafficking in Persons in Tunisia: Assessing the Scope and Manifestations*. Tunis: IOM Tunisia.
IOM. 2013b. *OIM Moyen-Orient et Afrique du Nord: Flash Info*. Cairo: IOM MENA Regional Office.
IOM. 2014a. *Lettre d'Information N°22*. Rabat: IOM Morocco.
IOM. 2014b. *IOM Middle East and North Africa: Flash Report*. Cairo: IOM MENA Regional Office.
IOM. 2014c. *Newsletter OIM Tunisie, Juillet 2014*. Tunis: IOM Tunisia.
IOM. 2015a. *Migration in Egypt, Morocco and Tunisia. Overview of the Complex Migratory Flows in the Region*. Cairo: IOM MENA Regional Office.

IOM. 2015b. *Traites des Personnes: 160 Magistrats Tunisiens Sont Sensibilisés par l'OIM sur le Problème de la Traite des Personnes en Tunisie*. Tunis: IOM Tunisia.
IOM. 2015c. *Assistance de Court Terme et Aide au Retour Volontaire des Migrants Rescapé de la Mer*. Tunis: IOM Tunisia.
IOM. 2015d. *Une Délégation de l'OIM se Réunit Avec l'Assemblée des Représentants du Peuple Autour du Projet de Loi Organique Contre la Traite des Personnes en Tunisie*. Tunis: IOM Tunisia.
IOM, and African Development Bank (ADB). 2012. *Migration of Tunisians to Libya: Dynamics, Challenges, and Prospects*. Tunis: IOM Tunisia/ADB.
Jackson, Peter. 2009. "Pierre Bourdieu." In *Critical Theorists and International Relations*, edited by Jenny Edkins and Nick Vaughan-Williams, 102–113. London and New York: Routledge.
Kapur, Ratna. 2005. *Erotic Justice. Law and the New Politics of Postcolonialism*. London: Routledge-Cavendish. doi:10.4324/9781843146193.
Karakayalı, Serhat. 2008. *Gespenster der Migration. Zur Genealogie illegaler Einwanderung in der Bundesrepublik Deutschland*. Bielefeld: transcript. doi:10.14361/9783839408957.
Korneev, Oleg. 2014. "Exchanging Knowledge, Enhancing Capacities, Developing Mechanisms: IOM's Role in the Implementation of the EU–Russia Readmission Agreement." *Journal of Ethnic and Migration Studies* 40 (6): 888–904. doi:10.1080/1369183X.2013.855072.
MSF. 2013. *Violence, Vulnerability and Migration: Trapped at the Gates of Europe*. MSF. https://www.msf.org/violence-vulnerability-and-migration-trapped-gates-europe [01.04.2021].
Neuhauser, Johanna, Sabine Hess, and Helen Schwenken. 2017. "Unter- oder überbelichtet: Die Kategorie Geschlecht in medialen und wissenschaftlichen Diskursen zu Flucht." In *Der lange Sommer der Migration. Grenzregime III*, edited by Sabine Hess, Bernd Kasparek, Stefanie Kron, Mathias Rodatz, Maria Schwertl, and Simon Sontowski, 176–195. Berlin and Hamburg: Assoziation A.
No Borders Morocco. 2015. "Update III on Detentions and Deportations of Sub-Saharan Migrants in Morocco." February 25th, 2015. https://beatingborders.wordpress.com/2015/02/23/update-iii-on-detentions-and-deportations-of-sub-saharan-migrants-in-morocco/ [30.01.2018].
O'Connell Davidson, Julia. 2016. "De-Canting 'Trafficking in Human Beings', Re-Centering the State." *The International Spectator* 51 (1): 58–73. doi:10.1080/03932729.2016.1121685.
Pandofli, Marinella, and Laurence McFalls. 2010. "Global Bureaucracy: Irresponsible but not Indifferent." In *Conflict, Security, and the Reshaping of Society*, edited by Alessandro Dal Lago and Salvatore Palidda, 171–185. London: Routledge. doi:10.4324/9780203846315-20.
Pécoud, Antoine. 2015. *Depoliticizing Migration: Global Governance and International Migration Narratives*. Basingstoke: Palgrave Macmillan.
Schatral, Susanne. 2010. "Awareness Raising Campaigns against Human Trafficking in the Russian Federation: Simply Adding Males or Redefining a Gendered Issue?" *Anthropology of East Europe Review* 28 (1): 239–267.
Schatral, Susanne. 2011. "Categorization and Instruction: IOM's Role in Preventing Human Trafficking in the Russian Federation." In *Perpetual Motion? Transformation and Transition in Central and Eastern Europe & Russia*, edited by Tul'si

Bhambry, Clare Griffin, Titus Hjelm, Christopher Nicholson, and Olga G. Voronina, 2–15. London: School of Slavonic and East European Studies, UCL.
Sharma, Nandita. 2003. "Travel Agency: A Critique of Anti-Trafficking Campaigns." *Refuge* 21 (3): 53–65. doi:10.25071/1920-7336.21302.
Sullivan, Barbara. 2010. "Trafficking in Human Beings." In *Gender Matters in Global Politics. A Feminist Introduction to International Relations*, edited by Laura J. Shepherd, 89–102. London and New York: Routledge.
Ticktin, Miriam. 2008. "Sexual Violence as the Language of Border Control: Where French Feminist and Anti-Immigrant Rhetoric Meet." *Signs* 33 (4): 863–889. doi:10.1086/528851.
UN. 2000. *United Nations Convention against Transnational Organized Crime*. Geneva: UN.
Yurdakul, Gökce. 2010. "Governance Feminism und Rassismus: Wie führende Vertreterinnen von Immigranten die antimuslimische Diskussion in Westeuropa und Nordamerika befördern." In *Staatsbürgerschaft, Migration und Minderheiten. Inklusion und Ausgrenzungsstrategien im Vergleich*, edited by Gökce Yurdakul and Michael Bodemann, 111–125. Wiesbaden: VS Springer. doi:10.1007/978-3-531-92223-2_5.

Conclusion

In its examination of the International Organization for Migration's (IOM) practices in Morocco and Tunisia, this book has shown that migration management in North Africa aims to teach (potential) migrants and state actors to view the control of migration as their own problem and to take actions that are in line with the dominant logics of the field, namely neoliberalism, humanitarianism, and security. The IOM supports this process through social work and education, aid and assistance, knowledge production and dissemination, and capacity building. In this conclusion, I summarize the empirical findings of this study and reflect on its theoretical framework.

In the first part of the conclusion, I give a condensed overview of the transformations in migration control practices and discuss how these transformations affect stability and change in the *trans-Mediterranean field of migration management*. I argue that the IOM's soft techniques of governing migration—based on participation, offers, and incentives—exercise a *symbolic power* and *symbolic violence* that helped stabilize the *European border regime* in times of instability and fading legitimization. At the same time, I highlight that the implementation of the IOM's migration management practices remains contested by the *struggles of migration* and by the *strategies* and *stakes* of diverse actors in the field that necessitate the reinvention of new control practices. Against this background, I outline general trends in international migration governance that increasingly expand on the African continent today.

In the second part, I focus on the IOM's *position* and *relations* in the trans-Mediterranean field of migration management. I characterize the IOM as a global expert (not only) on migration issues and draw conclusions about the organization's growing influence in the arranging of migration control in sending and transit countries. I argue that the *symbolic capital* that the IOM holds as an apolitical, technical service provider of international expertise helps the organization promote its work and establish itself as a widely recognized actor in the field. As shown in this book, IOM projects are based on a humanitarian, neoliberal, and thus progressive self-understanding that are well suited to meeting the structural requirements of an increasingly economized and transnationalized international migration governance.

DOI: 10.4324/9781003204169-7

230 *Conclusion*

This *fit* with the dominant logics and their flexible application in its practical work account for the organization's success.

In the final part, I reflect on the use of Bourdieu's *Theory of Practice* to study international organizations (IOs) and international migration governance. In the study of IOs within a certain field, Bourdieu's relational approach accounts for both the agency and the influence of IOs vis-à-vis other actors as well as for the structures that constrain their action. This praxeological perspective does not regard IOs as monolithic actors but considers the stakes, strategies, and knowledges within an organization. In sum, Bourdieu's Theory of Practice allows conceptualizing change and stability in international migration governance as resulting from various interrelated struggles *among* and *within* collective actors at different levels of a transnational field.

Change and stability in the trans-Mediterranean field of migration management

The IOM's services were increasingly demanded by its member states in the context of the so-called migration crises in Morocco in 2005 and in Tunisia in 2011. These 'crises' were in fact crises of the European border regime, which was built on militarized measures and on cooperation with North African states that had agreed to stop migrants by repressive means. When the security-oriented border regime was challenged by the struggles of migration, the EU and its member states searched for new actors and instruments to exercise control over unauthorized migration movements and to stabilize their external borders in the Mediterranean. In these moments of instability and fading legitimacy of the border regime, the IOM promoted its services, promising more effective, sustainable, and humane techniques to govern migration movements before migrants reached the borders of Europe. The organization announced that they would take care of what European states perceived as the 'problem of irregular migration' within the North Africa borderlands, using projects that would work through incentives, voluntary offers, and the participation of those groups who should be protected, returned, or prevented from leaving. In this respect, the IOM distinguished its work from dominant means of repressive state control that stop migrants through the use of physical violence.

However, looking at the implementation and negotiation of IOM projects in North Africa, this book has shown that migration control through *repression*—notably by state actors—and migration control through *compassion*—notably by international and non-state actors—are two elements of the same border regime. IOM projects rely on and profit from the precarious situations of (potential) migrants at the external borders of the EU, their lack of prospects in their countries of origin, and their strong beliefs and material needs to reach Europe. To different degrees, these conditions enabling IOM projects to succeed are produced by the same European states that fund IOM projects to manage the situation in the North African borderlands. According to Loïc Wacquant (2010), the combination of economic and penal elements is inherent to the neoliberal state. With a conceptualization of migration management as a "market-conforming state crafting" project (ibid. 2012, 71), these elements can be regarded as core features of the neoliberal governance of migration. For the trans-Mediterranean field of migration management, this means that the "boundaries between protection and coercion, attention and persuasion, help and control" are increasingly blurred, so that different interventions become difficult to distinguish and to critically evaluate (Brachet 2016, 286).

In analyzing concrete practices of prevention, voluntary return, and anti-trafficking, this study has demonstrated how IOM interventions help foster and expand the border regime in both *symbolical* and *material* terms. Examining the IOM's information campaigns, Chapter 3 has focused on practices of education, empowerment, and social work. It has shown how the IOM uses innovative, participatory methods to encourage potential North African emigrants to voluntarily participate in their own management and to believe in its benefits. They are addressed as entrepreneurial, neoliberal subjects who need to be informed in order to make responsible decisions about their lives and about the development of their countries. Control over migration is pursued through practices of (in)formation that seek to influence potential migrants' future behavior and choices. These practices exercise symbolic power that makes use of morals and emotions to mobilize marginalized youth to cooperate in what the IOM perceives as orderly projects of life—and thereby stay in their country. These practices aim to change individuals in the Global South rather than the global social inequalities that account for their desires and needs to migrate. Therefore, migration management can be interpreted as a *global duty to educate* young people in North Africa about their proper place in an asymmetrically structured field of international mobility rights. The IOM's individualized risk management through prevention thereby prioritizes a *neoliberal logic* over a *logic of rights* in the trans-Mediterranean field of migration management.

The chapter on voluntary return (Chapter 4) has directed attention to the IOM's practices of humanitarian aid and assistance. It has shown how the IOM is implicated in the sorting and reorienting of Sub-Saharan migrants in transit along the lines of flexible, employed target groups defined by the donors of its services. Through practices of categorizing and classifying people on the move into different profiles, the IOM contributes to a wider humanitarian trend in international migration politics of offering material assistance to vulnerable groups who are perceived as passive recipients of aid, rather than of granting rights to asylum to individuals who flee political persecution. Through its voluntary return program, the organization thus seeks to gain control over migration through practices of care. In this respect, migration management can be described as a *moral responsibility to protect* vulnerable migrants who are blocked at the external borders of the

EU rather than to question the causes and conditions of their vulnerability. Thus, the IOM's politics of return contribute to a shift away from a logic of rights to an emphasis on the *logic of humanitarianism* in the field.

Focusing on the IOM's anti-trafficking politics, Chapter 5 has paid particular attention to practices of knowledge production and capacity building. It has shown how the IOM contributes to the perception of human trafficking as a relevant issue in Morocco and Tunisia by means of counting, mapping, locating, and categorizing. Based on its symbolic capital as an international expert, the organization is able to stimulate North African actors to learn how to 'fight human trafficking' according to international standards. The IOM helped to establish national policies, laws, and institutions to address the phenomenon through measures of criminal justice and humanitarian protection. In this way, the organization emphasizes both *security* and *humanitarian logics* over a rights-based approach. Migration control is mainstreamed in the North African borderlands by making state actors accountable for combating human trafficking according to these logics. In its endeavor for *hard facts and soft influence*, the IOM's anti-trafficking politics in North Africa strengthened the organization's position in the field as a humanitarian actor and as a liberal advocate for women's rights.

These developments in trans-Mediterranean migration politics have not been presented as a linear path of evolution toward more sophisticated control technologies; rather, the book has shown how different practices of migration management were implemented in parallel, reinforcing and sometimes contradicting each other. In sum, a combination of neoliberal, humanitarian, and security logics dominates the trans-Mediterranean field of migration management. To start, a neoliberal logic, which has been addressed by much of the literature on the politics of international migration management (see Chapter 2), informs the IOM's work in North Africa. In this respect, the IOM promotes its services as effective and sustainable instruments that productively channel migration into orderly ways that mutually benefit migrants and states, drawing on an economic discourse based on a neoliberal rationality. Moreover, its practices of engaging (potential) migrants but also North African actors in the transnational management of migration represent neoliberal arts of governing at distance. The IOM's migration management thus works by outsourcing responsibility and by disciplining those who should be controlled and those who should learn how to control. It creates competition among Moroccan and Tunisian actors looking to become its partners but also among (potential) migrants looking to participate in and profit from its services. At the same time, the IOM's constant concern with the marketing of its services indicates how its work is part of a competitive business of migration control.

However, the study of the IOM's practices of migration management has also shown that these are neither the expression of a purely economic rationality nor the outcome of a totalizing neoliberal project. Chapter 4 has revealed how neoliberal logic combines with humanitarian ambitions, and Chapter 5 has highlighted how it is entangled with unquestioned security concerns. In North Africa, migration is not primarily managed for the purpose of becoming economically productive. Legal instruments to select migrants who could be economically beneficial to European labor markets hardly exist; instead, migration movements are filtered according to humanitarian and risk criteria. 'Vulnerable' groups of Sub-Saharan migrants are selected to be cared for in the North African borderlands, and North African youth 'at risk' of emigration are educated on caring for themselves, their future, their family, and/or their country. The IOM engages multiple actors in the governance of migration who would themselves believe in the stakes of migration management—whether economic, humanitarian, security, or other. These actors are mobilized to take action and responsibility for creating what the IOM promotes as orderly and smooth processes of migration and its control. Yet, a rights-based logic is not promoted by the IOM but rather pushed to the margins of the field.

Managing migration according to the dominant logics entails bringing migration under the effective authority of states—preferably without producing too much turbulence, criticism, and deaths. Through flexible (re)combination and distinction of these logics, the IOM's practices helped the European border regime reinvent and even expand itself in a time of fading legitimization of existing control practices. As new actors emerged, practices changed, and logics shifted, these reconfigurations in migration control stabilized the border regime in the Mediterranean. As demonstrated in this book, the IOM's practices in Morocco and Tunisia provide a new normative orientation along with innovative methods for states to gain control over unauthorized movements of migration. They promise international expert knowledge and new forms of authority that draw on the complicity of those who are governed. Moreover, in the long term, the IOM's migration management contributes to maintaining the existing symbolic and material orders without the use of physical force and/or obvious means of repression. Practices of pedagogic prevention and humanitarian aid compensate for the brutal effects of migration control and normalize more visible forms of violence at the border. In emphasizing humanitarian and neoliberal logics, the IOM makes the externalization of migration control less prone to public criticism.

Furthermore, the IOM's practices contributed to incorporating countries outside Europe into the expanding project of international migration management. This externalization operates less through the building of walls and fences and more through the introduction of the discourses, categories, and procedures of migration management to new contexts. For one thing, the IOM itself is implicated in the practical sorting of migration movements in transit; the organization filters and reorients the trajectories of people on the move according to rather flexible categories, without provoking international protest and outside the domain of European asylum procedures. In this way, its practical work introduces new forms of differential inclusion according to humanitarian concerns rather than to political rights or economic utility. It fosters a global trend of turning the protection of migrants and refugees from an issue of rights into an act of mercy, thereby contributing to the marginalization of the logic of rights in international migration governance.

For another thing, the organization teaches state and non-state actors in the Global South to recognize the control of migration and human trafficking as their problem and to design themselves appropriate policies, laws, and institutions according to the dominant logics of the field. Notably, the Tunisian context has shown how the IOM's migration management interferes with processes of state (re)building and of stabilizing a model country within an unstable region. Consequently, Morocco and Tunisia are expected to become countries that are safe enough for the return, rescue, and accommodation of migrants that Europe does not want on its territory. Thus, the IOM seeks to make state actors accountable for managing migration and for becoming reliable partners for international cooperation. This is possible because the IOM is not perceived as an external force with a colonial past intervening in these countries but as a somewhat neutral international expert. The IOM's practices also affect North African politics and societies beyond issues that are directly linked to migration. Projects that aim to disseminate knowledge and build capacities to manage migration or to fight human trafficking often entail implicit assumptions, such as those around (neo)liberal values or gender norms. Through the education of supposedly uninformed migrants and state actors, the IOM's practices reproduce colonial and patriarchal relations between so-called international experts or aid workers on the one hand and the recipients of their information and aid on the other.

The IOM's practices of migration management do not only reveal changing *modes* of migration control; they also provide insights into the (not so new) *content* of these arts of governing. In other words, they indicate who is to be managed, educated, cared for, or criminalized. The IOM's definitions of target groups for its programs reveal whose suffering is regarded as worthy of protection; whose behavior is considered as suspicious, deviant, or a risk; and whose mobility across borders is criminalized as 'illegal' and 'trafficked'—while the mobility of internationals and expats is welcomed. The IOM contributes not only to the symbolic production and elaboration of these different categories of people on the move but also to sorting migration movements accordingly. The organization thus establishes and fosters new hierarchies of legitimate claims to international mobility and protection and is responsible for their very material consequences.

The IOM's anti-trafficking politics are particularly influential in this regard: through its production and dissemination of knowledge on human trafficking, the organization has established a prominent discourse in North African politics and societies that depicts figures of mostly female 'victims of trafficking' and male 'criminal traffickers' (Chapter 5). In this way, the IOM fosters perceptions of women in the Global South as best protected if they stay 'at home' or if they are 'voluntarily' returned there, along with perceptions of men who exploit women if they support them in moving on. While this picture is certainly true for many situations along the routes of migration to Europe, it especially leaves out the agency of female migrants from the Global South and their networks and economies of self-help and support, as well as the structural conditions of the expanding border regime on the African continent that make it necessary to rely on smuggling services in the first place. By establishing such predefined gendered and racialized categorizations in international migration management, the IOM supports policies, laws, and institutions that differentiate people's movements and govern different groups through varying practices of care, control, and criminalization. While the IOM acts in the name of saving or preventing migrants (especially female migrants in the Global South) from suffering, its projects actualize racialized colonial modes and patriarchal practices of governing people on the African continent.

This example shows that both states and IOs play a crucial role in the struggles over the legitimate vision and division of the social world (Bourdieu 2003). The global discourses, international standards, and common categories of migration management that the IOM mainstreams into North African politics and societies are powerful instruments that "impose universalist claims" about who is entitled to migrate and who must be prevented and controlled (ibid.). Through practices of naming, categorizing, and sorting people on the move, the IOM exercises a *symbolic violence* in the trans-Mediterranean field of migration management. This concept directs attention to the ways that the IOM's practices of migration management reproduce and legitimize existing social hierarchies and power relations without being recognized as doing so (Jackson 2009, 102). Through its knowledge production and dissemination, the IOM is able to create a certain reality or 'problem' that calls for specific measures, which can be provided by the IOM's services.

Finally, whether symbolic or material, practices of migration management nevertheless remain contested. The IOM's different projects have shown how migrants continue to struggle with the practices of their management. The regime concept allows us to regard these struggles as not external to migration governance but as an integral part that challenges, co-opts, and actualizes its practices, thereby leading to its redefinition and further development. Since IOM projects rely on the voluntary participation of other actors in order to be effective, their implementation remains a particularly fragile negotiation process. While the IOM's migration management rests on and actualizes an *illusio* of migration as controllable, this book has shown that its implementation remains subject to unpredictable struggles. These struggles necessitate the development of new control practices and logics to stabilize social and political orders in the trans-Mediterranean field of migration management.

The IOM as a global expert for (not only) migration

The IOM's symbolic power is based on its symbolic capital gained as an international expert in migration and human trafficking. As the empirical chapters have demonstrated, the organization is able to direct international attention and political action to certain phenomena and to make invisible those issues that are (at risk of becoming) out of (the IOM's) control. Numbers and statistics are important resources in this regard (Guild, Grant, and Groenendijk 2017, 15); published in the organizations' reports, websites, press releases, etc., they are powerful tools in the *symbolic struggles* over the definition of crises, risks, and crimes. These publications commonly include recommendations for management: the production of a crisis necessitates exceptional, humanitarian measures; a risk calls for neoliberal forms of prevention; and a crime requires repressive measures to persecute the criminal. Thus, the IOM is able to promote a dominant view on migration and its appropriate management in North Africa, along with a demand for its own services. Its symbolic interventions are particularly effective, since they are not perceived as an imposition by external forces but as offers that can be appropriated by different actors to pursuit their own projects. Its reputation as a somewhat neutral and objective international expert is a main advantage of the IOM in comparison to European states, whose interventions are often viewed by North African actors in the field in light of their colonial pasts.

This study revealed that the organization's practices of migration management are often in contrast to its discourses, which promote and justify its work as being mutually beneficial for sending and receiving states and migrants alike. Analysis of its practices of prevention, voluntary return, and anti-trafficking has shown that the organization is not able to fulfill the promises that it makes in its multiple forms of self-presentation. Nevertheless, the IOM continuously expands its activities and influence in the trans-Mediterranean field of migration management and beyond. Despite the contested character of its programs and the dubious impact of its projects in Morocco and Tunisia, the IOM has succeeded in establishing itself as a relevant actor in North Africa. This success can be explained with the help of Bourdieu's concepts on two interlinked levels: first, by analyzing the IOM's position and relations in the trans-Mediterranean field of migration management; second, by looking inside the organization and investigating the collectively shared *habitus*, assumptions, and knowledge that account for the organization's performance in the field (see next section).

With regard to the IOM's position and relations in the field, this book has shown that the organization is neither a mere instrument of powerful states nor an actor that is totally independent of them. Contrary to assumptions about neoliberal governance, the increasing involvement of IOs in the politics of international migration management does not necessarily dismantle state politics; rather, it intervenes in the complex relations among diverse actors in transnationalized fields. The work of IOs is conditioned by the rules and logic of these fields, which they are also able to shape. For example, the IOM's activities are conditioned by and reproduce neoliberal logic by its constant competition with other IOs and non-governmental organizations (NGOs) over funding from donors.

The IOM is not the only organization that implements projects governing migration in North Africa: the United Nations High Commissioner for Refugees (UNHCR), the International Labor Organization (ILO), and the International Centre for Migration Policy Development (ICMPD) all entered the field in the beginning of the century. While they officially cooperate in different projects, release common statements, and conduct joint missions, they take great pains to formally distinguish their mandates, target groups, and spheres of influence. The UNHCR is the main partner but also the main opponent of the IOM in the field. In my observations, the relationship of the two organizations seemed ambivalent: while staff spoke on behalf of each other's organization at official events, they were very keen to delineate their own responsibilities—especially in critical situations, such as the struggles of Choucha (Chapter 4). Generally, the UNHCR received more attention than the IOM, but also more criticism. As shown in this book, the IOM had to make itself known in the field and take an equally prominent position in the beginning of the century. It put forward its neoliberal assets—such as its flexibility, time-, and cost-effectiveness—to compete with what was perceived as a cumbersome UN bureaucracy acting in the name of humanitarianism, which was a marginal logic at that time.

Once the IOM itself began to work according to the logic of humanitarianism in 2011, it also had to compete with humanitarian NGOs, such as the Red Crescent, Caritas, and the Islamic Relief, to name a few. In this case, it was less its *economic capital* and more its *social capital* that was used to the IOM's advantage. While NGOs each had to demonstrate their own expertise, the IOM was already known among donors from its work in other countries or projects. IOM services were "not cheap," as some representatives complained during interviews, yet the IOM was known to be trustworthy, reliable, and professional enough to absorb large funds. Instead of all the work of distributing funds among many smaller projects implemented by NGOs, donors preferred to fund one large program—here, the IOM—that could then redistribute the money among its implementing partners.

At the same time, the IOM also had to distinguish itself from newly founded agencies, such as Frontex, which works directly under the EU. In its competition with Frontex, the IOM has increasingly played the humanitarian card. For example, counting and denouncing the deaths of migrants at the EU's external borders became a central practice through which the organization sought to ensure that its work was perceived as less brutal and deadly.

The rules of competition among international and non-state actors are, to a large extent, defined by the donors that finance projects of migration management in North Africa, as IOs and NGOs must play by these rules in order to gain funding. The IOM was particularly successful because it gained recognition as a flexible and reliable service provider. Its constant concern with the visibility of its interventions and with quantifiable results of its projects—even for issues that are hardly measurable, such as irregularized migration or human trafficking—can be explained by the neoliberal logic of economization and projectization in international migration governance. Nevertheless, IOs can improvise within these structural constraints on the field and enlarge its boundaries, such as by producing knowledge that suggests new target groups or new needs for projects. The IOM's work in North Africa has demonstrated how the organization has developed a *feel for this game*, proposing new activities that European states are willing to fund. This *practical sense* has helped the organization extend its activities even beyond its core business of migration management to include, for example, social work activities to educate marginalized Moroccan and Tunisian youth (Chapter 3). By inventing new practices, the IOM stretched the boundaries of the field of migration management to include new modes and contents, such as social prophylaxes for marginalized people.

At the same time, the IOM implements the rules of the field vis-à-vis migrants, such as by selecting participants for its programs according to the categories defined by donors. Even though the IOM hardly makes these rules explicit, migrants learn how to play by them through close observation of the IOM's practices. Migrants are not recognized as relevant players, and the logic of their struggles for rights is marginalized in the field. However, my analysis of the voluntary return program in Morocco has shown how migrants share their knowledge about the humanitarian categories that are eligible to participate and how they try to perform these categories in order to profit from IOM services (Chapter 4). In contrast, in Tunisia, migrants rejected the same services, since they did not offer migrants the rights they demanded. While migrants in Morocco protested for the continuation of the voluntary return program, migrants in Tunisia protested against it. Both contexts revealed how the IOM sought to adapt its program to migrants' practices of appropriation and resistance. Therefore, the organization's relations to migrants cannot be framed in simple terms of contestation or complicity, but are complex and ambivalent, changing across contexts and over time.

Finally, the IOM also has to cooperate with Moroccan and Tunisian state actors to implement its programs. While these are recognized as relevant actors in the field, they are not regarded as equals, as their security-oriented approach is not accepted by European states and international actors as innovative or humane enough. Through practices of counseling, education, and capacity building, the IOM assigns Moroccan and Tunisian actors a subordinate position in the field. These practices help reproduce an asymmetrical relationship between mostly White European experts and African apprentices that echoes a colonial past. Based on a self-understanding as a global expert, the IOM intervenes in the Global South in the name of educating the apparently backward politicians and societies. From this relational perspective, it becomes clear that the IOM can indeed follow its own interests vis-à-vis states, but this is much easier to do so with respect to the (weaker) sovereignty of states in the Global South (Pécoud 2020, 7). At the same time, these states bring their own strategies and stakes into the negotiation processes with IOs. For example, the IOM's anti-trafficking politics provide insight into why North African state actors would cooperate and how they have learned how to play by the rules of international migration management (Chapter 5). The Moroccan context demonstrated how self-confident state actors strategically cooperated with the organization when it helped them gain economic, social, and/or cultural capital to reinvest in other policy fields. Moreover, the Tunisian context revealed what it means for the IOM to intervene in a field undergoing a transition that is marked by temporary and provisional structures and ongoing struggles over positions and responsibilities. Therefore, the IOM's relations with North African state actors can be characterized as situational alliances and flexible modes of cooperation.

In sum, an investigation of the IOM's position and relations in the trans-Mediterranean field of migration management reveals that the externalization of migration control is not a smooth, top-down process but rather a relational and conflictual negotiation process to which many state and non-state actors (must) contribute. The IOM's success in this field is partly based on its ability to interact with these different actors and to flexibly combine security with neoliberal and humanitarian logics at the expense of a rights-based approach.

The praxeological approach reconsidered

This praxeological study of the IOM's migration management in Morocco and Tunisia has stressed that such management is not implemented in a vacuum but instead in dynamic fields that are structured by the power relations among diverse actors that condition its *making*. North African actors are not passive recipients of IOM services; rather, they actively participate in service implementation for their own purposes and with their own strategies. Different state and non-state actors take part in international migration management because they believe in its stakes for different reasons. Economic reasons are an important incentive, but they are not the only form of capital at stake. North African actors also cooperate with the IOM in order to gain social and cultural capital, such as by accumulating international contacts and expert knowledge that can be reinvested in the struggles over power and positions in national fields of migration politics. The status of being recognized by the IOM as a relevant actor can provide them with symbolic capital that strengthens their authority and influence in the field. Using Bourdieu's concepts thus enables us to study actors (such as the IOM) not in isolation but within the scope of their action and struggles. In terms of the analysis of transnational spaces, processes, and politics, these concepts allow us to conceptualize the interrelations of struggles among and within different actors at different levels.

While the IOM was successful in influencing other actors to participate in the field, cultivating these relationships means constant care and repair work for the organization. Looking inside this organization, this study has shown that its competitive habitus, flexible performance, and diplomatic and humanitarian self-understanding are well suited to meet expectations in the field. Interviews with IOM staff revealed that they perceive their work as innovative and efficient, often distinguishing it from the bureaucratic procedures of states and other IOs. Knowing that their jobs depend on project-based funding by European states, they seemed to have internalized their employer's logic of projectization and competitive fundraising. In this respect, IOM staff were not only concerned with marketing its services but also with constantly improving them. This concern manifested in their responsiveness to criticism and protests from other actors in the field, notably those that put forward the rights of migrants. The flexibility to seize critical positions and to adapt and reuse them according to a different logic was a remarkable skill of IOM staff in Morocco and Tunisia. These shared individual dispositions crystallized in a collective habitus that presented the organization as flexible and resourceful in monopolizing critical and creative ideas raised by other actors, if such ideas allowed the IOM to design innovative services. This way, claims for migrants' rights were transformed into, e.g., a call for humanitarian action (see Chapter 4).

While IOM staff insisted that they would 'work for governments,' they also highlighted that their work would 'help migrants in need.' From their perspective, it seemed possible to manage migration 'to the benefit of all,' They expected IOM services to have an impact on migrants' behavior and decisions—for example, that information campaigns would change young people's decisions to migrate (Chapter 3). In the most moderate terms, this means that without the IOM, the situation for (potential) migrants in North Africa would be worse. This view is underpinned by a strong humanitarian motivation for their work. Moreover, a self-understanding as international experts who can bring progressive, mostly (neo)liberal changes to supposedly uninformed North African politics and societies provided an unquestioned *illusio* to their work. Speaking with enthusiasm about the aid and assistance they offer to migrants, IOM staff shared good intentions for and apolitical perceptions of their work. During the interviews, it was noticeable that they considered it not only necessary but also possible to effectively and sustainably manage migration in North Africa. In this way, the IOM plays an active part in spreading a worldwide *illusio* of bureaucratic efficiency in migration control (Brachet 2016, 285). However, since the organization 'works for governments,' it is limited by the project guidelines, capacities, and resources provided by donors. Consequently, the humanitarian bureaucrats of the IOM often emphasized that critical issues were beyond their responsibilities.

With regard to the individuals who work for the IOM in North Africa, this study has shown that the IOM is not a monolithic actor whose work can be derived from one central logic, but that multiple forces, stakes, and strategies are at play inside the organization. While the various internal logics that orient the practical work of IOM staff do not coexist without tension, they account for the organization's collective habitus and social practices in the field. Its 'international' (mostly young, Western, and White) employees believe in the humanitarian and progressive mission of their organization and share a hardworking, mobile, and flexible habitus and a *doxic belief* in the global political and economic system that frames their work. Their individual dispositions fit and foster the three dominant logics of neoliberalism, humanitarianism, and security in field. To draw on Bourdieu, this *homology* accounts for the IOM's increasingly influential position in the trans-Mediterranean field of migration management.

Examining the making of international migration management in North Africa from a praxeological perspective has revealed that the IOM's practices barely fulfill the objectives promised in its glamorous discourses. However, Bourdieu's concepts helped to show how the IOM was nevertheless able to establish itself as a relevant actor that seeks to position itself for more important tasks in the future, as a result of the negotiations of positions, relations, and capitals among and inside the different actors in the trans-Mediterranean field of migration management. Bourdieu's Theory of Practice has been particularly helpful in analyzing the interdependence between structural developments in the field and the corresponding structures and strategies within an organization. While this book has empirically focused on the particular position, strategies, and stakes of the IOM in Morocco and Tunisia, the praxeological approach made it possible to analyze change and stability in international migration politics as the outcomes of situated struggles at different levels of a transnational field, as well as to question the implicit assumptions and taken-for-granted knowledge of (one of) the actors involved.

Literature cited

Bourdieu, Pierre. 2003. *Méditations Pascaliennes*. Paris: Seuil.
Brachet, Julien. 2016. "Policing the Desert: The IOM in Libya beyond War and Peace." *Antipode* 48 (2): 272–292. doi:10.1111/anti.12176.
Guild, Elspeth, Stefanie Grant, and Kees Groenendijk. 2017. *IOM and the UN: Unfinished Business*. SSRN Scholarly Paper ID 2927414. Rochester, NY: Social Science Research Network.
Jackson, Peter. 2009. "Pierre Bourdieu." In *Critical Theorists and International Relations*, edited by Jenny Edkins and Nick Vaughan-Williams, 102–113. London and New York: Routledge.
Pécoud, Antoine. 2020. "Introduction: The International Organization for Migration as the New 'UN Migration Agency.'" In *The International Organization for Migration: The New 'UN Migration Agency' in Critical Perspective*, edited by

Martin Geiger and Antoine Pécoud, 1–27. Cham: Springer International Publishing. doi:10.1007/978-3-030-32976-1_1.

Wacquant, Loïc. 2010. "Crafting the Neoliberal State: Workfare, Prisonfare, and Social Insecurity." *Sociological Forum* 25 (2): 197–220. doi:10.1111/j.1573-7861.2010.01173.x.

Wacquant, Loïc. 2012. "Three Steps to a Historical Anthropology of Actually Existing Neoliberalism." *Social Anthropology* 20 (1): 66–79. doi:10.1111/j.1469-8676.2011.00189.x.

Index

Note: Page numbers followed by "n" denote endnotes.

Adler-Nissen, Rebecca 47
AECID *see* Spanish Agency for International Development Cooperation (AECID)
Algeria 217
Andrijasevic, Rutvica 62
anti-trafficking politics 63, 185–225; capacity building 209–220; IOM's position and influence, perceptions of 218–220; mainstreaming 188–202, 220–224; negotiating laws 209–220; and repressive migration control 214–218; victims of trafficking 202–209
Arab Spring 5, 155
Assisted Voluntary Return and Reintegration (AVRR) program 124, 126, 128, 130, 131, 133, 134, 136, 138–144, 147–149, 153, 157, 160, 164, 167, 171–176, 177n1, 177n3, 177n4, 179n25, 206
Australia 155
Autonomy of Migration 10, 25, 46, 71; border regime 25–30
AVRR *see* Assisted Voluntary Return and Reintegration (AVRR) program

Bartels, Inken 78n13
Bayat, Asef 27
Ben Ali, Zine El Abidine 6, 68, 69
Bernstein, Elizabeth 223–224
Bigo, Didier 48, 92, 112
border/migration regime 24; European border regime 2; crises and conflicts of expanding 3–6; framework of 25–30
Boswell, Christina 78n10, 88
Bourdieu, Pierre 11, 34, 48, 50, 51n8, 51n9, 52n10, 241; *Theory of Practice* 2, 25, 34, 35, 48, 230; *see also* Bourdieusian perspective on politics of international migration management
Bourdieusian perspective on politics of international migration management 34–47; field 36–39; habitus 39–41; stability and change 45–47; symbolic capital 41–45; symbolic power 41–45; symbolic violence 41–45
Braudel, Fernand 38
Bueger, Christian 51n4, 51n5

camps 4, 149, 151, 153–159, 161–164, 168–170
capacity building 209–220
capital 40; cultural 92, 135, 168, 170; economic 35, 195, 237; forms of 11; social 134, 198, 237; symbolic 41–45, 115, 124, 187, 229
Caritas 237
Cassarino, Jean-Pierre 70
commodity of labor power 73
compassion 220–224, 230
conditionality, positive 68
conferences, play of international 195–202
constructivist structuralism 35
Convention against Transnational Organized Crime 186
Convention of the European Council for the Fight against Human Trafficking 188
Convention on Action against Trafficking in Human Beings 197
criminalization 235; of human trafficking 189; voluntary return and 165–167
crises 1–6, 46, 124, 148–171

Index

Critical Border and Migration Studies 24
cultural capital 92, 135, 168, 170
culture 31; definition of 51n3

Danish Refugee Council 155
Davidson, Julia O'Connell 216, 222
Declaration of the Summit of Laeken (2001) 78n9
De Genova, Nicholas 26, 74
deportability 15, 139, 166
deportation 125–128
discourse theory 28
Doctors without Borders (Médecins Sans Frontières, MSF) 177
donor influence 133–138
doxa 36, 119, 188
Dünnwald, Stephan 38, 177n1

Eastern Europe 61, 62, 68, 100, 111, 188
economic capital 135, 195, 237
ethnography 29
EU *see* European Union (EU)
Europe 27, 61, 117, 125; European border regime 2–6; Global Approach to Migration 7; refugee crisis (2015) 2
European Neighbourhood Policy (ENP) 63, 68
European Union (EU) 3–5, 11, 28, 38, 46, 51n7, 62, 63, 69–71, 74, 88, 124, 164, 167, 169, 173, 187, 197, 232; Council of Ministers 119n1; Neighbourhood Strategy Action Plans (2004 and 2005) 78n9; Security Strategy (2003) 78n9
externalization of migration control 65–68

Fassin, Didier 49, 50, 150, 173–175
female suffering, defining VoTs through 203–205
Ferguson, James 98
field 36–39
FitzGerald, Sharron 210–211
Foucault, Michel 28–29, 48
Frontex 76, 165, 190, 201, 237
funding rationalities, international play of 133–138

GADEM 217
Gadhafi, Muammar al 5, 6, 102
Gadinger, Frank 51n4, 51n5
GAM *see* Global Approach to Migration (GAM)

Garelli, Glenda 100
Geertz, Clifford 51n3
Geiger, Martin 7–8, 16n1, 61, 62, 73, 113
genealogy 28
Geneva Convention 60, 69, 78n12, 128, 153, 154, 206
geopolitics 38
Ghosh, Bimal 72
Global Approach to Migration (GAM) 7, 63, 72, 88
Global Compact on Safe, Orderly and Regular Migration 60
global governmentality 8
Global North 124, 155, 223
Global Resettlement Solidarity Initiative 154
Global South 1, 119, 155, 174, 196, 208, 221, 234, 235, 238, 239
governmentality 28; global 8
Gupta, Akhil 98

habitus 11, 34–36, 39–41, 199, 236; definition of 39
Hess, Sabine 27, 51n2, 187
Humanitarian Assistance and Voluntary Return for Vulnerable Migrants Rescued on the High Seas 165
humanitarian crisis management, voluntary return as 148–177; and charity 167–171; criminalization and illegalization 165–167; *illusio* 156–158; rumors and hope 163–165; symbolic production of humanitarian crisis 149–152
humanitarianism 16, 149, 149, 151, 158, 173–176, 229, 232, 237, 241

ICMPD *see* International Centre for Migration Policy Development (ICMPD)
illegalization, voluntary return and 165–167
illusio 36, 92, 101, 173, 176, 235, 240; of humanitarian migration management 156–158
ILO *see* International Labor Organization (ILO)
implicit knowledge 77
information campaigns 87–120; definition of 94–95
International Centre for Migration Policy Development (ICMPD) 61, 237
International Labor Organization (ILO) 61, 237

international migration management:
Bourdieusian perspective 34–47;
in North Africa 63–71; practice-
theoretical approaches to international
politics 30–34; praxeological approach
to politics of 24–52,
239–241
International Organization for
Migration (IOM) 3, 5, 9, 11–15, 27,
29, 30, 33, 38, 41–43, 46, 49, 50, 73;
anti-trafficking politics 185–224;
AVRR program 124, 126, 128, 130,
131, 133, 134, 136, 138–144, 147–149,
153, 157, 160, 164, 167, 171–176,
177n1, 177n3, 177n4, 179n25, 206;
cost-effective and humane alternative
to deportation 125–128; foundation of
16n1; as global expert for migration
236–239; on humanitarian crisis
management 148–171; information
campaigns 87–106; migrants'
encounters with 129–133; as migration
agency 61, 192; in North Africa 1–2;
politics of anti-trafficking 15–16;
in transnational field of migration
management 59–78; as travel agency
145–148; voluntary return programs
123–179
international organizations (IO) 1, 3,
5, 12, 29, 33, 41, 44, 45, 47, 60, 114,
129, 142, 155, 167–169, 196, 199,
205, 212, 213, 230, 238; and politics
of migration management in North
Africa 6–9; relationship with third-
countries 8; retreat from the field
158–163
International Political Sociology 24
international politics, practice-
theoretical approaches to 30–34
International Relations (IR) 9, 10, 24,
28, 35, 47; constructivist approaches
in 31
IO *see* international
organizations (IO)
IOM *see* International Organization for
Migration (IOM)
IR *see* International Relations (IR)
Islamic Relief 153
Italian Development Cooperation (IDC)
91, 96

Karakayalı, Serhat 51n2
knowledge production 13, 34, 93,
190–195, 211, 221, 235

Lavenex, Sandra 70
legitimacy/legitimization 2, 125, 229
Libya 7, 102, 160, 168; migration crisis
5–6

managerial language 75
McKinley, Brunson 59
Mediterranean Sea 165
mental orders 31
Mezzadra, Sandro 73
migration control 3–6, 8; in the
Mediterranean, praxeological
perspective to 9–13; securitization and
externalization of 65–68
migration industry 76
migration management 3, 233; as global
duty for education 87–120; as moral
responsibility to protect 123–179;
in North Africa, policies of 6–9;
praxeological approach to politics of
24–52, 239–241; trans-Mediterranean
field of 2, 10–12, 25, 36, 42, 45, 46, 48
migration politics in times of transition
188–202
misrecognition 43, 44, 202
Mobility Partnership 201; in Eastern
Europe and West Africa 62
Moroccans Residing Abroad (Marocains
Résidants à l'Étranger, MRE) 89
Morocco 2, 7, 9, 11, 12, 39, 50, 78n5,
87–89, 103, 116; anti-trafficking
politics 185–224; Association
Agreement 69; border regime, crises
and conflicts of expanding 3–6;
contested positions and relations
in migration politics 68–71;
Department of Migration and Border
Surveillance 188; funding rationalities,
international play of 133–138; IOM
in 63–65, 68, 77; migrants' encounters
with an international bureaucracy
129–131; migration 71–72; Ministry
for Migration 144; Ministry for
Moroccans Residing Abroad and
Migration Affairs 142, 143, 200,
215–216, 218; Ministry of Interior
143, 188, 198; Ministry of National
Education 91; Ministry of Youth and
Sports 91; Moroccan Action Plan
of the High Level Working Group
119n1, 142, 143; National Council for
Human Rights 215; National Strategy
Against Smuggling of Human Beings
188, 190; New Migration Policy

246 *Index*

196, 200, 217; politics of migration management in 29, 50–51; preventing populations at risk of migration in 90–102; repressive migration control 214–218; SALEM project 91–93, 98, 99; symbolic violence of constructing and infantilizing risk groups 93–94
MRE *see* Moroccans Residing Abroad (Marocains Résidants à l'Étranger, MRE)

National Human Rights Council (Conseil National des Droits de l'Homme, CNDH) 141
neoliberal governance of migration 2, 41, 48, 59, 72, 75, 231
neoliberal logic of marketization 124–125
neoliberal risk management, symbolic power of 115–119
New Migration Policy 141–143
NGOization 76
NGOs *see* non-governmental organizations (NGOs)
No Borders Morocco 216, 217
non-governmental organizations (NGOs) 6, 28, 61, 170, 192, 195, 198, 201, 237
nonmovements 27
non-refoulement 126
North Africa 3, 5. 11, 13–15, 34, 38, 50, 51, 88, 89, 102, 124, 175; human trafficking in 187; information campaigns in 117, 118; international migration management 63–71; IOM in 1–2; migration control policies 3; migration in and from 64–65; politics of migration management in 6–9, 29, 43; securitization 63–71; Sub-Saharan migrants in 4

Office of Tunisians Abroad (Office des Tunisiens à l'Étranger, OTE) 69, 78n5, 103–105
Organization for Africa Unity (OAU): Convention for Refugees in Africa 69; Convention of 1969 78n12
outsourcing 75
ownership, negotiating 141–145

Palermo Protocols 186, 189, 191, 215, 224–225n11
Pécoud, Antoine 8, 16n1, 61, 73, 90, 95, 100, 111

Poulantzas, Nicos 28
Pouliot, Vincent 32
practical orders 31
praxeography: practice-theoretical approaches to international politics 30–34; praxeographic border regime analysis 24–52, 239–241
prevention 90–102, 207–209
PRIRAC *see* Promoting the Return and Reintegration of Rejected Asylum Seekers (PRIRAC)
privatization 75
projectization 60, 238, 240
Promoting the Return and Reintegration of Rejected Asylum Seekers (PRIRAC) 153, 165
Protocol on the Smuggling of Migrants by Land, Sea and Air 191
Protocol to Prevent Suppress and Punish Trafficking of Persons, in Particular Women and Children 68, 69, 186, 191
Provisional Committee for the Movement of Migrants from Europe 60

readmission agreements 65
Reckwitz, Andreas 31
repression 220–224, 230
repressive migration control 214–218
returnability 125, 139, 143–144, 166
risk groups, prevention of 207–209
risk management 87, 90–93, 97, 115–119, 207–209, 222, 231

safe third countries 65
SALEM *see* Solidarity with the Children in Morocco (SALEM) project
SALEMM *see* Solidarity with the Children of the Maghreb and the Mashriq (SALEMM) project
Sayad, Abdelmalek 51n6
Schatzki, Theodore 31
Scheel, Stephan 78n13
Schengen Agreement (1985) 65; Article 7 78n6
Schengen Area 7
Sciortino, Giuseppe 26
securitization: of migration control 65–68; in North Africa 63–71
SHARE (Support and Hand-over of Assistance and Referral mechanism as well as Exchange of practices in Anti-trafficking) project 210, 211
social anthropology 29

Index

social capital 134, 198, 237
social epistemology 34
Solidarity with the Children in Morocco (SALEM) project 91–93, 98, 99
Solidarity with the Children of the Maghreb and the Mashriq (SALEMM) project 102, 106–113
Spain 4, 72–73
Spanish Agency for International Development Cooperation (AECID) 99, 142
START project (Stabilizing At-Risk Communities and Reinforcing Migration Management to Enable Smooth Transitions in Egypt, Tunisia and Libya) 102, 106
structuralist constructivism 35
struggles of migration 26–27, 37, 42–43, 45, 50, 96, 167–171, 185–225, 229, 236; as engine of stability and change 45–47
Sub-Saharan Africa 46, 156
Swiss Development Cooperation (SDC) 165
symbolic capital 41–45, 115, 124, 187, 229
symbolic domination 43, 151
symbolic power 2, 41–45, 98, 229; of law 209–214; of neoliberal risk management 115–119
symbolic violence 16, 92, 127, 202, 229, 235; of constructing and infantilizing risk groups 93–94

tacit knowledge 51
textual orders 31
Theory of Practice (Bourdieu) 2, 25, 34, 35, 48, 230
Ticktin, Miriam 174
Transit Migration Research Group 27
trans-Mediterranean field of migration management 115, 124, 229; change and stability in 230–235; shifting discourses, practices, and actors in 71–77
trans-Mediterranean migration politics 68–71
transnational field of migration management 2, 10–12, 25, 36, 42, 45, 46, 48; emergence of 60–63; IOM in 59–78; securitization 63–71
transnationalization 75
Treaty of Amsterdam (1997) 78n8
Treaty of Maastricht (1992) 78n8

Tsianos, Vasilis 27, 52n1
Tunisia 2, 7, 9, 11, 12, 39, 50, 88, 116; anti-trafficking politics 185–224; Border Department 68; border regime, crises and conflicts of expanding 3–6; IOM in 63–65, 68–71, 77; Local Integration Program 158–164, 166, 178n17; Migration Department 213; Migration Resource Centers 103–105; Ministry of Development and International Cooperation 6, 159–160, 168; Ministry of External Relations 213; Ministry of Foreign Affairs 198; Ministry of Interior 68–70, 198, 213; Ministry of Justice 178n11; Ministry of Social Affairs 104, 198, 213; National Action Plan against Trafficking 210; and Palermo Protocols 189; participatory migration management in 102–115; policy-making in 209–214; politics of migration management in 29, 50–51; Red Crescent 114, 144, 153, 162, 165, 166, 170, 212, 237; SALEM project 102–106; SHARE project 210, 211; virtual migration management 113–115; voluntary return as humanitarian crisis management in 148–171
Tunisian–Libyan border 149–152

United Nations (UN) 16n1, 60, 76, 196; Commission on Global Governance 72; Convention on Transnational Organized Crime 68; Geneva Convention of 1951 69; Protocol to Prevent Suppress and Punish Trafficking of Persons, in Particular Women and Children 68, 69, 186
United Nations High Commissioner for Refugees (UNHCR) 60, 61, 69, 70, 78n13, 127, 129, 136, 152–155, 160–166, 169, 171, 178n11, 203, 205, 206, 212, 215, 219, 237
United States (US) 155, 220; anti-trafficking politics 186; Provisional Committee for the Movement of Migrants from Europe 60

Valluy, Jerome 78n13
venue shopping 76
victims of trafficking (VoTs) 186, 193–195, 211, 216, 218, 220–222, 234; as new target group of migration management 202–209; risk groups,

prevention of 207–209; through female suffering, defining 203–205; vulnerable migrants, protection of 205–207
violence 41–45; physical 43; symbolic 92–94, 202, 229, 235; systemic 16, 127
virtual migration management 113–115
visa system 65
voluntary return 2, 15. 46, 203, 205, 206, 216, 219–221, 231, 236, 238; competition in 128–129; donor influence in 133–138; humanitarian politics of 171–177: migrants' encounters with an international bureaucracy 129–133; ownership and responsibility, negotiating 141–145; programs 123–179; protesting for right to 139–141
VoTs *see* victims of trafficking (VoTs)
vulnerability 107, 146, 153, 163, 168, 174, 175, 203, 205, 206, 232
vulnerable migrants, protection of 205–207

Wacquant, Loïc 11, 36, 37, 39, 41–43, 46, 51n6, 224
Walters, William 62, 175
West Africa 4, 145
World Social Forum (WSF) 169, 170

Yurdakul, Gökce 223

Printed in the United States
by Baker & Taylor Publisher Services